IDENTITY AND SUBSISTENCE

GENDER AND ARCHAEOLOGY SERIES

Series Editor
Sarah Milledge Nelson
University of Denver

This series focuses on ways to understand gender in the past through archaeology. This is a topic poised for significant advances in both method and theory, which in turn can improve all archaeology. The possibilities of new methodological rigor as well as new insights into past cultures are what make gendered archaeology a vigorous and thriving subfield.

The series welcomes single authored books on themes in this topical area, particularly ones with a comparative focus. Edited collections with a strong theoretical or methodological orientation will also be considered. Audiences are practicing archaeologists and advanced students in the field.

EDITORIAL BOARD

Philip Duke, *Fort Lewis College*
Alice Kehoe, *Marquette University*
Janet Levy, *University of North Carolina, Charlotte*
Margaret Nelson, *Arizona State University*
Thomas Patterson, *University of California, Riverside*
K. Anne Pyburn, *Indiana University*
Ruth Whitehouse, *University College London*

BOOKS IN THE SERIES

Volume 1, *In Pursuit of Gender: Worldwide Archaeological Approaches*, Sarah Milledge Nelson and Myriam Rosen-Ayalon, Editors
Volume 2, *Gender and the Archaeology of Death*, Bettina Arnold and Nancy L. Wicker, Editors
Volume 3, *Ancient Maya Women*, Traci Ardren, Editor
Volume 4, *Sexual Revolutions: Gender and Labor at the Dawn of Agriculture*, by Jane Peterson
Volume 5, *Ancient Queens: Archaeological Explorations*, Sarah M. Nelson, Editor
Volume 6, *Gender in Ancient Cyprus: Narratives of Social Change on a Mediterranean Island*, by Diane Bolger
Volume 7, *Ambiguous Images: Gender and Rock Art*, by Kelley Hays-Gilpin
Volume 8, *Gender and Chinese Archaeology*, Katheryn M. Linduff and Yan Sun, Editors
Volume 9, *Gender in Archaeology: Analyzing Power and Prestige, Second Edition*, by Sarah Milledge Nelson
Volume 10, *The Archaeology of Childhood: Children, Gender, and Material Culture*, by Jane Eva Baxter
Volume 11, *Gender and Hide Production*, edited by Lisa Frink and Kathryn Weedman
Volume 12, *Handbook of Gender in Archaeology*, Sarah Milledge Nelson, Editor
Volume 13, *Women in Antiquity: Theoretical Approaches to Gender and Archaeology*, Edited and Introduced by Sarah Milledge Nelson
Volume 14, *Worlds of Gender: The Archaeology of Women's Lives Around the Globe*, Edited and Introduced by Sarah Milledge Nelson
Volume 15, *Identity and Subsistence: Gender Strategies for Archaeology*, Edited and Introduced by Sarah Milledge Nelson

SUBMISSION GUIDELINES

Prospective authors of single or co-authored books and editors of anthologies should submit a letter of introduction, the manuscript or a four to ten page proposal, a book outline, and a curriculum vitae. Please send your book manuscript/proposal packet to:

Gender and Archaeology Series
AltaMira Press
4501 Forbes Blvd Suite 200
Lanham, MD 20706
www.altamirapress.com

IDENTITY AND SUBSISTENCE

Gender Strategies for Archaeology

EDITED BY
SARAH MILLEDGE NELSON

A Division of
ROWMAN & LITTLEFIELD PUBLISHERS, INC.
Lanham • New York • Toronto • Plymouth, UK

ALTAMIRA PRESS
A division of Rowman & Littlefield Publishers, Inc.
A wholly owned subsidary of
The Rowman & Littlefield Publishing Group, Inc.
4501 Forbes Boulevard, Suite 200
Lanham, MD 20706
www.altamirapress.com

Estover Road
Plymouth PL6 7PY
United Kingdom

British Library Cataloguing in Publication Information Available

Library of Congress Cataloguing-in-Publication Data

Identity and subsistence : gender strategies for archaeology / edited by Sarah Milledge Nelson.
    p.   cm.— (Gender and archaeology series)
  Includes bibliographical references and index.
  ISBN-13: 978-0-7591-1114-1 (cloth : alk. paper)
  ISBN-10: 0-7591-1114-6 (cloth : alk. paper)
  ISBN-13: 978-0-7591-1115-8 (pbk. : alk. paper)
  ISBN-10: 0-7591-1115-4 (pbk. : alk. paper)
    1. Social archaeology.   2. Feminist archaeology.   3. Identity (Psychology)—History.
  4. Sex—Social aspects—History.   5. Sex role—History.   6. Masculinity—History.   ꜰ
  7. Prehistoric peoples.   8. Human evolution.   9. Agriculture—Social aspects—History.
  10. Pastoral systems—Social aspects—History.   I. Nelson, Sarah M., 1931–
  CC72.4.I33   2007
  930.1—dc22   2007013539

Printed in the United States of America

♾ ™ The paper used in this publication meets the minimum requirements of American National Standard for Information Sciences—Permanence of Paper for Printed Library Materials, ANSI/ NISO Z39.48–1992.

$80.05

Contents

Introduction

SARAH MILLEDGE NELSON

A NALYZING GENDER in archaeological sites has proven to be basic for understanding all facets of archaeology. The chapters in this book are divided into two sections. The first group of chapters demonstrates how important gender is in postprocessual archaeology, and the second group shows the value of gender for processual research designs. These chapters are adapted from the sections titled "Identities" and "Subsistence Strategies" in the *Handbook of Gender in Archaeology*. Their juxtaposition in this volume will be useful for classes in archaeological theory, in cultural evolution, and in gender research. The chapters show the variety of ways that a focus on gender reveals new facets of well-worn archaeological topics as well as opening up new vistas in archaeological discoveries.

Gender is one of the ways in which identities are formed, but it is not the only way. The section on identities considers intersections between gender and other ways of experiencing the self as well as the ways societies may sub-divide people into ethnicities, ages, sexualities, classes, races, and other classifications, which then become part of their identities. These are topics that have been difficult to pursue with archaeological data, but these chapters illuminate that path.

Bonnie Clark and Laurie Wilkie use data from historical archeology to highlight these intersections. With sophisticated examples, they show how the various elements that make up a person's social identity are interactive and complex, not merely additive. They use the concept of personhood to incorporate these various identities into a single framework that allows them to be considered simultaneously. In using the concept of "personhood," Clark and Wilkie specifically include the social aspects of identity, avoiding the notion of "individuals" in which the social context is undertheorized. Personhood importantly includes the embodiedness of humans as persons in societies. The variety of ways in which societies at different times and in different places allow personhood to be constructed is critical for this type of analysis. The authors present archaeological examples of several facets of personhood, building on previous work on gender in archaeology and clarifying the process of archaeological interpretation.

Barbara Voss summarizes recent research on sexuality and the ways it has affected archaeological practice. She discusses sexology, the sex/gender system, and gender performance theory as the theoretical bases of the archaeology of sexuality. Her discussion of Judith Butler's work is particularly illuminating. Voss goes beyond these concepts to point out their limitations for archaeology. She summarizes what has been accomplished by archaeologists in five areas of sexuality: the management of fertility; homosexuality and transsexuality; prostitution; architecture and space; and representations of the erotic or sexual. Each of these topics has contributed to widening the understanding of sexuality beyond recent Euro-American concepts. Finally, Voss shows that archaeology can counter political assertions that the past offers a stable model of sexual practices.

One of the chief reasons for developing an archaeology of gender was that archaeological explanations were androcentric, that is, that they explained cultures from an exclusively male point of view. However, that does not preclude an awareness of males as well as part of engendered relationships. "The Archaeology of Men and Masculinities" is the subject of Benjamin Alberti's chapter, addressing the kinds of questions that have been raised when gender research seems to be just about women. Alberti suggests that there is no need for a new archaeological field of study, but that it is useful to consider the ways that masculinity and men have been construed in archaeological research. The argument in favor of including an archaeology of masculinity is similar to that about personhood—otherwise it is assumed that masculinity is more important than all other social facets of a person, such as age, class, ethnicity, and so forth. The argument against partly returns to an early feminist stance, that it reifies masculinity rather than viewing it as part of a social and cultural setting. Masculinity, Alberti emphasizes, is not a stable category.

Sandra Hollimon takes on the question of nonbinary genders: bisexualism, transsexualism, and transvestitism. Since ethnography of Native Americans points to these as categories that archaeologists who work in the Americas should be alert to, she focuses on this region. Hollimon notes that age is a part of understanding Native American gender, and that a category such as "shaman" may have no gender, or be considered a gender in itself. She describes various ways through which archaeologists have attempted to discover third and fourth genders: through bioarchaeology, the analysis of households and space, and through imagery.

Under the category "Subsistence Strategies," I asked the authors to consider the differences for genders of the various ways that groups have fed themselves, since the division of labor has been said to underlie various kinds of gender arrangements. The chapters admirably dispel the notion that subsistence strategies necessarily underlie gendered expectations of behavior, or gendered social structures.

One of the most basic misuses of human evolution has been to insist that gender structures are "hard-wired" into humans, because they constituted adaptive behaviors. Food is at the heart of this narrative. The chapter by Diane Bolger on "Gender and Human Evolution" takes on the challenge of refuting this type of essentialist thinking. She presents a historical narrative of the earlier Man the Hunter myth, which dominated archaeological interpretation for decades and still has its adherents. The Woman as Gatherer and the Food Sharing models are also critiqued. Bolger then casts a critical eye on sociobiology, especially evolutionary psychology, and its impact on archaeological interpretations. The notion that cognitive sex differences are real and are a result of evolutionary processes is the most recent attempt to interpret sex differences as the same throughout time and place. This is the opposite of current feminist research, which examines differences through time, space, and types of societies rather than trying to construct gender distinctions for all of humanity. Bolger concludes with some suggestions about the potential role of archaeology in correcting the gender stereotypes that are implicit in most research on human evolution.

Gender dynamics in more recent hunter-gatherer societies are the focus of the chapter by Hetty Jo Brumbach and Robert Jarvenpa. They use ethnoarchaeological studies, the ethnohistoric record, and ethnography to discuss the ways that hunter-gatherers organized their societies. Their questions are rooted in material culture, making them of maximal value for archaeological research. Whether tools and space were gendered, and whether they can be so understood in archaeological sites, have been vexing questions in gender research. Brumbach and Jarvenpa importantly demonstrate the variability and flexibility in divisions of labor, and question the stereotypes of both women and men and their activities.

Early farming societies are discussed by Jane Peterson, who considers past uses of gender in understanding these societies. The evolution of farming societies turns out to be much more complex than early studies implied. Peterson begins by pointing out that gendered cross-cultural comparisons are not useful, because farming developed quite differently in different regions. It follows that the different regions—broadly speaking Europe, Africa, Northern China, the Southern Levant, Coastal Ecuador, and the Pre-Hispanic Southwest—show critical differences in the meanings and practice of gender.

Pastoralism is the topic of the chapter by Pam Crabtree. She discusses the domestication of animals, and the subsequent caring for animals, as important gendered topics, but ones that have often been based on stereotypes, when they are discussed at all. This seems to be an area ripe for serious investigations into gender ideology and roles.

All of these chapters call for more systematic studies of gender, as well as attention to the nuances of gender differences in various kinds of societies. They point out, on the one hand, that gender is more than the study of women and men, and, on the other hand, that the contexts of gender in ancient societies need more scrutiny. They open the way to future studies that will be more sophisticated and attuned to variation, but grounded in archaeological data.

The Prism of Self: Gender and Personhood   I

BONNIE J. CLARK AND LAURIE A. WILKIE

A S FEMINIST ARCHAEOLOGISTS have continued to develop more sophisticated approaches and understandings of gender, they have recognized with increasing frequency that gender intersects with and is shaped by a range of other social identities. This intellectual position is drawn from the works of third-wave feminists (e.g., Butler 1990, 1993; Collins 2000; Giddings 1984; Spelman 1988), particularly those who examine the experiences of minority women. Spelman (1988:15) articulated this most eloquently when she observed, "One's gender identity is not related to one's racial and class identity as the parts of pop-bead necklaces are related, separable and insertable in other 'strands' with different racial and class 'parts.'" Instead, these facets of social identity are articulated and interface in complex ways that lead to the embodied experience of self. This is not to say that gender is not an important construct but, rather, that we weaken our interpretations when we fail to recognize how gender is shaped by life course, status, and other social positions.

Like many other archaeologists (e.g., Fowler 2004; Gillespie 2000; Joyce 2000a, 2004, 2006; Knapp 1988; Meskell 1999, 2002, 2004; Meskell and Joyce 2003), we have come to believe that the pursuit of archaeologies of "personhood" will allow us to better realize the potentials of engendered and feminist archaeologies. One way to construct multidimensional archaeological interpretations is to create archaeologies that recognize finer grains of social difference. Gender, age, rank, race, and other identities would be all part of a socially situated and performed persona. Such an approach would allow us to shift from considerations of gross categories, such as "woman," to a consideration of socially constructed roles that incorporate gender, such as "mother." In this chapter, we will also argue that the concept of personhood provides a new avenue of interpretive inquiry for understanding sexism and racism in the material record.

While there are a growing number of archaeologists who are explicitly constructing archaeologies of personhood, there are other archaeological projects that are also complementary to this work. For instance, a growing number of studies focus on archaeologies of childhood (e.g., Ardren and Hutson, 2006; Joyce 2000b; Moore and Scott 1997; Sofaer-Derevenski 2000; Yamin 2002). These studies examine a particular stage in the life cycle while also exploring how children learn gender and other roles. Still other scholars are studying other aspects of social difference, such as racism (e.g., Epperson 2004; Orser 2000), ethnogenesis and creolization (e.g., Ferguson 1992; Lightfoot et al. 1997; Wilkie and Farnsworth 1999), and social stratification or class identities (e.g., Wood 2004; Wurst and Fitts 1999). There exists, of course, a large body of literature on gender (e.g., Galle and Young 2004; Gero and Conkey 1991; Gilchrist 1999) and sexuality (e.g., Schmidt and Voss 2000; Voss 2000).

These works (and others like them) are looking at particular aspects of social identity that are components of personhood. Archaeologies of personhood should not be seen as replacing archaeologies of gender, sexuality, life course, or other axes of difference. Instead, archaeologies of personhood should be seen as a framework of understanding through which anthropological archaeology can integrate these dimensions of social identity in a meaningful and holistic way.

Archaeologists have been drawn to the notion of personhood for a variety of reasons. "Personhood" provides an important alternative to the Western notion of the "individual"—an autonomous and independently motivated and intentioned actor. Archaeologists have often been guilty of projecting the notion of individualism into the pasts they study. To do so ignores the complex ways of knowing and being that shape social life in other cultural and chronological settings. Personhood emphasizes humans as situated in a series of social relations and entanglements that define who they are within a community (Gillespie 2000; Meskell 1999). Personhood recognizes that the human experience is an embodied one (Joyce 2004, 2006; Meskell and Joyce 2003). Susan Gillespie (2000) sees archaeologies of personhood as conceptual means of bridging the divide between actor and society in a way that focuses on social dimensions of actors. Fowler (2004:5) sees the study of personhood as a necessary component of a humanized archaeology that recognizes culture as "socially manipulated and consumed in heterogeneous ways."

Despite differences in theoretical orientation, archaeologies of personhood share several important features. First, authors are concerned about shedding the Western notion of the individual as well as the Western notion of the mind/body dichotomy (see especially Meskell and Joyce 2003). Instead, personhood is seen as a way of interrogating materials for evidence of how embodied actors engaged in discursive social relationships. Second, scholars recognize that there are two facets to personhood—the person as a socially constructed collection of identities versus the unique lived life experiences of particular persons. This is an important distinction, for it is fully possible to be a unique individual person but not have personhood, just as personhood can be conveyed on animals or objects that are clearly not human beings. Ethnographers, particularly explicitly feminist ones, have conducted detailed investigations of the interplay of gender and elements of personhood (for overviews, see Collier and Yanagisako 1987; di Leonardo 1991; Howell and Melhuus 1993). Like other scholars, we turn to ethnographic examples to illustrate the rich and diverse ways that personhood is constructed cross-culturally, briefly discussing examples from the Ashanti, Navajo, and Tchambuli.

Ashanti and the Life Course

Working among the Ashanti people of Ghana in the early twentieth century, R. S. Rattray (1932) found that personhood did not begin at birth, for the physical world parallels that of the spirit world. When a child is born into this world, a ghost mother is losing her baby. Following birth, the infant occupies an uncertain space, between two worlds, not fully rooted in either. Hair is cut from the baby's head and is called ghost hair; the first excrement is referred to as "ghost excreta." Armlets and amulets are put on the baby. These actions serve to root the child in this world. The eight days following birth are crucial, for, in Rattray's words, "During this period no one is very certain whether the infant is going to turn out a human child or prove, by dying before this period has elapsed, that it was never anything more than some wandering ghost" (59). If the child dies before the eighth day, the body may be disfigured and buried in the village midden heap, which also served as the women's latrine. Children who had not achieved the age of puberty were buried in a similar way and referred to as "pot children," based on the nature of their burial in ceramic pots. These individuals were not afforded the full funeral rites reserved for adolescents and adults. In the case of infant death, parents gave the appearance of celebrating to discourage the ghost mother from sending another child it had no intention of leaving to live in the world.

In this example, we can see that personhood is developed as part of a maturation process. Only on achieving certain rites of passage is Ashanti personhood fully established. There are clear material correlates with each step. Life cycle is too often ignored in archaeological interpretations. There are important exceptions (see Gilchrist 1999, 2000; Joyce 2000a, 2004; Meskell 1999, 2002, 2004; Meskell and Joyce 2003; Wilkie 2003). Indeed, King (2006) suggests that residents of early post-Classic coastal Oaxaca may have held ideas about children and personhood similar to that of the Ashanti. Her excavations revealed that while adults were kept linked to households through burial under house floors, children were buried outside, either under patios or even beyond the residential areas. While some archaeologists have begun to look at childhood (e.g., Ardren and Hutson, 2006; Sofaer-Derevenski 2000), there is little consideration of other stages of life; in effect, to borrow Tringham's (1991) descriptor, the archaeological past is peopled with ageless blobs. Archaeologists must attempt, then, to identify transformative moments in the life cycle, whether marked by rites of passage or other course of life events. This is not an impossible task. In studying an African American midwife's assemblage, Wilkie (2004) has correlated the ritualized use of particular materials to specific stages of labor, delivery, and postpartum protection of the infant.

The Navajo and the Personhood of Nonhumans

Personhood is not limited to people. In Navajo life, aspects of personhood can be attributed to plants, animals, and objects that other cultures might define as inanimate. Schwarz (1997) argues that the ways that Navajo personhood is entwined with the physical space of the matrilineal home is an underlying tension in the Navajo–Hopi land dispute. The connection to one's matrilineal home is established prenatally and then in infancy, when the afterbirth and umbilical cord are buried at the matrilineal home.

The placement of the umbilical cord is particularly important for the child's future occupation. One informant told Schwarz that umbilical cords anchor babies to the earth. Navajo return to the matrilineal home frequently, including for ceremonies. Schwarz observes that the physical relocation of Navajo from their matrilineal homes literally leaves them anchorless in the world, leading to increased incidence of alcoholism, depression, and family instability. The relocatees are literally robbed of their personhood.

This case makes two important points for our consideration. First, personhood is a quality that can be conferred on inanimate objects and places. In addition, human body parts and substances can also be conferred with the status of personhood. This is not as foreign a concept to Western culture as it may first appear. After all, the abortion debate in the United States makes clear that some would confer personhood on embryos rather than on adult women. Similarly, death does not necessarily denote the end of a person's social obligations, but may only mark another transformation in their personhood. This is clearly illustrated in Gillespie's (2000) consideration of funerary ritual in Mesoamerica and Meskell and Joyce's (2003) discussion of human–animal hybrids in Egyptian and Mesoamerican art and religion.

The Tchumbali and Depersonalized Persons

Being a person does not guarantee one personhood. Among the Tchumbali of Papua New Guinea, Gewertz (1984) found that to allow for her to move in both the men's and the women's houses of this society, the elders had redefined her as a nonperson. She writes, "They agreed that I was probably not a woman at all, but a strange creature who grew male genitals upon donning trousers. My husband, they thought, was a '*man bilong sem*'—a man of shame—meaning a feminized male. And our daughter, they decided, was not born of our union but had been acquired unnaturally, perhaps purchased from a stranger who needed money. After all, two normally fertile people would have produced many more children by our advanced ages" (618). Gewertz was at first confused by this description and first tried to understand it as a redefining of her gender position. In time, she came to understand that, as an ambiguously sexed creature who was unable to contribute offspring to a patriclan, she was a social nonentity. "I was . . . a differentiated individual, an autonomous self. . . . Yet from the Tchambuli perspective, an individual has no significant reality, and hence no power, apart from his or her relationships" (618).

This example is of particular interest to this work because it illustrates an aspect of personhood not always discussed in the archaeological literature. Not only can society convey personhood, but it can also deny it. For those of us who grapple with racism, sexism, and class inequalities in the archaeology of the recent past, this allows us to recognize that these are not dehumanizing processes as much as they are depersonalizing processes. Patterson (1982) has written about slavery cross-culturally and through time being the experience of "social death." The Maya execution of prisoners of war has been presented as a ritualized stripping of their personhood (Meskell and Joyce 2003). Handler (1996) has suggested that treatment of one woman's grave at Newton Plantation was in keeping with the treatment of witch's burials in Africa. Even in death, this person had much potential for harm to her community, and her burial was designed to contain the malevolence of her person.

Archaeologies of the Contextualized Self and Archaeobiography

For our purposes, we consider an archaeology of personhood to be the archaeology of a socially contextualized self. This contextual self encompasses the experiences, expectations, and rights a person derives from ascribed and achieved statuses or identities. Gender, age, lineal associations, marriage, parental, occupation, political, caste, and other statuses converge to create a socially situated persona. We are explicit on this point because we think it is necessary for archaeologists to recognize that personhood is constructed within the constraints of a given community. Achievement, for some individuals, may be explicitly limited by their ascribed statuses. For instance, consider an enslaved person—the recognition of their achievements will always be shaped by perceptions of the potentials of persons in that ascribed role. Aspects of personhood, such as race, sex, age, ethnicity, and occupation, can be ascribed by society. Subaltern groups may hold notions of their own community's personhood that are in conflict with dominant ideologies. Archaeology, then, has the opportunity to explore the discursive relationship between structure and agent through competing personhoods. "Personhood" provides a framework through which we can look at responses to racism and sexism.

The goal of studying the contextual self is not so much to identify specific persons or the "smallest social unit" (see Flannery 1976; Hill and Gunn 1977) as to recognize at a finer grain of analysis the diversity of subject positions that existed in past societies. Within any society, there will be multiple people who occupy similar social statuses and spaces. In our consideration of personhood, we also want to discuss an additional dimension—that of the actual self. The actual self is the differentiated individual whose own experiences, attitudes, and inherent human uniqueness distinguish one from others who may occupy the same social statuses and spaces. This is not to say that the actual self is without social situatedness; rather, because of particular archaeological circumstances, dimensions of that person's unique humanity and agency are available to us. We will refer to archaeologies that include considerations of the actual self (in addition to the contextual self) as "archaeobiographies" (Clark 1996). The actual self cannot be studied, however, without consideration of the contextual self. Archaeobiography, then, represents the consideration of a completely embodied person and their lived life.

Amache Ochinee Prowers: A Case Study in Archaeobiography

Archaeobiography is perhaps most easily pursued within historical archaeology. Certainly that was implied when the concept was originally conceived as "a narrative that uses documentary records, material culture and excavated artifacts to tell the story of a specific person during a specific time" (Clark 1996:14). The first examination termed an archaeobiography (although certainly not the first to pursue this line of research) focused on the life of Amache Ochinee Prowers (Clark

1996). Her story was one particularly well suited to an approach that combined a concern for a specific lived life (biography) and the materials remains associated with that life (archaeology).

Born on the Great Plains of North America in the mid-1840s, Amache was the daughter of Ochinee or Lone Bear (*Nah'ku'uk'ihu'us*), a Southern Cheyenne subchief. In her teens, Amache married John Prowers, a Euroamerican Indian trader. While in her twenties, Amache and her growing family moved to the small town of Boggsville, Colorado. Located along the Mountain Branch of the Santa Fe Trail, Boggsville served as the center for several ranching operations as well as a destination on the trail. Amache's husband John built on his trading experience by opening a store in the Prowers' house to serve travelers on the trail. Amache would host such travelers as well as accommodate the visits of her own family. Her natal band often pitched their tipis adjacent to her house on their travels between the newly established Southern Cheyenne reservation in Oklahoma and traditional hunting and fishing grounds in Colorado.

Amache lived at a time of great change for the Cheyenne and for the country in which they uneasily resided. The choices she made, especially to marry outside her tribe but to continue relations with them, placed her in a delicate position, especially when her father was one of the over 200 Southern Cheyenne killed in the Sand Creek Massacre of 1864. If individual lives can contribute to our understanding of history, hers is certainly one of import. But history alone cannot tell her story. Although Amache could fluently speak three languages—Cheyenne, English, and Spanish—she was illiterate. The documents of her life include a scattering of legal papers regarding her husband's estate, several photographs, and the remembrances of her children and grandchildren. Historical syntheses and public memory (prior to archaeological research) focused on Amache's assimilation into Euroamerican society. A plaque below her picture in the Bent County courthouse claims that she was respected by that society "due to the strenuous effort of the Cheyenne woman to adapt herself to white man's ways." To truly understand her personhood, unfiltered by racism or nostalgia, we must turn to the material record.

A series of excavations both inside and surrounding the Prowers house at Boggsville have helped to recover the material record of Amache's life (Carrillo et al. 1993, 1994). Despite public memory of an assimilated Amache, her children's private memories suggest that Amache was not, in fact, "giving up her own way of life" (Hurd 1957). She continued to practice elements of Cheyenne foodways, including the gathering and processing of wild plants and game. To date, no botanical studies have been performed at the site, but the recovery of a broken pestle from the deposits implies that Amache engaged in Cheyenne methods of food preparation often enough to require replenishing her tools. Seed beads were recovered throughout the house and yard, suggesting that Amache continued to either wear or produce beaded clothing. That she had this skill is supported by accounts that state that her marriage arrangements included gifts of items she beaded herself (Hurd 1957).

The material record, however, also speaks to some of Amache's activities that were completely undocumented. Of import for wider disciplinary discussions is that fact that a number of lithics were recovered from discretely historic deposits at the Prowers house. These include fragments of two formal tools, several utilized flakes, and a number of pieces of debitage. The ethnographic record points out that a number of lithic tools were part of Cheyenne women's tool kits, including hide scrapers, implements for cutting meat, and knives with which to sharpen their digging sticks. Anthropologist Stan Hoig (1989:25) asserts, "The many chores performed by Cheyenne women required a variety of tools that they devised themselves."

We have, it is hoped, moved forward as a discipline since 1991, when Joan Gero, rhetorically speaking, had to jump up and down to call attention to the fact that women, whose tasks so often involve the use of stone tools, were likely making them as well (Gero 1991). Certainly recent research on hide workers in Ethiopia indicates that women there are involved in all stages of lithic procurement, production, and use (Brandt and Weedman 2000). Amache spent much of her time significantly spatially separated from other Cheyenne. If her stone tools needed sharpening or refurbishing, she would have had to do it herself. That Amache would have continued to use and maintain stone tools at Boggsville fits into what we know of her from written and material sources.

Individual artifacts are tangible pieces of the past. Yet when we are trying to say something about cultural continuity and change and especially the creation and manipulation of ethnic identities, their meanings can be ambiguous. As Lightfoot (1995:207) has contended, when it comes to ethnically pluralistic settlements like Boggsville, "it is clear that simply computing the percentage of European and native artifacts in archaeological deposits tells us little about the process of culture change." Indeed, many "traditional" activities can be more than adequately pursued using adopted material culture. However, an emphasis on the organization and use of space can allow us to identify key cultural values less likely to be masked by outward material signs.

Boggsville, at first blush, is not visibly different from settlements in Missouri, where John Prowers hailed from (fig. 10.1). The buildings there exhibit the symmetry of typical Anglo structures of the time, at least as seen from the front. Both the Prowers' house and that of their neighbors, the Boggses, feature the neoclassi-

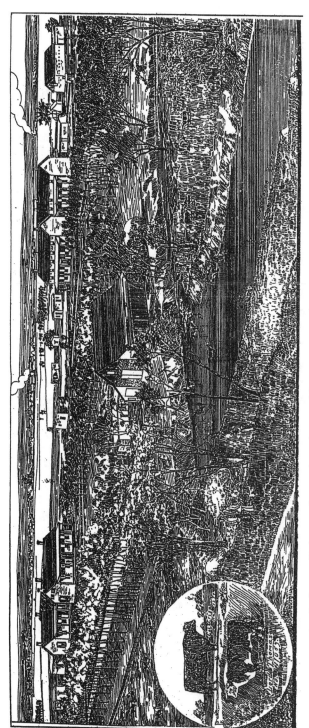

Figure 1.1.   Historic sketch of Boggsville from an illustrated supplement of the *Bent County Democrat*, Spring 1888.

cal touches that identify them as territorial-style architecture. However, both houses are made of adobe—not surprising given that the majority of women who lived at this site were Hispanic women from Taos, New Mexico (Clark 1997). That the Anglo veneer was very important to the settlers is clear in that both houses were "tattooed," the plaster painted with a design to make them look, from a distance, like they were built of cut stone. In addition to the use of adobe, another Hispanic element of the houses was their U-shape plans, with rooms built around a courtyard in hacienda style.

The orientation of the courtyard at the Boggs house makes sense according to the formal layout of the settlement and from an environmental standpoint. As one approaches from the river following the formal, tree-lined entry, the symmetry of the Boggs house holds. The courtyard faces south and is thus both warmed by the sun and protected from the wind. The Prowers courtyard, on the other hand, conforms to neither that layout nor environmental factors. As one approached the settlement, one would have seen right into the courtyard. Facing east as it does, it is almost always in the shade.

If one takes into account only the elements of Hispanic and Anglo architecture, the orientation of the Prowers house makes no sense. But if one factors in Cheyenne practice, it becomes much more legible. Domestic space reflects the rituals of daily life. One of the rituals that is the most critical to everyday Cheyenne functioning is *niv'stan'y'vo*, the supplications to the cardinal points of the compass. Like members of many Plains Indian groups, Amache was probably always aware of her orientation to cardinal directions. The Prowers house, with its east-facing courtyard, mirrors a Cheyenne encampment. The camp circle and the tipis themselves opened to the east or southeast. That configuration allowed the Cheyenne to greet the sun daily as it rose in the east (Grinnell 1962). The U-shaped Prowers house similarly opened up to the east, enabling Amache to continue this ritual in her daily practice. Despite the almost inconceivable nature of such a proposition, it appears that the Prowers house is a blending of Anglo and Cheyenne architecture.

This case study of an archaeobiography speaks to some of the promise of the approach. Rather than telling a story about personhood in the abstract, it examines the idea through the lived experience of a real, embodied person. It is one thing to say that the United States has always been a place of ethnic diversity. It is another to envision Amache Prowers sitting in her Victorian-era house grinding buffalo meat and greeting both travelers on the Santa Fe Trail and the rising sun in the east.

This course of research coincides with Beaudry's (1991) call to reinvent historical archaeology. We must recognize, she claims, that "the details of human life are as important as broad generalizations" (3). In fact, she goes on, the greatest potential of historical archaeology is "to help us bring to light and to understand the life history of one site and its inhabitants," eventually creating "a more and more complex mosaic" (20). Such work shifts the attention of the field from "totalizing frameworks . . . to cultural actors" (21). Archaeobiography, where it is possible, shifts the focus to an even smaller scale, telling us about not just cultural actors but also a specific, embodied, cultural actor and their lived experience.

As Meskell (1998, 2002, 2004), Meskell and Joyce (2003), and Gillespie (2000) have amply demonstrated, this level of archaeological resolution is not limited to archaeologies of the recent past. These archaeologies do require, however, a commitment to drawing on a wide range of evidentiary lines. For instance, textual archaeologies, by which we mean archaeologies that draw on written or oral sources as an evidentiary line, are in a unique situation regarding the study of personhood. Texts can provide insights into the variety of social identities and positions recognized by a group. In addition, through texts, we can come to understand the important transitions used to mark different stages in the life cycle. Through textual sources, we can find ourselves in the position of studying historically documented persons, thus allowing for the study of actual selves.

Bioarchaeology provides another line of evidence that provides a window into differentiated individuals. Hodder's (2000) consideration of the ice man is an outstanding example of such work. Bioarchaeologists have been able to do very particular kinds of archaeobiography. They construct individual life histories from skeletal materials, compiling both a catalog of single-episode life misfortunes or alternations, like a fracture or tooth shaping, and a chronicle of ongoing routines resulting in long-term changes to skeletal health or form. Arthritis, joint deterioration, malnutrition, excessive musculature, foot binding, ongoing health problems, and so on leave a documentary record inscribed on the bone. Combined with what Blakey (2001) refers to as a biocultural approach, the individual's embodied experiences can be understood within the time and place one lived.

Gender and Personhood Collide: Mothering and Childhood in the Archaeological Record

"Mother" is a cross-culturally constructed social persona that has received little attention from archaeologists. It is also a role situated in webs of generational, gender, kinship, and rank relations. One of the shortcomings of many archaeologies of childhood has been the isolation of children in the analyses from the wider social community that ultimately defined them as children. We will discuss mothering and childhood as examples of lived and embodied social relationships at two very different sites: La Placita in Colorado and Clifton Plantation in the Bahamas. In both case studies, the people at the center of the study have been denied some aspect of personhood by the larger society of which they are a part.

For the enslaved people of Clifton, the British legal system defined them as nonpersons—chattel—with no rights over their children or families. They had no rights over even their own bodies. As many feminist scholars have demonstrated (e.g., Collins 2000; Davis 1983; Giddings 1984; Roberts 1997), for women this denial of personhood led to the most outrageous sexual exploitation and abuse. Within the quarters, the enslaved people were a culturally heterogeneous group and, on the basis of ethnohistoric literature from West and Central Africa, were likely to have held a variety of conflicting notions of personhood. In the slave quarters, then, we have the potential to see how new understandings of personhood and value are constructed within a Creole community situated within the system of British enslavement.

The Hispanic population of La Placita faced racism as well, although of a systemically less structured nature than that experienced by enslaved peoples. Hispanics, too, were denied their full share of rights, especially those related to citizenship. In particular, the territorial expansion of the United States into what was once Mexico led to a spiral of disenfranchisement and land loss. Hispanic families in this area continue to pursue social and economic strategies in the face of disempowerment, strategies that in their material component are available to archaeologists. In these case studies, we demonstrate how we can begin the project of the study of personhood in subaltern groups.

Mothering and Childhood at Clifton Plantation

Clifton was one of three plantations owned by Loyalist William Wylly. Wylly was the attorney general of the Bahamas, and, while not an abolitionist, he was an advocate of the amelioration movement that swept through the Caribbean in the late eighteenth and early nineteenth centuries. Clifton, home to somewhere around seventy enslaved and apprenticed persons at its peak, was Wylly's grand social experiment—a place where he could put into practice what he considered to be an enlightened slaveholding philosophy (Wilkie and Farnsworth 2005).

Clifton was managed according to the "Rules of Clifton Plantation," which outlined labor and behavioral expectations to which Wylly held his enslaved people and what treatment they could expect if they followed the rules. The rules emphasized monogamy, faithfulness in marriage, engagement in Christian worship, commitment to a strong work ethic, and the demonstration of economic initiative on the part of the enslaved people. In return, Wylly promised Clifton's population opportunities for outside work and trade, good accommodations, set rations, land for families to farm, and literacy training. It is interesting to note that while Wylly dictated many aspects of proper behavior, he did not dictate any policies about child rearing (Wilkie and Farnsworth 2005).

While punishments for adultery are detailed, notably missing from the rules are any exemptions from work or other considerations for pregnant or lactating women. The later dispersal of the slave community by Wylly when he left the Bahamas demonstrated that he had no qualms about separating husbands from wives or parents from children. For enslaved Africans and their descendants whose native cultures emphasized the importance of ancestors and lineal relationships, the threat of separation was particularly cruel. Although the rules are silent on the role of children within the plantation community, from other documentary evidence we can derive some insight into mothering arrangements at Clifton.

To preface this case study, we want to emphasize that we are here defining mothering as a relationship between a child and an adult that provides physical and emotional nurturing, protection, and enculturation. These are needs of children that are cross-culturally universal and necessary for successful social reproduction. While in our society we often understand mothering responsibilities for a particular child or set of children as falling to a single female, this is a culturally and chronologically specific definition. Mothering duties need not fall to biological kin or, for that matter, even to women. Collins (1994) has forcefully demonstrated that many African American women perform mothering work in a variety of ways for their communities, taking responsibility for African American children in a variety of social arenas. Likewise, among the white elite in the plantation Caribbean and American South, many mothering responsibilities for white children, including such intimate acts as breast feeding, were provided by enslaved African American women (Wilkie 2003).

Wylly clearly saw labor as being sexually divided. Women were most likely to be employed as cooks and house servants, with men more likely to be fieldworkers, carpenters, and masons. In one document, Wylly clearly states that he saw the maintenance of the provisioning grounds located adjacent to the houses to be the duty of women, with assistance of their children, while men and their able sons were to pursue outside employment such as wall building (Wilkie and Farnsworth 2005). Wylly's attitudes allowed the women of Clifton a rare opportunity to be physically close to their children during their work when farming.

Children were a large part of the Clifton population. In 1818, of the at least fifty-three persons known to have been living at Clifton, at least twenty-two were children under the age of eighteen. Six children are recorded as being employed on the plantation. They worked as shepherds, cowherds, and servants and cared for milk cows. Wylly was entitled to the labor of any child over the age of five, and at least one child of this age seems to be employed attending to milk cows and dairy, with the other person in this position at Clifton being a child of age eleven. Cowherds were children between the ages of eleven and fifteen or older men and women over the age of fifty. Servants were also young, with one on Clifton being eleven (Wilkie and Farnsworth 2005). Boys were more likely than girls to be employed at a younger age. Only one girl under the age of eighteen was employed in a set task for Wylly. Young male children and nearly all female children were an important labor resource, then, for their families, not Wylly.

Given the organization of women's labor supported by Wylly as well as his underutilization of children's labor, the women of Clifton plantation would have had the ability to keep their children near them during much of the workday. Accounts from the American South and Caribbean suggest that, when possible, enslaved women preferred to keep infants and very small children with them while working, particularly children still breast-feeding (Wilkie 2003). Most ethnographic data supports Corruccini et al.'s (1985) skeletal study, which estimated weaning age to be two to three years for enslaved children. After that age, children could be more comfortably separated from their mothers, but until they were older, they would still require supervision by an older child or adult. Older children could assist in the provisioning grounds, as envisioned by Wylly, or could engage in alternate economic activities for the good of their households.

To what degree, then, does the archaeology suggest patterns of caregiving and child oversight? We will briefly focus on three areas in which archaeological evidence is suggestive of mothering practices and children's activities: the organization of house yards, the acquisition of shellfish and marine resources, and the realm of spiritual well-being and protection.

The living space immediately surrounding the house constituted the house yard and was a distinct space in both use and organization from provisioning grounds (Pulsipher 1993). House yards tend to be swept areas where activities such as cooking, eating, cleaning, weaving, socializing, and child care took place.

At Clifton, there are eight standing structures in the slave village (fig. 10.2). Extensive excavation around four of these structures by Farnsworth and Wilkie from 1996 to 2000 allowed for the study of the size and construction of house yards (Wilkie and Farnsworth 2005). Wilkie and Farnsworth found that house yards are typically swept surfaces that are slightly wider than the width of the house structure and extend as far as fifteen meters from the rear of the house. The perimeters of the yards are typified by a ring of higher trash concentrations, with the greatest amount of accumulation corresponding to the rear of the yard.

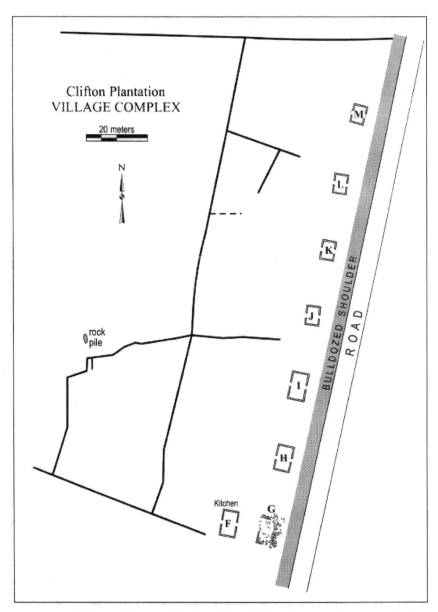

Figure 1.2.   The layout of houses in the Slave Village of Clifton Plantation. Locus G was the driver's house; Locus F served as both a house and village kitchen. The remainder of the structures were single family homes.

The yard contains at least a cooking surface or structure, food preparation area, barrels for storage of drinking and washing water, and an area for eating, which in at least one case was marked by a canopy-covered structure. In the yards where kitchen buildings were identified, they tend to be located on the edge of the yard with the center areas being used for other activities. The areas immediately behind the houses featured the lowest concentrations of artifacts. Materials such as ceramics, clothing- and tobacco-related items, and food remains are typically found distributed throughout the yards despite sweeping.

At one house, a sixty-square-meter block of the yard was excavated, providing the most complete information on internal yard structure (fig. 10.3). It was this yard that provided some insight into how mothering considerations shaped the organization of space. Once the distribution of different artifact types across the extent of the yard was plotted, overlapping densities of artifacts were explored to define internal activity areas and to look at associations between architectural features in the yard and materials. A platform for a kitchen structure was found at the southern edge of the yard, and a sheltered dining area was located at the western edge. While ceramics, pipes, food remains, barrel parts, and laundry items were differentially clustered throughout the yard in patterns suggestive of different use areas, glass was recovered from only one section of the yard—a naturally occurring hole located just at the yard perimeter. From this one location, all the glass was recovered—numbering over 700 large (at least three by three centimeters) sherds.

Various reasons for this depositional pattern were contemplated. Perhaps the household was attempting to hide visible evidence of liquor consumption from the planter. Wylly had expressed disgust in a newspaper article with sailors who traded rum for provisions with the people of Clifton. There is little evidence, however, that Wylly ever spent time in the quarters but instead seems to have left all details of management up to his free-black overseer. Likewise, there were many innocent reuses for bottles that would not require them to be hidden. No bottles were recovered whole, which would have been likely if the bottles had been deposited in the hole directly after being emptied of their primary contents.

Suppose, however, that the glass was removed from the yard not because of the perceived danger of the contents but because of the perceived danger of the glass to yard occupants. Ceramics found in the yard tended to be small and did not include porcelain vessels, which may have very sharp edges when broken. Even after nearly 200 years, the edges on the glass remained sharp enough to injure excavators. If any number of small but mobile children had been tended in the yard, the glass would have been a danger to bare feet and small, curious hands.

The organization of the yard, with food preparation and consumption and

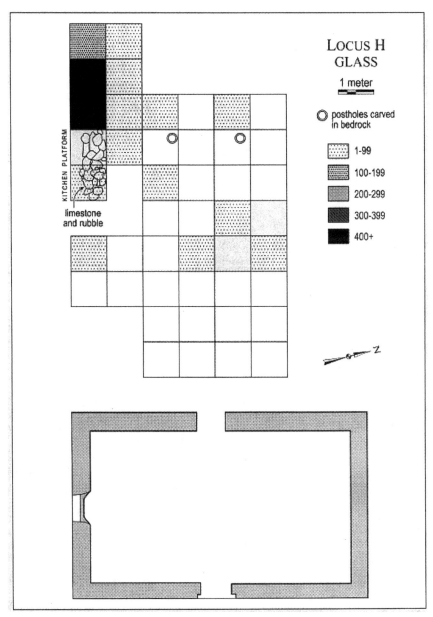

Figure 1.3.   Distribution of glass recovered from the yard of Locus H, Clifton Plantation.

laundry activities consolidated along the perimeters, created an ideal surveillance zone for anyone working in those areas while facing the house. Even though employed mainly in labor benefiting her family or community rather than the planter, an enslaved person at Clifton caring for children still would have been busy with a range of other tasks. The organization of the yard space maintained a structured play zone for children that could be watched while other activities were performed. Though not at the same density, Wilkie and Farnsworth found glass to be tightly concentrated in other yards as well. This suggests that child care took place in each yard at different times, not just in one house area under a single caretaker.

Based on documentary evidence, there is reason to believe that the house at H was occupied at least through 1821 by a young African apprentice, Cudjoe, and his enslaved wife, Esther. According to an 1818 plantation slave list, the couple had two of the youngest children on the plantation, perhaps accounting for the fastidiousness of the glass collection. It may also be that Esther, as a young mother caring for two very small children, was not an efficient farmworker and instead watched other women's children in her yard. This might have led to the greater attention to potential dangers there.

Concerns for child well-being may have also shaped dietary practices at Clifton. Clifton is a coastal plantation, and the bay adjacent to the shore contains what remains one of the richest reef resources on the island of New Providence today. Shellfish and marine fish are abundant in the area. As Wilkie and Farnsworth (2005) detail elsewhere, the people of Clifton subsisted mainly on wild resources while selling domestic animals they raised in their yards and provisioning grounds at the local market. Men seemed to have taken advantage of the opportunity to earn cash from Wylly by building walls, and accounts of provisioning grounds indicate that a wide range of crops were being raised as well. Older people unable to do strenuous work and children were the most likely providers of marine resources consumed by the households. The compositions of the shellfish and fish assemblages support this contention. The vast majority of the fish recovered from Clifton were pan-sized species such as grunts, small snappers, porgies, and hinds. The fish, no matter the species, are consistent in size, suggesting the use of fishing pots. Clifton features a cliff area that abuts the sea, with the water below ranging ten to twenty feet in depth. In this area, fish swim immediately next to shore. This area would be perfect for dropping pots. Although larger fish, such as Nassau groupers and blue parrot fish, can be caught by spearfishing just a few meters from shore, these species are rare in the assemblage. Not only can pots be left unattended, thus minimizing labor involved, but, if dropped from the shore, they do not involve the same kind of risk of drowning associated with swimming.

The shellfish assemblage also supports the idea that safety concerns shaped the procurement strategy. Queen conch, a rich marine resource, is very abundant off Clifton's shore. While conch was an important part of the diet in Clifton's households, chiton, periwinkle, West Indian top shell, and tiger lucines occur to a degree not encountered at other Bahamian plantations. These are much smaller mollusks compared to conch and today are typically eaten at the beach as a snack rather than harvested for home consumption. Periwinkle and chiton are particularly difficult to harvest in any numbers because they nestle in the depths of the honeycomb rock that characterizes the shoreline. They are best removed by persons with small hands. Unlike conch, which is recovered by diving, each of the abundant species recovered from Clifton are accessible from shore. By directing that no one could enter the water while fishing or shellfish gathering, nurturers could protect children even when out of their direct oversight. Children would have been able to contribute to the family's dietary needs, but in a way that did not needlessly endanger them.

Finally, a small series of artifacts recovered from each of the houses at Clifton, beads and other potential protective devices may also be related to child care and mothering. In West Africa, beads are used to communicate multiple meanings and functions, ranging from gender or age status, ethnic identity, or religious affiliation or status (Carey 1997).

The use of "charms" or "fetishes" by African peoples was often remarked on (and misunderstood) by European visitors. Describing a group living on the Gambia River, Gray wrote in 1825, "Like all other pagans, they are very superstitious, and wear a great number of grigres, or charms round their necks, arms and legs. They are inordinately fond of red cloth, which they make use of in covering those charms." Rattray (1932) spent a great deal of effort trying to contextualize and explain the use of *suman* among the Ashanti. The *suman* is an object or series of objects that have been endowed with powers by a spiritual force, such as a deity, through a religious specialist. The components of a *suman* can widely vary but often incorporate animal parts, such as hide, bone, teeth, or claws, vegetable or animal shells, beads of different materials, fabric, and cord. The uses for *suman* can also widely vary but tend toward protective in nature and are intended for use by a single individual rather than for the protection of a corporate group (such as a lineage or a village) as shrines may be. Similar traditions of protective devices are well documented in the American South, and archaeologists have recovered materials believed to be components of such objects (Brown and Cooper 1990; Orser 1994; Wilkie 1997). Throughout the New World, the common West African practice of delaying the naming of a child until its ninth day of life was followed. Following birth, protective ornaments are placed on a newborn as a means of helping to root the child spiritually in this world.

One particular set of artifacts from House I drew our attention. From adjacent units (that otherwise contained few materials) a brass bell, a brass button, a shell button, and a comb bittersweet with a hole drilled through it—as if it were intended for stringing—were recovered. Both the bell and the shell bead are unique to the site, the only ones of their kind recovered in four excavation seasons. Comb bittersweets are very common on Clifton's beaches, and if this were a desirable ornamental object, more would have been found during excavation. The materials are not unlike protective devices described for infants and children. Were these and similar objects used to protect children from the spiritual harm that surrounded them? There are a range of objects recovered from Clifton that appear to have had uses as protective magic, including glass beads, buried coins, and other objects (Wilkie and Farnsworth 2005). The people of Clifton clearly maintained communication with persons in the spiritual realm, suggesting that indigenous understandings of personhood continued to shape discourse in the quarters.

In this case, we have briefly dealt with one aspect of mothering—that of the protection of children from harm, be that harm derived from physical or metaphysical sources. The materials from Clifton suggest much about the embodied experience of both motherhood and childhood in the context of enslavement. Arrangements of yards suggest that children were supervised in the yard spaces of homes, most likely under the surveillance of their own kin. Despite the dominant discourses that portrayed enslaved people as poor caregivers, the community employed its own value system in this arena. Likewise, food acquisition patterns also suggest a tendency toward caution and protectiveness toward young hunters and fisherfolk. Finally, the recovery of a probable protective device suggests that traditional ways of thinking about children's personhood persisted in the New World despite encounters with the religious teachings of Methodism.

Mothering and Childhood at La Placita

Although almost half a world away, the material evidence of mothering and childhood at La Placita, Colorado, bears a striking resemblance to Clifton Plantation. In particular, two elements—structured play zones and children's contributions to foodways—suggest that the strategies of subaltern families during the 1800s coalesce in instructive ways.

La Placita was a small Hispanic settlement just south of what had once been the border between Mexico and the United States. Although within U.S. territory when it was occupied in the 1880s and 1890s, the region remained part of what has been conceptualized as the "Hispano Homeland" (Nostrand 1992), and Hispanics were its majority population. Now consisting of the clustered ruins of native stone structures, La Placita was probably home to at least three different households, likely related to one another. Like the majority of Hispanic occupants of the region at that time, the people who built and occupied this settlement did not own their land. These squatters, however, are perhaps better thought of as subaltern settlers (Clark 2005), as they were pursuing traditional Hispanic land occupancy patterns legislated out of existence by the incoming U.S. government (Van Ness 1991).

Like Clifton, the work of mothering at La Placita fell almost exclusively to women but for different reasons. Indeed, not just mothering but almost all the tasks required to keep the settlement going on a day-to-day basis would have fallen on its female residents. While the enslaved men of Clifton worked the fields away from home, men in the area of the Hispano Homeland (centered in New Mexico but extending to adjacent states) were gradually less and less present in their settlements. The process whereby Hispanic men were pulled into transient labor has been elaborated by Deutsch (1987). Prior to the American takeover, many of the men of New Mexico spent time traveling either as freighters on the Santa Fe Trail or as buffalo hunters or traders with local Indians. With the American takeover came the subsequent removal of native groups, followed in the 1870s by the completion of railroads through the region. This resulted in the evaporation of many entrepreneurial opportunities for Hispanic men. Additionally, ethnocentric policies of the conquering U.S. government closed off many administrative positions formerly held by Hispanics.

This narrowing of opportunity could not have come at a worse time. The American takeover made Hispanic settlements less and less self-sufficient both through the imposition of taxes and grazing fees and through the enclosure of communal lands that had supported villages. As Deutsch (1987) documents, between 1880 and 1920, the adult and adolescent men of villages spent more and more time away as sojourning wage laborers, whether on the railroad, in mines, or as cowboys for large Anglo ranching syndicates. This is certainly suggested by the region's 1880 census, which indicates that only two of those fifteen households with male heads had as their primary occupation rancher or farmer. The other thirteen heads of household appear to be wage laborers: two are listed as farm laborers, six as general laborers, and five as herders. In six of these same households, male children were occupied as herders or laborers. Men come and go, but women and children make up the core of most households.

Material evidence at the site suggests that, like many of their neighbors, the men and possibly older boys of La Placita sojourned as wage laborers elsewhere. Although many of the site's features relate to animal husbandry, including a barn and corral, a lambing pen rock shelter, and a sheep drive line, overall the facilities at the site were modest. What was not modest were the remains of consumer goods. Over 1,100 ceramic sherds, representing a minimum of ninety-five vessels, were recovered, as well as mass-produced footwear, clothing, and tools. It is clear that the residents of the site had access to cash, more of it than could have been produced by the sheep raised there.

When women became the de facto heads of household, their workload must have increased. Not only did they need to raise children, cook, clean, and garden (all elements of established gendered divisions of labor), but they also needed to keep an eye on the stock and contend with visitors, both human and nonhuman. The material evidence of daily life at the site is a record of how women got by in a world where their work expanded because their personhood was diminished.

Child rearing, which was traditionally a dominant part of the gendered role of Hispanas, competed with new jobs they had to do, especially taking care of grazing animals. In such a situation, we might envision such women spending some of the pool of available money on items to keep children entertained. However, the artifactual evidence of toys at La Placita is quite minimal. A collapsed rubber ball and two fragments of a porcelain bisque doll were all that were recovered. Given that there are thousands of artifacts from the site, they are rare items indeed. One could use such a paucity to argue not that few toys were purchased but rather that few children were on the site. Yet in the 1880 census of the region, Hispanic households had an average of three children. Given that this was a multihousehold occupation, it is likely that there were quite a few children living at La Placita.

Children at the site seem to have figured out other ways to entertain themselves. Evidence from prehistoric sites suggests that items considered trash by adults are often used as playthings by children (Hutson and Magnoni 2002). The recycling of trash as toys would help explain some of the more puzzling items found at La Placita. It seems that a particular joy was expressed in the promise of wire. At La Placita, it gets wrapped around a range of broken items. Indeed, one of the most enigmatic of features from the site features wire wrapped around a small arch eroded out of the soft sandstone surrounding the site. Below the wire is small rock overhang enclosed with an irregular rock wall. This activity area likely represents a children's play feature, something brought up in oral histories about children's life in this area (Louden 1992). Although perhaps the work of children, the mothers of the site likely exerted influence over the feature's placement; it is on a clear line of sight from one of the domestic structures. One would, with merely a raised voice, be able to call out and be heard between the two features.

When investigating habitation areas, archaeologists should keep the spatial implications of childhood and mothering in mind. The structures of La Placita are loosely grouped around three sides of a flat terrace area. The fourth side is demarcated by a topographic break in slope that in some areas is quite steep. This settlement plan created an open arena in which the movement of children would be visible from almost all areas of the site. However, keeping the smallest children of the site from tumbling into the canyon below would have been a potential concern. Analysis of the spatial patterning of architecture and trash disposal at the site strongly suggests that the residents of the site constructed and used the open area of the site as a traditional plaza, keeping the area free from trash. A close look at the distribution of ceramic sherds (fig. 10.4) highlights that, although the majority of trash is found down the canyon, in actuality the dump begins a meter or two before the break in slope. As such, the trash could have served as a marker to smaller children that the plaza, their "safe" area of play, ended just shy of the actual terrace edge. Like those of Clifton, the mothers of La Placita were providing a structured play zone for their children, one designed for easy surveillance by busy adults.

Thinking about child rearing means thinking about children's work in addition to their play. Historians suggest that our understanding of children and childhood are radically contingent (Ariès 1962). Exactly what was expected of children in Hispanic families of this time period can at least be suggested by oral histories and ethnographies gathered during the early part of the twentieth century. These accounts imply that Hispanic children were expected to both work and play. Children assisted with many household duties, including cooking, sewing, and agricultural labors. Many chores were specifically conceptualized as children's work, particularly fetching water and tending to small animals like chickens or rabbits (Brown et al. 1978; García 1997). Alice Lopez Russell, who grew up in the early 1900s near La Placita, provides us with a firsthand account of childhood in the region (Louden 1992). Like all the children in her family regardless of gender, Alice was expected to help her mother in the kitchen. She also recalled fetching water as one of her main chores. Photographs taken in New Mexico during the early twentieth century show girls hauling water at a young age (Brown et al. 1978).

At La Placita, the water source was an enclosed seep, located off the canyon edge, below the majority of the site. The residents created a path from the edge of the plaza down to the seep, the steepest portion of which angles across a rock

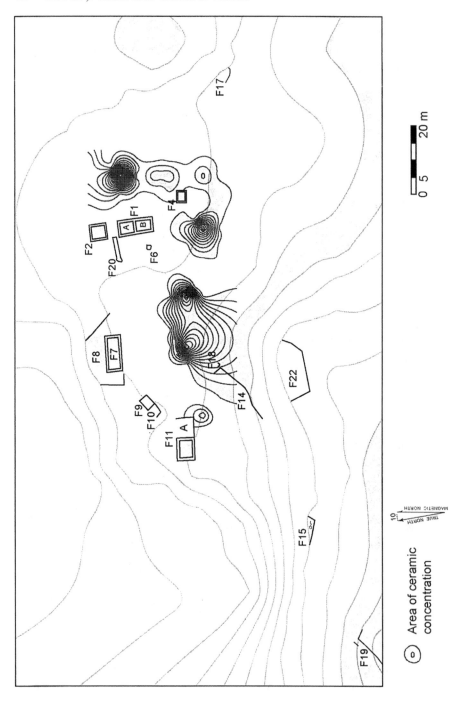

Figure 1.4.   La Placita site map showing ceramic distribution.

face. Where it crosses dirt, the path is merely cleared of vegetation, but some parts exhibit serious labor investment, especially a series of steps carved into the rock. A low rock wall edges the pathway as it drops across the rock face. It would seem to serve little purpose. However, if fetching water is primarily the task of children, it takes on more import. The low rock wall made the pathway more visible and provided a psychological comfort if not actually making the path more safe. The small steps carved into the lower edge of the path are most effective for small feet and short strides.

It is clear that the mothers of La Placita invested in spatial infrastructure to increase the safety of their children. But what other compensatory measures were taken to deal with increased demands on their labor? Deutsch (1987:55) suggests that one such measure was the acquisition of new technology, in particular sewing machines and wood-burning stoves. No evidence of sewing machines was recovered from La Placita, although straight pins recovered from multiple contexts do speak to the importance of sewing. There does appear to have been a wood-burning stove used in one household, but two others went without.

The women of La Placita seem to have pursued another strategy to lessen their workload, one not envisioned by Deutsch but noted by ethnographers as common in postcolonial settings (Klein 2003). Rather than relying solely on technology, these women manipulated the social obligations of labor. Faunal evidence from the site indicates that the major sources of protein for the site's residents were wild rabbits and chickens. Both are animals associated with Hispanic children's labor. Nasario García grew up in northern New Mexico with a sojourning father. On the weekends, it was his job to kill either a chicken or a rabbit so that there would be meat with supper on the night of his father's return. As he writes, "Killing rabbits was especially painful, since I raised them; but I learned to appreciate that slaughtering or butchering animals was necessary for one's survival" (García 1997:10). There is no evidence that the cottontail rabbits at La Placita were being raised in a hutch, but it seems likely that the work of snaring or shooting them fell to children, as did the care of chickens, including gathering eggs. It is likely that children also gathered nearby wild plants, particularly piñon seeds from the tree near the seep. The overwhelming evidence of small animals at La Placita indicates that women there were delegating much of the labor of subsistence to their children. Such a strategy allowed them to focus on other aspects of their newly expanded roles.

The archaeology of both the Clifton Plantation and La Placita provides powerful insight into the lives of two very different subaltern groups. That they share so much in common speaks to the pressures of personhood under siege. When powerful outside groups claim the labor of men and older boys, it has a significant impact on women's lives. As their labor increases, women often compensate in part by relying on the work of children. Yet what children were allowed to do was conscripted, carefully managed to help ensure their safety. The safety of children was also of concern nearer the home. There, busy mothers needed to perform labor while keeping an eye on the youngest children. These mothers did their best to create structured and safe play zones for those children who had yet to be pressed into service. The results of these studies provide powerful evidence for feminist anthropologists. Modern politicians and ideologues continue to suggest the incompatibility of certain elements of personhood, especially around mothering. Although most do not overtly suggest that certain racial or ethnic positions prevent true motherhood, they blame a variety of ills on mothers who work. Of course, the wealth inequity that is one of the legacies of racism and colonization means that many mothers must work. The archaeological evidence cited here suggests that work and motherhood have never been incompatible.

Directions for the Future

The study of personhood in the past is a promising form of investigation, one that has greatly expanded in the twenty-first century. It coincides with other avenues of research both within and beyond anthropology, including studies of embodiment and postcolonial theory. Additionally, it engages with thought about agency, given that elements of a contextualized self often either conscribe or expand the potential of individual actors to engage in various social practices. Archaeologists can continue to contribute to the growing body of research in these areas, particularly given their access to data that greatly expand the temporal reach of social thought and ground it in material and spatial practices.

We hope this chapter has made it clear that for those interested in gender, archaeologies of personhood hold great potential. They promise to decenter yet at the same time reinvigorate gendered archaeology. By thinking about the prism of self, of people not with just gender but also age, kin, class, and ethnicity, we move from talking about women or men in the past to more fully realized social actors: mothers and fathers, young women, and elite elder men. The material record holds great promise for investigating the spatial elements of gendered personhood, be it the locations of rites of passage such as burials or the household spaces of parenting and childhood. When people's personhood is denied through sexism, racism, and other forms of oppression, the material world is the location of struggles and yields the evidence of strategies of resistance.

Clearly our agenda has much in common with our fellow authors in this volume. Like them—and fellow feminist researchers throughout the social sciences—we aim to expand but not abandon the goals of decades of research into gender. In 1994, feminist philosopher of science Helen Longino investigated what feminist researchers actually do. She identified a number of "theoretical virtues" (Longino 1994:476) in feminist work, including embracing complexity and eschewing single-factor causal models, trying to diffuse power, and doing work that addresses current human needs. A critical contribution of the piece is that in it Longino identifies something she calls the "bottom line requirement of feminist knowers . . . namely that they reveal or prevent the disappearing of gender" (481). Echoing Longino, we believe that an archaeology of personhood can move us forward only if pursued in such a manner that it never forgets its roots in feminist thought and never disappears gender.

References

Ardren, Traci, and Scott Hutson, eds.
    2006   *The Social Experience of Childhood in Ancient Mesoamerica.* Boulder: University Press of Colorado.
Ariès, Philippe
    1962   *Centuries of Childhood.* London: Jonathan Cape.
Beaudry, Mary C.
    1991   Reinventing Historical Archaeology. In *Historical Archaeology and the Study of American Culture.* L. A. d. Cunzo and B. L. Herman, eds. Proceedings, 1991 Winterthur Conference. Pp. 473–497. Winterthur, DE: Henry Francis du Pont Winterthur Museum.
Blakey, Michael
    2001   Bioarchaeology of the African Diaspora in the Americas: Its Origins and Scope. *Annual Review of Anthropology* 30:387–422.
Brandt, Steven A., and Kathryn J. Weedman
    2000   *Hide-Working Practices and Material Culture of Southern Ethiopia: A Cross-Cultural Comparison.* Gainesville: Department of Anthropology, University of Florida.
Brown, Kenneth, and Doreen Cooper
    1990   Structural Continuity in an African American Slave and Tenant Community. *Historical Archaeology* 24(4):7–19.
Brown, Lorin W., Charles W. Biggs, and Marta Weigle
    1978   *Hispano Folklife of New Mexico.* Albuquerque: University of New Mexico Press.
Butler, Judith
    1990   *Gender Trouble: Feminism and the Subversion of Identity.* New York: Routledge.
    1993   *Bodies That Matter: On the Discursive Limits of "Sex."* New York: Routledge.
Carey, Margaret
    1997   Gender in African Beadwork: An Overview. In *Beads and Beadmakers: Gender, Material Culture and Meaning.* L. D. Sciama and J. B. Eicher, eds. Pp. 83–93. Oxford: Berg.

Carrillo, Richard, Stephen M. Kalasz, Stephen A. Brown, Phillip L. Petersen, and Christian J. Zier
    1994   Archaeological Excavations at the Prowers House, Boggsville Historic Site (5BN363), Bent County, Colorado. Manuscript available from author.

Carrillo, Richard, Lori E. Rhodes, and Phillip L. Petersen
    1993   Historical Archaeology at Boggsville Historic Site (5BN363): Excavations Conducted to Facilitate the Restoration and Reconstruction of the Prowers House, Bent County, Colorado. Manuscript available from author.

Clark, Bonnie J.
    1996   Amache Ochinee Prowers: The Archaeobiography of a Cheyenne Woman. Master's thesis, University of Denver.
    2003   On the Edge of Purgatory: An Archaeology of Ethnicity and Gender in Hispanic Colorado. Ph.D. dissertation, University of California, Berkeley.
    2005   Lived Ethnicity: Archaeology and Identity in *Mexicano* America. *World Archaeology* 37(3):440–52.

Collier, Jane, and Sylvia J. Yanagisako, eds.
    1987   *Gender and Kinship: Essays toward a Unified Analysis.* Stanford, CA: Stanford University Press.

Collins, Patricia Hill
    1994   Shifting the Center: Race, Class, and Feminist Theorizing about Motherhood. In *Mothering: Ideology, Experience and Agency.* E. N. Glenn, G. Chang, and R. Forcey, eds. Pp. 45–66. New York: Routledge.
    2000   *Black Feminist Thought: Knowledge, Consciousness and the Politics of Empowerment.* New York: Routledge.

Corruccini, R., J. Handler, and K. Jacobi
    1985   Chronological Distribution of Enamel Hypoplasias and Weaning in a Caribbean Slave Population. *Human Biology* 57:699–711.

Davis, Angela
    1983   *Women, Race and Class.* New York: Vintage Books.

Deutsch, Sarah
    1987   *No Separate Refuge: Culture, Class, and Gender on an Anglo-Hispanic Frontier.* New York: Oxford University Press.

di Leonardo, Micaela
    1991   Introduction: Gender, Culture, and Political Economy: Feminist Anthropology in Historical Perspective. In *Gender and the Crossroads of Knowledge: Feminist Anthropology in the Postmodern Era.* M. di Leonardo, ed. Pp. 1–48. Berkeley: University of California Press.

Epperson, Terrence
    2004   Critical Race Theory and the Archaeology of the African Diaspora. *Historical Archaeology* 38(1):101–8.

Ferguson, Leland
    1992   *Uncommon Ground.* Washington, DC: Smithsonian Institution Press.

Flannery, Kent, ed.

1976   *The Early Mesoamerican Village.* New York: Academic Press.

Fowler, Chris

2004   *The Archaeology of Personhood: An Anthropological Approach.* London: Routledge.

Galle, J. E., and A. L. Young, eds.

2004   *Engendering African-American Archaeology: A Southern Perspective.* Knoxville: University of Tennessee Press.

García, Nasario, ed.

1997   *Comadres: Hispanic Women of the Rio Puerco Valley.* Albuquerque: University of New Mexico Press.

Gero, Joan

1991   Genderlithics: Women's Roles in Stone Tool Production. In *Engendering Archaeology: Women and Prehistory.* Joan M. Gero and Margaret W. Conkey, eds. Pp. 163–93. Oxford: Blackwell.

Gero, Joan, and Margaret Conkey, eds.

1991   *Engendering Archaeology.* Oxford: Blackwell.

Gewertz, Deborah

1984   The Tchambuli View of Persons: A Critique of Individualism in the Works of Mead and Chodorow. *American Anthropologist* 86(3):615–29.

Giddings, Paula

1984   *When and Where I Enter: The Impact of Black Women on Race and Sex in America.* New York: William Morrow.

Gilchrist, Roberta

1999   *Gender and Archaeology: Contesting the Past.* London: Routledge.

2000   Archaeological Biographies: Realizing Human Lifecycles, -Courses, and -Histories. *World Archaeology* 31(3):325–28.

Gillespie, Susan

2000   Personhood, Agency, and Mortuary Ritual: A Case Study from the Ancient Maya. *Journal of Anthropological Archaeology* 20:71–112.

Gray, William

1825   *Travels in Western Africa in the Years 1818, 19, 20, and 21 from the River Gambia to the River Niger.* London: John Murray.

Grinnell, George Bird

1962   *The Cheyenne Indians: Their History and Ways of Life* I. New York: Cooper Square.

Handler, Jerome

1996   A Prone Burial from a Plantation Slave Cemetery in Barbados, West Indies: Possible Evidence for an African-Type Witch or Other Negatively Viewed Person. *Historical Archaeology* 30(3):76–86.

Hill, James, and James Gunn, eds.

1977   *The Individual in Prehistory: Studies of Variability in Style in Prehistoric Technologies.* New York: Academic Press.

Hodder, Ian
    2000   Agency and Individuals in Long-Term Processes. In *Agency in Archaeology*. Mar-
            cia-Anne Dobres and John Robb, eds. Pp. 21–33. London: Routledge.
Hoig, Stan
    1989   *The Cheyenne*. Indians of North America. New York: Chelsea House Pub-
            lishers.
Howell, Signe, and Marit Melhuus
    1993   The Study of Kinship; the Study of Person; a Study of Gender? In *Gendered
            Anthropology*. T. del Valle, ed. Pp. 38–53. London: Routledge.
Hudnall, Mary Prowers
    1945   Early History of Bent County. *Colorado Magazine* 22(6):233–47.
Hurd, C. W.
    1957   *Boggsville: Cradle of the Colorado Cattle Industry*. Las Animas, CO: Boggsville Com-
            mittee.
Hutson, Scott, and Aline Magnoni
    2002   Children Not at Ancient Chunchucmil, Yucatan, Mexico. Paper presented
            at the Annual Meeting of the American Anthropological Association, New
            Orleans.
Joyce, Rosemary
    2000a   *Gender and Power in Prehispanic Mesoamerica*. Texas: University of Texas.
    2000b   Girling the Girl and Boying the Boy: The Production of Adulthood in
            Ancient Mesoamerica. *World Archaeology* 31(3):473–83.
    2004   Embodied Subjectivity: Gender, Femininity, Masculinity, Sexuality. In *Com-
            panion to Social Archaeology*. Lynn Meskell, ed. Pp. 81–91. Oxford: Blackwell.
    2006   Feminist Theories of Embodiment and Anthropological Imagination: Mak-
            ing Bodies Matter. In *Feminist Anthropology: Past, Present and Future*. P. Geller and
            M. Stocking, eds. Philadelphia: University of Pennsylvania Press.
King, Stacie
    2006   The Marking of Age in Ancient Coastal Oaxaca. In *The Social Experience of
            Childhood in Ancient Mesoamerica*. T. Ardren and S. Hutson, eds. Boulder: Univer-
            sity Press of Colorado.
Klein, Laura
    2003   *Women and Men in World Cultures*. Boston: McGraw-Hill.
Knapp, A. Bernard
    1998   Boys Will Be Boys: Masculinist Approaches to a Gendered Archaeology. In
            Reader in Gender Archaeology. K. Hays-Gilpin and D. S. Whitley, eds. Pp. 365–
            73. London: Routledge.
Lightfoot, Kent G.
    1995   Culture Contact Studies: Redefining the Relationship between Prehistoric
            and Historical Archaeology. *American Antiquity* 60(2):199–217.

Lightfoot, K., A. Martinez, and A. M. Schiff
  1997   Daily Practice and Material Culture in Pluralistic Social Settings: An Archae-
            ological Study of Culture Change and Persistence from Fort Ross, California.
            American Antiquity 63(2):199–222.
Longino, Helen
  1994   In Search of Feminist Epistemology. *The Monist* 77(4):472–85.
Louden, Dick
  1992   Alice Lopez Russell interview. Manuscript available from the author.
Meskell, Lynn A.
  1999   *Archaeologies of Social Life*. Oxford: Blackwell.
  2002   *Private Life in New Kingdom Egypt*. Princeton, NJ: Princeton University Press.
  2004   *Object Worlds in Ancient Egypt: Material Biographies Past and Present*. London: Berg.
Meskell, Lynn A., and Rosemary A. Joyce
  2003   *Embodied Lives: Figuring Ancient Maya and Egyptian Experience*. London: Routledge.
Moore, Jenny, and Eleanor Scott, eds.
  1997   *Invisible People and Processes: Writing Gender and Childhood into European Archaeology*.
            London: Leicester University Press.
Nostrand, Richard
  1992   *The Hispano Homeland*. Norman: University of Oklahoma Press.
Orser, Charles E., Jr.
  1994   The Archaeology of African American Slave Religion in the Antebellum
            South. *Cambridge Archaeological Journal* 4(1):33–45.
Orser, Charles E., Jr., ed.
  2000   *Race and the Archaeology of Identity*. Salt Lake City: University of Utah Press.
Patterson, Orlando
  1982   *Slavery and Social Death: A Comparative Study*. Cambridge, MA: Harvard Univer-
            sity Press.
Pulsipher, Lydia
  1993   Changing Roles in the Life Cycles of Women in Traditional West Indian
            Houseyards. In *Women and Change in the Caribbean: A Caribbean Perspective*. J. J.
            Momsen, ed. Pp. 50–64. Bloomington: Indiana University Press.
Rattray, R. S.
  1932   *The Tribes of the Ashanti Hinterland*. 2 vols. Oxford: Clarendon Press.
Roberts, Dorothy
  1997   *Killing the Black Body*. New York: Pantheon.
Schmidt, Robert, and Barbara Voss, eds.
  2000   *Archaeologies of Sexuality*. London: Routledge.
Schwarz, Maureen T.
  1996   Unraveling the Anchoring Cord: Navajo Relocation, 1974–1996. *American
            Anthropologist* 99(1):43–55.

Sofaer-Derevenski, Joanne, ed.
　　2000　*Children and Material Culture*. London: Routledge.
Spelman, Elizabeth
　　1988　*Inessential Woman: Problems of Exclusion in Feminist Thought*. Boston: Beacon Press.
Tringham, Ruth
　　1990　Households with Faces: The Challenge of Gender in Prehistoric Architectural
　　　　　Remains. In *Engendering Archaeology*. Joan Gero and Margaret Conkey, eds. Pp.
　　　　　93–131. Oxford: Blackwell.
Van Ness, John R.
　　1991　*Hispanos in Northern New Mexico: The Development of Corporate Community and Multi-
　　　　　community*. New York: AMS Press.
Voss, Barbara
　　2000　Feminisms, Queer Theories, and the Archaeological Study of Past Sexualities.
　　　　　World Archaeology 32(2):180–92.
Wilkie, Laurie A.
　　1997　Secret and Sacred: Contextualizing the Artifacts of African-American Magic
　　　　　and Religion. *Historical Archaeology* 31(4):81–106.
　　2003　*The Archaeology of Mothering: An African-American Midwife's Tale*. New York:
　　　　　Routledge.
Wilkie, Laurie A., and Paul Farnsworth
　　1999　Trade and the Construction of Bahamian Identity: A Multiscalar Exploration.
　　　　　International Journal of Historical Archaeology 3(4):283–320.
　　2005　*Sampling Many Pots: An Archaeology of Memory and Tradition at a Bahamian Plantation*.
　　　　　Gainesville: University Press of Florida.
Wood, Margaret C.
　　2001　Working-Class Households as Sites of Social Change. In *Household Chores and
　　　　　Household Choices: Theorizing the Domestic Sphere in Historical Archaeology*. K. S. Barile
　　　　　and J. C. Brandon, eds. Pp. 210–32. Tuscaloosa: University of Alabama
　　　　　Press.
Wurst, LuAnn, and Robert Fitts, eds.
　　1999　Confronting Class. *Historical Archaeology* 33(1):1–195.
Yamin, Rebecca
　　2002　Children's Strikes, Parent's Rights: Paterson and Five Points. *International Jour-
　　　　　nal of Historical Archaeology* 6(2):113–26.

Sexuality in Archaeology

2

BARBARA L. VOSS

F
OR CENTURIES, archaeologists have encountered sexually explicit materials from past cultures, but their sexual content has been either minimized or treated lasciviously. In the early 1990s, however, this situation began to change, largely through the development of feminist and gender studies in archaeology. Initially, there was little published work; individual researchers, working mainly in isolation from each other, began to circulate manuscripts and give conference papers on sex-focused research. Then, in 1996, Taylor published his ambitiously conceived and controversial monograph *The Prehistory of Sex: Four Million Years of Human Sexual Culture*. In 2000, Schmidt and Voss published their edited volume *Archaeologies of Sexuality*, and Dowson edited a *World Archaeology* issue titled "Queer Archaeologies." In the five years since then, a growing number of articles and book chapters have been published, and archaeological conferences frequently include presentations and symposia centered on sexual themes. Archaeologists are increasingly conducting investigations in which sexuality is examined as an integral aspect of the cultures they study.

The first section of this chapter, "Sexual Theories," considers the ways in which archaeologists conceptualize sexuality. It traces the relationship between sexuality studies and engendered archaeology and then turns to consider three major theories of sexuality: sexology, the sex/gender system, and queer theory. Then the chapter turns to "Sexual Topics." To date, archaeological research on sexuality can be loosely grouped around five major (and at times overlapping) themes: fertility management, homosexuality/transsexuality, prostitution, architecture and space, and sexual or erotic representations. The third section, "Sexual Cultures," discusses the work of two archaeologists—Rosemary Joyce and Lynn Meskell—who have developed rich, nuanced archaeological interpretations of sexual life in two very different times and places: Classic Maya Mesoamerica and New Kingdom Egypt.

Sexual Theories

In the mid-1980s, feminist critiques of androcentric biases in archaeology established a firm foundation for future research on sexuality. Prior to feminist interventions, most archaeological studies interpreted the past through gender stereotypes that, among other aspects, presumed a heterosexual norm, linked men to production and toolmaking and women to reproduction and child rearing, and identified men as sexually dominant and women as passive sexual objects. The feminist critique in archaeology challenged the universal applicability of these stereotypes and in doing so created possibilities for archaeological research not only on gender but also on sexuality (Conkey and Spector 1984:3–13; Gilchrist 1991; Nelson 1997:113–29; Sørensen 1988, 2000:45–52; Voss and Schmidt 2000:14–18). By separating gender roles from biological reproduction, these early feminist studies created possibilities for researching sexuality independently of reproduction. Additionally, feminist attention to the microscale demonstrated that research on interpersonal relationships—including sexual acts, sexual relations, and sexual ideologies—is neither trivial nor particularistic but instead is essential to understanding so-called macroscale topics ranging from subsistence and settlement systems to state formation and imperialism.

These early feminist archaeological studies fostered a climate within which research on sexuality became increasingly possible. As Claassen (1992:4) wrote, "There is another social function of gender to be considered and that is the social marking of sexually appropriate partners . . . if the reader accepts this social function of gender, then an archaeology of gender is an archaeology of *sexuality.*" Further, it is clear through bibliographic citations that early feminist and gender-focused archaeological research was engaged with a wide range of theories of sexuality (Voss 2000b). Yet, for the most part, the topic of sexuality was rarely addressed directly. For example, many researchers examined marriage primarily as a locus of the gendered organization of labor but not as a mechanism for the social regulation of sexuality. Others used the concept of the *berdache* (Native American two-spirit) as an example of a "culturally defined gender category" (Conkey and Spector 1984:15) without discussing the ways in which two-spirit identities also reference cultural categories of sexuality. In other words, as the feminist critique matured into a program of archaeological research on gender (Conkey and Gero 1997), sexuality took a backseat. Although this may in part be attributed to what Rubin has called "sex essentialism" and "sex negativity" (Rubin 1984:275, 278; see also Voss and Schmidt 2000:3–5), it is perhaps equally attributed to the ways that certain social theories have shaped archaeological investigations of gender and sexuality.

Like all archaeological research, investigations of sexuality interpret the past through the lens of the present: deliberately, through the use of ethnographic analogies; and, less consciously, through the ways that present-day sexual norms, politics, ideologies, and identities affect researchers' conceptualization of the past. The language used to discuss sexuality today can seem so self-evident that terms such as "heterosexual," "homosexual," "masochist," or "cross-dresser" are often taken to be universal, transhistorical identity categories. Archaeological researchers without specific training in the field of sexuality studies may not be aware of the extent to which these modern, largely Euro-American sexual identity categories are relatively recent cultural phenomena. Here, I briefly discuss three of the major intellectual projects that have shaped present-day conceptions of sexuality: sexology, the sex/gender system, and gender performance theory.

Sexology

All modern academic studies of sexuality, including archaeological ones, are a legacy of sexology, a discipline that emerged in the late 1800s as part of the general expansion of taxonomic and medical sciences (Bland and Doan 1998a, 1998b). Although the research goals and practices of sexologists were diverse, a shared premise of sexology was that sexuality was an essential, enduring determinant of a person's character or identity. While religious and civil frameworks of the time focused primarily on the regulation of sexual acts and sexualized behaviors, sexologists argued that sexual acts and practices were the symptomatic expressions of durable underlying sexual dispositions. Further, these sexual dispositions were thought to cause not just sexual desires and behaviors but nonsexual preferences, habits, and behaviors as well.

Sexologists generally used the medical case-study method, in which interviews and examinations of afflicted patients were used to build profiles of the symptoms and progressions of specific diseases. Observations gathered from multiple case studies were used to develop elaborate sexual typologies. Common variables that sexologists evaluated when constructing these typologies included the patient's apparent genital sex at birth, the physical attributes of the patient's adult genitalia and other parts of the body, the patient's degree of conformance to gender norms in appearance and behavior, and the patient's sexual behavior and desires, with a specific focus on the gender(s) of the patient's real and desired sexual partners. While the case studies used were drawn primarily from urban European and American populations, they also included observations from early ethnographic studies and from reports submitted by colonial officials and missionaries working abroad (e.g., Casella 2000a). The resulting typologies were thus generally presented as universal and transhistorical categories that had been discovered through scientific research, resulting in a speciation of sexual subjects loosely parallel to the Linnaean speciation of plant and animal organisms. Most sexual identity terms used today (e.g., pedophile, transvestite, heterosexual, or homosexual) are an enduring legacy of these medical typologies.

The Sex/Gender System

If sexology generated a universalizing model of sexuality, cultural anthropology provides an alternative legacy that highlights cross-cultural variation in sexual behaviors and identities. In particular, anthropological research has focused on how sexual subjectivities are integral to cultural systems. While sexologists argued that sexuality was central to individual identity, the work of anthropologists— from Mead and Malinowski onward—expanded this premise to argue that sexuality is implicated in "almost every aspect of culture" (Malinowski 1929:xxiii).

These anthropological studies provided the empirical basis for the second dominant model operating today in sexuality studies: the sex/gender system. First articulated in Rubin's (1975) article "The Traffic in Women," the sex/gender system distinguished between sex (biological—male, female) and gender (cultural—man, woman, masculine, feminine). Subsequent anthropological research inspired by the sex/gender model focused initially on documenting the cross-cultural variability of gender roles, a project that greatly shaped the emergence of feminist and gender-focused archaeologies.

Within the sex/gender model, sexuality lurks uncomfortably in the interstices between biology and culture. Studies of sexuality within this framework have focused primarily on cultural attitudes toward men's and women's sexuality and the power dynamics of sexual relationships. Rubin (1984:267) herself articulated the limitations of the sex/gender model in this regard, intoning, "The time has come to think about sex." Rubin called for historical and political analyses to demonstrate how sexuality in general has been constructed as a stigmatized aspect of modern life and how specific sexual practices have been constructed as benign or malignant. Through reference to sexological research, Rubin advocated a "concept of benign sexual variation" in which differences in sexual practices should be viewed through an appreciation of "variation [as] a fundamental property of all life, from the simplest biological organism to the most complex human social formations" (283). As in the sex/gender system, this conceptualization of varied sexualities that are suppressed or promoted through cultural mechanisms embraces a nature/culture duality.

The theoretical prominence of the sex/gender system within archaeological studies has specific implications for the ways in which sexuality has been conceptualized in archaeological interpretations. Most positively, the sex/gender model has encouraged research on ways that sexuality varies across culture and time. However, these sexual practices and sexual identities have been treated predominantly as a function of gender rather than as a distinct aspect of social relations. Additionally, the conceptualization of sexuality as the product of a nature/cultural duality has unwittingly supported a tendency to treat reproductive, heterosexual sexual acts as natural and constant while emphasizing the cultural production of nonreproductive sexual practices and identities.

Gender Performance Theory

The nature/culture duality of the sex/gender system has been challenged by Butler's theory of gender performance. First outlined in her landmark text *Gender Trouble* (1990, reprinted in 1999) and further elaborated in various articles (e.g., Butler 1993b, 1994) and the book *Bodies That Matter* (1993a), Butler's theory of gender performativity challenges both the analytical distinction between gender and sexuality and the biological/cultural dualism of the sex/gender system model.

Butler's performance theory is complex and multifaceted and cannot be easily summarized; however, a few key points are particularly relevant here. First, Butler rejects the categorical distinction between gender and sexuality, instead arguing that both are mutually produced through a heterosexual matrix (Butler 1999:chaps. 1 and 2). The dominant discourse of heterosexuality requires a division of persons into two gender categories and simultaneously legitimizes sexual desires for the opposite gender. Through this matrix, both those with nonnormative gender identities and those whose sexual desires and practices deviate from heterosexuality are simultaneously constructed as abject persons. The heterosexual matrix is sustained by defining itself against those practices and identities that it stigmatizes and thus relies on the abject for its own existence (Butler 1993b).

Butler also questions the distinction between biological and cultural aspects of sexuality and gender. The sex/gender system rests, for example, on a claim that certain aspects of being a woman or a man are natural, yet the line between what is "cultural" or "natural" about gender and sexuality is highly contested and debated in cultural discourse. Butler thus argues that what is perceived as "natural" is delineated and fixed through cultural practices and that it is perhaps more productive to see the distinction between natural and cultural as a disciplining practice that seeks to establish certain aspects of identity as irreducible and unchangeable (Butler 1999:7–12). "There is," Butler notes, "an insistent materiality of the body, but . . . it never makes itself known or legible outside of the cultural articulation in which it appears" (Breen and Blumenfeld 2001:12).

A third element of Butler's theory is that gender and sexual identities are continually produced through social performances. Although gender and sexual identities may appear stable, the appearance of continuity is an illusion created by an endless series of mimetic repetitions, much as a film projector creates an illusion of continuity through a rapid sequence of still images being flashed on a screen. These gendered and sexual performances are not volitional in the sense that an actor might assume the identity of a character she is playing; rather, these performances are "a set of repeated acts within a highly rigid regulatory frame" (Butler 1999:43–44). It is within the gaps between these repetitions that Butler identifies potential for agency, as subjects may be able to subtly transform these mimetic performances through subversive practices like mimicry, satire, drag, exaggeration, and so on (e.g., Butler 1993a:121–40, 1999:173–77).

It would not be an understatement to note that Butler's theories of gender performance have transformed the fields of feminist/gender/sexuality studies and have shifted the terms of sexual and feminist political and social activism. One of the key effects of Butler's theories has been a profound change in sexual identification practices, especially the reclamation of the epithet "queer" (de Lauretis 1991:v). Broadly conceptualized as being oppositional to the normative heterosexual matrix, queer practices of identification generally celebrate fluidity and instability in both gender and sexual identities. Many people who previously identified (or would have been identified) as gay or lesbian or bisexual or transgendered/transsexual have adopted the moniker "queer" as a form of resistance to the taxonomic sexual identity categories that were codified and given medical and legal legitimacy through sexology (Warner 1993).

Theorizing Archaeologies of Sexuality

Archaeological research on sexual identities thus operates within this triple legacy of sexology, the sex/gender system, and gender performance theory. The greatest liability of these theories is that they were all developed to address relatively recent conditions in European and American cultures. These theories may tell us more about how we understand our sexual selves in the present day than about how people in the past may have experienced and shaped the sexual aspects of their lives. For archaeologists, this shortcoming is an opportunity. Archaeological studies of sexuality are important precisely because they illuminate the assumptions and limitations of modern theories of sexuality and, in doing so, aid in developing a practice of sexuality studies that more accurately engages with the full range and potentials of human subjectivity.

One of the biggest challenges facing archaeologists is that the categorization of "sexuality" as a distinct aspect of social relations and the premise that sexuality is a central component of social identity may both be historic products of Western modernity (Foucault 1978). On one hand, sexology, the sex/gender system, and gender performance theory provide conceptual tools that enable us to investigate sexuality in the past; on the other hand, our own predilection to view sexuality as a discrete category may blind us to other ways that sexualities were enacted in past cultures. By being aware of the historical and cultural limitation of current sexual theories, archaeologists may be able to remain open to the possibility that what we think of as "sexuality" may have been quite differently organized in the past.

A second challenge that archaeologists face in our research on sexuality consists of the tensions and contradictions among the theories of sexuality outlined here. Sexology provides a universal, medical model of sexuality; the sex/gender system provides a means for considering the ways that sexuality is biologically structured but culturally contingent; and performance theory emphasizes the social construction of sexuality. But we need not resolve the extent to which sexuality is shaped by biology or culture in order to conduct archaeological investigations of sexuality. For example, few would argue that food consumption is unrelated to biology or lacks an adaptive function, yet archaeologists also investigate how culture—including social organization, economic relationships, ethnic identities, gender ideologies, and religion, to name a few—shapes the ways that social groups and individuals produce, process, prepare, and consume food. Likewise, cultural responses to sexual desires and behaviors are so profound and varied that the relationship between biology and a specific sexual identity or practice is at most likely to be correlative rather than determinate.

Sexual Topics

These three bodies of sexuality theory—sexology, the sex/gender system, and performance theory—have provided important foundations for archaeological investigations of sexual identities. To date, archaeological research on sexuality can be loosely grouped around five major (and at times overlapping) themes: fertility management, homosexuality/transsexuality, prostitution, architecture and space, and sexual or erotic representations. This section summarizes the work that has been undertaken within each of these arenas in turn.

Reproduction in Culture: Fertility Management

Some of the earliest archaeological investigations of sexuality have centered on fertility management—a term that broadly encompasses both the production of cultural knowledge about fertility and actions that may be taken to promote or avoid conception and/or live birth of viable offspring. However, in considering fertility management as a topic within archaeological research on sexuality, it is critical not to conflate sexuality with reproduction or vice versa. There is, of course, a physiological link between reproduction and certain sexual practices— notably those that involve what Abelove (1989:126) has termed "cross-sex genital intercourse (penis in vagina, vagina around penis, with seminal emission uninterrupted)." But sexual activity is by no means limited to such practices, nor do those participating in such practices always desire conception as the outcome of sexual acts. Taylor (1996:7) posits that "for the past four million years the human line has been able to consciously separate sex from reproduction." The evidence Taylor produces to substantiate this claim is ambiguous at best, but his point that biological reproduction and sexual intercourse may have been culturally shaped long before the advent of anatomically modern humans is an important one. A growing number of studies have demonstrated that members of many animal species generally (Baghemil 2000) and of nonhuman primate species more particularly (de Waal 1989, 1995; McDonald Pavelka 1995; Vasey 1995, 1998) regularly engage in nonreproductive sexual behaviors. Vasey (1998:416–17) in particular argues that both reproductive and nonreproductive sexual behaviors are motivated largely by "mutual sexual attraction and gratification." Likewise, Taylor (1996:75) argues that for all primates (including humans), sexuality is a learned source for the exploration and expression of pleasure and power. Fertility management thus provides a means by which the reproductive aspects of sexual practices can be either enhanced or suppressed within a broader cultural context of sexuality.

Cultural practices related to fertility management include both bodily practices that are unlikely to be represented in the archaeological record and material practices that are more likely to have been preserved archaeologically. One of the most contested debates in archaeological research on sexuality centers around whether figurines and rock art from Paleolithic, Neolithic, and Mesolithic Europe and the Near East constitute evidence of rituals related to prehistoric fertility management. Selected figurines, such as the famous Venus of Willendorf, have been interpreted by some as evidence of fertility rituals or beliefs about a cosmological link between fertility and female deities—an argument that has most recently been promulgated through so-called Goddess archaeology but has its roots in earlier, nineteenth-century interpretations. As Conkey and Tringham (1995:212) have synthesized, the central argument made by many authors is that "female figurines . . . with large stomachs and so-called pendulous breasts depicted pregnancy and or lactation and therefore signified fertility and the magical desires for sexual births." Other archaeologists have extended this argument by attributing sexual meanings to other forms of prehistoric European art (e.g., Kokkinidou and Nikolaidou 1997; for discussions of varied approaches, see Bahn 1986; Bahn and Vertut 1988; Conkey 1989). The broad interpretations of prehistoric symbolic images as evidence of fertility ritual complexes have been widely challenged on both empirical and methodological grounds (Conkey and Tringham 1995; Dobres 1992; Handsman 1991; Meskell 1995, 1998b; Nelson 1990). This debate has been particularly important to the development of archaeologies of sexuality because it has introduced feminist theories of representation, the sexual gaze, and the body into archaeological interpretation.

Other archaeological investigations of fertility management have focused less on spiritual/magical practices and more on physical techniques. Taylor's survey of archaeological evidence of contraception in prehistoric Egyptian, Greek, and Bronze Age European contexts reveals a wide variety of materials used to prevent or promote reproduction. These included caustic or blocking vaginal pessaries, herbal medicines, mechanical devices used in abortions, and condoms (Taylor 1996:85–96). Archaeological investigations of more recent historical contexts in Britain and the United States have similarly recovered artifacts associated with fertility management. One of the most rigorous of these is a study of ten animal-membrane condoms recovered from a seventeenth-century garderobe (latrine) from Dudley Castle (Gaimster et al. 1996). The investigators' detailed physical analysis of the Dudley Castle specimens proved that professional production of standard-sized condoms was a well-developed craft at least a century earlier than historical records alone suggested.

Perhaps the most comprehensive archaeological study of fertility management is Wilkie's (2000, 2003) research on African American sexual magic and midwifery. Wilkie takes as her starting point a collection of artifacts that she excavated from trash deposits associated with the Perrymans, an African American family living in Mobile, Alabama, in the late nineteenth and early twentieth centuries. The maternal head of the family, Lucrecia Perryman, turned to midwifery as a means of supporting her family after her husband's death. Lay midwives in the American South served not only as medical practitioners but also as "generational and gender mediators for their communities" (Wilkie 2003:xix). Wilkie's distinctive contribution to the archaeology of fertility management and sexuality is her investigation of the ways that women during this period made decisions "to mother or not to mother" and her recognition that spiritual and medicinal practices were seamlessly integrated in the "ethnomedical tool kit" (Wilkie 2000:138) that women and men employed in preventing and promoting childbearing and in mediating tensions between the sexes. "All of these magical-medical cures indicated from the midwifery site incorporated symbols that were strongly connected with regulating sexual activity or treating the consequences of such activity. . . . The contents of a single jar of Vaseline could have been bought for use as a hair pomade, used to help cure a bout of impotence, and then used to treat a diaper rash" (Wilkie 2000:139, 133). Further, she demonstrates that fertility management can be understood only within the specific historical and cultural context within which it is practiced—in this case, within the context of the legacies of slavery, the challenges of African American life in the postbellum South, and the rise of discourses of "scientific mothering" and the increasing persecution of mid-wives by the American Medical Association.

Within sexuality studies as a whole, the archaeology of fertility management reminds us that even in its most "biological" moments, sexuality is produced through culture. Whether these cultural practices are spiritual, material, or both, they often involve material objects that at times literally mediate the physical surfaces of human sexual interaction. As Wilkie so powerfully demonstrates, even the most mundane, everyday artifacts can have sexual meanings and sexual functions for the people who used them.

Challenging Heteronormativity: Investigations of Homosexuality / Transsexuality

Another prominent theme in sexuality studies is research that challenges the pervasive heterosexist biases of most archaeological interpretations. The vast majority of archaeological research—including much work conducted within the framework of feminist or gender-focused archaeology—presumes heterosexual relationships (especially the nuclear family) to be the foundation of social life in past cultures. This bias persists despite the vast corpus of anthropological and historical evidence to the contrary. Heterosexism has a debilitating effect on archaeological research: in some cases, the presumption of universal heterosexuality blinds researchers to alternative and equally plausible explanations; in others, archaeological data are even distorted to support implausible interpretations (Dowson 2000; Schmidt 2002; Voss, in press; Voss and Schmidt 2000).

Efforts to correct this heterosexist bias in archaeological interpretation have been twofold. First, a body of work has emerged that seeks to expose the sexual assumptions behind archaeological interpretations. Yates's (1993) analysis of sexual representations in Scandinavian prehistoric rock art is a particularly salient example of this; he questions the conventional interpretation of certain images as a representation of heterosexual intercourse, arguing that the images could just as plausibly represent a sex act between two people of the same gender. Schmidt

(2002) traces the relationship between archaeological evidence (or lack thereof) and scholarly and popular debates about the sexuality of Ötzi, the Tyrolean "Ice Man." Reeder (2000) points out that heterosexual bias has led Egyptologists to interpret images of men in socially affectionate poses as brothers or friends, while images of men and women in similar poses are interpreted as married couples. Danielsson (2002) similarly notes that analyses of gold foil images in late Iron Age Scandinavia describe images of opposite-sex pairs as depictions of "loving couples," while same-sex pairs in similar poses are not interpreted as sexual partners. McCafferty and McCafferty (in press) examine textual and archaeological sources for evidence of nonnormative gender identities in preconquest Mexico and conclude that there existed a "range of intermediate identities" some of which were gender ambiguous (hunchbacks and dwarfs) and others sexually "deviant" (homosexuals and harlots). Cobb (in press) critiques the ways in which hunter-gatherer studies in archaeology presume the transhistorical existence of the heterosexual family group. Likewise, Dowson (in press) draws attention to the ways that museum displays and archaeological reports perpetuate a mistaken image of the heterosexual family group as the enduring constant in British history from the Mesolithic to the Anglo-Saxon period.

Second, several researchers have undertaken investigations aimed at recovering evidence of nonheterosexual identities and practices in the past. These investigations have generally focused on two modern identity categories: homosexuality (sexual desire for persons of the same gender) and transgender/transsexuality (identifying with the gender role normally performed by persons of the opposite biological sex). At times, as will be seen later in this chapter, archaeologists have conflated these two categories. This confusion is problematic but understandable. The clinical separation of gender identity from sexual object choice in modern sexual identities was one of the major intellectual products of sexology; however, many modern folk categories tend to view them as inseparable (e.g., a "fairy" is simultaneously an effeminate male and a homosexual). Here again, archaeological research struggles within the legacy of sexology while simultaneously exposing the limitations of modern sexual taxonomies.

In North America, most research challenging heteronormative biases has centered on the archaeology of so-called *berdache* and two-spirit indigenous identities. *Berdache* and two-spirit (also third- and fourth-gender) are generic anthropological terms used to conceptualize gender and sexual variance among Native North Americans. Such terms encompass a wide range of identification practices that varied significantly among different tribes. Broadly speaking, two-spirit identities are often associated with same-sex sexual practices, hermaphroditism, and transsexuality. Archaeological and ethnographic research suggest that multiple-gender/

sexuality systems may have great antiquity in North America, perhaps even originating in gendered and shamanistic practices of populations that migrated from eastern Asia and Siberia to the Americas over 10,000 years ago (Hollimon 2001).

In archaeological research, two-spirit identities were first discussed as an example of the potential diversity of sex/gender systems in the past (Claassen 1992; Duke 1991; Hollimon 1991, 1992; Whelan 1991). The earliest empirical studies of two-spirit identities centered on the analysis of mortuary evidence as a means to identify individuals in the past whose cultural gender (as identified through grave goods) differed from their physical sex (Whelan 1991). Hollimon's analysis of prehistoric Chumash burials expanded this approach by combining analysis of skeletal pathologies with distributional analysis of associated artifacts to identify a possible 'Aqí (two-spirit) burial (Hollimon 1996, 1997). This methodology has also been used in European archaeological contexts to evaluate measures of gender dichotomy and to identify gender diversity within a cemetery population (e.g., Lucy 1997; Rega 1997; Schmidt 2000, 2001); most recently, Arnold (2002) has identified ancient DNA analysis as an additional line of evidence that can be used to investigate sex/gender configurations in mortuary contexts. These approaches to "finding" two-spirits in the archaeological record emphasize transsexuality (or, per Arnold [2002], "gender transformers") as the determinant characteristic of two-spirit identity.

More recent archaeological research has taken a more holistic view of two-spirit identities. Hollimon has reexamined the Chumash burial case to consider the relationship between gender, sexuality, religion, and occupation in 'Aqí identity. Noting that the Chumash 'Aqí are usually members of an undertaking guild that involves occupational, spiritual, and kin-based obligations and privileges, Hollimon suggests that designation as an 'Aqí may relate more directly to abstinence from procreative sex acts than to a particular gendered or sexual identity. 'Aqí, she suggests, included biological men who were transsexual, men who had sex with other men, men without children, celibates, and postmenopausal women (Hollimon 2000, in press). Prine has similarly examined two-spirit Hidatsa miati through close readings of ethnohistoric, ethnographic, and archaeological records. Her research indicates that miati individuals, who were identified as male at birth, were differentiated from their age and sex cohorts in six different ways: they changed gender at adolescence, they had specific spiritual roles, they were highly respected, they created households focused on relationships with men, they were highly productive, and they were cultural innovators. Within Hidatsa culture, miati played a key role in earth lodge–building ceremonies, mediating the tension between feminine earth and masculine sky. Prine thus finds archaeological indicators of the miati through a study of architectural remains, identifying a double-posted earth lodge that might have been a *miati* household (Prine 1997, 2000). The role of space and architecture in the production of two-spirit identities has also been considered by Perry and Joyce (2001) in their examination of Zuni *lhamana* identities. Ethnographically and historically documented *lhamana* identities evince a broad diversity of traits but generally involve biological males and females who participated in a mixture of labor and cultural practices associated with both genders and who took the role of the bigendered *Kolhamana* katsina in public ritual performances. Perry and Joyce consider the possibility that a shift in architectural practices that occurred in the Zuni region around 1200 to 1300 c.e. may also signal the crystallization of *lhamana* identities. The shift involved the construction of large plaza-oriented settlements and the movement of gender-specific everyday activities from locations inside rooms into communal plazas where rituals were also held. The public performance of gender—through both daily labor and ceremonial ritual in communal plazas—may have formalized the status of what Perry and Joyce term "gender transgressive persons."

The archaeological study of Native American two-spirit identities demonstrates the limitations of modern sexual theories. Two-spirit identities may involve sexual or gendered practices that are stigmatized today in many contexts, but within their own societies, two-spirits were as "normal" as other people. Further, it is not clear that concepts such as homosexuality or transsexuality are pertinent here. *'Aqí*, *miati*, and *lhamana* identities appear to have been shaped as much by spirituality and occupation as by gender and sexuality; further, if two-spirits occupied a *different* gender than the culturally specific categories of man or woman, they were not transsexual or transgendered, nor were their sexual relations with members of the same gender. Archaeological research on identity variation in Native North American contexts thus illuminates the methodological challenges facing archaeological research on sexuality in the past.

The same methodological challenges emerge in other studies aimed at the investigation of homosexuality in the past. How can archaeologists counter heteronormative biases without replicating the problematic ways that nonheterosexual and nonreproductive sexualities are conceptualized in the present? Unfortunately, not all archaeological research on the topic is successful in this regard. Matthews (1999:7), for example, has argued that "there is an ahistorical element in homosexual behaviour" and posits that researchers should be able to identity "common themes in the material culture of gay men," such as transvestism or exaggerated masculinity in clothing, meeting spaces where sexual encounters and exchange of partners could occur, and sex toys (which Matthews states are used "more frequently in the gay world than in the straight" [11]). While the desire to identify cross-cultural "traits" of homosexuality is understandable, such projects rely on troubling stereotypes of modern gay male life and obscure the cultural specificity of sexual practices and sexual identities. Other researchers have painstakingly worked to avoid these pitfalls. Schmidt (2002:161), in his research on Mesolithic Siberian sexuality, provides an alternative to the prevalent gender/sexual binarism, arguing instead for a "multiple sex/gender paradigm" in which the "number of sex and/or gender categories . . . cannot be assumed before analysis. Nor is there any requirement specifying the nature of categorical boundaries. In addition to discrete, non-overlapping sets, categorical variation may be continuous, such that categories grade into one another." Within this framework, Schmidt turns to the study of shamanistic identities and practices as a way of understanding prehistoric sexuality. He focuses on the "sensuous bodily experiences of shamans, and the role of the shaman as a bridge between various levels of existence" (226), including the ability to harness both male and female sexual potentials. Such work could be ephemeral or more permanent and might involve same-sex sexual relationships. But this is not an archaeology of "homosexuality"; to the contrary, Schmidt argues that for both men and women, for shamans, and for the sexual partners of all these, "sexuality in the Mesolithic was about more than mating networks. As instantiations of a sexualized cosmology, meaningful patterns of sexuality shaped how people lived and experienced their lives" (231).

Danielsson similarly turns to imagery associated with shamans in the Late Iron Age in Scandinavia. Focusing her analysis on gold foil artifacts that contain iconographic depictions of humanoid forms, she notes that such objects initially portrayed a single, mask-wearing individual of ambiguous gender. These masked figures, Danielsson suggests, most likely were representations of shamanic acts and performances in a variety of sexualized gender- and species-bending ecstatic states. In later periods, however, the gold foils increasingly depicted two individuals locked in an embrace. The unmasked figures on these later foils represented "stereotyped, aristocratic, well-to-do bodies of a man and a woman . . . (re)presenting them with conservative traits, in choice of clothes or total appearance" (Danielsson 2002:193). Danielsson argues that this transition is isometric with a literary shift that increasingly represented transgender/homosexual practices as godly rather than human practices; the changing images on the gold foil artifacts sustained "a stricter and more rigid division of gender roles in every day life, recognizable through punishment against cross-dressing, and the more easily discernible genders in grave material in the Late Iron Age compared to the Early Iron Age" (196). Archaeology, then, can not only challenge heteronormative biases of the present but also trace the historical production of disciplinary regimes that enforced gendered and sexual norms.

Historical archaeology at eighteenth- and nineteenth-century sites is contributing to a greater understanding of how the sexological terms now in common use were historically produced. Davis, for example, explores the erotic and sexual dimensions of Fonthill Abbey, a residence constructed in the early 1800s by shunned sodomite William Courtenay. At the time, Davis (2000:109) notes, "sodomy was routinely conceived rhetorically as 'pre-posterousness,' as putting ahead or before what should come below or after, inverting the natural order of social relations." Davis turns to Courtenay's unusual construction of sight lines both within and outside the building as an engagement of the desiring gaze with tropes of inversions of front and back. A second example is Casella's archaeological investigation of a nineteenth-century women's prison in Australia. Casella's excavations there revealed evidence of a black-market sexual economy—one in which both same-gender and cross-gender sexual services were part of a dense network of exchanges of food, indulgences, money, clothing, and transportation. The apex of this underground sexual economy was, paradoxically, the solitary cells, which were constructed specifically to punish repeat sexual offenders. Within the prison, Casella (2000b:214) argues, "women's sexual expression remained both opportunistic and fluidly defined. Convicts did not possess 'sexual identities' or exclusive 'persuasions,'" although most colonial officials interpreted long-term same-sex relationships among convict women as a transgressive form of heterosexuality, with a member of each couple being identified as a "pseudo-male." Just as Casella's and Davis's research provides material evidence of under-documented historic sexualities, so too has anthropologist Rubin (1991, 2000, 2002) turned to archaeological methodologies in her study of twentieth-century leathermen in San Francisco. Her diachronic and spatial analyses of gay and leather "settlement patterns" and "sites" reveals the historical production and transformation of sexual identities and practices within the shifting context of urban development.

Sexual Economies: Prostitution

As Casella's research on the sexual economy of a nineteenth-century prison suggests, commercial sex has also been central to archaeological investigations of sexuality. Archaeological studies of prostitution in North America have been spurred by the discovery of deposits from Victorian-era and turn-of-the-century brothels, parlor houses, and cribs. Significant studies include excavations of brothel sites in East Blairmore, Alberta (Lawrence Cheney 1991, 1993); Washington, D.C. (Cheek and Seifert 1994; Seifert 1991, 1994; Seifert et al. 2000); Los Angeles (Costello 2000, 2002; Costello and Praetzellis 1999; Costello et al. 1998, 1999); and Oakland (Solari 1997). Most recently, the journal *Historical Archaeology* has published a thematic issue ("Sin City") on the archaeology of prostitution (Seifert 2005).

In nearly all cases, these investigations have focused on artifacts recovered from hollow features such as privies and kitchen waste pits that are known through historic records to have been associated with brothels. In some cases, the structural remains of brothels have been recovered and recorded as well. Many of these investigations have focused on the working conditions of prostitutes and their relative economic status compared to nonbrothel households. For example, materials recovered from Los Angeles indicate that parlor house prostitutes enjoyed a substantially higher standard of living than their working-class neighbors, while the material record of crib prostitutes reflects spartan, nonresidential working conditions (Costello et al. 1998, 1999). Studies in Washington, D.C., have shown that initially, in the late 1800s, the living conditions of brothel prostitutes were roughly identical to that in adjacent nonbrothel households. However, by the early 1900s, the relative economic status of prostitutes had increased (Seifert 1994). Archaeological studies have also documented the occupational hazards of sex work through the recovery of panel medicine bottles that once contained "cures for venereal disease and pain-numbing tinctures of opium and morphine" (Costello 2002:177). The economic and occupational emphases in archaeological research on prostitution are suggestive of feminist organizing around sex work as labor from the 1970s on (Bell 1987, Nagle 1997).

Archaeological studies of prostitution have also problematized conventional scholarship about gender ideologies of the Victorian era, noting the permeability of the "separate spheres" usually associated with the female cult of domesticity (Poovey 1988, Smith-Rosenberg 1979). For example, Seifert (1991) has noted that for white working-class women in Hooker's Division, economic well-being and sexual activity were intertwined through marriage, on-the-job sexual harassment, sexual reciprocation for gifts from male friends, and sex for pay. Solari (1997) has likewise noted that for many women, prostitution was a conscious choice among a series of unattractive and equally dehumanizing alternatives. Solari has also traced the ways in which prostitution sustained the economic fabric of entire communities: people made money as brokers (procurers, pimps, and madams) and by supplying food, clothing, medicines, and liquor to brothels (Solari 1997:277–78). De Cunzo's (1995) excavation of the Magdalen Society in nineteenth-century Philadelphia expands this point by investigating the institutions that formed to oppose the spread of commercial sexuality and to provide "reform, respite, and ritual" to the "fallen" women involved in the trade.

Overwhelmingly, however, these archaeological investigations of prostitution sites have focused on the economic aspects of prostitution. What are curiously sidestepped are the sexual subjectivities of the people who lived at, worked in, and patronized these businesses. The performance piece "Red Light Voices: An Archaeological Drama of Late Nineteenth Century Prostitution" (Costello 2000) demonstrates how archaeological interpretations are radically changed when sexual subjectivities are included. Performed by Costello and her colleagues at several archaeological conferences in North America, "Red Light Voices" is a spoken-word archaeological narrative that juxtaposes historic photographs and images of artifacts from Los Angeles brothel sites with selections from oral histories and letters of prostitutes, johns, and pimps. Costello's aim in producing this drama was "to expose the human face behind our data . . . to arrive at a deeper understanding of past events by humanizing them" (Costello 2000:163).

"Red Light Voices" is notable within the genre of archaeological studies on prostitution not only in its humanistic approach but also because the drama engages with the experiences not only of women prostitutes but also of their male clients. With this one exception, archaeological studies of prostitution have focused on women—the standard of living and health practices of female prostitutes and the business acumen of madams. These studies have also presumed that the sexual transactions at brothel sites were wholly heterosexual. Here again, the legacy of sexological studies has biased archaeological research. With few exceptions, sexologists confined their discussions of prostitution to diagnosing the underlying causes of female prostitution; male patronage of female prostitutes was framed as a normal, unremarkable outgrowth of men's naturally vigorous sexual drive. Female prostitutes, on the other hand, were variously characterized in sexology as degenerate and immoral, as evidence of evolutionary atavism among the lower classes, and as the female equivalent of the male born criminal (Caplan 1998, Greenway 1998).

It is interesting that most archaeological studies of prostitution have been conducted at North American sites dating to the nineteenth and early twentieth centuries. Recently, a few papers about archaeological investigations of prostitution in other historical and geographical contexts have been presented at conferences (Chávez 2004, Levin-Richardson 2005), and it is clear from these works that there is great potential for further investigation of commercial sexuality in other archaeological settings.

Architecture and Space

Another common theme among archaeological studies in sexuality concerns architecture and space. Several examples of this have already been noted: Perry and Joyce (2001) and Prine (1997, 2000) view architecture and space as a means through which two-spirit identities were enacted and performed; Casella (1999, 2000a, 2000b, 2001), Davis (2000), Rubin (1991, 2000, 2002), and Eger (in press) likewise examine landscape, settlement patterns, viewshed, and architecture as contexts that produced and supported nonheterosexual identities and practices. Others (Chase 1991, Croucher 2004) have explored ways in which architecture and landscape participate in polygamous sexual relationships. Investigations of architecture and space provide a means for archaeologists to study the intersections between practice and representation; sexualized spaces both serve as social metaphors for sexuality and are the contexts that enable sexual performances and sexual acts.

Buchli (2000) has documented perhaps the earliest use of architectural data in an archaeology of sexuality: Soviet archaeologists in the 1920s and the 1930s turned to archaeological evidence of Paleolithic architecture as evidence of sexual relations within Friedrich Engels's vision of prehistoric communalism. The archaeological remains of Paleolithic households had immense significance for the newly formed communist society and its quest to imagine new communistic social formations, identities, and sexualities. The archaeological data recovered by Soviet archaeologists were thus used as resources by architects and planners whose designs aimed to materialize "a radical reworking of heterosexuality" (Buchli 2000:240). Buchli's archaeology of twentieth-century socialism traces the lives of individuals who lived in one such master-planned community, the Narkomfin Communal House, a structure designed and built to "ease an individual's transition towards fully socialized life" (Buchli 2000:67) through a variety of communal facilities and living quarters. Buchli's painstaking, diachronic analysis demonstrates that all space, however mundane—from laundry facilities to gymnasiums to kitchens—are constructed and experienced through shifting sexual ideologies.

Meskell (1998a, 2000) has also examined the sexualization of household space in the planned community of Dier El Medina, which housed tomb workers in New Kingdom Egypt. Her analysis of the architectural remains of workers' houses and the artifacts and imagery they contained suggest that activities in one type of room in particular—the *lit clos*, or "day bed" room—centered on married, elite, sexually potent, fertile females. The *lit clos* may have been a ritual location for sexual intercourse, conception, and childbirth; the murals usually found there incorporate erotic motifs—especially those associated with "the lives of women, and the sexual lives of mature women, at that" (Meskell 1998a:227). Meskell demonstrates that the sexual meanings of spaces are mutually produced through the physicality of the spaces themselves, the activities that occur within them, and the imagery and material culture that co-occurs within the space.

Several archaeologists have extended this argument to examine the ways in which architecture not only facilitates certain sexual meanings and practices but can also be used to control sexuality. Both Gilchrist (1994, 2000) and Voss (2000a) have particularly examined the ways that the architecture of religious institutions shaped the sexual subjectivities of the people who lived within them. Gilchrist's investigation of medieval British monasteries explores the embodied qualities of the celibacy of religious women. Architectural practices of physical enclosure—a "glorious prison" (Gilchrist 2000:93) according to one eleventh-century abbot—contributed to a process through which "the sexuality of medieval religious women was turned inside out: sexuality became an interior space, a place of elevated senses and ecstatic states of consciousness" (Gilchrist 2000:89). The enclosed environment and practices of physical asceticism enhanced the importance of visual culture, especially images of the suffering of Christ's body, which likewise showed a concern with interiority—"inner spaces, inner suffering" (Gilchrist 2000:99).

Yet, while the enclosure of medieval religious women was largely voluntary, Voss (2000a) examines the sexual confinement experienced by Native Californians in religious Spanish-colonial missions in the late 1700s and early 1800s. Colonial missionaries used architecture as a technology of sexual control. Unmarried women were prevented from having sex through confinement in a *monjerío*, or locked barracks; interethnic sexual activity was discouraged by physically segregating colonial soldiers from indigenous neighborhoods; and long adobe buildings containing single-room apartments were one means by which missionaries policed conjugal heterosexuality and enforced Catholic prohibitions against same-sex and polygamous sexual relations. Yet Native Californian oral histories highlight the contrast between official architectural intentions and the actual practices that occurred in these spaces. In particular, the locked *monjerío*, designed to protect female sexual "virtue," was in practice a space within which native girls and women were particularly vulnerable to sexual molestation by mission priests. Oral histories also recount ways that Native Californian residents of the missions were unwilling to let architectural impediments prevent sexual pleasure, arranging covert liaisons and sexual parties in the very spaces designed to effect sexual control.

Ambiguous Images: Representations of the Sexual and Erotic

Sexual and erotic representations form another body of evidence through which much archaeological research on sexuality has been produced. Several examples of this have already been discussed. Imagery from Paleolithic, Neolithic, and Mesolithic sites in Europe and the Near East are often interpreted as evidence of cultural practices related to fertility management. Critiques of heterosexism in archaeological interpretation also frequently center on reanalysis of imagery that has been previously assumed to represent heterosexual identities or practices. Gilchrist's (1994, 2000) research on medieval monasticism powerfully demonstrates how architecture and imagery together participate in the production of specific sexual subjectivities. These studies have all raised critical points in the archaeological interpretation of sexual imagery. First, they have highlighted the danger of interpreting imagery from the past through the sexual standards of the present. Today in the United States, for example, certain kinds of bodily display (exposure of the pubic region, buttocks, and female breasts) are sexually charged, but it would be a grave ethnocentric error to assume that this was always the case. Further, the sexual meanings of representations are context dependent, so that a naked human figure in a medical textbook is experienced differently by its viewers than in an art museum or a porn magazine. Second, archaeological studies of imagery need emphasize not only the context of imagery but also the production and consumption of such images. Images are not seamless reproductions of social behaviors; they are culturally constructed representations that may participate in ideological and political agendas. Viewers actively engage with visual imagery from the different subject positions they occupy. The sexual "meanings" of archaeologically recovered imagery are thus inherently ambiguous and multifaceted.

A particularly salient case in point are the so-called sex pots of ancient Peru. These sexually explicit ceramic vessels, recovered primarily from Moche funerary contexts, "are both functional clay pots, with hollow chambers for holding liquid and stirrup-shaped spouts for pouring, and works of three-dimensional sculpture [depicting] lively little figures engaged in a startling variety of acts involving the hands, nipples, genitals, anus, mouth, and tongue" (Weismantel 2004:495). The sex pots have attracted scholarly comment for decades (Gero 2004:19 provides a useful listing of previous studies). The sexual imagery on the pots centers on autoerotic and heterosexual sex acts with an emphasis on masturbation, fellatio, and anal sex; vaginal/penile intercourse is almost never depicted. This "absence" of what is generally assumed to be procreative sex has been the focus of many scholarly interpretations of the pots, which have been variously interpreted as portrayals of birth control techniques, as admonitions against forbidden sexual practices, or, because the pots are found largely in mortuary contexts, as representations of funerary sex rituals in which nonprocreative sex is symbolically associated with death.

Recently, Gero (2004) and Weismantel (2004) have each undertaken studies of the Moche sex pots that draw explicitly on feminist and queer theory. Although their approaches are quite different, both share a concern that while the pots have attracted much commentary, "the topic remains under-theorized and connotations of the 'erotic' unexamined" (Gero 2004:19). They also draw careful attention to the pots' archaeological context as funerary offerings found in burial contexts, especially the tombs of elites. The pots must be interpreted as objects commissioned by and made for elite consumers; the sexual "meanings" of the pots are thus unlikely to have been shared by all classes or ethnic groups (Weismantel 2004:500).

Weismantel's analysis of the Moche sex pots focuses on ceramics depicting heterosexual anal sex, with the man and woman lying on their sides facing the same direction (belly to back). Most Moche ceramic anal sex scenes also commonly include a tiny and shapeless third figure "who lies next to the woman's chest to breast-feed while she has sex" (Weismantel 2004:496). Weismantel challenges the commonly asserted premise that the figures on the anal sex pots are not engaged in reproductive sex. Instead, she argues, the figures might be seen as being involved in transfers of reproductive substances. Many anthropological studies have documented cultures in which sexual reproduction is seen not as a single event (of sperm meeting egg) but as a series of practices that occur over a long period of time, often involving various transfers of bodily fluids (semen, milk, or blood) into different orifices (mouth, anus, or vagina). Hence, one possible reading of the Moche anal sex pots is that "the substance that is transmitted from the man's body into the woman's as seminal fluid is the same substance that passes through her nipple into the baby's mouth; the scene depicts the movement of this nurturing fluid between three bodies, to the ultimate benefit of the infant" (499). Within this framework, other "nonreproductive" sex acts depicted on Moche pots may be similarly reinterpreted: for example, another frequent motif, that of the masturbating skeleton, may represent the intergenerational transfer of reproductive bodily fluids from the ancestors to the living (501). Weismantel concludes that Moche elite may have used these visual representations of bodily fluid transfers "to alter the definition of the reproductive act . . . [to] position the ancestors, elders, and the most powerful lineages at the center of the system that flows" (502), thus sustaining and legitimating the growing centralization of power among elite Moche lineages.

Gero's analysis of the Moche sex pots provides a different yet complementary perspective to Weismantel's. Gero compares the Moche sex pots with another assemblage of erotically charged Peruvian pottery: "copulation pots" recovered from Recuay contexts. Recuay and Moche polities were roughly contemporary, with the Moche located in coastal areas and the Recuay in the Andes. The Recuay pots, which are also found almost exclusively in mortuary contexts, represent sexuality quite differently than the Moche ones. The Recuay depict heterosexual pairs copulating belly to belly; both the male and the female figures are well dressed, but this, Gero argues, does not indicate sexual modesty but instead provides a means of marking the elite status of the copulating pair. The copulation scenes often include representations of public architecture and additional figures suggesting that the copulation was observed by an audience. "We must conclude," Gero posits, "that the Recuay copulations . . . are profoundly ritual" involving a distinctive class and status of participants. Like Weismantel, Gero views the pots as representations used by elites in their growing consolidation of power, but her comparison of the Recuay and Moche sex pots leads her to suggest that the gender politics of elite life were significantly different in the two polities: while Recuay sex pots depict complementary male–female pairs, the Moche sex pots typically depict anal and oral sex scenes in which "the focus of the interactive activity is not union and mutual pleasure but a celebration of the male orgasm . . . male orgasm emerges as both a powerful and a political act, a co-joining of maleness and powerfulness and pleasure (Gero 2004:19–20). This contrast, Gero concludes, demonstrates the significant role of "bodily ritual and embodied sensuous practice in the constitution of society" (19).

Weismantal's and Gero's reexaminations of the famed Peruvian sex pots are exemplary of other feminist archaeological research on sexually explicit representations. Marshall's (2000) reconsideration of sexually explicit prehistoric stone objects from the North American Pacific Northwest challenges earlier readings that divided these artifacts into "male" and "female" forms. Instead, she notes, the objects connote ambiguity on several registers: function is interwoven with form, aspects of woman and man are combined, and vulva and phallus intermingle. The images, Marshall suggests, refuse the binary divisions of sexuality that are often presumed in present-day cultural politics. Mayan representations of the phallus, in images of human bodies and in disembodied forms, are also regular topics of archaeological investigation; Houston (2001) has explored representations of emotions such as lust, sexual longing, and sexual disgust in phallic imagery. Many others have drawn connections between Mayan phallocentric representations of masculinity (especially penile bloodletting) and the reinforcement of male identity and state authority (Ardren, in press; Ardren and Hixson, in press; Joyce 2000a, 2000c; Meskell and Joyce 2003).

Sexual Cultures

Although the archaeology of sexuality is a relatively new undertaking, the corpus of research discussed previously fully demonstrates that archaeological remains provide a rich source of information about past sexualities. Further, archaeological investigations of past sexualities are expanding our understanding of human sexuality beyond what is imaginable from observations in the present day. The ultimate challenge for archaeologists is to integrate questions of sexuality into our studies of the whole fabric of social life in the past cultures we investigate—to fully consider Malinowski's (1929:xxiii) claim that sexuality participates in "almost every aspect of culture." This closing section discusses the research conducted by two archaeologists, Lynn Meskell and Rosemary Joyce, who perhaps have been most successful in achieving this objective. Joyce researches the Classic Maya in Mesoamerica; Meskell studies New Kingdom Egypt. Their individual scholarship on gender and sexuality in these societies is impressive in itself (Joyce 1996, 1998, 2000a, 2000b, 2000c, 2002; Meskell 1996, 1998a, 1999, 2000, 2001; Perry and Joyce 2001); most recently, they have jointly undertaken a comparative work (Meskell and Joyce 2003) that explores the embodied lives of Classic Mayan and New Kingdom Egyptian subjects.

The core project in Meskell and Joyce's comparative work is to examine "the centrality of embodied life in all its sensual and sexual specificity" (Meskell and Joyce 2003:162). In doing so, they strive to think beyond the constraints of Cartesian dualism and its foundational premise that the mind and body are ontologically separate. Classic Mayan and New Kingdom Egyptian societies existed "before and separate from the tradition that runs from Platonic to Cartesian thought, [and] give us a potential window on other ways of framing embodiment, distinct from concepts of duality, hierarchy, and rational privilege" (17). For Joyce and Meskell, sexuality and material culture are both integral to and indivisible from this investigation of embodiment: the objects that survive in the archaeological record, they argue, are not mere costumes or props or representations but "extensions of the materiality of the embodied person. This leads us to a consideration of the play of desire implied by the materialities of embodiment" (10).

Because much of the archaeological material that Meskell and Joyce engage with consists of texts and imagery, their analysis involves a substantial consideration of the sexual politics of representation. In New Kingdom Egypt, the abundant corpus of textual and iconographic materials and durable monuments and tombs have skewed archaeological interpretation to emphasize the elite perspective, which was very different from that of the majority of the populace who were illiterate and lived "in relative poverty and simplicity" (Meskell and Joyce 2003:2). Likewise, among the Classic Maya, representations are a "powerful and ambiguous source of evidence" that present "stereotypes of a universe populated primarily by young, male, subjects. They thus systematically bias our vision of ancient Maya experience" (23). In both cases, texts and representations are shaped not only by status but also by gender, specifically that of elite males. Such representations must be viewed as projects that seek to influence the ways that people understand the cultural norms they are expected to emulate and a means by which actual practices can be measured against the represented ideal (Perry and Joyce 2001:65–66). Archaeology, Meskell and Joyce (2003:4) argue, provides a valuable counterperspective that highlights household and domestic life and can "hint at more subversive trends" within each culture.

Central to this political analysis is their examination of "phallic culture" in both Mayan and Egyptian contexts. "The representation of male sexuality, although quite distinct in nature, occupies central place in both traditions, signified literally by the objectification of the penis as subject for textual and visual discourse" (Meskell and Joyce 2003:10). The Egyptian worldview centers on a "motif of bodily self-creation" (13) in which the world and many of its gods were literally brought into being through masturbatory ejaculation by the god Atum. Phallic culture was not limited to the mythical but was tied to the everyday through material objects in the form of the phallus and through representations of male bodies that emphasize or exaggerate the penis. Egyptian phallic culture was also reinforced through tropes of bodily perfection in which the female form was represented as "inherently sexualized and directed by the male gaze" (53). Unlike many cultures in which girls are asexualized, Egyptian representations show girls wearing the sexualized signifiers of female adulthood. Egyptian female sexuality, Meskell and Joyce consider, might be best understood as a continuum without sharp demarcations or rites of passage that are common in other cultures.

The centrality of the phallus in representations in the Classic Mayan world stands in contrast to that in New Kingdom Egypt, cautioning against tendencies toward universalizing or totalizing interpretations. Classic Maya representations provide images of the exposed bodies of athletic young men on homoerotic display for a politically dominant individual male. These include representations of ball-game playing, dancing, and warfare in which the erotics of the male body are highlighted through exposure of the flesh and strategic clothing that highlights the penis as it conceals it. The phallus is further emphasized through the images of penile piercing and bloodletting and "by phallic ornamentation, including three-dimensional sculptures of erect phalli up to 3 meters long" (Meskell and Joyce 2003:125). In contrast, most representations depict the female body as unsexualized and draped in clothing, with the exception of small figurines showing careful depictions of breasts and suckling infants (120–27). Further, representations of men and women figures together are unusual and when present usually depict the female gaze as directed toward the male groin. In sum, Meskell and Joyce conclude, "the bodies of young males are represented as objects for the gaze of other, centrally posed, male figures within the picture plane, and of male and female viewers of these works" (125).

In both New Kingdom Egypt and Classic Maya worlds, "phallic culture" is both complemented and contradicted by other images and texts. For example, the Egyptian worldview of phallic creation is balanced by a female sexualization of the cycle of daily life, in which the goddess Nut continuously swallows the sun and stars through her mouth and births them through her vagina. Among the Maya, there is a parallel between penile bloodletting among men and the perforation of the female tongue. The penis and semen were conceptualized as integral parts of "fluid economies," in which the emissions and emanations of the body were central to the transmission and expression of culture and power. Egyptian subjectivities emphasized the porous nature of the body, distinguishing between *mtw* (conduits for semen, air, milk, blood, urine, sweat, fragrance, disease, and spirits) and *iwf*, or flesh, including skin and genitalia. Classic Maya concepts of the body emphasized the interplay of solid and vapor, of breath, blood, and bone: raw materials that "extended personhood beyond the bounds of individual subjects" (Meskell and Joyce 2003:75). Bone, semen, spittle, blood, milk, and vaporous emanations circulated in manners that linked the living to the dead, people to animals, nobles to commoners, and kin and cohort to each other. The realm of sexual and sensual embodiment, so bounded in Western concepts of the individual subject, resists delimitation in both New Kingdom Egypt and Classic Maya contexts.

Meskell and Joyce's individual and comparative research thus demonstrates the promise of archaeological research to provide a radical perspective in sexuality studies, one that can expose and denaturalize the disciplining practices of sexology, its present-day successors, and their constraining effect on current sexualities. The very materiality of the archaeological record provides "evocative fragments of past life to think through our own cultural contexts, to understand the importance of our different legacies and refigure our own taxonomies and experiences with the recognition of cultural difference firmly in mind" (Meskell and Joyce 2003:162).

The politics of the present—as well as those of the past—have always been central to the feminist project of engendering archaeology. Archaeological research on sexuality is necessary not only because it is an integral aspect of the past cultures that archaeologists study but also because in the sexual politics of the present moment, the past is being used as a devastating rhetorical weapon by those who seek to control the sexual identities, expressions, and relationships of others. One need only consider the debates about "gay marriage" in the United States to understand this; the alleged sexual practices of ancient Greeks and

Romans, medieval Europeans, prehistoric Native Americans, and Pacific Islanders have perhaps never been received so much media attention. President Bush's call for a "marriage amendment" to the Constitution claimed that monogamous heterosexual marriage was "one of the most fundamental, enduring institutions of our civilization" (State of the Union Address, January 20, 2004). Bush's adviser, Karl Rove, later told reporters that this constitutional amendment is necessary because "we cannot allow activist local elected officials to thumb their nose at 5,000 years of human history" (Saunders 2004:B11). The research reviewed in this chapter demonstrates that archaeology is already providing an empirically rich body of knowledge that challenges the premise that any form of sexual subjectivity is inherently natural or constant. Instead, the archaeology of sexuality is demonstrating that human sexuality is more richly varied, across cultures and across time, than could have ever been imagined.

Acknowledgments

Invitations from Thomas Dowson, Eleanor Casella and Chris Fowler, Kath Sterling, and the organizers of the 2004 Chacmool Conference provided important opportunities to develop work that informed the writing of this chapter. Thanks also to Deb Cohler, Meg Conkey, Sandy Hollimon, Rosemary Joyce, Purnima Mankekar, Lynn Meskell, Robert Schmidt, Sarah Nelson, and Laurie Wilkie for many conversations and inspiration on this topic.

References

Abelove, Henry
     1989   Some Speculations on the History of Sexual Intercourse during the Long Eighteenth Century in England. *Genders* 6(fall):125–30.
Ardren, Traci
     In press   Masculinity in Classic Maya Culture. In *Que(e)rying Archaeology: The 15th Anniversary Gender Conference*. Proceedings of the 37th Annual Chacmool Archaeological Conference. Calgary: University of Calgary.
Ardren, Traci, and David R. Hixson
     In press   The Unusual Sculptures of Telantunich, Phalli and the Concept of Masculinity in Ancient Maya Thought. *Cambridge Archaeological Journal* 16(1).
Arnold, Bettina
     2002   "Sein und Werden": Gender as a Process in Mortuary Ritual. In *In Pursuit of Gender: Worldwide Archaeological Approaches*. Sarah Milledge Nelson and Myriam Rosen-Ayalon, eds. Pp. 239–56. Walnut Creek, CA: AltaMira Press.
Baghemil, Bruce
     2000   *Biological Exuberance: Animal Homosexuality and Natural Diversity*. New York: St. Martin's Press.

Bahn, P.

1986   No Sex, Please, We're Aurignacians. *Rock Art Research* 3(2):99–120.

Bahn, P., and J. Vertut

1988   *Images of the Ice Age.* Leicester: Winward.

Bell, Laurie, ed.

1987   *Good Girls/Bad Girls: Feminists and Sex Trade Workers Face to Face.* Seattle: Seal Press.

Bland, Lucy, and Laura Doan, eds.

1998a   *Sexology in Culture: Labeling Bodies and Desires.* Chicago: University of Chicago Press.

1998b   *Sexology Uncensored: The Documents of Sexual Science.* Chicago: University of Chicago Press.

Breen, Margaret Soenser, and Warren J. Blumenfeld

2001   "There Is a Person Here": An Interview with Judith Butler. *International Journal of Sexuality and Gender Studies* 6(1/2):7–23.

Buchli, Victor

2000   Constructing Utopian Sexualities: The Archaeology and Architecture of the Early Soviet State. In *Archaeologies of Sexuality.* Robert A. Schmidt and Barbara L. Voss, eds. Pp. 236–49. London: Routledge.

Butler, Judith

1990   *Gender Trouble: Feminism and the Subversion of Identity.* New York: Routledge.

1993a   *Bodies That Matter: On the Discursive Limits of "Sex."* New York: Routledge.

1993b   Imitation and Gender Insubordination. In *The Lesbian and Gay Studies Reader.* Henry Abelove, Michele A. Barale, and David Halpern, eds. Pp. 307–20. New York: Routledge.

1994   Against Proper Objects. *differences* 6(2 + 3):1–26.

1999   *Gender Trouble: Feminism and the Subversion of Identity.* 2nd ed. New York: Routledge.

Caplan, Jane

1998   "Educating the Eye": The Tattooed Prostitute. In *Sexology in Culture: Labeling Bodies and Desires.* Lucy Bland and Laura Doan, eds. Pp. 100–115. Chicago: University of Chicago Press.

Casella, Eleanor Conlin

1999   Dangerous Girls and Gentle Ladies: Archaeology and Nineteenth Century Australian Female Convicts. Ph.D. dissertation, University of California, Berkeley.

2000a   Bulldaggers and Gentle Ladies: Archaeological Approaches to Female Homosexuality in Convict Era Australia. In *Archaeologies of Sexuality.* Robert A. Schmidt and Barbara L. Voss, eds. Pp. 142–59. London: Routledge.

2000b   "Doing Trade": A Sexual Economy of 19th Century Australian Female Convict Prisons. *World Archaeology* 32(2):209–21.

2001   Landscapes of Punishment and Resistance: A Female Convict Settlement in

Tasmania. In *Contested Landscapes: Landscapes of Movement and Exile*. Barbara Bender and Margot Winer, eds. Pp. 103–20. Oxford: Berg.

Chase, Sabrina M.
  1991   Polygyny, Architecture and Meaning. In *The Archaeology of Gender*. Proceedings of the 22nd Annual Chacmool Conference. Dale Walde and Noreen D. Willows, eds. Pp. 150–58. Calgary: Department of Archaeology, University of Calgary.

Chávez, Ulises
  2004   Cuanto Cuesta Tu Amor: La Prostitucion Entre Los Azteca. Paper presented at the Chacmool Conference: Que(e)rying Archaeology—The 15th Anniversary Gender Conference, University of Calgary, Alberta.

Cheek, Charles D., and Donna J. Seifert
  1994   Neighborhoods and Household Types in Nineteenth-Century Washington, DC: Fannie Hill and Mary McNamara in Hooker's Division. In *Historical Archaeology of the Chesapeake*. Paul A. Shackel and Barbara J. Little, eds. Pp. 267–81. Washington, DC: Smithsonian Institution Press.

Claassen, Cheryl
  1992   Questioning Gender: An Introduction. In *Exploring Gender through Archaeology: Selected Papers from the 1991 Boone Conference*. Cheryl Claassen, ed. Pp. 1–10. Madison, WI: Prehistory Press.

Cobb, Hannah
  In press   A Queer Eye for the Straight Hunter Gatherer. In *Que(e)rying Archaeology: The 15th Anniversary Gender Conference*. Proceedings of the 37th Annual Chacmool Archaeological Conference. Calgary: University of Calgary.

Conkey, Margaret W.
  1989   The Structural Analysis of Paleolithic Art. In *Archaeological Thought in America*. C. C. Lamberg-Karlovsky, ed. Pp. 135–54. Cambridge: Cambridge University Press.

Conkey, Margaret W., and Ruth E. Tringham
  1995   Archaeology and the Goddess: Exploring the Contours of Feminist Archaeology. In *Feminisms in the Academy*. Donna C. Stanton and Abigail J. Stewart, eds. Pp. 199–247. Ann Arbor: University of Michigan Press.

Conkey, Margaret W., and Joan Gero
  1997   From Programme to Practice: Gender and Feminism in Archaeology. *Annual Review of Anthropology* 26:411–37.

Conkey, Margaret W., and Janet D. Spector
  1984   Archaeology and the Study of Gender. *Advances in Archaeological Method and Theory* 7:1–32.

Costello, Julia G.
  2000   Red Light Voices: An Archaeological Drama of Late Nineteenth Century Prostitution. In *Archaeologies of Sexuality*. Robert A. Schmidt and Barbara L. Voss, eds. Pp. 160–75. London: Routledge.

2002   Life Behind the Red Lights: Prostitution in Los Angeles, 1880–1910. In *Restoring Women's History through Historic Preservation*. Gail Dubrow and Jennifer Goodman, eds. Pp. 177–96. Baltimore: The Johns Hopkins University Press.

Costello, Julia G., and Adrian Praetzellis

1999   *Excavating L.A.'s Brothels*. Venice, CA: Furman Films.

Costello, Julia G., with Adrian Praetzellis, Mary Praetzellis, Judith Marvin, Michael D. Meyer, Erica S. Gibson, and Grace H. Ziesing

1998   *Historical Archaeology at the Headquarters Facility Project Site, the Metropolitan Water District of Southern California, Volume 1, Data Report: Recovered Data, Stratigraphy, Artifacts and Documents*. Los Angeles: Submitted to Union Station Partners on behalf of the Metropolitan Water District of Southern California, Environmental Planning Branch.

Costello, Julia G., with Adrian Praetzellis, Mary Praetzellis, Erica S. Gibson, Judith Marvin, Michael D. Meyer, Grace H. Ziesing, Sherri M. Gust, Madeleine Hirn, Bill Mason, Elain-Maryse Solari, and Suzanne B. Stewart

1999   *Historical Archaeology at the Headquarters Facility Project Site, the Metropolitan Water District of Southern California, Volume 2, Interpretive Report*. Los Angeles: Submitted to Union Station Partners on behalf of the Metropolitan Water District of Southern California, Environmental Planning Branch.

Croucher, Sarah

2004   Complex Identities on 19th Century Zanzibar. Paper presented at Theoretical Archaeology Group Conference, University of Glasgow, December 18.

Danielsson, Ing-Marie Back

2002   (Un)Masking Gender—Gold Foil (Dis)Embodiments in Late Iron Age Scandinavia. In *Thinking through the Body: Archaeologies of Corporeality*. Yannis Hamilakis, Mark Pluciennik, and Sarah Tarlow, eds. Pp. 85–97. New York: Kluwer Academic/Plenum.

Davis, Whitney

2000   The Site of Sexuality: William Beckford's Fonthill Abbey, 1780–1824. In *Archaeologies of Sexuality*. Robert A. Schmidt and Barbara L. Voss, eds. Pp. 104–13. London: Routledge.

De Cunzo, Lu Ann

1995   Reform, Respite, Ritual: An Archaeology of Institutions; the Magdalen Society of Philadelphia, 1800–1850. *Historical Archaeology* 29(3):1–164.

de Lauretis, Teresa

1991   Queer Theory: Lesbian and Gay Sexualities: An Introduction. *differences* 3(2):iii–xviii.

de Waal, Frans

1989   *Peacemaking among Primates*. Cambridge, MA: Harvard University Press.

1995   Sex as an Alternative to Aggression in the Bonobo. In *Sexual Nature/Sexual Culture*. Paul R. Abramson and Steven D. Pinkerton, eds. Pp. 37–56. Chicago: University of Chicago Press.

Dobres, Marcia-Anne

1992   Reconsidering Venus Figurines: A Feminist Inspired Re-Analysis. In *Ancient Images, Ancient Thought: The Archaeology of Ideology*. A. Sean Goldsmith, Sandra Garvie, David Selin, and Jeannette Smith, eds. Pp. 245–62. Calgary: Archaeological Association of the University of Calgary.

Dowson, Thomas A.

2000   Why Queer Archaeology? An Introduction. *World Archaeology* 32(2):161–65.

In press   Que(e)rying Archaeology's Loss of Innocence. In *Que(e)rying Archaeology: The 15th Anniversary Gender Conference*. Proceedings of the 37th Annual Chacmool Archaeological Conference. Calgary: University of Calgary.

Duke, Philip

1991   Recognizing Gender in Plains Hunting Groups: Is It Possible or Even Necessary? In *The Archaeology of Gender*. Proceedings of the 22nd Annual Chacmool Conference. Dale Walde and Noreen D. Willows, eds. Pp. 280–83. Calgary: Department of Archaeology, University of Calgary.

Eger, A. Asa

In press   Does Function Follow Form? Architectures of Queered Space in the Roman Bathhouse. In *Que(e)rying Archaeology: The 15th Anniversary Gender Conference*. Proceedings of the 37th Annual Chacmool Archaeological Conference. Calgary: University of Calgary.

Foucault, Michel

1978   *The History of Sexuality, Volume I: An Introduction*. Robert Hurley, trans. New York: Pantheon.

Gaimster, David, Peter Boland, Steve Linnane, and Caroline Cartwright

1996   The Archaeology of Private Life: The Dudley Castle Condoms. *Post-Medieval Archaeology* 30:129–42.

Gero, Joan M.

2004   Sex Pots of Ancient Peru: Post-Gender Reflections. In *Combining the Past and the Present: Archaeological Perspectives on Society*. Terje Oestigaard, Nils Anfinset, and Tore Saetersdal, eds. Pp. 3–22. BAR International Series 1210. Oxford: British Archaeological Reports.

Gilchrist, Roberta

1991   Women's Archaeology? Political Feminism, Gender Theory and Historical Revision. *Antiquity* 65:495–501.

1994   *Gender and Material Culture: The Archaeology of Religious Women*. New York: Routledge.

2000   Unsexing the Body: The Interior Sexuality of Medieval Religious Women. In *Archaeologies of Sexuality*. Robert A. Schmidt and Barbara L. Voss, eds. Pp. 89–103. London: Routledge.

Greenway, Judy

1998   It's What You Do with It That Counts: Interpretations of Otto Weininger.

In *Sexology in Culture: Labeling Bodies and Desires*. Lucy Bland and Laura Doan, eds. Pp. 26–43. Chicago: University of Chicago Press.

Handsman, Russell G.

1991   Whose Art Was Found at Lepenski Vir? Gender Relations and Power in Archaeology. In *Engendering Archaeology: Women and Prehistory*. Joan M. Gero and Margaret W. Conkey, eds. Pp. 329–65. Cambridge, MA: Basil Blackwell.

Hollimon, Sandra E.

1991   Health Consequences of the Division of Labor among the Chumash Indians of Southern California. In *The Archaeology of Gender*. Proceedings of the 22nd Annual Chacmool Conference. Dale Walde and Noreen D. Willows, eds. Pp. 462–69. Calgary: Department of Archaeology, University of Calgary.

1992   Health Consequences of Sexual Division of Labor among Prehistoric Native Americans: The Chumash of California and the Arikara of the North Plains. In *Exploring Gender through Archaeology: Selected Papers from the 1991 Boone Conference*. Cheryl Claassen, ed. Pp. 81–88. Madison, WI: Prehistory Press.

1996   Sex, Gender, and Health among the Chumash: An Archaeological Examination of Prehistoric Gender Roles. *Proceedings of the Society for California Archaeology* 9:205–8.

1997   The Third Gender in Native California: Two-Spirit Undertakers among the Chumash and Their Neighbors. In *Women in Prehistory North American and Mesoamerica*. Cheryl Claassen and Rosemary A. Joyce, eds. Pp. 173–88. Philadelphia: University of Pennsylvania Press.

2000   Archaeology of the 'Aqi: Gender and Sexuality in Prehistoric Chumash Society. In *Archaeologies of Sexuality*. Robert A. Schmidt and Barbara L. Voss, eds. Pp. 179–96. London: Routledge.

2001   The Gendered Peopling of America: Addressing the Antiquity of Systems of Multiple Genders. In *The Archaeology of Shamanism*. Neil Price, ed. Pp. 123–34. London: Routledge.

In press   Examining Third and Fourth Genders in Mortuary Contexts. In *Que(e)rying Archaeology: The 15th Anniversary Gender Conference*. Proceedings of the 37th Annual Chacmool Archaeological Conference. Calgary: University of Calgary.

Houston, Stephen D.

2001   Decorous Bodies and Disordered Passions: Representations of Emotion among the Classic Maya. *World Archaeology* 33(2):206–19.

Joyce, Rosemary A.

1996   The Construction of Gender in Classic Maya Monuments. In *Gender and Archaeology*. Rita P. Wright, ed. Pp. 167–98. Philadelphia: University of Pennsylvania Press.

1998   Performing Gender in Prehispanic Central America. *RES: Anthropological Aesthetics* 33:147–65.

2000a   *Gender and Power in Prehispanic Mesoamerica*. Austin: University of Texas Press.

2000b   Girling the Girl and Boying the Boy: The Production of Adulthood in Ancient Mesoamerica. *World Archaeology* 31(3):473–83.

2000c   A Precolumbian Gaze: Male Sexuality among the Ancient Maya. In *Archaeologies of Sexuality*. Robert A. Schmidt and Barbara L. Voss, eds. Pp. 263–83. London: Routledge.

2002   Desiring Women: Classic Maya Sexualities. In *Ancient Maya Gender Identity and Relations*. Lowell S. Gustafson and Amelia M. Trevelyan, eds. Pp. 329–44. Westport, CT: Greenwood Press.

Kokkinidou, Dimitra, and Maraianna Nikolaidou

1997   Body Imagery in the Aegean Mesolithic: Ideological Implications of Anthropomorphic Figurines. In *Invisible People and Processes: Writing Gender and Childhood into European Archaeology*. Jenny Moore and Eleanor Scott, eds. Pp. 88–112. London: Leicester University Press.

Lawrence Cheney, Susan

1991   Women and Alcohol: Female Influence on Recreational Patterns in the West 1880–1890. In *The Archaeology of Gender*. Proceedings of the 22nd Annual Chacmool Conference. Dale Walde and Noreen D. Willows, eds. Pp. 479–89. Calgary: Department of Archaeology, University of Calgary.

1993   Gender on Colonial Peripheries. In *Women in Archaeology: A Feminist Critique*. Hilary du Cros and Laurajane Smith, eds. Pp. 134–37. Canberra: Australian National University.

Levin-Richardson, Sarah

2005   Sex, Sight, and *Societas* in the Lupanar, Pompeii. Paper presented at Seeing the Past: Building Knowledge of the Past and Present through Acts of Seeing, Stanford Archaeology Center, Stanford University, Stanford, CA, February 5.

Lucy, S. J.

1997   Housewives, Warriors, and Slaves? Sex and Gender in Anglo-Saxon Burials. In *Invisible People and Processes: Writing Gender and Childhood into European Archaeology*. Jenny Moore and Eleanor Scott, eds. Pp. 150–68. London: Leicester University Press.

Malinowski, B.

1929   *The Sexual Life of Savages in North-Western Melanesia: An Ethnographic Account of Courtship, Marriage, and Family Life among the Natives of the Trobriand Islands, British New Guinea*. New York: Readers League of America, distributed by Eugenics Publishing Company.

Marshall, Yvonne

2000   Reading images stone b.c. *World Archaeology* 32(2):222–35.

Matthews, Keith

1999   The Material Culture of the Homosexual Male: A Case for Archaeological Exploration. In *Gender and Material Culture in Archaeological Perspective*. Moira Donald and Linda Hurcombe, eds. Pp. 3–19. London: Macmillan.

McCafferty, Sharisse D., and Geoffrey G. McCafferty

In press   Alternative and Ambiguous Gender Identities in Postclassic Central Mexico. In *Que(e)rying Archaeology: The 15th Anniversary Gender Conference*. Proceedings of the 37th Annual Chacmool Archaeological Conference. Calgary: University of Calgary.

McDonald Pavelka, Mary S.

1995   Sexual Nature: What Can We Learn from a Cross-Species Perspective? In *Sexual Nature/Sexual Culture*. Paul R. Abramson and Steven D. Pinkerton, eds. Pp. 16–36. Chicago: University of Chicago Press.

Meskell, Lynn

1995   Goddesses, Gimbutas, and New Age Archaeology. *Antiquity* 69:74–86.

1996   The Somatization of Archaeology: Institutions, Discourses, Corporeality. *Norwegian Archaeological Review* 29(1):2–16.

1998a   An Archaeology of Social Relations in an Egyptian Village. *Journal of Archaeological Method and Theory* 5(3):209–43.

1998b   Oh, My Goddess! Archaeology, Sexuality, and Ecofeminism. *Archaeological Dialogues* 5(2):126–42.

1999   *Archaeologies of Social Life: Age, Sex, Class* et cetera *in Ancient Egypt*. Oxford: Blackwell.

2000   Re-em(bed)ing Sex: Domesticity, Sexuality, and Ritual in New Kingdom Egypt. In *Archaeologies of Sexuality*. Robert A. Schmidt and Barbara L. Voss, eds. Pp. 253–62. London: Routledge.

2001   *Private Life in New Kingdom Egypt*. Princeton, NJ: Princeton University Press.

Meskell, Lynn, and Rosemary A. Joyce

2003   *Embodied Lives: Figuring Ancient Maya and Egyptian Experience*. London: Routledge.

Nagle, Jill, ed.

1997   *Whores and Other Feminists*. New York: Routledge.

Nelson, Sarah Milledge

1990   Diversity of the Upper Paleolithic "Venus" Figurines and Archaeological Mythology. In *Powers of Observation: Alternative Views in Archaeology*. Sarah Milledge Nelson and Alice Kehoe, eds. Pp. 11–22. Washington, DC: American Anthropological Association.

1997   *Gender in Archaeology: Analyzing Power and Prestige*. Walnut Creek, CA: AltaMira Press.

Perry, Elizabeth M., and Rosemary A. Joyce

2001   Providing a Past for "Bodies That Matter": Judith Butler's Impact on the Archaeology of Gender. *International Journal of Sexuality and Gender Studies* 6(1/2):63–76.

Poovey, Mary

1988   *Uneven Developments: The Ideological Work of Gender in Mid-Victorian England*. Chicago: University of Chicago Press.

Prine, Elizabeth P.
  1997   The Ethnography of Place: Landscape and Culture in Middle Missouri
          Archaeology. Ph.D. dissertation, University of California Berkeley.
  2000   Searching for Third Genders: Towards a Prehistory of Domestic Spaces in
          Middle Missouri Villages. In *Archaeologies of Sexuality*. Robert A. Schmidt and
          Barbara L. Voss, eds. Pp. 197–219. London: Routledge.
Reeder, Greg
  2000   Same-Sex Desire, Conjugal Constructs, and the Tomb of Niankhkhnum and
          Khnoumhotep. *World Archaeology* 32(2):193–208.
Rega, Elizabeth
  1997   Age, Gender, and Biological Reality in the Early Bronze Age Cemetery at
          Mokrin. In *Invisible People and Processes: Writing Gender and Childhood into European
          Archaeology*. Jenny Moore and Eleanor Scott, eds. Pp. 229–47. London: Leice-
          ster University Press.
Rubin, Gayle
  1975   The Traffic in Women: Notes on the "Political Economy" of Sex. In *Toward
          an Anthropology of Women*. R. R. Reiter, ed. Pp. 157–210. New York: Monthly
          Review Press.
  1984   Thinking Sex: Notes for a Radical Theory of the Politics of Sexuality. In
          Pleasure and Danger: Exploring Female Sexuality. C. S. Vance, ed. Pp. 267–319.
          London: Pandora.
  1991   The Catacombs: A Temple of the Butthole. In *Leather-Folk: Radical Sex, People,
          Politics, and Practice*. Mark Thompson, ed. Pp. 119–41. Boston: Alyson Publi-
          cations.
  2000   Sites, Settlements, and Urban Sex: Archaeology and the Study of Gay Leath-
          ermen in San Francisco, 1955–1995. In *Archaeologies of Sexuality*. Robert A.
          Schmidt and Barbara L. Voss, eds. Pp. 62–88. London: Routledge.
  2002   Studying Sexual Subcultures: Excavating the Ethnography of Gay Communi-
          ties in Urban North America. In *Out in Theory*. Ellen Lewin and William L.
          Leap, eds. Pp. 17–68. Chicago: University of Illinois Press.
Saunders, Debra J.
  2004   The Homophobic Party. *San Francisco Chronicle*, November 9, B11.
Schmidt, Robert A.
  2000   Shamans and Northern Cosmology: The Direct Historical Approach to Mes-
          olithic Sexuality. In *Archaeologies of Sexuality*. Robert A. Schmidt and Barbara L.
          Voss, eds. Pp. 220–35. London: Routledge.
  2001   Sex and Gender Variation in the Scandinavian Mesolithic. Ph.D. dissertation,
          University of California, Berkeley.
  2002   The Iceman Cometh: Queering the Archaeological Past. In *Out in Theory*.
          Ellen Lewin and William L. Leap, eds. Pp. 155–85. Chicago: University of
          Illinois Press.

Schmidt, Robert A., and Barbara L. Voss, eds.

2000 *Archaeologies of Sexuality*. London: Routledge.

Seifert, Donna J.

1991 Within Site of the White House: The Archaeology of Working Women. *Historical Archaeology* 25(4):82–107.

1994 Mrs. Starr's Profession. In *Those of Little Note: Gender, Race, and Class in Historical Archaeology*. Elizabeth M. Scott, ed. Pp. 149–73. Tucson: University of Arizona Press.

Seifert, Donna J., ed.

2005 Sin City. *Historical Archaeology* 39(1).

Seifert, Donna J., Elizabeth Barthold O'Brien, and Joseph Balicki

2000 Mary Ann Hall's First-Class House: The Archaeology of a Capital Brothel. In *Archaeologies of Sexuality*. Robert A. Schmidt and Barbara L. Voss, eds. Pp. 117–28. London: Routledge.

Smith-Rosenberg, Carroll

1979 The Female World of Love and Ritual: Relations between Women in Nineteenth-Century America. In *A Heritage of Her Own*. Nancy F. Cott and Elizabeth H. Pleck, eds. Pp. 311–42. New York: Simon and Schuster/Touchstone.

Solari, Elaine-Maryse

1997 A Way of Life: Prostitution in West Oakland. In *Sights and Sounds: Essays in Celebration of West Oakland—The Results of a Focused Research Program to Augment Cultural Resources Investigations for the I-880 Cypress Replacement Project, Alameda County*. Suzanne B. Stewart and Mary Praetzellis, eds. Pp. 277–94. Sacramento: Submitted by the Anthropological Studies Center, Sonoma State University Academic Foundation, Inc., to the California Department of Transportation, District 4.

Sørensen, Marie Louise Stig

1988 Is There a Feminist Contribution to Archaeology? *Archaeological Review from Cambridge* 7(1):9–20.

2000 *Gender Archaeology*. Cambridge: Polity Press.

Taylor, Timothy

1996 *The Prehistory of Sex: Four Million Years of Human Sexual Culture*. New York: Bantam Books.

Vasey, Paul L.

1995 Homosexual Behaviour in Primates: A Review of Evidence and Theory. *International Journal of Primatology* 16:173–203.

1998 Intimate Sexual Relations in Prehistoric: Lessons from the Japanese Macaques. *World Archaeology* 29(3):407–25.

Voss, Barbara L.

2000a Colonial Sex: Archaeology, Structured Space, and Sexuality in Alta California's Spanish-Colonial Missions. In *Archaeologies of Sexuality*. Robert A. Schmidt and Barbara L. Voss, eds. Pp. 35–61. London: Routledge.

2000b   Feminisms, Queer Theories, and the Archaeological Study of Past Sexualities. *World Archaeology* 32(2):180–92.

In press   Looking for Gender, Finding Sexuality: A Queer Politic of Archaeology, Fifteen Years Later. In *Que(e)rying Archaeology: The 15th Anniversary Gender Conference*. Proceedings of the 37th Annual Chacmool Archaeological Conference. Calgary: University of Calgary.

Voss, Barbara L., and Robert A. Schmidt

2000   Archaeologies of Sexuality: An Introduction. In *Archaeologies of Sexuality*. Robert A. Schmidt and Barbara L. Voss, eds. Pp. 1–32. London: Routledge.

Warner, Michael, ed.

1993   *Fear of a Queer Planet: Queer Politics and Social Theory*. Minneapolis: University of Minnesota Press.

Weismantel, Mary

2004   Moche Sex Pots: Reproduction and Temporality in Ancient South America. *American Anthropologist* 106(3):495–505.

Whelan, Mary K.

1991   Gender and Historical Archaeology: Eastern Dakota Patterns in the 19th Century. *Historical Archaeology* 25:17–32.

Wilkie, Laurie A.

2000   Magical Passions: Sexuality and African-American Archaeology. In *Archaeologies of Sexuality*. Robert A. Schmidt and Barbara L. Voss, eds. Pp. 129–42. London: Routledge.

2003   *The Archaeology of Mothering: An African-American Midwife's Tale*. New York: Routledge.

Yates, T.

1993   Frameworks for an Archaeology of the Body. In *Interpretive Archaeology*. Chris Tilley, ed. Pp. 31–72. Providence, RI: Berg.

Archaeology, Men, and Masculinities   3

BENJAMIN ALBERTI

S TUDYING MEN AND MASCULINITY in archaeology is a sticky proposition. While one's initial reaction may be, "Why of course! We must study masculinity alongside other aspects of gender," it quickly becomes apparent that it is not that simple. Feminist and gender archaeologies continue to reveal how "women" have been an invisible category in archaeological interpretation and history. "Men," in contrast, have always been visible, but their gender has been "unmarked." Their presence has been assumed—but assumed on the basis of a "neutral" body, unmarked by gender, race, or any other category of identity (Conkey and Spector 1984; Joyce 2004; Knapp 1998b:92; Nelson 1997:16; Wylie 1991). The genderless man comes to stand for society as a whole. The question then becomes, Can we "mark" men—give them a gender—without reinstating "man" as the universal historical subject, which would once again exclude women and subordinate men? Moreover, the inequality and violence that result from current ideas and practices associated with men and masculinity mean that to speak of "masculinity" is to invite engagement with the politics of knowledge.

The first part of the chapter considers the not entirely rhetorical question of whether we need an archaeology of masculinity at all. I argue that we need a critical study of past men and masculinities but that the framework for such studies is already in place. There is no need for a new subfield; such a move is potentially exclusionary. I further examine definitions of masculinity and point out that a certain degree of conceptual confusion exists. By disentangling such confusion, we can gain a better understanding of the ways in which masculinity and men have been understood in archaeological research. The next part of the chapter is an introduction to how men and masculinity have been understood and interpreted in archaeology. Most work on masculinity in archaeology must be inferred from general works or from work within gender archaeology. What clearly comes into focus is that issues around male bodies are at the forefront of recent work on masculinity. Ironically, this potentially presents a foundational challenge to the nascent studies of masculinity in archaeology.

A crucial issue that emerges from my discussion, addressed in the final part of the chapter, is the status of the category "masculinity." I suggest that "masculinity" or "men" may not always be the most appropriate interpretive frameworks. Indeed, the decision of whether to use the categories hinges on methodological and political concerns. I suggest two ways to proceed: either admitting the contingency of the category but using it anyway (a kind of "strategic essentialism") or being prepared to let go of the category and allow apparent ambiguity or difference in the material to drive interpretation. Borrowing a term from Fox (1998), I argue that reflexivity and the issue of "critical need"—the tension between what we want from our material and what it can tell us—should guide our decision on which path to take. The search for complete narratives of past social lives is more likely to efface differences by reproducing the historical male subject, whereas admitting the fragmentary nature of our material may prevent reification of the category "masculinity."

Do We Need an Archaeology of Masculinity?

Gutmann's (1997) observation for the status of studies of masculinity in anthropology still stands for archaeology: a quick perusal of indices in archaeological works may show women as an entry but not men. Instead, men's presence is assumed. Moreover, there are few works that focus explicitly on masculinity in archaeology. Regardless, this chapter is not intended to be a clarion call for "an" archaeology of masculinity; it is not "men's turn" (see Gutmann 1997:403). I advocate a more cautious approach by asking, Do we need an archaeology of masculinity? I argue there are compelling reasons why it is important to study masculinity in archaeology. However, there are also important qualifiers, including interpretive and conceptual issues, such as whether there is anything we can recognize as "masculinity" in the archaeological record.

It has been widely recognized that accounts of past peoples have actually been accounts of normative masculinity (e.g., Conkey and Spector 1984; Scott 1997:8). Simultaneously, men have long been presented as gender neutral in archaeological accounts of the past. Archaeologists arguing for the inclusion of masculinities in archaeology echo this point, stating that to ignore masculinity is to leave the idea of an undifferentiated, universal "man" in place (Caesar 1999b:115; Foxhall 1998a; Joyce 2004; Knapp 1998b:92, 1998a). Caesar (1999b:115) states that "archaeology has neglected the complexity of masculinity and made the prehistoric man invisible through the stereotypical way of interpreting and representing the male sex." Others argue that focusing on women to the exclusion of men has had the unfortunate side effect of reinforcing the idea of a monolithic masculinity (Cornwall and Lindisfarne 1994; Knapp 1998b). Conceptually, therefore, there is a need to deconstruct the dominant concepts of "masculinity" and "man" as universal norms. Making past men's gender explicit reveals them as gendered subjects—rather than representing the whole of humanity, they can stand only for themselves.

Archaeological knowledge tends to reproduce an image of the contemporary dominant form of masculinity (see Caesar 1999a:133). The past is used as a repository of idealized archetypes that are called on by popular culture to reinforce essentialist ideas (see Joyce 2004). Caesar (1999b) points out that such "myths and stories" of man in prehistory then become active components in contemporary men's identity projects (e.g., the mythopoetic men's movement; Bly 1990; see also Middleton 1993). For example, essentialist arguments about the roots of men's aggressive sexuality that appear in the popular media use simplistic stereotyped notions of prehistoric gender arrangements to give their ideas the spurious credibility of time depth (e.g., Vedantam 2003). More sinisterly, nationalist and religious rhetoric frequently cites ideals of past male warriors and heroes (see Archetti 1998; Gutmann 1996; Mosse 1996). Thus, the "invisible man," the positive norm of masculinity in prehistory, is "a dynamic and active component in the present production of gender" (Caesar 1999a:115).

Making men's gender explicit has its own dangers. Hence, I argue that there is no need for a separate subfield ("the" archaeology of masculinity), as the necessary theoretical and conceptual frameworks are in place in feminist-inspired archaeology. Moreover, inaugurating an archaeology of masculinity has the potential to lend further solidity to an object ("masculinity") that, as discussed in this chapter, may not be a stable object of inquiry. The development of studies of masculinity in the social sciences and humanities disciplines (for overviews, see Clatterbaugh 2000; Connell 2000; Petersen 2003; in anthropology, see Gutmann 1997) has been met with skepticism by some feminists and pro-feminists (Braidotti 1994). For example, Solomon-Godeau (1995:76) signals the danger of approaching masculinity as a "newly discovered discursive object" when the fundamentals do not change but rather a newly expanded field for their deployment is offered. Moreover, as a simple "corrective" measure, it is flawed because the concepts of "men" and "masculinity" are already overvalued in Western society. Some authors have argued that the danger in creating a false equivalence between women's studies and men's studies is that men will once again be taken as representative of society as a whole (Hearn 2004; Solomon-Godeau 1995).

Carving out a disciplinary niche, or subfield, can be an aggressive process, setting up exclusions or effacements as "proper objects" (Braidotti 1994) of study are defined and boundaries are established. One of the founding fathers of the field known as New Men's Studies, Harry Brod (1987; see Cornwall and Lindisfarne 1994:29–30), reveals such a process. He argues that only men can truly understand men (Brod 1987) and ignores years of feminist scholarship, resulting in reactionary rather than critical theory and debate (Canaan and Griffin 1990; Hanmer 1990; Hearn 2004:63; Solomon-Godeau 1995:20). As Almeida (1996:143) remarks in the case of anthropology, without feminist theory and women's studies, "masculinity" would never have made an appearance on the research agenda.

Knapp (1998a, 1998b; see also Knapp and Meskell 1997) has argued for a "masculinist" archaeology informed by feminism. He states that we must include the work of "masculinist" writers partially as a corrective measure, to avoid a "gynocentric," "exclusionary, feminist world-view" (Knapp 1998a:365). In much the same way, Brod argues that "New Men's Studies can offer the necessary corrective to the 'female bias'" in feminist-inspired work (Cornwall and Lindisfarne 1994:30). The implication in both cases is that a "masculinist" perspective can challenge both androcentric and gynocentric accounts, whereas a feminist perspective merely replaces an androcentric account with a gynocentric one. Knapp's (1998a, 1998b) choice of terms is also curious; "masculinist" is not widely used in critical men's studies. In addition, it could be taken as unnecessarily antagonistic, its more common meaning being restricted to androcentric material and beliefs.

"Masculinist" perspectives have not caught on in archaeology. With Gutmann (1998:113–14), I agree that the inclusion of "masculinist" theory is not a prerequisite for either a feminist archaeology or critical studies of men and masculinity within archaeology. However, there are contributions to be made by the men's studies literature, as Knapp (1998a, 1998b) indicates. What are required, I argue, are both critical engagements with the concept of "masculinity" and the development of the means of conceptualizing sexual difference that go beyond the assumption of fixed binary categories of identity. Both these goals can be achieved through extant conceptual and theoretical frameworks within the discipline.

Defining Masculinity

There are two broad ways in which the category "masculinity" has been understood: as an "object" open to empirical analysis or as "configurations of practices" (Connell 1995, 2000). The status of the body is central to the distinction between these approaches. Practice-based approaches suggest the possibility that the category "male" is not beyond cultural intervention. Consequently, the categories on which contemporary studies of masculinity are founded may not be universally significant, in which case "masculinity" may not always be a relevant dimension of analysis in archaeological contexts.

Any interpretation of past social worlds implies an understanding of what "masculinity" means, although few authors define the term. That task is notoriously difficult—studies of men and masculinity are riddled with imprecise definitions (Connell 2000:15; Hearn 2004; MacInnes 1998; Petersen 2003). Authors frequently entirely ignore any attempt at definition, relying on implied or taken-for-granted meanings (Clatterbaugh 1998; Connell 2000:16; Gutmann 1997:385–86; Petersen 2003:58). Some of the confusion stems from whether you consider the term a descriptive or an analytical one. Problems arise when the two usages are seen as equivalent or are not clearly separated. If the term is purely descriptive, then to define masculinity is to best describe the attributes that epitomize masculine identity (i.e., a measurable list of qualities). This can lead to essentialist notions of masculinity in which certain key attributes are said to define what it means to be a man in all times and places. It quickly becomes apparent that any such description is limited to one time, one place, and one type of man. Consequently, masculinity is currently more commonly conceived of as an analytical category the content of which is culturally and historically specific. Masculinity consists of traits, behaviors, beliefs, expectations, and so on that are commonly associated with males in specific cultures and, when internalized, are a constitutive part of their identities. At the root of the term as it is conventionally used is the assumption that one's behavior reflects the type of person one is (Connell 1995:67). In effect, descriptions of masculinity often appear as a list of qualities said to characterize the category. Aggression, competitiveness, and emotional detachment are common core elements for contemporary Western countries (Petersen 2003:58), with variations of the list for other cultures. As a result, "masculinity appears as an essence or commodity, which can be measured, possessed or lost" (Cornwall and Lindisfarne 1994:12).

Even if used analytically, there remains the problem that this is a Western category of relatively recent genesis—a similar category that can be recognized as "masculinity" does not exist in many cultures (Connell 1995). Some have questioned, therefore, whether masculinity is generally applicable as a concept (Hearn 2004; MacInnes 1998). Others have argued that the inability to pin down a definition is because masculinity is not an object that can be studied empirically (Connell 1995). More recent theories of masculinity posit practice-based definitions in which the category is enacted rather than predefined by culture or society. For example, Connell (1995:44), a leading theorist in men's studies, understands masculinities to be "configurations of practice within gender relations." Ideas that have been developed to encompass this more flexible definition include "multiple masculinities," in which the term is relativized, and "hegemonic masculinity" (Carrigan et al. 1987; Connell 1987, 1995), which gets at power differentials among groups of men and between men and women as well as how the dominant form of masculinity (often elided as the way to be a man in popular discourse) maintains its position of social, economic, and political privilege. Rather than conceive of masculinity in terms of a fixed list of traits, these traits can be best understood as "tendencies and possibilities . . . that individuals have access to at different points in time" (MacInnes 1998:15). As such, there are many different notions of masculinity, often contradictory and in tension. Furthermore, in practice-based approaches, it is understood that "completely variant notions of masculinity can refer simultaneously or sequentially to the same individual" (Cornwall and Lindisfarne 1994:12).

At the heart of the tension between masculinity-as-object and masculinity-as-practice lies the sex/gender division, in which sex is a biological constant and gender is the meaning given to each sex by culture. This formulation has been challenged, opening up the category "male" to critique (see the discussion later in this chapter). Once "male" is challenged as a natural foundation for gender, it becomes hard to think of the category masculinity as universally applicable because the male–female binary is no longer a given. As Petersen (2003:58) points out, it is difficult to speak of masculinity without implying a binary notion of gender.

Archaeological Approaches to Masculinities

The following critical review of approaches to masculinity and men in archaeology reveals how the previously mentioned definitions of masculinity lie hidden in our interpretations of gender. Little of this work investigates masculinity directly. Therefore, I make explicit the understandings of masculinity implied in archaeological interpretation. I embed discussion of archaeological texts within a framework of research from other disciplines that address more directly questions of masculinity and include developments that are of interest to the archaeological study of masculinities. Also drawing from this work, recent research in archaeology brings the complexity of the category to the forefront, demonstrating the existence of a plurality of masculinities and forms of masculine identity formation. However, the underlying understanding of masculinity remains that of a quantifiable object. Other work has begun to challenge the stability and universality of the category "male," thereby exposing the interpretive limitations of the category "masculinity." What becomes clear is that it cannot be assumed that what we understand as "masculinity" is inherent in the material. Feminist-inspired theories of embodiment indicate how sexual difference may be explored without resorting to the categories "masculinity" or "male."

Work that focuses explicitly on masculinity includes general theoretical works (Alberti 1997; Caesar 1999a, 1999b; Knapp 1998a, 1998b; Knapp and Meskell 1997; Meskell 1996; Nordbladh and Yates 1990), investigations into the formation of specific masculine identities (Harrison 2002; Joyce 2000; Shanks 1996; Treherne 1995; Yates 1993), and critical research into classical masculinities (contributions to Foxhall and Salmon 1998a, 1998b; Shanks 1996). Historical periods have also produced archaeological research on masculinity (e.g., Hadley 1998a; Harrison 2002; Wilkie 1998). Furthermore, Harrison (2002) has explored experimental modes of presentation in the form of fictionalized vignettes, following the work of feminist archaeologists (e.g., Spector 1993).

"Universal Man": Essentialist Approaches to Masculinity

Essentialist approaches to masculinity have played a dual role in archaeology. First, most interpretations of masculinity in archaeology were essentialist until the advent of gender archaeology. Second, even though soundly critiqued, such approaches demonstrate the political role of interpretations of past masculinities. The search for certain key attributes of masculinity was part of the driving force behind early archaeological explorations. In terms of a framework for interpreting masculinity in the past, essentialism is limited by an inability to account for cultural or historical variation. Masculinity is seen as firmly rooted in an undifferentiated male body.

Essentialist approaches highlight key characteristics that are said to define masculinity. Irrespective of culture, history, or experience, the basis for men's behavior and identities is linked to hypothetically innate psychobiological structures, or cultural universals. Sociopolitical arrangements, such as the division of labor or organization of sexuality and reproduction, are considered epiphenomena of these innate gendered behaviors. These forms of determinism appear in many archaeological interpretations, often subtextually. They have their roots in post-Enlightenment thought and are coeval with the emergence of archaeology as a discipline. Essentialism has recently experienced a renaissance in the form of sociobiological arguments about genetically programmed behavior.

In the nineteenth and early twentieth centuries, masculinity was given a psychohistorical dimension. Protestantism and belief in scientific progress and knowledge encouraged a distinction to be made between nature and reason in which men and modernity were increasingly associated with the latter (Mosse 1996; Petersen 2003). Successful masculinity involved dominating base, animal urges through rational thought (see Connell 1994, 1995; Lloyd 1993; Seidler 1994). It was assumed that men everywhere faced the same challenge. Models of social evolution, proposed by Spencer, Morgan, and Tyler (see Trigger 1989), among others, in which human groups evolved through stages of increasing social complexity toward civilization implied a corollary psychohistorical model of the development of "mind." The psychic unity of mankind implied that all men had the potential for "cultured" (civilized) behavior and thought. Differences among men from different cultural contexts were of the nature of psychohistorical depth rather than due to individual or historicocultural difference. As such, nineteenth-century evolutionary models imply that "primitive" or prehistoric man reflected an earlier stage in the development of "modern man" both culturally and psychically.

There is an intimate relationship between masculinity and the emergence of archaeology as a discipline. The analytical structures used by archaeologists are embedded in post-Enlightenment thought, which is deeply complicit with nineteenth-century ideals of masculinity (Baker 1997:183–84; Hearn and Morgan 1990:4; Seidler 1989:2–4; Thomas 2004). This is clearly seen in the relationship among classical archaeology, contemporary ideals of masculinity, and theories of masculinity. Classical "man" was the focus of early archaeological work, the classical world being considered a gold mine of attributes of ideal masculinity, such as notions of reason, and questions of aesthetic judgment and idealized masculine beauty (Gutmann 1998; Mosse 1996). More directly, classical myths and philosophy were the inspiration for psychoanalytical theories of masculine sexual identity, including essentialist perspectives (Foxhall 1998b:2–3). Similarly, Harrison (2002) has shown how colonial ideal masculinity was consciously created through material culture. Harrison (2002) examines the manufacture of Kimberly spear points in northern Australia as a case of the mutual constitution of hybrid masculinities, those of the local Aborigine men and colonial collectors. The collector aspired to capture for himself some essence of the Aborigine man's "primitive" masculinity. An important project for future work on masculinity in archaeology, therefore, must be to critique the role played by archaeological knowledge in the contemporary identity projects of men (see Caesar 1999b).

Essentialist ideas about masculinity have reemerged in academia and in popular culture. The racism of early socioevolutionary theories has been replaced by evolutionary perspectives that root behavior in DNA and genes. This form of essentialism is particularly pervasive in popular scientific accounts of sexual difference (e.g., Baker 2000; Buss 2003). Common themes include exploring the genetic or socioevolutionary reasons for sexual behavior, violence, and hunting (e.g., Lovejoy 1981; Tiger 1969, 2000; Washburn and Lancaster 1968). There is little convincing evidence that genes or evolutionary adaptive behaviors predispose men to particular conduct or capabilities (for critiques of gender in human origins research, see Fedigan 1982; Hager 1997).

Essentialist ideas about masculinity are difficult to defend. Even if there are measurable, biological differences between men and women, trying to tie down such differences to specific conduct or capacities has proven unsuccessful (Connell 1995:46–52; Fausto-Sterling 1992). Similarly, the choice of "essence" is fairly arbitrary, depending on the theoretical leanings of the author in question (Connell 1995:69). In practice, essentialist approaches tend to focus on contemporary dominant ideals of masculinity (e.g., Gilmore 1990; see critique in Cornwall and Lindisfarne 1994:27). Archaeologically, we could only hope to find evidence of a fixed masculine "essence." Most essentialist work pre-dated the introduction of the sex/gender split into archaeology. As such, the essential attributes of masculinity were thought to emanate from within a clearly defined, universal male body.

Relativizing Masculinity: Social Construction

Social construction provided a way of thinking about masculinity that offered far greater flexibility. Most theories of social construction are based on the idea that sex and gender are two separate entities. Gendered identities and conduct are constructed by culture rather than existing within the body. Thus, variation in social arrangements and men's and women's roles cross-culturally can be explored. A limitation of this approach for exploring masculinity lies in the concept of gender used. Even though variation in "men" can be recognized, a form of essentialism remains in that the category "male" is unexplored.

A social construction theory of gender was adopted by archaeology in the 1980s (Conkey and Spector 1984) that opened the door for studies of masculinity in archaeology. However, such studies failed to materialize during this period. Given this paucity, the following is necessarily a schematic account. The meaning of "masculinity" is generally inferred rather than read directly from the texts. The focus in this section is on initial work within gender archaeology, which I inevitably falsely homogenize.

In the initial formulations of gender archaeology, "masculinity" referred to the actions and values habitually associated with males in a given culture (Conkey and Spector 1984). As such, masculinity can adhere to other people or things but must ultimately refer back to men. At times, "masculine" is used in a quantitative fashion: one can have more or less of it, as can things that are described as "masculine" (e.g., Osborne 1998). Therefore, "masculinity" can be treated as a clearly defined object that can be measured empirically and so is open to positivist approaches within archaeology (compare Joyce 2004). Material culture could be observed in association with evidence of a "male," leading to a quantifiable list of attributes that defined masculinity in that particular context. Mortuary studies, figurine analyses, and artworks were obvious realms in which such attribution could take place, as is the case with gender archaeology more broadly (Joyce 2004; Marshall 1995).

Gender was also conceived of as dichotomous, implying structural analyses: men's and women's activities could be inferred by the absence of that activity within the repertoire of the other sex. Similarly, symbolic analyses could be made by the association between "masculine" and "feminine" meanings and objects. A focus on gender "roles," combined with a general interest in materialist analysis (Voss 2000:182), and the ability to determine use wear on human skeletal remains lead to a number of studies focused on the division of labor. The relationship between material culture and gender was seen as one of reflection or ascription: particular activities, objects, and images were attributed to one or other gender. Those objects and activities then served to define "masculinity" or "femininity."

The concept of gender "identity" largely adopted in gender archaeology—that it reflects one's own feeling of being a man or a woman (Conkey and Spector 1984)—stems from work within psychoanalysis in the 1950s and 1960s, Robert Stoller (1964) being especially influential. In archaeological terms, material that is attributed to one or other sex—therefore assigning that sex a gender—is treated as the external manifestations of a stable, internal identity. Research on identity within men's studies and anthropology has also relied on Stoller's work (e.g., Gilmore 1990; Herdt 1987). Another influential source has been object-relations theories of identity formation, especially the work of Nancy Chodorow. Chodorow (1978) emphasized family dynamics as the root cause of masculine identity. She argued that boys are pushed to break their primary identification with their mothers, resulting in structures of personality that emphasize boundaries with people (see Connell 1995:20).

Chodorow's theories have been applied in archaeology to an innovative exploration of masculinity as a force for historical change. Caesar (1999b) proposes a general model of masculinity and social change based on the existence of separate male and female spheres of influence. When women attempt to occupy the male sphere, this results in the removal of the male sphere to a place where women do not yet have access, thereby maintaining male dominance and causing historical change. At the roots of her theory of gender dichotomy and hierarchy is Chodorow's notion of the boy abandoning identification with the mother (i.e., the female sphere) in search of a male object of identification. As such, masculine identity formation drives historical change.

Social construction allows for the analysis of a dynamic relationship between men and women. Gender archaeology has always focused on questions of power through the notion of gender ideology. Following Conkey and Spector (1984), gender ideologies are taken to be the meaning of male, female, sex, and reproduction in specific cultural and social contexts. In practice, ideology in gender archaeology has operated to include issues of power in a broad-based sense in which the genders interact much like classes. The relations that dominate are those between two large blocks. Often questions revolve around male domination and perhaps evidence for women's resistance and alternative ideologies (McCafferty and McCafferty 1998). Men often remain the undifferentiated dominant block or group. "Masculinity" becomes virtually synonymous with male domination (see Shanks 1996; Treherne 1995). In effect, masculinity is conflated with ideology, which is taken to be the material (often symbolic) manifestations of the undifferentiated group "men."

There are limitations to this formulation of gender. Social construction can result in a notion of gender that is static and normative. The taking on of a gendered identity through socialization or psychological development is uncomplicated and quasi-automatic. Masculine or feminine identities adhere to a man or woman through their life cycle. Questions remain concerning how to account for differences among men and for differences through the life cycle of one man. Moreover, the formulation fails to come to grips with the complexities of individual identity formation in which other categories of identity are implicated, such as race, class, age, and so on (see Meskell 2002). Men's studies authors working within this framework found that men never actually achieve "normal" masculinity, which begs the question whether these are norms at all (e.g., Metcalf and Humphries 1985). Rather, they would appear to resemble unattainable ideals. Commenting on this paradox, Connell (1995:70) asks whether the majority of men are therefore unmasculine. Even in the case of pseudo-Freudian (e.g., Stoller 1964) and object-relations theories of identity formation, in which internal conflict is at the root of the process, the assumption that there is a single structure common to the formation of masculine identity in all times and places straitjackets the theory within universalism and ethnocentrism, a criticism that has been leveled at some studies of masculinity within anthropology (e.g., Gilmore 1990; Herdt 1981, 1987; see also Cornwall and Lindisfarne 1994:32–33).

Other problems revolve around the conceptualization of "men" and "women" as dichotomous. Neither is implicated in the maintenance of the other, as they are essentially unitary and self-contained. This obscures the mutually constitutive or relational aspects of the creation of identity as well as the overlaps and commonalities between men and women (Cornwall and Lindisfarne 1994:36). Relations of power tend to be categorical: all men have power, and all women lack power. Even when questions of class are introduced into the equation, which they often are when addressing issues such as ideology, power still operates between homogeneous blocks of people.

An important limiting factor in this understanding of masculinity is the status of the body. It has been commented that fear of biologisms prevents the categories "male" and "female" from being scrutinized or considered as social constructions (Cornwall and Lindisfarne 1994:35–36; Moore 1994). In practice, sex and gender are often conflated in archaeology. Frustration has been expressed at the limitations of separately identifying sex or gender, leading some to suggest that an archaeology of gender is in fact an archaeology of sex (e.g., Marshall 1995; Sørensen 1992:35).

Multiple Masculinities: Disaggregating Men

The following work still fits within the general rubric of social construction but attempts to address some of the problems outlined in the previous section. The recognition of differences among men had previously been limited to the axes of cultural or historical difference. Research in men's studies, anthropology, and history introduced the idea that men also varied within cultures—there could be competing masculinities within a single cultural context. However, "masculinity" is still conceptualized as an identifiable, empirically measurable object residing in a "male" body. As such, the nature of the biological category "male" is not interrogated.

The weaknesses in conceiving of "man" as an undifferentiated, monolithic category in dichotomous relationship to an equally monolithic, undifferentiated "woman" quickly led to studies that began to consider variation both in terms of different kinds of men and in terms of how male subjects incorporate multiple influences in the process of identity formation. Knapp (1998a:93) has commented that the main contribution of men's studies literature to archaeology is to highlight the existence of "divergent, multiple masculinities." Historical studies have demonstrated both the contingent nature of masculinity and the plurality of forms of masculinities that exist, often side by side (e.g., Mosse 1996; Roper and Tosh 1991). Hadley, in an edited volume on masculinities in the medieval world, explores varying ideas about what men were in different historical contexts in order to "disaggregate the generality of the term 'men'" (Hadley 1998b:2) in the literature on the Middle Ages.

Historicizing the category "man" and introducing the idea of multiple masculinities breaks down the idea of men as a single oppositional category. However, it also risks producing a series of self-contained masculinities divided by race, class, sexuality, and culture. In men's studies, the concept of "hegemonic masculinity" was developed to account for relations of power and hierarchy among men as well as those between men and women (see Carrigan et al. 1987:89–100; Connell 1987, 1995; Kauffman 1994; in anthropology, see Almeida 1996). Hegemonic masculinity refers to how "particular groups of men inhabit positions of power and wealth, and how they legitimate and reproduce the social relations that generate dominance" (Carrigan et al. 1987:92). The concept has been fine-tuned to include analytic categories such as "subordinated masculinities" (e.g., homosexual men), men who are not the "frontline troops" of domination but benefit nonetheless ("complicit masculinities"), and men, often from other classes or races, who can as individuals embody the hegemonic form but lack social authority ("marginalized masculinities") (see Connell 1995:76–81).

In archaeology, the concept of "ideology," when given a gendered dimension, has sometimes been used in a broadly similar way. For instance, Robb's (1994) analysis of the development of inequality in prehistoric Italy bears a striking resemblance to Connell's formulation of the structure of hegemonic gender relationships. Robb (1994) argues for the existence of a single "male ideology" in the Eneolithic and Bronze Age in Italy. This ideology was initially used to justify male dominance over women but developed to support a male warrior elite's domination of a commoner class in the Iron Age. The same ideological model was used to justify the domination of both women and subordinate groups of men by an elite group of men. Likewise, Connell's work relies on the theoretical principle that "the relationships within genders are centered on, and can be explained by, the relationships between genders" (Demetriou 2001:343) such that the dominance of women by men provides the model or structure for the internal hierarchical ordering of masculinity and femininity.

Thinking of men's power and its ideological underpinnings in terms of the hegemony of specific groups of men or types of masculinity gets away from categorical notions of power. Connell's (1987, 1995) work on hegemonic masculinities has been developed further by Demetriou (2001; see also Archetti 1998), who, drawing on Gramsci's notion of "hegemonic bloc" and Bhabha's notion of "hybridity," formulates the concept of hegemonic masculinity as a "hybrid bloc" that unites practices from diverse masculinities rather than merely excluding or ghettoizing the subordinate and marginalized elements. The advantage of the author's approach is that it challenges the idea that masculine power is a closed, coherent and unified totality that includes no contradiction. Hybridity, Demetriou (2001) argues, leads to cunning transformations and the continuation of masculine hegemony.

The idea of a fixed, stable male identity has similarly been challenged by recognizing that the formation of the male subject is complex (Petersen 2003; Rogoff and Van Leer 1993). Object-relations theories of identity formation prioritize a unitary subject, defined by sex. Differences within a single gender category (through race, class, sexual orientation, and so on) are treated as add-ons rather than equally constitutive of the subject (see Cornwall and Lindisfarne 1994:32–33). Work by black, Chicano, and Asian men (e.g., Baca Zinn 2003; Espiritu 2003; Mac an Ghaill 1994) has led to the recognition that identity is an interpolation of differences. Similar ideas have been developed by archaeologists. Foxhall (1998a:1, 1998b) argues that a plurality of male selves existed in the classical Greek and Roman worlds. She argues that "each male self strives to be central" (Foxhall 1998a:1) by excluding others, such as effeminate men, slaves, and especially women, from the subject position. Excluded men and women have different positions in relation to the male subject. "Non-masculine" men may be derided, subjected to violence, and used as "anti-subjects" (Foxhall 1998a), but they are still men. They share a male body with their hegemonic counterparts. Subordinated men still collude with male power, whereas women's bodies disqualify them from ever becoming true subjects (Foxhall 1998b:4–5). The contributors to Foxhall and Salmon (1998a, 1998b) show clearly the nonunitary status of the category "masculinity" in antiquity.

Foxhall (1998a, 1998b) argues that the material culture and texts that constitute archaeological evidence in the classical world are complicit in the formation of ancient, male subjects. The monolithic facade—the appearance of coherence and wholeness—is an effect of reflexive male subject formation. The involvement of material culture in the active creation of dominant male subjectivity has been examined in other cultural contexts. Joyce (1996, 2000) takes figural and textual representations of male–male sexual practices in Classic Maya society as evidence of identification by a male audience with the powerful male bodies that are represented. Ritualized male bodies presented as powerful, youthful, and elaborately costumed were depicted in scenes representing all-male socialization events designed for exclusively male audiences. Joyce (2000) relates this imagery to a sexualization of masculinity and a generalized desire (by both men and women) for the male body rather than as evidence of stigmatized practices.

Bodies and the category "male" in fact occupy a slightly ambiguous status in the work on multiplicities and hegemony. On the one hand, this work shows that different bodies can be taken as evidence of different types of masculinity. For example, Foxhall (1998a:2) shows how effeminate men and slaves' bodies in the ancient world acted as antibodies. They displayed characteristics that were positively male but were negatively construed when used to typify an "Other," a non-hegemonic male. On the other hand, even though situated and marked by multiple facets of identity, the body and the sexed binary as fixed categories are still present. In men's studies, some of this confusion is revealed by Hearn's (2004) suggestion that we should be talking about "the hegemony of men" rather than hegemonic masculinities. Cornwall and Lindisfarne (1994:20) have pointed out that in their formulation of "hegemonic masculinity," Carrigan et al. (1987) elide the terms "male" and "masculinity," making that relationship seem natural and inevitable, in much the same way that sex and gender are often (unintentionally) conflated in gender archaeology. Other authors have recognized that masculinity formulated in this way becomes static, resulting in discrete blocks—groups of men and women—vying for dominance (Demetriou 2001:359; Hearn 2004:58).

Talking in terms of "masculinities" is an important step, but it does not automatically do away with masculinity as stable and unified—one simply has more stable, unitary subjects (see Dudink 1998:421). Furthermore, Petersen (2003:57) remarks that hegemonic masculinity has lost its dimension of power, simply standing for plurality or diversity. Connell has admitted that, in practice, masculinities tend to be posited as fixed "character types" battling it out for dominance (Demetriou 2001:347, n. 65). Definitions of masculinity become "additive" in the form of a fixed list of variables that are separate and relatively stable (Petersen 2003). In summary, sociological studies of men that focus on multiplicity and hegemony have added a typology of different men but have not challenged the status of the category itself (Cornwall and Lindisfarne 1994:2).

Deconstructing the Category "Male"

Essentialist and social construction approaches imply a stable object of inquiry, that there is such a thing as "masculinity" that can be measured or discovered in various cultural contexts. Social construction suggests that the specific form of masculinity may change through time but that the category itself is stable and in some sense predefined. The idea of a unitary category "man" has been challenged, but the essentialist categories "male" and "female" continue to provide the grounds for much archaeological research into gender. Recent trends in feminist-inspired archaeology and such areas as queer studies and explorations of sexuality have called into question these essentialist categories. Interestingly, the little research that deals explicitly with issues of masculinity in archaeology almost exclusively falls here, both theoretical surveys of the masculinity literature (Alberti 1997; Knapp and Meskell 1997) and specific case studies on masculinity in archaeology (Alberti 1997; Joyce 2000; Knapp and Meskell 1997; Treherne 1995; Yates 1993). I argue that the logical outcome of the critique of fixed categories is that "masculinity" becomes a highly problematic foundation for research. Consequently, I indicate research that enables us to work beyond the category yet still focus on sexed differences as an aspect of past identities.

The sex/gender division has been widely criticized for the way it essentializes sex, taken as a biological constant (Butler 1990, 1993:1–12; Grosz 1994, 1995; Moore 1994; Yanagisako and Collier 1987; in archaeology, see Alberti 2002; Joyce 2004; Meskell 1996; Nordbladh and Yates 1990; Yates 1993). Supporting social construction has led to ignoring biology as a field of inquiry. By equating sex with biology, sex and the body are seen as historically and culturally invariant. The category sex is merely a vehicle for gender. The result is that masculinity is seen as derivative of this supposed natural binary division of bodies. Furthermore, identity is thought of in terms of an internal "core" rather than as the result of active engagements with the material world (Alberti 2001; Joyce 2004).

It is widely argued that sex as much as gender is culturally constructed (see Meskell 1996). Bodies are understood and arranged according to historically and culturally specific meanings (e.g., Busby 2000; Lacqueur 1990; Strathern 1988). Anthropology has provided examples of this process, such as models of how gender can be a relational aspect of identity, in which neither masculine nor feminine essences "stick" to a body but rather pass between contextually sexed bodies (Strathern 1988). There is also evidence that, in some cultures, possession of a male body at birth is no guarantor that a child will physically develop into a male adult (e.g., Herdt 1987; Roscoe 1993). Historical studies into men's bodies also reveal that notions of male embodiment are historically contingent (Bourke 1996; Lacqueur 1990; Mosse 1996; Petersen 2003:64). As such, there are various culturally distinct ways of conceptualizing male bodies that may call into question "male" and therefore "masculinity."

The influence of culture on bodies—and the power of discourse to shape them—has been explored in archaeology through poststructuralist and practice-based theories, drawing from authors such as Foucault, Lacan, and Bourdieu, and feminist theories of embodiment, based principally on the work of Butler and Grosz (for overviews, see Joyce 2004; Meskell and Joyce 2003; Perry and Joyce 2001). There are two related ideas that run through this work that have implications for studying masculinity through archaeology: first, that bodies can escape simple sexed dichotomies, and, second, that sexual difference (and, by extension, genitality) is not always central to identity. The approach shares with other "post-processual" work in archaeology an understanding that material culture is not just a passive medium but is actively involved in shaping human action and identity (e.g., Barrett 1988; Joyce 1998, 2001; Thomas 2000).

The limits of a binary understanding of sexual difference has been explored by Yates (1993), who has produced a densely theoretical account of the construction of male subjectivity in prehistoric Sweden. He used Lacanian and neo-Lacanian theories of the role of the body in the process of subject formation to reinterpret rock art from Göteborgs och Bohuslän. The images include representations of figure with swords, horns, and phalluses and other figures that lack these features. There are also representations of isolated calves, boats, and animals. Traditional interpretations had taken the rock art as evidence of an aggressive warrior society. Figures without weapons or phalluses were interpreted as women. According to Yates (1993:67), the formation of an aggressive masculinity resulted from certain body parts acting as "points of focus and intensity." He argues that there is no natural arrangement of the body or greater significance being accorded one part or another. Rather, society imposes an image of the body on the self, which then organizes desire and attachments. Masculinity is channeled through signs rather than being a basic property of the body. According to Yates, "Masculine identity must be guaranteed by signs applied to the surface of the body, and these signs are detachable—they do not inhere in the body, but can be separated from it" (66). He argues that identities are presented as aggressive masculinity versus ambiguity, where the second category could encompass either males or females. As such, he recognizes that a particular identity is not dependent solely on the absence or presence of genitals but rather requires other "detachable" signs to guarantee that identity. Yates's approach shares in common with Foxhall's (1998a, 1998b) work on male subjectivity a concern with how a unitary male subject is formed through the active exclusion of other possible subjects, whether male or female. This may be because both authors rely on theories of identity formation derived from Lacan, which tend toward a universal structure. The "achievement" of male subjective formation through separation and exclusion is also reminiscent of Gilmore's (1990) global model of the "achievement of masculinity" (see also Foxhall 1998b:7).

Yates has been critiqued for overrelativizing the body (Joyce 2004; Treherne 1995), a common criticism of poststructuralist theory. Connell (1995) argues that a wholly cultural account of gender is no more tenable than one based on biological determinism, as the body provides resistance to its inscription. He proposes the notion of "body reflexive practices" to bridge the gap between biological essentialism and extreme social constructionism. Connell (1995:61) argues that "bodies [are] both objects and agents of practice" and that the practices themselves form the social structures within which bodies are "appropriated and defined." In archaeology, Treherne (1995) develops a similar practice-based theory of masculine subject formation for Bronze Age European warrior societies. The warrior societies he describes show evidence that notions of beauty and the preparation and care for the body became central to male ideology during a general shift in Bronze Age Europe from a focus on communality to one in which masculine self-awareness is paramount. He argues that the body is an active part of the process of subjectification rather than being dominated by culture and language (Treherne 1995).

Treherne's work points to ways in which male identity is constituted through the interaction of bodies and material culture. However, what is missing from Connell's and Treherne's accounts is a sense of how the body can escape dualisms. Moreover, Treherne's interpretation can be criticized for being overly general and for arguing that the experience of violence is a universal constitutive element in male subject formation (Joyce 2004). The same criticism could be directed at Shanks's (1996) interpretation of proto-Korinthian imagery of hoplites.

The idea of "bodily reflexive practices" and the interplay between material culture and self-conscious subject creation are useful ways of looking at how "embodiment" is achieved. Combined with Yates's (1993:48–49) argument that the binary male–female is only one way of conceptualizing the structure of sexual identity, bodies are freed to signify in new ways. Approaches to embodiment in archaeology that draw on feminist scholarship are pushing in this direction. Central to this work is the recognition that material culture does not reflect certain categories of identity, or fixed, stable gendered divisions among people. Rather, material culture is intimately involved in the production of these categories. For example, Joyce (2004) has shown how embodiment is amenable to archaeological investigation through analyses of the connections among representations of bodies, bodily adornments that may imply physical alterations of bodies, and the development of subject positions within pre-Columbian Mesoamerican societies (Joyce 2001, 2004; Meskell and Joyce 2003). Joyce (e.g., 1998, 2001) investigates the actual process through which bodies become categorized as subjects—how they are materialized into categories—and the active role that material culture played in that process. Certain material items demonstrate a closeness and intimacy with the body that provide clues to their roles in the creation of ancient subjects. Images and representations of the body provided precedents that were called on in the reiteration of certain bodily practices. The result is a reconstruction of past subject positions that takes the materiality of their embodied existence seriously and fully integrates material culture into that process.

Questioning the universality of a binary structure to sex opens up the possibility that body parts other than genitalia may have had especial significance. For example, Alberti (2001, 2002) has noted that in Late Bronze Age Cretan art, a physical binary structure to gender is not a consistent aspect of the imagery. All bodies exhibit a similar hourglass body shape. The only clearly marked sexed characteristics are breasts, which appear in conjunction with certain clothing in the images, leading Alberti (2001) to suggest that sexed differences are only a transient aspect of categorical differences as presented in the art. In fact, thumbs appear to be of greater significance in the artwork than penises, which are entirely absent (Alberti 1997). Drawing on similar theoretical sources, Knapp and Meskell (1997) argue that androgynous figures and the lack of figures clearly represented as male among Chalcolithic (Cypriot Bronze Age) figurines is evidence that individuality was of greater contextual significance than group differences based on sex. In the case of Mesoamerican sculpture, Joyce (1998:160) recognizes hands rather than genitalia as the "bodily locus" of gender.

Deconstruction of the categories "male" and "female" has led to archaeological interpretations that stress the contingent and context-dependent formation of sexed categories and the active involvement of material culture in that process. However, bodies do not disappear when the categories are questioned. Rather, the focus moves from material culture as reflective of fixed categories of identity to one where material culture is constitutive of categories of identity. Furthermore, the terms of the debate are broadened to include the relationship between sexual difference and other forms of difference without assuming a priori that one is more central. Masculinity becomes a far less stable concept as a result. Suggesting that "male" and "masculinity" may not be relevant dimensions of analysis merely removes these objects, not the body or embodied experience of genitally differentiated bodies. Nonetheless, this work does suggest that there are logical limits to the use of "masculinity" as an analytical category.

Negotiating Masculinity

Arguing for the exclusion of "masculinity" as an a priori dimension of analysis is not merely an exercise in abstract thought. If the category is used—even when the objective is to "mark" men by giving them a gender—there is the possibility that it takes on the appearance of a universal structure. More nuanced understandings of "masculinities" do not guarantee that ideal forms will not reemerge. However, this need not mean that "masculinity" disappear entirely from interpretation. I argue there are two ways to proceed. Either the category is accepted and used as a kind of "heuristic fiction," or it is dispensed with entirely. The material evidence should drive the decision of which path to take. Adopting a reflexive approach by admitting the tension between the limitations of your material and what you desire from it may prevent the category from becoming reified.

Categorical Dilemmas

Cornwall and Lindisfarne (1994:2) argue that men's studies authors have consistently failed to dismantle categories that they take for granted. This is partly understandable. The antiessentialist critique creates quiet a dilemma for studies of masculinity, as "male" and "masculinity" can no longer be guaranteed to be universally present. An obvious reaction is the fear of erasing the categories altogether, one that I suspect is holding back men's studies from engaging fully with the implications of the poststructural critique of bodies (see Alberti 1997; Petersen 2003). This parallels Voss's (2000:186) comments on the reluctance of gender archaeology to fully critique sex, which would result in it having to relinquish its proper object, gender.

A further difficulty emerges when "masculinity" becomes the focus of inquiry, even in contexts where its presence can be assumed. At the beginning of this chapter, I stated that the concept "masculinity" must come under critical scrutiny to critique the idea of a monolithic man as well as to mark men as gendered. Ironically, this very strategy may have an undesirable side effect: by focusing attention explicitly on men, "masculinity" can become stabilized rather than destabilized. This process has been commented on in the case of historical works on masculinity, where the effort to "mark" the category has, paradoxically, led to it being reinforced (e.g., Dudink 1998, critiquing Mosse 1996). By showing masculinity as a specific historical category, it becomes stable and perhaps, once again, beyond history: "Apparently, wanting to write a history of masculinity by focusing on masculinity easily produces a perverse effect in that masculinity then quickly becomes a category of either incredible stability or a category that is somehow beyond history" (Dudink 1998:430).

The deployment of the term "masculinity" in archaeological work may be having the same effect. It is notable that the work produced to date has concentrated on violent men (e.g., Shanks 1996; Treherne 1995; Yates 1993; contributions to Foxhall and Salmon 1998a, 1998b; and work in sociobiology). A further tendency has been to conflate representations of idealized masculinity with masculinity in general. Masculinity, as it has been studied in archaeology, becomes exclusively associated with the ideal or normative form, hence losing its ability to differentiate among "masculinities."

Increased research on the connections between violence and masculinity, in both sociology and anthropology, is a crucial resource for archaeologists if we want to either disassemble the idea that masculinity and violence are synonymous or better understand that process. This focus on violent masculinity in archaeology is partly explained by the preponderance of representations of violent men as well as material culture to do with warfare. The nature of the material remains encourages a focus on images, burials, and "gendered" artifacts that suggest a connection between men and such activities, in which case we may be repeating a distortion left us by a struggle for hegemony among various forms of masculinity in the past, the hegemonic male subject leaving us evidence of his success (see Fox 1998; Foxhall 1998a). It is a mistake, therefore, to equate such evidence with a generalized masculine identity. A focus on men and violence has also privileged certain types of evidence and representations over others, leading to a lack of research on men who were not warriors, priest-kings, and the like.

If hegemonic masculinity maintains its position of privilege precisely by forcing out alternatives and declaring one type of masculinity as the normative and positively valued (in this case, violent men), then archaeology would appear to be unwittingly supporting this process by excluding alternative masculinities from research. Ironically, these alternative masculinities tend to be studied within other areas of archaeological research, including work on sexualities and queer studies.

Strategic Essentialism

Is it inevitable that when masculinity does come under scrutiny in archaeology, it restabilizes the category, lending it an air of being beyond history? Both abandoning the category altogether and continuing to use it as a heuristic device present difficulties. The former approach begs the question, With what do we replace "masculinity"? The latter runs the risk of falling foul of the tendency to associate positive values and power with the term, again subsuming marginalized or subordinated masculinities, not to mention women, however contingent the categories. Which approach is adopted should depend on the nature of the material under investigation. As such, I am in agreement with those archaeologists who contend that grand theories and overgeneralized frameworks tend to obscure rather than bring out the difference inherent in much archaeological material. A single, authoritative account of past social life is beyond our grasp (see Thomas 1996, 2000; compare Cornwall and Lindisfarne 1994:45–46). Theoretical and methodological models should be responsive enough to grow out of a hermeneutic relationship with the material evidence.

Even if masculinity is a relatively recent invention (MacInnes 1998), there is clearly cause for its use as a descriptive or analytical category in historical periods.

Dudink (1998:430) suggests that what is required is an "outflanking move" by not starting from the presumption of the historical presence of a thing identifiable as "masculinity." Dudink (1998:430) writes, "One should study around the object, questioning evidence that may or may not imply its presence; in other words, a history of masculinity that does not focus on masculinity." Such a back-door route to studying masculinity may avoid restabilizing the category. Following this strategy suggests that we look for types of masculinities that may not be as exciting as warriors or kings. In other words, the pacifists, "stay-at-home dads," "wimps" and "layabouts" must come into interpretive focus. Contributors to Foxhall and Salmon (1998a, 1998b) have begun to address this issue for the classical world, as has Hadley (1998a) for medieval masculinities. Anthropology can provide concrete examples of practices that are not usually considered part of normative masculinity, such as alternative fathering roles, the couvade (e.g., Rival 1998), and homosexuality (e.g., Gutmann 1997:394–95; Herdt 1987, 1993). Simply recognizing the existence of practices that appear antithetical to normative masculinity (see Dowson 2000; Kimmell 1994) will broaden the terms of the debate (e.g., Joyce 2000; Voss and Schmidt 2000). In men's studies, Hearn (2004:50) argues that the category should be retained, but to avoid reifying it or refocusing our gazes exclusively on ideal forms, we should only refer to the category in relation to women, children, other forms of masculinity, race, and so on. Locating masculinity in this way demands that attention be paid to explicitly situated subjects (see also Joyce 2004).

There will be many contexts in which the appropriateness of the category will not be clear. For example, to talk of "masculinity" in remote prehistory may make little sense. However, there is an argument to be made for its use as a heuristic device, or a "controlled fiction" (Strathern 1988). A common criticism of the antiessentialist critique is that political action becomes paralyzed if identity categories are destabilized. A response has been to use such categories strategically, employing them to achieve specific goals (Butler 1990; Petersen 2003:57). If used explicitly and critically, masculinity may serve a similar purpose in archaeological interpretation. A word of caution, though. Terms such as "queer" have been successfully strategically redeployed (see Butler 1993). But the category "masculinity" starts from a position of privilege, which puts it in a completely different relationship to power and knowledge. It is unclear whether it is possible to retain its use analytically without reinstating that same relationship of power in our interpretations.

A Methodological Corrective

The second possibility is to dispense with the category altogether. It has been remarked that archaeological evidence is inherently ambiguous (e.g., Knapp

1998a). A full critique of "masculinity" would take that ambiguity as a "tangible aspect" of the meaning of the archaeological evidence rather than a problem of methodology (see Alberti 1997; Yates 1993:47). One would not, therefore, start from the assumption that what we recognize as masculinity exists or that the analytical category "masculinity" is necessarily appropriate. Such assumptions could result in our trying to squeeze material into inappropriate interpretive frameworks. As argued previously, the sex/gender division implies a binary organization of bodies into male and female. Yates (1993) and Alberti (2001, 2002) have demonstrated how such an assumption can straitjacket the material, forcing a dualism and associated interpretations that are not inherent in the material.

To say that ridding ourselves of the category "masculinity" leaves us with few options to talk about "men" in the past would be disingenuous. Any mention of past identities is necessarily fragmentary, incomplete, and underdetermined by the evidence. Using terms that do not refer to a specific "masculine" identity but do refer to a sexed body—whether that sex is central to the identities represented or explored—is less likely to produce distortion than to redeploy a category that is heavy with meaning in the present but may not have had meaning in the past. Instead, identities and relations among persons can be built from the ground up using models that respond and are sensitive to the material in question (e.g., Joyce 2001; Meskell and Joyce 2003). Moreover, we should not expect all classes of material to be involved in every aspect of past life. For example, where monumental two-dimensional art may be involved in the enactment of power cut through with issues of hierarchy and dominance, it may not speak primarily to aspects of sexual identities. Similarly, burial goods and use-wear analyses of bones might indicate another level of interaction between things and people. Both are incomplete and will involve different usage of theory and different conceptualizations of the interrelationship between material and identity. For example, in a critique and reinterpretation of artwork from Late Bronze Age Knossos, Alberti (2001, 2002) argued that sexual difference was not central to the imagery. Consequently, the category "masculinity" seemed to be an imposition in talking about the art. This need not imply, however, that another body of material from the same period on Crete may not warrant mobilization of the category (bearing in mind the dangers of reification). Phallic imagery found at contemporary Cretan "peak sanctuaries" could indicate just such a possibility (see Peatfield 1992). Different material has different relationships to identity and sociopolitical structure, which begs for theoretical and conceptual flexibility and pluralism in approach.

Reflexivity and "Critical Need"

Studying masculinities in archaeology demands reflexivity on the part of the researcher to avoid interpretations that are reactionary rather than critical. Reflexivity refers to the process of acknowledging what it is that we want from the material and being aware of the standpoint from which knowledge is produced. Feminists and anthropologists have written on the importance of the politics of location (see Cornwall and Lindisfarne 1994:45), as have men's studies authors (e.g., Hearn 2004:62). Gender archaeology and postprocessual approaches have shown how knowledge claims are embedded in sociopolitical experience (Conkey and Gero 1991; Engelstad 1991; Shanks and Tilley 1987; Thomas 2000:3; Voss and Schmidt 2000). The gap between what our evidence says clearly and what we say of it is obviously considerable. Being open to the ambiguity of the material and to the possibility that masculinity is inappropriate for modeling past gendered lives addresses part of the issue. To further avoid exclusions inherent in the use of dominant categories, men's studies authors are following a feminist lead by calling for greater attention to be paid to the politics of knowledge and the need for reflexivity on the part of (especially male) researchers (Hearn 2004:62; Petersen 2003:55; see also Haraway 1988). Men, in general, have greater access to resources and are able to make their voices heard more easily than women, although this tendency is heavily mitigated by other aspect of social identity. This requires a degree of self-reflexivity when studying issues such as masculinity, itself so heavily involved in systems of inequality (see Hearn 2004). Men are notoriously bad at being reflexive, especially when they think they are good at being reflexive. Middleton (1993:11) has noted that "reflexivity works imperfectly for men because they don't see what they're seeing when they see themselves."

Fox (1998) has addressed the issue of reflexivity in archaeological investigations of masculinity. Even though he focuses his critique on interpretations of Athenian men, his commentary on what is at stake by attempting to study men while simultaneously not allowing the categories of "man" or "men" to eclipse historical difference has general implications. The example Fox (1998:7) examines is the thesis of the ancient Athenian as the "constrained man," proposed by Winkler (1990). Fox (1998:12) states that Winkler's enthusiasm for his object—Athenian man—led him to prematurely create a historical subject based on readings of texts without first asking what kind of subject the texts themselves were creating. In order to explain why this happened, Fox introduces the concept of "critical need"—how the desires that motivate research into past social worlds influence "the boundaries of what we study and the kinds of analysis we produce" (12). He compares the position of ancient historians who focus on gender to feminist critics who deconstruct the category "woman," the basis of the political goal that they wish to further. A parallel can also be drawn with archaeologists who deconstruct the categories "man" and "woman." Echoing my argument, Fox states that "it is the insistence upon historical difference which will prevent the category

of man from emerging" (12–13). Either we admit the contingency of our categories but readmit them because we consider them so important, hence dispensing
with historicity, or we adhere to the goal of "reconstructing social realities" but
with material that is so incomplete that clear "answers" are hard to come by (12–
13). This is where "critical need" comes into play: our objectives in studying men
are inseparable from the analysis. Drawing on Fox (1998:13), it may be that the
category "masculinity" is present in our material only because of our desire to see
it there. He argues that it is "a fantasy of narrative completion that motivates the
attempts to produce a cohesive picture of the ancient self, when it is the cracks
themselves which are a clear mark of a distinct historical character" (19).

Conclusions

Self-reflection on issues such as "critical need" may reduce what we say about the
past, but it will also mitigate potentially destructive effects when addressing the
study of masculinity. Moreover, ambiguity and uncertainty in the material may
be the "cracks," or the "outflanking move," required to write a history of "men"
through archaeology. Undeniably, research has successfully demonstrated the
complexity wrapped up in the categories "man," "masculinity," and "male" for
historical periods and in the classical world. Even so, Fox (1998) and Dudink
(1998) alert us to the potential for such studies to lend greater solidity to a
singular historical male subject, a process I suggest may be occurring in other
areas of archaeology. Contexts that rely exclusively on nontextual evidence are
even more vulnerable to imposing a category onto the material. As such, an
important axiom to adopt, I suggest, is the willingness to admit that "masculinity"
may not be salient in a given context. Even if we wish to afford it strategic value,
I argue that there can be no archaeology of masculinity that is not simultaneously
an archaeology of other historically situated and constructed subjects. The decision on whether to use the term will depend on each researcher's "critical need"
and whether the local material and context warrant it.

Acknowledgments

Thank you to Sarah Nelson for providing an opportunity to develop my thinking
around the issue of how to study men and masculinities through archaeology and
for her patience and support. I am grateful to Rosemary Joyce for sending me
unpublished work and for inspiration. My colleagues at Framingham State College provided valuable input in departmental seminars where some of these ideas
were presented. Ira Silver and Lisa Eck gave continuous support and insightful
commentary, for which I am hugely grateful. Many thanks to Ing-Marie Back

Danielson and Camilla Caesar, who searched for and sent materials. Thank you to Thomas Dowson and Cassie Richardson. Without Karen Alberti, this chapter would not have been completed.

References

Alberti, Benjamin
  1997   Archaeology and Masculinity in Bronze Age Knossos. Ph.D. dissertation, University of Southampton.
  2001   Faience Goddesses and Ivory Bull-Leapers: The Aesthetics of Sexual Difference at Late Bronze Age Knossos. *World Archaeology* 33(2):189–205.
  2002   Gender and the Figurative Art of Late Bronze Age Knossos. In *Labyrinth Revisited: Rethinking Minoan Archaeology*. Yannis Hamilakis, ed. Pp. 98–117. Oxford: Oxbow.
Almeida, Miguel Vale de
  1996   *The Hegemonic Male: Masculinity in a Portuguese Town*. Providence, RI: Berghahn Books.
Archetti, Eduardo
  1998   *Masculinities: An Anthropology of Football, Polo and Tango*. Oxford: Berg.
Baca Zinn, Maxine
  2003   Chicano Men and Masculinity. In *Men's Lives*. Michael S. Kimmel and Michael A. Messner, eds. Pp. 25–34. Boston: Allyn and Bacon.
Baker, Mary
  1997   Invisibility as a Symptom of Gender Categories in Archaeology. In *Invisible People and Processes: Writing Gender and Childhood into European Prehistory*. Jenny Moore and Eleanor Scott, eds. Pp. 183–91. London: Leicester University Press.
Baker, Robin
  2000   *Sperm Wars*. London: Pan Books.
Barrett, John
  1988   Fields of Discourse: Reconstituting a Social Archaeology. *Critique of Anthropology* 7:5–16.
Bly, Robert
  1990   *Iron John: A Book about Men*. New York: Addison-Wesley.
Bourke, Joanna
  1996   *Dismembering the Male: Men's Bodies, Britain and the Great War*. London: Reaktion Books.
Braidotti, Rosi
  1994   Radical Philosophies of Sexual Difference. In *The Polity Reader in Gender Studies*. Pp. 62–70. Oxford: Blackwell.
Brod, Harry
  1987   The Case for Men's Studies. In *The Making of Masculinities: The New Men's Studies*. Harry Brod, ed. Pp. 39–62. Winchester: Allen and Unwin.

Busby, Cecilia
 2000   *The Performance of Gender: An Anthropology of Everyday Life in a South Indian Fishing Village.* London: Athlone Press.
Buss, David
 2003   *The Evolution of Desire: Strategies of Human Mating.* Philadelphia: Basic Books.
Butler, Judith
 1990   *Gender Trouble: Feminism and the Subversion of Identity.* London: Routledge.
 1993   *Bodies That Matter: On the Discursive Limits of Sex.* London: Routledge.
Caesar, Camilla
 1999a   The Construction of Masculinity—The Driving Force of History: A New Way of Understanding Change in the Past. *Lund Archaeological Review* 5:117–36.
 1999b   Urmannen—Den Osynliga Normen: Maskulinitetsforskning Inom Arkeologin [The Ancient Man—The Invisible Norm]. In *Han Hon Den Det: Att Integrera Genus Och Kön i Arkeologi.* Camilla Caeser, Ingrid Gustin, Elisabeth Iregren, Bodil Petersson, Elisabeth Rudebeck, Eriak Räf, and Louise Ströbeck, eds. Pp. 115–25. Institute of Archaeology Report Series 65. Lund: University of Lund.
Canaan, Joyce, and Christine Griffin
 1990   The New Men's Studies: Part of the Problem or Part of the Solution? In *Men, Masculinities and Social Theory.* Jeff Hearn and David Morgan, eds. Pp. 206–14. London: Unwin Hyman.
Carrigan, Tim, Bob Connell, and John Lee
 1987   Toward a New Sociology of Masculinity. In *The Making of Masculinities: The New Men's Studies.* Harry Brod, ed. Pp. 63–100. Winchester: Allen and Unwin.
Chodorow, Nancy
 1978   *The Reproduction of Mothering: Psychoanalysis and the Sociology of Gender.* Berkeley: University of California Press.
Clatterbaugh, Kenneth
 1998   What Is Problematic about Masculinities? *Men and Masculinities* 1(1):24–45.
 2000   Literature of the U.S. Men's Movements. *Signs: Journal of Women in Culture and Society* 25(3):883–94.
Conkey, Margaret, and Joan Gero
 1991   Tensions, Pluralities and Engendering Archaeology: Women and Prehistory. In *Engendering Archaeology.* Joan Gero and Margaret Conkey, eds. Pp. 3–30. Oxford: Basil Blackwell.
Conkey, Margaret, and Janet Spector
 1984   Archaeology and the Study of Gender. In *Advances in Archaeological Method and Theory.* Vol. 7. Michael Schiffer, ed. Pp. 1–38. New York: Academic Press.
Connell, Robert
 1987   *Gender and Power.* Cambridge: Polity Press.

1994   Psychoanalysis on Masculinity. In *Theorizing Masculinities*. Harry Brod and Michael Kaufman, eds. Pp. 11–38. Thousand Oaks, CA: Sage.

1995   *Masculinities*. Berkeley: University of California Press.

2000   *The Men and the Boys*. Berkeley: University of California Press.

Cornwall, Andrea, and Nancy Lindisfarne

1994   Dislocating Masculinity: Gender, Power, and Anthropology. In *Dislocating Masculinity: Comparative Ethnographies*. Andrea Cornwall and Nancy Lindisfarne, eds. Pp. 11–47. London: Routledge.

Demetriou, Demetrakis Z.

2001   Connell's Concept of Hegemonic Masculinity: A Critique. *Theory and Society* 30:337–61.

Dowson, Thomas

2000   Why Queer Archaeology? An Introduction. *World Archaeology* 32(2):161–65.

Dudink, Stefan

1998   The Trouble with Men: Problems in the History of "Masculinity." *European Journal of Cultural Studies* 1(3):419–31.

Engelstad, Erika

1991   Feminist Theory and Post-Processual Archaeology. In *The Archaeology of Gender*. Proceedings of the 22nd Annual Chacmool Conference. Dale Walde and Noreen D. Willows, eds. Pp. 116–20. Calgary: Department of Archaeology, University of Calgary.

Espiritu, Yen Le

2003   All Men Are *Not* Created Equal: Asian Men in U.S. History. In *Men's Lives*. Michael S. Kimmel and Michael A. Messner, eds. Pp. 35–44. Boston: Allyn and Bacon.

Fausto-Sterling, Anne

1992   *Myths of Gender: Biological Theories about Women and Men*. New York: Basic Books.

Fedigan, Linda

1982   *Primate Paradigms: Sex Roles and Social Bonds*. Montreal: Eden Press.

Fox, Matthew

1998   The Constrained Man. In *Thinking Men: Masculinity and Its Self-Representation in the Classical Tradition*. Lin Foxhall and John Salmon, eds. Pp. 6–22. London: Routledge.

Foxhall, Lin

1998a   Introduction. In *Thinking Men: Masculinity and Its Self-Representation in the Classical Tradition*. Lin Foxhall and John Salmon, eds. Pp. 1–5. London: Routledge.

1998b   Introduction. In *When Men Were Men: Masculinity, Power, and Identity in Classical Antiquity*. Lin Foxhall and John Salmon, eds. Pp. 1–9. London: Routledge.

Foxhall, Lin, and John Salmon, eds.

1998a   *Thinking Men: Masculinity and Its Self-Representation in the Classical Tradition*. London: Routledge.

1998b   *When Men Were Men: Masculinity, Power, and Identity in Classical Antiquity*. London: Routledge.

Gilmore, David
1990   *Manhood in the Making: Cultural Concepts of Masculinity*. New Haven, CT: Yale University Press.

Grosz, Elizabeth
1994   *Volatile Bodies: Toward a Corporeal Feminism*. Bloomington: Indiana University Press.

1995   *Space, Time and Perversion: Essays on the Politics of Bodies*. London: Routledge.

Gutmann, Matthew
1996   *The Meanings of Macho: Being a Man in Mexico City*. Berkeley: University of California Press.

1997   Trafficking in Men: The Anthropology of Masculinity. *Annual Review of Anthropology* 26:385–409.

1998   Do We Need "Masculinist" (Manly?) Defenses of Feminist Archaeology? *Archaeological Dialogues* 5(2):112–15.

Hadley, Dawn, ed.
1998a   *Masculinity in Medieval Europe*. London: Longman.

Hadley, Dawn
1998b   Medieval Masculinities. In *Masculinity in Medieval Europe*. Dawn Hadley, ed. Pp. 1–18. London: Longman.

Hager, Lori D., ed.
1997   *Women in Human Evolution*. London: Routledge.

Hanmer, Jalna
1990   Men, Power and the Exploitation of Women. *Women's Studies International Forum* 13(5):443–56.

Haraway, Donna
1988   Situated Knowledge: The Science Question in Feminism as a Site of Discourse on the Privilege of Partial Perspective. *Feminist Studies* 14(3):575–99.

Harrison, Rodney
2002   Archaeology and the Colonial Encounter: Kimberley Spearpoints, Cultural Identity and Masculinity in the North of Australia. *Journal of Social Archaeology* 2(3):352–77.

Hearn, Jeff
2004   From Hegemonic Masculinity to the Hegemony of Men. *Feminist Theory* 5(1):49–72.

Hearn, Jeff, and David Morgan
1990   Men Masculinities and Social Theory. In *Men, Masculinities and Social Theory*. Jeff Hearn and David Morgan, eds. Pp. 1–17. London: Unwin Hyman.

Herdt, Gilbert
1981   *Guardians of the Flute: Idioms of Masculinity*. Chicago: University of Chicago Press.

1987   *The Sambia: Ritual and Gender in New Guinea.* New York: Holt, Rinehart and Winston.

Herdt, Gilbert, ed.

1993   *Third Sex, Third Gender: Beyond Sexual Dimorphism in Culture and History.* New York: Zone Books.

Joyce, Rosemary

1996   The Construction of Gender in Classic Maya Monuments. In *Gender in Archaeology: Essays in Research and Practice.* Rita Wright, ed. Pp. 167–95. Philadelphia: University of Pennsylvania Press.

1998   Performing Gender in Pre-Hispanic Central America: Ornamentation, Representation and the Construction of the Body. *RES: Anthropological Aesthetics* 33:147–65.

2000   A Precolumbian Gaze: Male Sexuality among the Ancient Maya. In *Archaeologies of Sexuality.* Barbara L. Voss and Robert A. Schmidt, eds. Pp. 263–83. London: Routledge.

2001   *Gender and Power in Prehispanic Mesoamerica.* Austin: University of Texas Press.

2004   Embodied Subjectivity: Gender, Femininity, Masculinity, Sexuality. In *Blackwell Companion to Social Archaeology.* Lynn Meskell and Robert Preucel, eds. Pp. 82–95. Oxford: Blackwell.

Kauffman, Michael

1994   Men, Feminism, and Men's Contradictory Experiences of Power. In *Theorizing Masculinities.* Harry Brod and Michael Kaufman, eds. Pp. 142–63. Thousand Oaks, CA: Sage.

Kimmell, Michael S.

1994   Masculinity as Homophobia: Fear, Shame, and Silence in the Construction of Gender Identity. In *Theorizing Masculinities.* Harry Brod and Michael Kaufman, eds. Pp. 119–41. Thousand Oaks, CA: Sage.

Knapp, A. Bernard

1998a   Boys Will Be Boys: Masculinist Approaches to a Gendered Archaeology. In *Reader in Gender Archaeology.* Kelley Hays-Gilpin and David S. Whitley, eds. Pp. 365–73. London: Routledge.

1998b   Who's Come a Long Way Baby? Masculinist Approaches to a Gendered Archaeology. *Archaeological Dialogues* 5(2):91–106.

Knapp, A. Bernard, and Lynn Meskell

1997   Bodies of Evidence on Prehistoric Cyprus. *Cambridge Archaeological Journal* 7(2):183–204.

Laqueur, Thomas

1990   *Making Sex: Body and Gender from the Greeks to Freud.* Cambridge, MA: Harvard University Press.

Lloyd, Genevieve

1993   *The Man of Reason: "Male" and "Female" in Western Philosophy.* St. Paul: University of Minnesota Press.

Lovejoy, C. Owen
　　1981　　The Origins of Man. *Science* 211:341–50.
Mac an Ghaill, Mairtin
　　1994　　The Making of Black English Masculinities. In *Theorizing Masculinities*. Harry
　　　　　　Brod and Michael Kaufman, eds. Pp. 183–99. Thousand Oaks, CA: Sage.
MacInnes, John
　　1998　　*End of Masculinity*. Buckingham: Open University Press.
Marshall, Yvonne
　　1995　　Why Do We Need Feminist Theory? Paper presented at the Institute of
　　　　　　Field Archaeologists Annual Conference, Bradford, April 11–13.
McCafferty, Sharisse D., and Geoffrey G. McCafferty
　　1998　　Spinning and Weaving as Female Gender Identity in Post-Classic Mexico. In
　　　　　　Reader in Gender Archaeology. Kelley Hays-Gilpin and David S. Whitley, eds. Pp.
　　　　　　213–30. London: Routledge.
Meskell, Lynn
　　1996　　The Somatization of Archaeology: Institutions, Discourses, Corporeality.
　　　　　　Norwegian Archaeological Review 29(1):1–16.
　　2002　　The Intersections of Identity and Politics in Archaeology. *Annual Review of
　　　　　　Anthropology* 31:279–301.
Meskell, Lynn, and Rosemary A. Joyce
　　2003　　*Embodied Lives: Figuring Ancient Maya and Egyptian Experience*. London: Routledge.
Metcalf, Andy, and Martin Humphries, eds.
　　1985　　*The Sexuality of Men*. London: Pluto Press.
Middleton, Peter
　　1993　　*The Inward Gaze: Masculinity and Subjectivity in Modern Culture*. London: Routledge.
Moore, Henrietta L.
　　1994　　*A Passion for Difference: Essays in Anthropology and Gender*. Cambridge: Polity Press.
Mosse, George L.
　　1996　　*The Image of Man: The Creation of Modern Masculinities*. New York: Oxford Univer-
　　　　　　sity Press.
Nelson, Sarah
　　1997　　*Gender in Archaeology: Analyzing Power and Prestige*. Walnut Creek, CA: AltaMira
　　　　　　Press.
Nordbladh, Jarl, and Timothy Yates
　　1990　　This Perfect Body, This Virgin Text: Between Sex and Gender in Archaeol-
　　　　　　ogy. In *Archaeology after Structuralism*. Ian Bapty and Timothy Yates, eds. Pp.
　　　　　　222–37. London: Routledge.
Osborne, Robin
　　1998　　Sculpted Men of Athens: Masculinity and Power in the Field of Vision. In
　　　　　　Thinking Men: Masculinity and Its Self-Representation in the Classical Tradition. Lin Fox-
　　　　　　hall and John Salmon, eds. Pp. 23–42. London: Routledge.

Peatfield, Alan
    1992   Rural Ritual in Bronze Age Crete: The Peak Sanctuary at Atsipadhes. *Cambridge Archaeological Journal* 2(1):59–87.
Perry, Elizabeth M., and Rosemary A. Joyce
    2001   Providing a Past for *Bodies That Matter.* Judith Butler's Impact on the Archaeology of Gender. Theme Issue, "Butler Matters: Judith Butler's Impact on Feminist and Queer Studies since *Gender Trouble,*" *International Journal of Sexuality and Gender Studies* 6(1–2):63–76.
Petersen, Alan
    2003   Research on Men and Masculinities: Some Implications of Recent Theory for Future Work. *Men and Masculinities* 6(1):54–69.
Rival, Laura
    1998   Androgynous Parents and Guest Children: The Huaorani Couvade. *Journal of the Royal Anthropological Institute* 4(3):619–42.
Robb, John
    1994   Gender Contradictions, Moral Coalitions, and Inequality in Prehistoric Italy. *Journal of European Archaeology* 2(1):20–49.
Rogoff, Irit, and David Van Leer
    1993   Afterthoughts . . . A Dossier on Masculinities. *Theory and Society* 22(5): 731–62.
Roper, Michael, and John Tosh, eds.
    1991   *Manful Assertions: Masculinities in Britain since 1800.* London: Routledge.
Roscoe, Will
    1993   How to Become a Berdache: Toward a Unified Analysis. In *Third Sex, Third Gender: Beyond Sexual Dimorphism in Culture and History.* Gilbert Herdt, ed. Pp. 329–72. New York: Zone Books.
Scott, Eleanor
    1997   Introduction: On the Incompleteness of Archaeological Narratives. In *Invisible People and Processes: Writing Gender and Childhood into European Archaeology.* Jenny Moore and Eleanor Scott, eds. Pp. 1–12. London: Leicester University Press.
Seidler, Victor
    1989   *Rediscovering Masculinity: Reason, Language and Sexuality.* London: Routledge.
    1994   *Unreasonable Men: Masculinity and Social Theory.* London: Routledge.
Shanks, Michael
    1996   Style and the Design of a Perfume Jar from an Archaic Greek City State. In *Contemporary Archaeology in Theory: A Reader.* Robert W. Preucel and Ian Hodder, eds. Pp. 364–93. Oxford: Blackwell.
Shanks, Michael, and Christopher Tilley
    1987   *Reconstructing Archaeology: Theory and Practice.* Cambridge: Cambridge University Press.
Solomon-Godeau, Abigail
    1995   Male Trouble. In *Constructing Masculinity.* Maurice Berger, Brian Wallis, and Simon Watson, eds. Pp. 69–76. London: Routledge.

Sørensen, Marie Louise Stig
    1992   Gender Archaeology and Scandinavian Bronze Age Studies. *Norwegian Archaeo-logical Review* 25(1):31–49.
Spector, Janet
    1993   *What This Awl Means: Feminist Archaeology at a Wahpeton Dakota Village.* St. Paul: Minnesota Historical Society Press.
Stoller, Robert
    1964   A Contribution to the Study of Gender Identity. *International Journal of Psycho-analysis* 45:220–26.
Strathern, Marilyn
    1988   *The Gender of the Gift: Problems with Women and Problems with Society in Melanesia.* Berkeley: University of California Press.
Thomas, Julian
    1996   *Time, Culture and Identity: An Interpretive Archaeology.* London: Routledge.
    2000   Introduction: The Polarities of Post-Processual Archaeology. In *Interpretive Archaeology: A Reader.* Julian Thomas, ed. Pp. 1–18. London: Leicester University Press.
    2004   *Archaeology and Modernity.* London: Routledge.
Tiger, Lionel
    1969   *Men in Groups.* New York: Random House.
    2000   *The Decline of Males: The First Look at an Unexpected New World for Men and Women.* New York: St. Martin's Press.
Treherne, Paul
    1995   The Warrior's Beauty: The Masculine Body and Self-Identity in Bronze Age Europe. *Journal of European Archaeology* 3(1):105–44.
Trigger, Bruce
    1989   *A History of Archaeological Thought.* Cambridge: Cambridge University Press.
Vedantam, Shankar
    2003   Desire and DNA: Is Promiscuity Innate? New Study Sharpens Debate on Men, Sex and Gender Roles. *Washington Post,* August 1: A01.
Voss, Barbara L.
    2000   Feminisms, Queer Theories, and the Archaeological Study of Past Sexualities. *World Archaeology* 32(2):180–92.
Voss, Barbara L., and Robert A. Schmidt
    2000   Archaeologies of Sexuality: An Introduction. In *Archaeologies of Sexuality.* Robert A. Schmidt and Barbara L. Voss, eds. Pp. 1–32. London: Routledge.
Washburn, Sherwood, and C. S. Lancaster
    1968   The Evolution of Hunting. In *Man the Hunter.* R. B. Lee and Irvine DeVore, eds. Pp. 293–303. Chicago: Aldine.
Wilkie, Laurie
    1998   The Other Gender: The Archaeology of an Early 20th Century Fraternity. *Proceedings of the Society for California Archaeology* 11:7–11.

Winkler, John J.
  1990   *The Constraints of Desire: The Anthropology of Sex and Desire in Ancient Greece.* London: Routledge.
Wylie, Alison
  1991   Gender Theory and the Archaeological Record: Why Is There No Archaeology of Gender? In *Engendering Archaeology.* Margaret Conkey and Joan Gero, eds. Pp. 31–54. Oxford: Basil Blackwell.
Yanagisako, Sylvia, and Jane Collier
  1987   Toward a Unified Analysis of Gender and Kinship. In *Gender and Kinship.* Jane Collier and Sylvia Yanagisako, eds. Pp. 1–50. Stanford, CA: Stanford University Press.
Yates, Timothy
  1993   Frameworks for an Archaeology of the Body. In *Interpretative Archaeology.* Christopher Tilley, ed. Pp. 31–72. Oxford: Berg.

The Archaeology of Nonbinary Genders in Native North American Societies

4

SANDRA E. HOLLIMON

IN THE TWENTY YEARS since the publication of Conkey and Spector's (1984) groundbreaking work on gender and archaeology, the examination of systems of multiple genders in the archaeological record has grown. Some theoretical advances in the realms of gender, sexuality, and identity construction have provided archaeologists with new conceptual approaches to their analyses. Following the feminist critiques of science in general and archaeological theory in particular, researchers have continued to debate the meanings and manifestations of gender in the archaeological record (Voss and Schmidt 2000:14–18; Wylie 2002:185–99). Many of the recent discussions can be found in the seminal volume *Archaeologies of Sexuality* (Schmidt and Voss 2000) and in Voss (this volume). The developing approaches in archaeology that employ sexuality, performance, and queer theory are described fully in Voss (2000, 2005) and Perry and Joyce (2001). Therefore, in this chapter, I confine my discussion to the archaeological investigation of nonbinary genders in Native North American societies, north of the present Mexico–U.S. border.

Ethnographic and ethnohistoric information from Native North American societies provides evidence of nonbinary third and fourth genders, in addition to the binary genders of "woman" and "man," as defined by the specific culture. For the purposes of this discussion, third genders are expressed by individuals who are biologically male but culturally not men. Fourth genders are expressed by persons who are biologically female, but are not recognized in their societies as women. If we recognize sex as a category of bodies and gender as a category of persons, we can better understand Native North American gender systems in which individual, acquired, and ascribed traits are more important in determining gender identity than biological sex assignment (Roscoe 1998:127). These systems frequently based gender on other variables than (but not necessarily exclusive of) biologically based primary and secondary sexual characteristics. Variables such as temperament, skill or preference for work, spiritual endowment, and reproductive status appear to have been more important gender markers for nonbinary persons than for normative women and men. I use the term "normative" advisedly, for I believe that it is somewhat misleading. What some anthropologists have called supernumerary or multiple genders are equally as normative as the two categories recognized in binary gender systems.

It has been suggested that nonbinary genders have a great time depth and were most likely recognized by the original colonizing groups of North America that migrated from northeastern Asia (Hollimon 2001b:123–24; Kirkpatrick 2000:397). Therefore, archaeologists who study the material record of Native North American groups should consider nonbinary genders in their interpretations of these social systems (see also Callender and Kochems 1983:444–46; Roscoe 1998:202–3). It is an astute criticism to note that the ethnographic data do not provide detailed information on gender roles in every instance. Nevertheless, the near ubiquity of nonbinary genders in Native American societies suggests that absence of evidence for these genders in some groups (e.g., the Northeast culture area) should not be read as evidence of absence.

The studies that mention ethnographically documented nonbinary genders in their interpretations of archaeological data continue to grow (e.g., Pate 2004). However, some do not necessarily address specific analytical approaches for identifying third and fourth genders at the outset; rather, they consider the possibility somewhat after the fact. In the remainder of this chapter, I discuss examples of some of the approaches that archaeologists have employed to examine nonbinary genders in Native North American societies. I also provide some suggestions about methods that could be employed in future research.

Gender and Other Social Identities

Meskell (2001, 2002) has discussed the overlapping axes of identity and how one can study them archaeologically. She makes the very important point that it may not be possible or even appropriate to try to disentangle the various aspects of "selfhood, embodiment, and being" that derived from gender, sexuality, ethnicity, status, and age (Meskell 2002:281; see also the following discussion). In particular, the role of age in the formation, maintenance, and performance of gender identity is of increasing interests to archaeologists (e.g., Gilchrist 2000).

The covariation of gender identity and age is culturally constructed, just as are all aspects of personhood. In some societies, full human status is not granted to juveniles until a particular milestone has been passed, whether that is weaning, walking, attending school, menarche, marking a significant birthday (e.g., thirteen, sixteen, eighteen, or twenty-one years), formal initiation, marriage, or becoming a parent. These rites of passage may be the most important arenas of gender marking in a culture, especially the passage between adolescence and adulthood. Cross-culturally, the attainment of adulthood includes instruction in the proper conduct expected of adults in the given society. As such, women learn their culturally expected roles and duties, as do men. It can also be seen cross-culturally that gender roles, behaviors, and identities, especially concerning child rearing, are emphasized in this rite of passage. However, it may be only during this passage, which is frequently followed shortly by marriage for girls or young women, that gender is strongly marked.

In many prehistoric Native American societies, it may have been that women and men did not require gender marking across the entire life cycle but that nonbinary gendered persons had their gender more strongly marked during everyday lived experience. This idea, based on Bourdieu's (1977) practice theory, explains that the quotidian activities of daily life form the material patterns that archaeologists study. Perhaps archaeologists can identify distinctive dress and ornamentation, labor practices or products, or changes to the skeleton that are distinctive of nonbinary genders.

If gender signification can vary among the genders recognized by a culture, then it can also vary throughout the life cycle as mentioned previously. The final rite of passage, death, may emphasize a person's identity in a way akin to a "final statement." Mortuary analyses by definition deal with the material correlates of behaviors exhibited by living persons at the end point of another's (physical) life. However, gender is only one aspect of identity among many that can be signified.

This idea presents interesting interpretive challenges for archaeologists who examine mortuary practices. As such, they may be severely limited in detecting and interpreting gender across the entire life course because they sample only a restricted point of time in an individual's (and community's) existence. An excellent example of overcoming this obstacle is the work of Schmidt (2000, 2001, 2002), who notes that in the Southern Scandinavian Mesolithic, gender apparently was weakly marked, if marked at all, in mortuary contexts. Nevertheless, he does not contend that gender was unimportant in these societies; instead, he posits that gender may have been emphasized in social contexts other than mortuary behavior, especially ritual practices.

The possible misconstruing of gender throughout the life cycle is exemplified when we consider some ethnographic studies. The etic categories "berdache," third-gender male, or two-spirit may not be applicable to a culture's designation of gender. Goulet's (1996, 1997) northern Athapaskan studies and Stewart's (2002) work among the Netsilik demonstrate that subsuming these gender "situations" under such a simplistic taxonomy misses the subtleties of the gender contexts. When a child's gender identity changes after killing a particular game animal as an adolescent rite of passage, it is not equivalent to the lifelong nonbinary gender identity of a third-gender male. If one were to try to discern this succession of genders in a mortuary context, for instance, the interpretation may ultimately become misleading (see Crass 2001).

Additional caution must be exercised when seemingly disparate identities combine in what appears to be a single category or axis of identity. Among the Chumash of coastal California, the occupational guild of undertakers (*'aqi*) appears to have been available to persons who were third-gender males, who were postmenopausal women, who were celibate, or who were biological males who had sexual relations with men. The feature that unites these apparently distinct gender/sexuality identities is that their sexual activities (or lack thereof among the celibates) were nonprocreative (Hollimon 2000a). The *'aqi* identity incorporates spirituality, occupational specialization, and sexuality, privileging these facets of personhood over either sex or gender despite the fact that Chumash eschatology is infused with gendered concepts and actors, both human and supernatural (Hollimon 2001a, 2004).

Mortuary Studies

Some archaeologists have been considering binary genders in examining native North American mortuary data for roughly the past twenty years. This is an advance beyond the consideration of mere biological sex in mortuary analyses. However, relatively few studies have deliberately considered nonbinary genders from the outset of the research program. Instead, a fairly common occurrence is the ascription of third or fourth gender to a burial that contains accompaniments associated with the "other biological sex." In some respects, interpretations that attempt to deal with "anomalous" data play a variation on a timeworn theme in archaeological analysis: if a specific function for a class of material culture is not readily apparent, the use or meaning of the material is attributed to "ritual" or "ceremonial" contexts. While the stereotype on which this joke is based may not be as prevalent as the nonarchaeological public believes, it is still a useful analogy for my point. Some archaeologists have employed nonbinary genders or identities as something of a "trash can category," explaining ambiguous gender attributions as possible reflections of these identities. I do not argue with the employment of such interpretations; on the contrary, it is heartening to see archaeologists consider nonbinary genders at all. Instead, I argue that some archaeological interpretations merely introduce the possibility that artifact X was associated in some way with a person of such a gender identity rather than providing a more subtle, nuanced, and ultimately more contextualized explanation.

As Voss (2005) describes this method, the initial step is the determination of a normative archaeological pattern; in this case, it is the distribution of grave accompaniments. Second, artifact distributions that vary from that norm are examined as possible evidence of third-, fourth-, or *n*th-gender identities or practices. Finally, the interpretation of evidence of nonbinary genders is then supported by ethnographic and ethnohistoric textual sources. While this approach is apparently sound, Voss (2005) makes the very important point that the example of nonbinary gender identities illustrates the need for archaeologists to make a critical, firm distinction between *social* deviance and *statistical* deviation. Are nonnormative mortuary treatments merely statistical outliers in a large population study, or are they examples of particularly rich treatments that do not conform to expectations about gender identities?

Arnold (1990) discusses just such a situation concerning "the deposed princess of Vix," a spectacular Iron Age burial in Germany. Excavated in 1953, some researchers were loath to accept the biological evidence of the female sex of the burial, instead choosing to interpret the burial as that of a transvestite priest (Arnold 1990:370). Weglian (2001) describes a comparable example of burial practices in the Neolithic/Bronze Age transition in Germany. Her interpretation of atypical burials supports the identification of more than two genders in these societies.

Similarly, in her examination of the nineteenth-century Blackdog burial site in Minnesota, Whelan (1991, 1993) statistically analyzed the correlation of mortuary goods and biologically sexed skeletal remains. Whelan's interpretation of the data included the possible presence of third-gender persons who were biologically male but did not display the "standard" mortuary treatment of normative males/men exhibited in the rest of the burial population.

I suggest that this approach may be useful in the examination of nonbinary genders because it is also possible that the conflation of occupational specialization and gender might be marked in mortuary contexts. As an example, a burial from the Bering Strait site of Ekven was interpreted by the excavators as a shaman's burial because drum handles and masks were found buried with the person. Additionally, the skeleton was sexed as female, but women's and men's tools made of ivory, wood, shell, stone, and bone were included as burial accompaniments. This was the most elaborate burial at the Ekven cemetery, a site that represents the Old Bering Sea complex dating to about 2500–1500 B.P. (Arutiunov and Fitzhugh 1988:126).

It is likely that this individual was not recognized as a woman or a man or even a fourth gender in the sense that it is defined at the outset of this chapter. It is probable that the person was gendered "shaman" (or culturally designated ritual specialist). In many circumboreal indigenous societies, including North America, the ritual/medical/social role of the shaman is considered analogous to a gender. Examples come from the Inuit (Saladin D'Anglure 1992), numerous Siberian cultures (Czaplicka 1914), and perhaps Mesolithic societies in Europe (Schmidt 2000).

When identities overlap, as among ritual specialists who display gender "difference" (Bean 1976; see also Hollimon 2001b), the approaches to studying nonbinary genders may also overlap in some aspects, such as combining bioarchaeological evidence and mortuary analysis. For example, the activity-induced pathologies or musculoskeletal stress markers (MSMs) associated with an occupational specialization bring in two types of skeletal evidence. These can be combined with an examination of mortuary practices. An occupational specialist's tools may be interred as offerings, allowing interpretations of the interplay among biological sex, gender identity, and occupation. An example from the Chumash of California is described later in this chapter.

Occupational Specialization

A recurrent theme in the ethnographic descriptions of Native North American third-gender males is that their skilled craft work was finely made and highly prized. Indeed, a hallmark of both third and fourth genders is the ability or preference for work associated with "the opposite" gender. Cross-culturally, it appears that most of these persons were identified by their societies when they expressed interest or aptitude and persistently engaged in the activities considered appropriate for women (in the case of third-gender males) or men (in the case of fourth-gender females). This often occurred well before puberty, indicating that sexual behavior was a less important defining trait for nonbinary genders (Roscoe 1998:8).

There are many references in the ethnographic literature to the innovations in arts and craft work that persons of nonbinary gender achieved. However, there are relatively few instances where a material product is said to have design elements that are specific to such persons or their gender identities. There are examples of stylistic changes that are associated with a single artist, such as Hastíín Klah. Klah's innovation was to take traditional Navajo sandpainting designs and weave very large tapestries incorporating ritually important *Yeibichai* figures. Klah (1867–1937), a Navajo *nádleehí*, combined the knowledge of weaving, a woman's art, with the knowledge of religion, a domain of men. Klah also took spiritual risks by making evanescent images from the sandpainting medium into permanent designs in the tapestry (Roscoe 1998:50–51).

Senior (2000), in her examination of pottery production techniques in the Southwest, suggests that it is just such innovation that is reflected in ceramic stylistic changes. Senior's "gender-shift model of craft innovation" posits that when one gender begins to practice "another gender's" craft, either the producer will change form or the product will change form. For example, she suggests that the "social institution" of the third-gender male in some Puebloan groups actually functioned to maintain a highly gendered division of labor because the (previously) male potter has his gender reclassified by virtue of the work performed (Senior 2000:73).

Third-gender males in many Native North American societies excelled at making pottery, weaving baskets, preparing skins and hides, and other skilled crafts associated with women. However, the ability to identify the products of the labors of nonbinary gender persons in the archaeological record seems elusive. One art in which we may be able to discern the handiwork of third-gender males is the porcupine quillwork of northern Plains groups. Males who dreamed of the supernatural entity Double Woman (or her cognates) experienced a shift in gender and became third-gender males (see also the discussion later in this chapter). The difficult tasks of preparing and embroidering the quills, as well as intricate beadwork, were expected of normative women, but only Double Woman dreamers were sanctioned to use design elements that depicted the figure (Wissler 1902, 1912). Even normative women who dreamed of Double Woman were granted sexual license, which is, in one aspect, a shift in gender/sexuality identity (see DeMallie 1983).

Other aspects of clothing may provide insight in identifying third-gender material culture. In a study of the physical dimensions of a particular Lakota dress, Logan and Schmittou (1996) suggested that if the dress was worn in a traditional belted style, the wearer would be exceptionally tall. They argue that this dress was worn by a Lakota third-gender male (*winkte*) who was taller than normative women in these societies. However, in both this case and the design elements associated with Double Woman dreamers, the nondurable quality of the materials makes preservation in the archaeological record an issue. An example of Double Woman crafts that can be preserved is presented later in this chapter.

Bioarchaeological Approaches

Skeletal remains can be viewed as material culture, and the biological indicators of sex might allow inferences about gender as well (Walker and Cook 1997).

Developing technologies in skeletal analysis may provide the ability to examine relationships among biological sex, culturally constructed gender identities, and the social dimensions of mortuary practices. For example, it is increasingly possible to determine the biological sex of skeletal remains using DNA and to compare this information with the treatment of the remains in mortuary contexts. In addition, bone chemistry analysis and the examination of some nutrition-implicated pathologies could shed light on the possibility that a past population fed their girls and boys differently. This in turn has implications for the interpretation of gender dynamics in that society.

Perry (2004) considers the bioarchaeological evidence of sex-based division of labor in skeletal remains from the pre-Hispanic Southwest. Her study examined MSMs, the remodeled bone that develops in response to repetitive motion. Habitual labor may leave traces on the skeleton, and these traces can be examined with regard to female and male patterns; activities such as weaving, food production, hunting, and ceramic manufacture may be reconstructed from these MSM patterns. Perry also considers the presence of typically female MSM patterns on skeletons that are morphologically sexed as male. These may indicate that the person performed the same types of work that normative females did and may be evidence of a socially recognized third gender.

Another example comes from the Chumash of coastal southern California. While there is generally a poor fit between the "gender" of the burial accompaniments and the biological sex of a skeleton in these archaeological sites, it may be possible to use other methods to assess gender. Specifically, the combination of tools associated with an occupational specialization and the presence of activity-induced pathologies, such as osteoarthritis, may provide another avenue of interpretation. I tentatively identified two third-gender burials of relatively young biological males that showed advanced spinal degeneration that was commonly found in female skeletons. These individuals may have incurred repeated stress to the spine by use of digging sticks for harvesting tubers or digging graves. Burial accompaniments suggest that these persons may have been undertakers, an occupation staffed by third-gender males and postmenopausal women; these two graves contained basketry impressions and digging stick weights and were the only male burials in the sample ($n = 210$) to contain both of these items in the undertaker's tool kit (Hollimon 1996, 1997, 2000a).

A promising approach to the examination of skeletal remains as material culture involves the identification of traumatic injuries in sexed skeletons. A number of studies of prehistoric skeletal populations have identified statistically significant sex differences in patterns of trauma (e.g., Lambert 1997; Martin 1997; Martin and Akins 2001; Walker 1997; Wilkinson 1997). Using these patterns, it may be possible to identify third- and fourth-gender persons in skeletal populations. Biologically sexed males who display female trauma patterns may be third-gender persons, while female-sexed skeletons displaying male patterns of injury may be fourth-gender persons. My work has tentatively identified possible fourth-gender females in precontact California and the protohistoric northern Plains. In both of these areas, traumatic injuries consistent with participation in warfare as combatants have been found in female skeletons (Hollimon 1999, 2000b, 2001c). Normative women in these societies could be combatants, but ethnographic evidence also supports the possibility that at least some of these persons were fourth-gender individuals.

Household and Architectural Analysis

Household analysis has long been a focus in feminist approaches to archaeological analysis (Voss and Schmidt 2000:15). Tringham (1991:99) points out that "the analysis of social change at a microscale of the household or co-residential group or family has long been recognized as an essential scale for the study of the social relations of production." Archaeologists examining gender systems in North America have also employed this perspective.

Prine's (1997, 2000) examination of eighteenth- and nineteenth-century Hidatsa earth lodges proposes a material correlate of third-gender activities in the upper Missouri River area. Grounded in ethnographic and ethnohistoric documentation, she suggests that the Hidatsa *miati*, as cultural-ritual innovators and earth lodge builders, would express their gender identity in the homes they built for themselves. A lodge that Prine (2000:210) named "Double Post" exhibits both structural elements and size differences that make it unique among excavated Hidatsa earth lodges. She interprets the doubled post elements as a possible expression of the doubled aspects of the *miati* life path, which combined culturally defined feminine and masculine traits.

In addition, the dimensions of Double Post may indicate an unusually small household by Hidatsa standards. While an older childless couple or an elder living alone would have a lodge with four posts, they lacked the peripheral posts and the floor space exhibited by Double Post. Despite its construction, Double Post is exceptionally small, suggesting that a *miati* and spouse (and perhaps their children, adoptive or other) resided there. In contrast, a typical Hidatsa earth lodge housed three generations and their in-marrying spouses, requiring much more space than that exhibited by Double Post (Prine 2000:211).

In addition to her analysis of skeletal material, Perry examined the plaza architecture of the Southwest to argue that the Zuni third gender, *lhamana*, may have its origins around A.D. 1275 (Perry and Joyce 2001:70–71). At roughly the same time, the Katsina religion was crystallizing, at least in terms of public perform-ances of rituals. The repetitive public performance of quotidian and ritual activi-ties in and around large plazas would serve to create highly dualistic gender roles. In addition, these activities would help create what Perry and Joyce (2001:69) term "gender transgressive performance." Domestic and ceremonial performances that were transgressive were reinforced in the plazas, where public, integrative activities were on display (Perry and Joyce 2001:69).

Imagery and Iconography

The anthropological study of rock art provides opportunities for examining gen-der in archaeological contexts. Imagery as defined here refers to pictures that rep-resent something in the physical or nonphysical world (Hays-Gilpin 2004:10). A complementary concept is that of iconography, which involves images with shared meanings and how those meanings function in particular cultural contexts (Hays-Gilpin 2004:10).

Hays-Gilpin (2004:127–46) uses such an approach to describe the iconogra-phy of certain gender/age categories in Southwest rock art. In addition to phallic flute players, she notes the wide distribution of figures with so-called butterfly hair whorls. These figures most likely depict unmarried postpubescent young women or girls and are often accompanied by female genitalia or string aprons, worn by women in ancestral Puebloan cultures. Two figures described by Hays-Gilpin may show hair whorls and penises. Although she entertains the possibility that these are depictions of female genitals or menstruation, she also considers the notion that these are representations of third-gender persons (Hays-Gilpin 2004:137).

Sundstrom (2002) has examined rock art of the northern Plains and has used oral traditions from the Lakota and Dakota to interpret the art's gender symbol-ism. In particular, she has focused on rock art that was most likely made by women who dreamed of Double Woman, a supernatural figure linked to dualistic aspects of womanhood (see also Hays-Gilpin 2004:93–98). These dualities include good and evil, modesty and promiscuity, and motherhood and childless-ness (Sundstrom 2002:100). Women who dreamed of Double Woman could receive supernatural assistance with their skilled crafts, such as quillwork, or might receive supernatural sanction to forgo marriage and childbearing. Sund-strom (2002:102) suggests that Double Woman could display a great deal of latitude with regard to her protégés, from conforming to feminine ideals to exem-plifying their exact opposites.

In addition to women, male persons might also dream of Double Woman. In this event, the person was able to adopt the clothing and lifestyle of a third gender, known in Lakota as *winkte*. The dream conferred powers similar to those attained by women who had Double Woman visions, including creativity in skilled crafts. *Winkte* also had the ability to predict the future and displayed their power by choosing auspicious names for children; parents sought the *winkte* to ensure good fortune for their children (Roscoe 1998:13–14). Although Sundstrom does not directly suggest this, it is possible to logically extend her argument. It is likely that some northern Plains rock art was made by Double Woman dreamers and that some of these persons were third gender; therefore, it is possible that third-gender persons may have been responsible for producing some of the art. The set of associated motifs that suggest Double Woman rock art include bison and deer tracks, human vulvas, handprints, footprints, and abraded grooves (Sundstrom 2002:107).

Summary

Several theoretical and methodological approaches show promise for identifying nonbinary genders in the archaeological record of Native North American societies. It is my hope that as researchers increase their examination of gender and sexuality in these cultures, they also consider the existence of nonbinary genders. In so doing, a more complete picture of these groups becomes possible.

The succession of paradigms in postprocessual archaeology has provided the opportunity for critical appraisal of many long-held and previously unexamined constructs. As an example, the use of queer theory allows us to problematize categories that were left unexamined by first-wave feminist archaeologies, such as men and masculinity (Voss 2000). As the archaeological study of gender continues its development, the subtleties and complexities of gender identities, practices, and their material manifestations will become clearer.

References

Arnold, Bettina
   1990   The Deposed Princess of Vix: The Need for an Engendered European Prehistory. In *The Archaeology of Gender.* Dale Walde and Noreen D. Willows, eds. Pp. 366–74. Calgary: University of Calgary Press.
Arutiunov, S. A., and William W. Fitzhugh
   1988   Prehistory of Siberia and the Bering Sea. In *Crossroads of Continents: Cultures of Siberia and Alaska.* William W. Fitzhugh and Aron Crowell, eds. Pp. 117–29. Washington, DC: Smithsonian Institution Press.

Bean, Lowell John
    1976   Power and Its Applications in Native California. In *Native Californians: A Theoretical Retrospective*. Lowell John Bean and Thomas C. Blackburn, eds. Pp. 407–20. Socorro, NM: Ballena Press.

Bourdieu, Pierre
    1977   *Outline of a Theory of Practice*. Cambridge: Cambridge University Press.

Callender, Charles, and Lee M. Kochems
    2000   The North American Berdache. *Current Anthropology* 24(4):443–70.

Conkey, Margaret W., and Janet D. Spector
    1984   Archaeology and the Study of Gender. *Advances in Archaeological Method and Theory* 7:1–38.

Crass, Barbara A.
    2001   Gender and Mortuary Analysis: What Can Grave Goods Really Tell Us? In *Gender and the Archaeology of Death*. Bettina Arnold and Nancy L. Wicker, eds. Pp. 105–18. Walnut Creek, CA: AltaMira Press.

Czaplicka, Marie A.
    1914   *Aboriginal Siberia*. London: Oxford University Press,.

DeMallie, Raymond J.
    1983   Male and Female in Traditional Lakota Culture. In *The Hidden Half: Studies of Plains Indian Women*. Patricia Albers and Beatrice Medicine, eds. Pp. 237–65. Lanham, MD: University Press of America.

Gilchrist, Roberta
    2000   Archaeological Biographies: Realizing Human Lifecycles, -Courses and -Histories. *World Archaeology* 31(3):325–28.

Goulet, Jean-Guy A.
    1996   The "Berdache"/"Two-Spirit": A Comparison of Anthropological and Native Constructions of Gendered Identities among the Northern Athapaskans. *Journal of the Royal Anthropological Institute* 2(4):683–701.
    1996   The Northern Athapaskan "Berdache" Reconsidered: On Reading More Than There Is in the Ethnographic Record. In *Two-Spirit People: Native American Gender Identity, Sexuality, and Spirituality*. Sue-Ellen Jacobs, Wesley Thomas, and Sabine Lang, eds. Pp. 45–68. Urbana: University of Illinois Press.

Hays-Gilpin, Kelley A.
    2004   *Ambiguous Images: Gender and Rock Art*. Walnut Creek, CA: AltaMira Press.

Hollimon, Sandra E.
    1996   Sex, Gender and Health among the Chumash of the Santa Barbara Channel Area. In *Proceedings of the Society for California Archaeology*. Vol. 9. Judith Reed, ed. Pp. 205–8. San Diego: Society for California Archaeology.
    1997   The Third Gender in Native California: Two-Spirit Undertakers among the Chumash and Their Neighbors. In *Women in Prehistory: North America and Mesoamerica*. Cheryl Claassen and Rosemary A. Joyce, eds. Pp. 173–88. Philadelphia: University of Pennsylvania Press.

1999   "They Usually Kill Some Woman": Warfare, Gender, and the Ethnographic Record in Studies of California Prehistory. Paper presented at the plenary session of the Annual Meetings of the Society for California Archaeology, Sacramento, April 3.

2000a   Archaeology of the '*Aqi*: Gender and Sexuality in Prehistoric Chumash Society. In *Archaeologies of Sexuality*. Robert Schmidt and Barbara Voss, eds. Pp. 179–96. London: Routledge.

2000b   Sex, Health, and Gender Roles among the Arikara of the Northern Plains. In *Reading the Body: Representations and Remains in the Archaeological Record*. Alison E. Rautman, ed. Pp. 25–37. Philadelphia: University of Pennsylvania Press.

2001a   Death, Gender and the Chumash Peoples: Mourning Ceremonialism as an Integrative Mechanism. In *Social Memory, Identity, and Death: Anthropological Perspectives on Mortuary Rituals*. Meredith Chesson, ed. Pp. 41–55. Archeological Papers of the American Anthropological Association 10. Washington, DC: American Anthropological Association.

2001b   The Gendered Peopling of North America: Addressing the Antiquity of Systems of Multiple Genders. In *The Archaeology of Shamanism*. Neil Price, ed. Pp. 123–34. London: Routledge.

2001c   Warfare and Gender in the Northern Plains: Osteological Evidence of Trauma Reconsidered. In *Gender and the Archaeology of Death*. Bettina Arnold and Nancy Wicker, eds. Pp. 179–93. Walnut Creek, CA: AltaMira Press.

2004   The Role of Ritual Specialization in the Evolution of Prehistoric Chumash Complexity. In *Foundations of Chumash Cultural Complexity*. Jeanne E. Arnold, ed. Pp. 53–63. Perspectives in California Archaeology, vol. 7. Los Angeles: Cotsen Institute of Archaeology, University of California.

Kirkpatrick, R. C.

2000   Evolution of Human Homosexual Behavior. *Current Anthropology* 41(3): 385–98.

Lambert, Patricia M.

1997   Patterns of Violence in Prehistoric Hunter-Gatherer Societies of Coastal Southern California. In *Troubled Times: Violence and Warfare in the Past*. Debra L. Martin and David Frayer, eds. Pp. 77–109. Amsterdam: Gordon and Breach.

Logan, Michael H., and Douglas A. Schmittou

1996   Identifying Berdache Material Culture: An Anthropometric Approach. *Tennessee Anthropologist* 21(1):67–79.

Martin, Debra L.

1997   Violence against Women in the La Plata River Valley (A.D. 1000–1300). In *Troubled Times: Violence and Warfare in the Past*. Debra L. Martin and David Frayer, eds. Pp. 45–75. Amsterdam: Gordon and Breach.

Martin, Debra L., and Nancy J. Akins

2001   Unequal Treatment in Life as in Death: Trauma and Mortuary Behavior at La Plata (A.D. 1000–1300). In *Ancient Burial Practices in the American Southwest*.

Douglas R. Mitchell and Judy L. Brunson-Hadley, eds. Pp. 223–48. Albuquerque: University of New Mexico Press.

Meskell, Lynn
2001   Archaeologies of Identity. In *Archaeological Theory Today*. Ian Hodder, ed. Pp. 187–213. Cambridge: Polity Press.
2002   The Intersections of Identity and Politics in Archaeology. *Annual Review of Anthropology* 31:279–301.

Pate, Laura
2004   The Use and Abuse of Ethnographic Analogies in Interpretations of Gender Systems at Cahokia. In *Ungendering Civilization*. K. Anne Pyburn, ed. Pp. 71–93. New York: Routledge.

Perry, Elizabeth M.
2004   Bioarchaeology of Labor and Gender in the Prehispanic American Southwest. Ph.D. dissertation, University of Arizona.

Perry, Elizabeth M., and Rosemary Joyce
2001   Providing a Past for "Bodies That Matter": Judith Butler's Impact on the Archaeology of Gender. *International Journal of Gender and Sexuality Studies* 6(1/2):63–76.

Prine, Elizabeth
1997   The Ethnography of Place: Landscape and Culture in Middle Missouri Archaeology. Ph.D. dissertation, University of California, Berkeley.
2000   Searching for Third Genders: Towards a Prehistory of Domestic Space in Middle Missouri Villages. In *Archaeologies of Sexuality*. Robert A. Schmidt and Barbara L. Voss, eds. Pp. 197–219. London: Routledge.

Roscoe, Will
1998   *Changing Ones: Third and Fourth Genders in Native North America*. New York: St. Martin's Press.

Saladin D'Anglure, Bernard
1992   Rethinking Inuit Shamanism through the Concept of "Third Gender." In *Northern Religions and Shamanism*. Mihaly Hoppál and Juha Pentikäinen, eds. Pp. 146–50. Budapest: Akadémiai Kiadó.

Schmidt, Robert A.
2000   Shamans and Northern Cosmology: The Direct Historical Approach to Mesolithic Sexuality. In *Archaeologies of Sexuality*. Robert A. Schmidt and Barbara L. Voss, eds. Pp. 1–32. London: Routledge.
2001   "What if Gender Didn't Matter?" Gender as a Structuring Principle of Identity in the Southern Scandinavian Mesolithic. Paper presented at the 7th Gender and Archaeology Conference, Sonoma State University, Rohnert Park, October 6.
2002   The Iceman Cometh: Queering the Archaeological Past. In *Out in Theory: The Emergence of Lesbian and Gay Anthropology*. Ellen Lewin and William L. Leap, eds. Pp. 155–85. Urbana: University of Illinois Press.

Schmidt, Robert A. and Barbara L. Voss, eds.

2000   *Archaeologies of Sexuality.* London: Routledge.

Senior, Louise M.

2000   Gender and Craft Innovation: Proposal of a Model. In *Gender and Material Culture in Archaeological Perspective.* Moira Donald and Linda Hurcombe, eds. Pp. 71–87. London: Macmillan.

Stewart, Henry

2002   *Kipijuituq* in Netsilik Society: Changing Patterns of Gender and Patterns of Changing Gender. In *Many Faces of Gender: Roles and Relationships through Time in Indigenous Northern Communities.* Lisa Frink, Rita S. Shepard, and Gregory A. Reinhardt, eds. Pp. 13–25. Boulder: University Press of Colorado.

Sundstrom, Linea

2002   Steel Awls for Stone Age Plainswomen: Rock Art, Women's Religion, and the Hide Trade on the Northern Plains. *Plains Anthropologist* 47:99–119.

Tringham, Ruth E.

1990   Households with Faces: The Challenge of Gender in Prehistoric Architectural Remains. In *Engendering Archaeology: Women and Prehistory.* Joan Gero and Margaret W. Conkey, eds. Pp. 93–131. Oxford: Blackwell.

Voss, Barbara L.

2000   Feminisms, Queer Theories, and the Archaeological Study of Past Sexualities. *World Archaeology* 32(2):180–92.

2005   Sexual Subjects: Identity and Taxonomy in Archaeological Research. In *The Archaeology of Plural and Changing Identities: Beyond Identification.* Eleanor Conlin Casella and Chris Fowler, eds. Pp. 55–78. New York: Springer.

Voss, Barbara L., and Robert A. Schmidt

2000   Archaeologies of Sexuality: An Introduction. In *Archaeologies of Sexuality.* Robert A. Schmidt and Barbara L.Voss, eds. Pp. 1–32. London: Routledge.

Walker, Phillip L.

1997   Wife Beating, Boxing, and Broken Noses: Skeletal Evidence for the Cultural Patterning of Violence. In *Troubled Times: Violence and Warfare in the Past.* Debra L. Martin and David Frayer, eds. Pp. 145–79. Amsterdam: Gordon and Breach.

Walker, Phillip L., and Della Collins Cook

1997   Gender and Sex: Vive la Difference. *American Journal of Physical Anthropology* 106:255–59.

Weglian, Emily

2000   Grave Goods Do Not a Gender Make: A Case Study from Singen am Hohentwiel, Germany. In *Gender and the Archaeology of Death.* Bettina Arnold and Nancy Wicker, eds. Pp. 137–55. Walnut Creek, CA: AltaMira Press.

Whelan, Mary K.

1991   Gender and Historical Archaeology: Eastern Dakota Patterns in the 19th Century. *Historical Archaeology* 25:17–32.

1992   Dakota Indian Economics and the Nineteenth-Century Fur Trade. *Ethnohistory* 40:246–76.

Wilkinson, Richard G.

1997   Violence against Women: Raiding and Abduction in Prehistoric Michigan. In *Troubled Times: Violence and Warfare in the Past*. Debra L. Martin and David Frayer, eds. Pp. 21–43. Amsterdam: Gordon and Breach.

Wissler, Clark

1902   Field Notes on the Dakota Indians. Department of Anthropology Archives, American Museum of Natural History, New York.

1912   Societies and Ceremonial Associations in the Oglala Division of the Teton-Dakota. *American Museum of Natural History Anthropological Papers* 11(pt. 1):1–99.

Wylie, Alison

2002   *Thinking from Things: Essays in the Philosophy of Archaeology*. Berkeley: University of California Press.

Gender and Human Evolution   5

DIANE BOLGER

IN THEIR GROUNDBREAKING ARTICLE "Archaeology and the Study of Gender," Conkey and Spector (1984:6) characterized reconstructions of early hominid behavior as "the most obvious case of androcentrism in archaeology both in conceptualization and mode of presentation." Unfortunately, this judgment still pertains to much of the research on human evolution today. While particular theoretical arguments and methodologies have changed in the intervening years, proponents of evolutionary theory continue to construct essentialist narratives of the human past. In terms of gender, these scenarios contain very powerful and compelling accounts of the genesis of separate spheres of male and female behavior based largely on fundamental biological differences—dichotomies, it is argued, that are so deeply rooted in the ancestral past as to be considered universally applicable to the social behavior and psychological outlook of modern humans regardless of variations between and among different social groups. Attempts to unravel or deconstruct these "origins narratives" lead directly to confrontation with many of the key issues in the archaeology of gender outlined by Conkey and Spector (1984:6–7): "presentist bias, essentialist models assuming a gendered division of labor early in prehistory, differential valuation of male and female activities, and models that generally fail to incorporate gender explicitly into constructs of the past." The principal aims of this chapter, therefore, are to examine some of the critical implications for gender of the study human origins and to assess the role of archaeological research in understanding the processes by which modern gender constructs are likely to have evolved. Although many of the critical debates about gender and evolutionary theory can be traced back to the nineteenth-century Darwinian landscape or even earlier, I have chosen as a starting point the rise of neoevolutionary theory in the early 1950s. The bulk of this chapter addresses the impact of neoevolutionary theory on the construction of two sets of biologically based narratives of human behavior that continue to exert a strong influence on archaeological interpretations of gender. The first of these traces the origin, development, and decline of "Man the Hunter," a rubric that comprises several hypothetical models of the gendered division of labor in early human societies that were extremely influential during the 1960s to 1980s. The second, more recent set of narratives consists of sociobiological models currently at the cutting edge of research in the cognitive sciences that have had an important impact on cognitive archaeology and Darwinian archaeology over the past decade. In the final section of this chapter, I explore some of the problems and prospects of constructing new explanatory models for the evolution of human behavior through which we might begin to overcome the androcentric, ethnocentric, and anachronistic bases of earlier research. I end with a detailed assessment of prospects for the participation by archaeologists in continuing debates on the conflicting roles of nature, culture, and environment in the development of hominid behavior. By engaging in these debates, archaeologists can measure the validity of current theories of gender relations in early adaptive environments by testing them against the record of our ancestral past as established by recent decades of fieldwork at a wide range of Pleistocene sites in Africa, Asia, and Europe.

In the Beginning: Modern Approaches to Human Origins

The modern study of human evolution owes its existence to a series of major developments during the 1940s and 1950s in the fields of biology, primatology, and anthropology that gave rise to new, process-oriented approaches that gradually came to replace the descriptive accounts of earlier decades. In doing so, the discipline acquired an integrated, multidisciplinary perspective that still characterizes the study of human origins today. Among these developments were the following:

- The emergence of modern evolutionary theory as a synthesis of traditional Darwinian theories of natural selection with principles of modern evolutionary biology.
- Primatological studies based on the study of animal behavior in the wild (rather than in a zoo or laboratory) that led to a greater appreciation of the social complexity of nonhuman primates and furnished new insights into similarities and differences between humans and other animals. The discovery that chimps and humans are 98 percent identical genetically has provided renewed impetus to these studies in recent years.
- The confirmation by le Gros Clark in 1949 of Dart's proposal in 1924

that *Australopithecus africanus* was a human ancestor as well as the revelation that Piltdown man was a forgery. These served as compelling challenges to racial and ethnocentric prejudices among laypersons and scientists alike that precluded the possibility that humans had evolved in Africa. Both were instrumental in establishing a more accurate account of the early stages of human development within the discipline of physical anthropology.

- The discovery by Louis and Mary Leakey at Olduvai Gorge in Tanzania of what then constituted the earliest known fossilized remains of hominids (in particular the discovery of *Zinjanthropus* in 1959 and *Homo habilis* in 1962). These discoveries quickly generated increased levels of funding for paleontological and archaeological research and created new research agendas for fossil hunters in Africa. The success of these operations is attested to by a number of outstanding discoveries such as "Lucy" and other specimens of *Australopithecus afarensis* in Ethiopia and Tanzania, the identification of several new hominid species by Meave and Richard Leakey's team at Lake Turkana in Kenya (e.g., *Australopithecus anamensis* and *Kenyanthropus platyops*), and the discovery in Chad in 2002 of a fossilized skull (provisionally classified as *Sahelanthropus tchadensis*) dating to nearly 7 million years ago.

As the result of these developments, there arose in the early 1960s a new impetus within the fields of paleoanthropology and prehistoric archaeology to explain the processes by which humans emerged as a separate species and to isolate the major factors that served as catalysts in that process, most notably an increase in brain size/intelligence as evidenced by increasing cranial capacities and the manufacture of increasingly complex stone-tool assemblages. The development of new subsistence strategies, in particular the regular inclusion of animal protein in the diet as the result of hunting, came to be regarded along with bipedality as a major factor distinguishing protohumans from nonhuman primates. In terms of sociocultural behavior, hunting was singled out as the primary reason for the greater intelligence, adaptive abilities, and social complexity of human primates. Links between hunting, intelligence, diet, and tool use, for example, were frequently diagrammed in various "feedback loops" that appeared regularly in college textbooks on physical anthropology from the 1970s to the early 1990s (e.g., Campbell 1992:249, figs. 9–11). Consequently, hunting as an adaptive strategy was allotted more evolutionary weight than simply a functional means of dietary improvement. For proponents of the hunting model, hunting technology and meat eating, together with aggression and dominance, came to be considered the very keys to the success of the genus *Homo*, and the hunting model was increasingly invoked not simply to characterize early modes of human subsistence but also to epitomize what it meant to be human. Embedded in this mode of thinking is the polarization of male and female labor and a hierarchical ranking of subsistence skills in which male activities (hunting) are positioned at the top of the evolutionary ladder and female activities (gathering) are marginalized. The development of these biased views into formal scientific hypotheses during the 1970s and 1980s is explored in detail in the following section.

Deconstructing "Man the Hunter": Technology, Subsistence, and the Sexual Division of Labor

A turning point in the study of human evolution occurred in 1950 when the eminent anthropologist and primatologist Sherwood Washburn and evolutionary biologist Theodosius Dobzhansky held a conference titled "The Origin of Man" at the renowned Symposium in Quantitative Biology at Cold Spring Harbor (Washburn 1951). One of the main objectives at this gathering of more than one hundred eminent geneticists and anthropologists was to begin to integrate modern evolutionary theory with anthropology and to shift the focus of research on human evolution from descriptive anatomy to the consideration of adaptive strategies, particularly those related to human reproduction and subsistence. Another tacit goal of the conference was political: the construction of a universal human history that was meant to combat the overt racism of American postwar society but that effectively bypassed issues of gender by lumping women and men under the generic rubric "man" (Haraway 1989:207). Several years later, Raymond Dart's imaginative reconstructions of australopithecines as aggressive hunters wielding weapons of bone, teeth, and horn (his so-called osteodontokeratic culture) captured the imagination of a number of scholars (e.g., Bartholemew and Birdsell 1953) and were adopted by the media to emphasize aggression, dominance, and territoriality—behaviors traditionally associated with males—as key factors in the success of human primates (Cartmill 1993:1–14). Later in the decade, a paper by Washburn and Avis (1958) linked the lack of estrus in females to the emergence of male–female pair bonding and monogamy, behaviors that they deemed to be hallmarks of humanity. At about the same time, primatological studies were beginning to be introduced into the emerging picture of early hominid society, first by Washburn at a Wenner-Gren conference titled "Social Life of Early Man" (1961), which included a much-cited chapter by Washburn and DeVore (1961) on the behavior of savanna baboons as a model for early hominid groups. A decade later, extensive research by Teleki (1973) drew on evidence of predation among chimpanzees to argue for the centrality of male aggression and domination as principal underlying causes of the successful emergence of humans.

The results of these and other like-minded studies were applied with increasing frequency during the 1970s and 1980s to investigations of early hominid social organization, which often focused on the differing biological and social roles of males and females. Much of this early research is now considered to be speculative, presentist, and extremely culture bound, as can readily be observed in the following fanciful reconstruction of early hominid life by French anthropologist F. M. Bergounioux, published in his contribution to *Social Life of Early Man* (1961:112):

> The first human societies were very small ethnic groups, the unit of which was the family clan. The chief at the head lived surrounded by his wife and children. His first duty was to provide for the immediate needs of his group and to defend it against anyone who attacked it. There was no need for any law except that of his will, and his authority was derived from his physical strength rather than from his intelligence or cunning.

The theoretical trajectory of these early androcentric narratives of prehistoric economic and social structures can be said to have culminated in the well-known symposium "Man the Hunter," organized by Washburn's students Lee and DeVore at Yale in 1966 (Lee and DeVore 1968), which for the first time integrated the disciplines of primatology, ethnology, archaeology, and paleoanthropology into research on early human subsistence. While explicit discussion of male and female roles in early hominid societies was curiously absent from almost all the conference papers, the importance attached to hunting, as well as the implicit assumption that a sexual division of labor existed from the time of the earliest protohumans, runs as an undercurrent throughout the book. Hunting, the collection and distribution of food and other resources at a central home base, monogamous pair bonding, a sex-based division of labor, and social organization based on a loose network of nuclear family groups were core elements in hypothetical reconstructions of the lives of our earliest ancestors, who already, it seems, bore a curious resemblance to our (modern Western) selves. With regard to subsistence and hence to the survival of the earliest known ancestral species of humans, hunting was regarded as the key factor separating humans from other primates. More than simply an innovative technological invention, hunting served as a powerful metaphor for emergent humanity in which larger brains, greater intelligence, more advanced technology, and communicative ability constituted a "great leap forward" in the struggle for the adaptive success of protohumans. "Man the Hunter" soon became a buzzword that connoted our very humanity, effectively summing up all that was important about the earliest phases of our past and helping to explain why we are who we are today.

Since men are more closely associated than women with hunting, aggression, and technological prowess in societies of the modern industrialized West, men's roles were implicitly given pride of place in these initial models of early hominid subsistence; women's roles, in contrast, appear to have been superfluous. Richard Lee's (1968) contribution to Man the Hunter was one of the few to place a high value on women's economic and social roles in hunting and gathering societies, a perspective he had gained from extensive ethnographic fieldwork among the Kala-hari !Kung (for related research, see Lee 1979; Lee and DeVore 1976 and Lee 1979). However, his conclusions regarding the sexual division of labor among hunter-gatherers, compelling though they seem today, failed to exert a decisive impact on the overall themes of the conference or even on general statements about hunting by Lee and DeVore themselves in the introductory chapter of the book: "to date the hunting way of life has been the most successful and persistent adaptation man has ever achieved" (Lee and DeVore 1968:3), and "hunting is so universal and so consistently a male activity that it must have been a basic part of the early cultural adaptation even if it provided only a modest proportion of the food supplies" (7). Such inflated views of the role of hunting in early hominid societies, which were scarcely balanced by brief acknowledgments of the benefits of food gathering, food sharing, and women's roles in subsistence, were echoed by statements in some of the other conference papers, such as the chapter by Washburn and Lancaster (1968:293), in which they claimed that "the success of the hunting way of life has dominated the course of evolution for hundreds of thousands of years" and that "the biology, psychology and customs that separate us from the apes—all these we owe to the hunters of time past" (303).

Among the several archaeologists in attendance, Lewis Binford's (1968) contribution to Man the Hunter is particularly significant in terms of his central role in the construction of theoretical agendas in archaeology during the decades that followed. Processual approaches in archaeology, which were coming into vogue at the time, claimed that archaeology's proper role was as a subdiscipline of anthropology, and many archaeologists had increasingly begun to draw on ethnographic evidence in their reconstructions of early human societies. One of the crucial effects of the "Man the Hunter" symposium on the discipline of archaeology, therefore, was the transmission of received ideas concerning the sexual division of labor, the social implications of presumed biological and physical differences between the sexes, and the predominance of males in evolving patterns of economic subsistence and technological progress (such as the invention and use of tools) from ethnography and primatology to paleontology and prehistory. Ironically, however, Binford's overriding concern with rigorous methodology in the interpretation of archaeological sites served ultimately to undermine the hunting hypothesis by calling attention to its lack of substantive data (see Binford 1981, 1985, 1986, 1988, 1989).

Another eminent archaeologist participating in the conference was Glynn Isaac, then a recent Cambridge Ph.D. who was soon to become the renowned excavator of a number of important early hominid sites in Africa and a leading authority on hominid prehistory. While his conference paper said little concerning the sexual division of labor, Isaac focused on the need for archaeology to "come of age" as a discipline by moving away from typological studies of stone tools to a consideration of paleoecological factors such as diet and technology (Isaac 1968). In contrast to Binford, Isaac objected to what he regarded as the "grafting of full-fleshed . . . depictions of primate and modern human lifestyles onto early hominid bones" (Blumenschein 1991:308), and he firmly believed that questions of early hominid behavior could be answered only as the result of painstaking archaeological investigation (Isaac 1968:253). It took Isaac more than a decade to develop and implement methods of excavation and analysis that were capable of generating sufficient evidence with which to formulate and test models of early hominid behavior, and that evidence was later used to construct an alternative model to "Man the Hunter: known as the food-sharing hypothesis (discussed later in this chapter). During most of the 1970s, however, the sole voices of dissent against the hunting hypothesis came from female primatologists and anthropologists rather than archaeologists, and very little of this research was accepted for publication in mainstream anthropological journals. While only a few of these women would have considered themselves feminists, it is highly likely that the women's movement played a central role for many of them in confronting the androcentric biases inherent in much of the existing anthropological research and in helping to formulate alternative models of hominid social organization that granted women central roles in economic subsistence and political decision making. Some of these alternatives are considered in the following sections.

Challenges to the Hunting Hypothesis

While the hunting hypothesis continued to be highly influential in anthropological circles throughout the late 1960s and well into the 1970s, its obvious gender biases came under increasing attack from feminist anthropologists and other scholars who questioned the assertion that early hominid females were dependent on males for survival and were unable to accept a theory that "leaves out half of the human species" (Slocum 1975:38). In one of the first published critiques of the model, Slocum characterized it as the ethnocentric discourse of social scientists who are white, Western, and male (Slocum 1975:37; published earlier as Linton 1971). Citing ethnographic evidence such as the work by Lee among the !Kung, Slocum emphasized the importance of gathering to the survival of preindustrial groups and noted the lack of evidence, among both human and nonhuman primates, for monogamous mating behavior. The primary social bonds among such groups, she argued, would have been between mothers and infants: males, if they did in fact bring back meat to kin, would have been more likely to provision parents and siblings than mates and offspring (Slocum 1975:44).

Other studies appearing at around the same time, such as Leibowitz (1975:7), carried these arguments a step further by noting the lack of clear sex role patterns among nonhuman primates and by questioning the equation of biological differences between the sexes with polarized male/female categories of social and economic behavior. Moreover, as she and others were quick to observe, studies that draw conclusions about the roles of men and women in prehistory on the basis of the social constructs of modernity are seriously flawed since they conflate the present with the past and therefore fail to comprehend the dynamics of gender relations. This important theme has been explored in greater depth in recent years, most notably by Conkey and Williams (1991), and we shall return to it again later in this chapter. A further line of attack was launched in the late 1970s by Marxist anthropologist Eleanor Leacock, who challenged the notion of binary social categories that polarized male and female behavior at an early stage of human evolution and created hierarchical relations between men and women by ascribing differential values to male and female labor, again on the basis of modern Western values (Leacock 1978, 1983). According to Leacock, the hunting hypothesis failed to consider the dynamics of social change and equally neglected the social, historical, and cultural (rather than simply the biological) factors that may have shaped the differences in status between males and females. "Instead," she observed, "the polarization of public male authority and private female influence is taken as a given of the human condition" (Leacock 1978:248).

The androcentric bias that characterizes much of the research on human origins has, until recently, been deepened and reinforced through the integration into discussions of human evolution of primatological research, which has served to extend the present even further back in time into the "natural" world of the animal kingdom (Fedigan 1986:38–43; Haraway 1978a, 1978b; Yanagisako and Delaney 1995). Conflation of human with nonhuman primate behavior has also opened the door to sociobiological interpretations of animal behavior, which often operate within the framework of the same limited set of evolutionary constraints associated with a narrow range of reproductive strategies. This reductionist view of processes of natural selection fails to consider possible alternative factors that may have helped shape our evolutionary history. Leibowitz (1975) notes, for example, that the selective pressure for sexual dimorphism, a physical characteristic noted in varying degrees among all species of primates, may have arisen for reasons other than the conventional explanation of male dominance and aggression in competition for food and females; factors linked to life cycle events, such as energy-saving requirements by pregnant females, may also account for slower rates of female growth at the attainment of sexual maturity. Finally, if primate studies are to be brought into arguments about human patterns of social integration and dominance, greater attention needs to be paid to recent behavioral studies of nonhuman primates that focus on networking and alliance-formation strategies among female members (see the discussion later in this chapter); it has recently been demonstrated, for example, that bonobo females form coalitions that create powerful alliances, often preventing male domination in a number of social situations. As Stanford (2001:116) has observed in a review of this research, "Under conditions of female coalitional behavior, sexual equality in political power may emerge. The result of course is a very different set of social relationships than among male-dominated primates."

Alternative Models of Early Subsistence: The Narrative of "Woman the Gatherer"

Armed with ample evidence from ethnology, primatology, and social theory, critics of *Man the Hunter* began in the mid-1970s to develop alternative models of human origins that granted women more substantive roles in the successful emergence of the hominid line. Among the most influential of these was the often-cited article by Tanner and Zihlman (1976), which aimed to establish a central role for women in human evolution by establishing gathering rather than hunting as the key economic innovation that led to the survival and success of the human species. According to these authors, the basic unit of kinship in early hominid societies was not the male–female pair bond but the mother–infant relationship. Adult females gathered food to share with their offspring and transmitted valuable technical skills and complex information about the environment (Tanner and Zihlman 1976:604). The long period of dependence by young on their mothers led to increased levels of maternal investment, which in turn led to greater discrimination by adult females in choosing their mates; sexual selection in human primates, therefore, was based on female rather than male choice (590). This line of argument was developed in further articles by Zihlman (1978, 1981) as well as in some of her more recent works (1997a, 1997b, 1998) in which she stresses the necessity of developing more flexible models that consider the roles of women, men, and children in reconstructions of early hominid life as well as "a range of activities throughout the lifecycle on which natural selection acts, rather than a narrower focus on one or two of them" (Zilhman 1998:103). The importance of life cycle approaches to the study of gender and human evolution is a theme that will be taken up later in this chapter.

The importance of gathering to the early hominid diet, particularly in the early stages of human evolution, is now widely accepted, but debates continue about when hunting may have become a more regular and effective subsistence strategy. Nevertheless, few anthropologists today would support the claim by Washburn and Lancaster (1968:293) that hunting has dominated the course of human evolution. The realization that hunting arrived rather late on the economic scene, millions of years after the emergence of the earliest protohumans, and that it is very likely to have been prefaced by a long period in which crude stone tools were used as aids in scavenging activities but certainly not to hunt is now commonplace (see, e.g., recent college textbooks in physical anthropology, such as Haviland 2000; Jurmain et al. 2000). Although it is difficult to gauge the extent to which the challenges posed by Tanner, Zihlman, Leibowitz, Slocum, Leacock, and others had an impact on the decline of the hunting hypothesis, it is likely that by exposing many of its weaknesses, they helped establish and promote new research agendas that opened the door to alternative narratives about the past and furnished a more balanced view of male and female roles in models of early human subsistence.

By 1980, however, there had been little reaction among mainstream anthropologists and prehistorians to what had come to be known as the gathering hypothesis. A conference organized by Dahlberg, "Woman the Gatherer," held at Yale University in the spring of that year, sought to provide the hypothesis with the higher profile its proponents believed it deserved. In her introduction to the publication of the conference proceedings, Dahlberg (1981:10) criticized the simplistic, binary approaches adopted by most research on the sexual division of labor and observed that cross-cultural evidence demonstrates a great variety of patterns with regard to the sexual division of labor, noting that even where task differentiation between men and women exists, it is rarely rigid and inflexible. Moreover, she argued that the claim that women are not hunters can be readily refuted by a number of important ethnographic examples, such as the Mbuti and the Agta (ethnographic examples that are discussed by others in subsequent chapters of the book). The fact that women in societies such as the Agta find hunting compatible with reproductive and child-rearing activities should have prompted anthropologists to reevaluate the assumption that the sexual division of labor served as a foundation for present human society (Estiokio-Griffin and Griffin 1981:146).

Although the publication of *Woman the Gatherer* should have generated a widespread reevaluation of male and female roles in hunting and gathering activities as well as a reconsideration of the presumed centrality of hunting in early hominid societies, it in fact received no more than scant mention in textbooks and mainstream journals. For many anthropologists, the gathering hypothesis was dismissed as a biased feminist reaction to the hunting hypothesis and was therefore marginalized or entirely ignored (ironically, these same critics had never sought to challenge the hunting hypothesis on the grounds of its evident androcentric biases). Given this poor reception, it is possible that the hunting hypothesis was more extensively undermined by its own empirical weaknesses, which became increasingly clear in the face of mounting evidence from careful excavation and analysis of early hominid sites in Africa. This research ultimately demonstrated that our earliest ancestors could not have been hunters, that tools from early hominid sites could not have been effective at hunting large game, and that the crude lithic assemblages known from these sites were probably used, among other purposes, for the extraction of marrow from bones rather than for hunting. Processual archaeologists also played an important role in the demise of "Man the Hunter," for they underscored the failure of the hunting hypothesis to produce any firm evidence for hunting prior to the Upper Paleolithic period. Lewis Binford was particularly critical of theories involving hunting, food sharing at a base camp, and complex social organization and spent much time challenging what he termed "just-so" stories about the behavior of our ancestors (e.g., Binford 1981, 1985, 1986). Despite these criticisms, however, fanciful stories about the early stages of our past continued to be written throughout the 1980s. Two of the most influential of these, Lovejoy's hypothesis of male provisioning and Isaac's food-sharing hypothesis, can be viewed (in slightly different ways) as variations on the theme of "Man the Hunter."

Active Males, Passive Females: Lovejoy's Myth of Male Provisioning

In 1981, Owen Lovejoy, a paleoanthropologist specializing in hominid locomotion, published an influential article in the journal *Science* in which he argued that bipedality rather than hunting and an enlarged brain was the principal trait that made us human since it is this feature that initially distinguished hominids from nonhuman primates and because it anticipated the earliest known stone-tool assemblages by several million years (the latter were found by Johansen's team in the Awash region of Ethiopia and date to about 2.6 million years ago, while bipedality is a physical feature of hominids now thought by some paleoanthropologists to have evolved as early as 6 to 7 million years ago). Since bipedal locomotion constitutes the initial point of bifurcation between apes and humans, Lovejoy argued that we should seek to build explanatory models of early hominid behavior that are centered on this major evolutionary innovation.

In a series of articles appearing in major anthropological journals in the 1980s, Lovejoy succeeded in establishing an alternative to "Man the Hunter" that until recent years was extremely popular and influential (e.g., Lovejoy 1981, 1988; Tague and Lovejoy 1986), appearing regularly in college textbooks on physical anthropology throughout the 1980s and into the early 1990s (see, e.g., Campbell 1992 and earlier editions; Jurmain et al. 1990 and earlier editions). In these works, Lovejoy used sociobiological arguments to account for the origins of bipedality by demonstrating the emergence of fully fledged bipedal locomotion at least 4 million years ago and by linking the latter to the establishment of male–female pair bonding and male provisioning of females and offspring at a home base. The ability of protohuman females to attract long-term partners was based on their continuous sexual receptivity and on successful competition with other females (for an alternative view, see Hamilton 1984).

According to Lovejoy, everyone gained something in the process. Because females no longer needed to expend energy in the search for food, they could increase their investment in pregnancy, birth, and child rearing and could produce a greater number of offspring by decreasing birthing intervals. Males, by provisioning mates and offspring and through what Lovejoy termed "copulatory vigilance" with women who were continually sexually receptive, would gain a regular outlet for sexual activity and could rest assured that the offspring they were providing for were their own progeny. In sum, Lovejoy's hypothesis is an attempt to explain a suite of evolutionary developments by integrating the emergence of bipedal locomotion with unmediated assumptions about gender relations; in doing so, it retains the androcentric perspectives of the hunting hypothesis while shifting the content of male subsistence from hunting to gathering. While these arguments seemed convincing to some anthropologists as the result of sociobiological models in ethology (e.g., Wilson 1975), which were gaining wide acceptance during the early 1980s, for others they represented a major step backward because of their reductionist, androcentric logic. In the words of one social scientist, Lovejoy had created a model of "Man the Gatherer" in which "early hominid females were left not only four-footed, pregnant, hungry and in fear of too much exercise in their central core area, but were also left 'waiting for their man'" (Falk 1997:114).

Extensive evidence from paleoanthropology and primatology now exists with which to effectively challenge many aspects of the "male provisioning" model. In the first place, several studies of fossilized remains earlier than 4.5 million years ago suggest the possibility of a long, slow transition to fully bipedal locomotion, with bipedality emerging in a forested rather than a savanna environment and anticipating the establishment of home bases and the hunter-gatherer lifestyles by millions of years (e.g., Kingdon 2003; Stern and Sussman 1983). Second, recent studies on bipedal locomotion show that less energy is expended in terrestrial movement (walking, not running), particularly for females; consequently, there is no need to invoke theories in which sedentary females are provisioned by males at a home base (Aiello and Wells 2002; Leonard and Robertson 1997). Third, female–female relationships may have been as or more important than male–female in terms of the evolution of social organization, a point that is addressed more fully later in this chapter (see Key and Aiello 1999). Finally, there is now evidence to suggest that accelerated birth intervals can harm rather than enhance reproductive success. The key to human reproductive success is "quality rather than quantity," and that is achieved through the steady production of offspring with adequate interbirth intervals. This contradicts more traditional interpretations, such as Lovejoy's, in which fertility rather than longevity is regarded as the key element in reproductive success. These arguments lay bare some of the weaknesses of narrow sociobiological models that define fitness solely in terms of reproductive output and demonstrate the importance of life history approaches to an understanding of human evolution. While Lovejoy's hypothesis figured prominently in textbooks of the 1980s and early 1990s, it has all but disappeared today in research on bipedality (the model is either given scant mention, cited as an unlikely scenario, or not mentioned at all, e.g., in Ember and Ember 1993; Haviland 2000; Jolly and White 1995; Jurmain et al. 2000; Kottak 2000; Stein and Rowe 1993).

Digging Up Difference: Isaac's Food-Sharing Hypothesis

At about the same time that Lovejoy's hypothesis was gaining wide acceptance, an alternative model of early hominid subsistence was being proposed by the prehistoric archaeologist Glynn Isaac, who was then engaged in the excavation of several hominid sites from about 1.5 million years ago near Lake Turkana in Kenya. On the basis of careful stratigraphic analyses of the remains from these and related sites (such as the so-called living floors at Olduvai Gorge) and the painstaking study of bone and stone-tool assemblages by specialist members of his team over the course of nearly a decade, Isaac constructed a model of early hominid adaptation that can be considered his most important contribution to paleoanthropology (first presented by Isaac in 1978; for a comprehensive list of his other published works as well as an assessment of Isaac's legacy, see Blumenschein 1991). The food-sharing model, as it came to be known, emphasized the exploitation of different environments by males and females who participated equally in subsistence activities and brought back food to a home base for distribution to the entire group. For Isaac, the key to the survival of early humans was not hunting or gathering but rather the sharing of food resources among the entire group, a characteristic behavior of humans that is not observed among nonhuman primates. Part of the appeal of the food-sharing model rested with its integration of a range of behaviors—the invention of tools, bipedalism, and greater levels of communication, intelligence, and social interaction, for example—without singling out any one factor as a "prime mover" (Isaac 1978:108). This more flexible model reflected Isaac's long-standing belief that a more broadly based model was "more readily compatible with models of human evolution that stress broadly based subsistence patterns rather than those involving intensive and voracious predation" (Isaac 1971:288).

While the food-sharing model certainly provided a more comprehensive, balanced model of early human behavior than the hunting hypothesis and the male provisioning model and managed to avoid some of their more blatant androcentric biases by acknowledging the importance of female subsistence activities in human evolution, it resembled the others in its unmediated, presentist assumptions about male and female social roles based largely on biological differences between the sexes, in its assumption of monogamous pair bonds and essentially modern "family-based" kinship structures, and in its inference of a sexual division of labor at an early stage of human evolution that associated women with the gathering of plant resources and men with the procurement of meat. As was the case with the earlier models, the polarization of male and female labor strengthened the claims of sociobiologists that disparities between men and women are inherent since they are traceable to the earliest stages of our emergence as a species; moreover, the food-sharing model failed to take into account important ethnographic evidence that demonstrates more flexible patterns of the division of labor among hunter-gatherer groups.

At around the time of his premature death in the mid-1980s, Isaac had begun to question and revise the food-sharing hypothesis, even changing its name to the "central place foraging process," which he felt made it more objective and hence more amenable to rigorous scientific testing (Blumenschein 1991:319). Even then, however, Isaac seemed to be increasingly skeptical of the ability of archaeology to provide the empirical evidence necessary to support such hypothetical reconstructions. Binford's hard-hitting criticisms of the results of Isaac's team (as well as of the Leakeys' work in East Africa) as overinterpretations of the material evidence had left unanswered the question of whether hunting existed at all among early hominid groups or whether the "sites" composed of scatters of animal bones and crude stone tools could truly be regarded as home bases (see Binford 1981, 1985, 1986, 1988, 1989). Indeed, these questions posed by Binford nearly twenty years ago remain at the forefront of archaeological inquiry into human origins today (Blumenschein 1991:320).

Current research trends in human evolution reflect to a certain degree the rigorous criticism made by nearly thirty years of research into the archaeology and anthropology of gender. One of the most influential pieces of research in this regard is an article by Gero (1991) on stone-tool production in hominid prehistory that challenges a number of long-standing, unmediated assumptions, such as the claim that males alone produced the tools that form such a large part of the archaeological record; that there was already a division of labor that excluded women from toolmaking tasks; that "tools" are equatable with "maleness" and male control of technology and the environment and, by implication, that women were somehow not strong or intelligent enough to make stone tools; that women's child care responsibilities restrict them to a limited range of repetitive, interruptible tasks that were not dangerous and did not require extensive travel; and that stone tools represent the pinnacle of prehistoric technology (with projectile points at the top of the hierarchy, bifaces in the middle, and flake tools at the bottom), thus endowing men's activities with greater social value. Elsewhere, Gero has shown that the division of labor and hierarchy of value imposed in these interpretations is highly reflective of modern gendered practices in the field of archaeology itself. To modify our interpretations of the past, we must therefore consciously change the processes and methods by which we construct those views (Gero 1985).

While remaining aware of these and other theoretical and methodological misconceptions, we must also agree with Isaac that archaeological inquiry is the discipline most capable of supplying the means by which theories about hunting, gathering, and the sexual division of labor can be fruitfully constructed. Unfortunately, just about every model proposed in previous decades to account for gender relations in the prehistoric past has been based on exaggerated distinctions between male and female anatomy, sexuality, and embodiment and on a priori inferences about the presumed behavioral correlates of those differences. The collective impact of this misengendered body of research has been enormous, and archaeologists have only just begun to deconstruct the most salient of its androcentric elements. As Conkey and Spector observed in their seminal article of

1984, "Theories of gender relations regarding production and distribution in early hominid societies should be subjects of scientific investigation rather than based on the unmediated assumptions regarding men's and women's economic roles" (7). As archaeologists continue to investigate many of these fundamental issues in the coming years, it is important that they consciously seek to avoid the many theoretical pitfalls and methodological biases that have dominated research on early hominid subsistence for more than half a century.

Gender, Cognition, and Evolution: Reconstructing the Prehistoric Mind

As the debates and controversies outlined in the previous section with regard to the gendered division of labor were in progress, new developments in evolutionary biology were beginning to filter into archaeological debate, providing fresh opportunities for incorporating sociobiological models into explanations of culture change. Although sociobiology was hardly a new idea, its reincarnation by Wilson (1975) and others in the mid-1970s, through the exploitation of concepts such as "inclusive fitness" (Hamilton 1964) and "reciprocal altruism" (Trivers 1972), began to exert a significant impact on archaeological theory since it now provided a vehicle for applying neo-Darwinian precepts to groups rather than individuals; it also threatened to sever the field of archaeology from its historical, cultural roots in the social sciences (especially anthropology) and to forge new links to the "harder" sciences of population genetics and evolutionary biology. By the early 1980s, these influences had crystallized into the formation of the subdiscipline known as neo-Darwinian archaeology, which soon split into two distinct branches known as evolutionary archaeology and behavioral ecology (for article-length reviews, see Boone and Smith 1998; Lyman and O'Brien 1998; Shennan 2004). While the intellectual focus of evolutionary archaeology has remained largely theoretical, with only a small proportion of articles devoted to specific applications (see Dunnell 1980 and the commentary by R. L. Kelly in Boone and Smith 1998:S161), research in behavioral ecology has tended to address issues of subsistence and human adaptation, such as optimal foraging models (e.g., Mithen 1990; Smith and Winterhalder 1992); in addition, since the marginal role accorded by evolutionary archaeology to cultural processes precludes the interpretation of gender categories as social constructs, behavioral ecology would appear to offer greater scope for gendered approaches since it acknowledges that the transmission of cultural variants can be attributed to factors other than natural selection (Boone and Smith 1998:S144). To date, however, it has produced very little research pertaining explicitly to gender.

In general, widespread charges by social scientists and biologists alike that sociobiological approaches (especially in their crudest forms) serve to promote sexist and racist agendas has not encouraged the integration of "naturist" principles into explanatory models of gender and human evolution. But in spite of the theoretical and methodological difficulties involved in grafting biological models onto archaeological evidence for culture change, the lack of clarity concerning the degree to which nonrandom transmission of cultural knowledge through mechanisms of social learning are deemed to have played a role in the evolution of human culture, and Dawkins's (1976:203–15) fuzzy and unsubstantiated concept of "memes" as heritable units of culture (see Shennan 2004), evolutionary approaches in archaeology have persisted as a subdiscipline of the field and have in fact been reinvigorated over the past ten to fifteen years. This is no doubt due to the assimilation of recent research in evolutionary and cognitive psychology by archaeologists who, for reasons that shall become clear later in this section, have managed to distance themselves from the more objectionable implications of sociobiological theory of the 1970s.

Cognitive aspects of human evolution have been adopted thus far by only a handful of prehistorians (e.g., Mithen 1996a; Renfrew and Scarre 1998; Shennan 2002; Steele and Shennan 1996), but they are widely regarded to be at the "cutting edge" of archaeological research and are currently receiving considerable support from academic funding bodies in the United States and the United Kingdom. Here, three major research strands have emerged: one with its roots firmly planted in traditional Darwinian principles of natural selection and reproductive success, which has been heavily influenced by recent research in evolutionary psychology (EP); another that is closely linked to cognitive psychology and concerns itself with the emergence and development of the cognitive structures ("architecture") of the human brain but is not as heavily selectionist in its outlook; and yet another, known as "dual inheritance" theory, that separates biological and cultural evolution into two distinct but interrelated strands and gives a prominent role to social learning in the diachronic transmission of culture (Boyd and Richerson 1985; Mithen 1996b). While models of cognitive evolution and dual inheritance theory are potentially important for investigating the relationships between gender and cognition in early human societies (see Hawkes 1996; Mithen 1990, 1996b), it is research in EP that is contributing most to current debates about male and female behavior within an evolutionary framework. It is therefore worthwhile to engage in a brief review of some of the central concepts of EP before turning to some of the archaeological data to which this research is currently being applied.

The Nature of Sexual Difference: Recent Developments in EP

Although many of the core elements of sociobiological theory, such as Hamilton's (1964) rule of inclusive fitness and Trivers's (1972) work on reciprocal altruism and parental investment are equally important to research in EP, current advocates of EP are at pains to show that they are not identical. For example, EP claims to have resolved the Cartesian mind–body split (often cited as a major theoretical weakness of earlier sociobiological models) by unifying the biological and nonbiological aspects of human existence. As Tooby and Cosmides (1992:21) have argued in a highly influential article, "The Psychological Foundations of Culture," which is widely acknowledged as the first comprehensive statement of the EP program, "The rich complexity of each individual is produced by a cognitive architecture, embodied in a physiological system, which interacts with the social and nonsocial world that surrounds it." Conceptual unification is attained by recognizing that "culture is the manufactured product of evolved psychological mechanisms situated in individuals living in groups" (24). Moreover, in linking social sciences with the "hard" sciences, EP claims to have overcome the inability of the social sciences to "causally locate their objects of study inside the larger network of scientific knowledge" (23). In opposition to "standard social science models," which are forever consigned by proponents of EP to the murky and rudderless realm of cultural relativism, the integrated models of EP promise the return to a principled universe replete with "grand laws and validated theories to rival those of the rest of science" (23). One does not need to consider these statements at great length, however, in order to realize that the "unification of social sciences with the rest of science" implies the assumption of the former by the latter, effectively negating "standard social science approaches" as valuable contributors to the understanding of human behavior. As a brand of sociobiology, EP reduces explanations of human behavior to static "laws" of natural selection and effectively relegates explanations of gender constructs to biological rather than cultural domains. For this reason, it has been labeled by a prominent critic in the social sciences as "neurogenetic determinism" (Rose 1998:272; see also articles in Rose and Rose 2001).

Today, more than a decade after the publication of Tooby and Cosmides's article, the literature on EP is vast and continues to grow. Limitations of space do not allow me to discuss this literature in any detail; however, mention should at least be made of some of the major works by principal proponents of EP discourse over the past ten to fifteen years: Buss (1999), Campbell (2002), Cronin (1991), Dennett (1995), Low (2000), Miller (2001), Pinker (1997), Ridley (1993, 2003), Sperber (1996), Thornhill and Palmer (2000), and Wright

(1994). While there are differences in scope and style of argumentation among these various works as well as in the degree to which they regard culture as a phenotype responsive to principles of Darwinian selection and the degree to which they vilify social science and feminist theory, they share a number of common characteristics. These include the accusation that "standard social science models" are wholly "nurturist" in orientation while ignoring the scientific "truths" of biology; the belief that the human mind is modular in its structure, a domain-specific rather than a multipurpose mechanism or a fitness-maximizing device; the consideration of a narrow range of adaptive behaviors as measures of human reproductive success, the most common being male/female differences in parental investment, sexual attraction, and strategies of mate selection; the claim that male and female adaptive behavior is essentially and fundamentally different and that the latter is linked to differences in male/female reproductive strategies that stem from basic biological differences between the sexes; a universalizing tendency that focuses exclusively on species-typical traits and ignores variation between and among different cultural groups; the speculative reconstruction of early hominid behavior without recourse to archaeological evidence; and the conflation of ancient and modern environments by using modern hunter-gatherer communities rather than early hominid species to characterize what is termed by proponents of EP as "the environment of evolutionary adaptation."

In the attempt to mollify those who would accuse EP of determinism and of failing to recognize individuals (particularly women) as active agents in their own destinies, a charge often leveled against advocates of sociobiological theory of the 1970s and 1980s, there is a growing body of research within the discipline that emphasizes the deliberate and conscious efforts (often described as "tactics" or "strategies") by individuals of both sexes to optimize their own reproductive success. For example, according to the principle of "expensive egg, cheap sperm," women are characterized in EP scenarios as "fussy" about selecting a mate since the latter will be free to exploit women's higher degree of parental investment (Campbell 2002:46). Men, on the other hand, are thought to be less fussy about mate selection since promiscuity (i.e., access to as many fertile females as possible) or even rape provides optimal conditions for male reproductive success (Campbell 2002:40; Thornhill and Palmer 2000). In another version of this scenario, Ridley (1993:236) speculates,

Deep in the mind of modern man is a simple male hunter-gatherer rule: strive to acquire power and use it to lure women who will bear heirs . . . likewise, deep in the mind of a modern woman is the same basic hunter-gatherer calculator, too recently evolved to have changed much: strive to acquire a provider husband who will invest food and care in her children; strive to find a lover who can give those children first-class genes.

While this line of argumentation appears to impart a mantle of apartheid egalitarianism to the disparate and often conflicting reproductive goals of males and females as defined by EP theory, the models employed by EP in the speculative reconstructions of male and female behavior (male hunting, provisioning of female mates and offspring, constant female sexual receptivity and sexual fidelity, pair bonding, and so on) scarcely differ from those proposed by proponents of "Man the Hunter" hypotheses of the previous generation. Moreover, the apparent alibi provided by the most extreme of these scenarios for the rape of females by males (see Thornhill and Palmer 2000) reveals strong links in some quarters of EP with the more misogynist elements of earlier sociobiological theory. From an archaeological perspective, subsistence models portraying active males and passive females are no longer acceptable for reasons that have been discussed in earlier sections of this chapter. In the remainder of this section, therefore, I wish to consider and assess critically from a gendered perspective several examples of recent archaeological research that have attempted to apply some of the basic concepts of EP to archaeological data of the Paleolithic and Mesolithic periods.

Genes, Memes, and Gender: Recent Research in Evolutionary Archaeology

The most wide-ranging application of evolutionary psychology to archaeology thus far has been Stephen Shennan's *Genes, Memes and Human History* (2002). At the beginning of the book, Shennan argues for the widespread adoption by archaeologists of evolutionary theory on many of the same grounds stated by proponents of EP, namely, that archaeology is in a crisis that has resulted largely from postmodernism's rejection of "grand narrative" throughout the social sciences (Shennan 2002:10). According to Shennan, this has led archaeology into a directionless state in which "scholars show more interest in unscientific attempts to empathize with ancient peoples than in obtaining valid knowledge about the past" (Shennan 2002:book jacket). After introductory chapters in which basic principles of evolutionary psychology, behavioral ecology, and life history approaches are presented, Shennan considers the role of natural selection in long-term patterns of human subsistence (chap. 6). He then turns (chap. 7) to the subject of the evolution of male–female relations.

Like other advocates of EP, Shennan (2002:17) begins this chapter by lamenting what he sees as the "ghettoization" of feminist research, which in his view has refused to acknowledge the fundamental role of biological factors in the construction of gender relations. Male–female relations, he argues, particularly sexual relations, are central to evolutionary archaeology since they constitute the behavioral matrix in which reproductive strategies are enacted to maximize reproductive success. From the perspective of natural selection, reproductive differences and their behavioral manifestations (e.g., gender-based differences in parental investment and mate selection) are all that really matter when considering cognitive differences between males and females and thus form the thrust of all subsequent discussion in this chapter. In sum, we are presented with many of the same arguments offered by EP, some of which have been summarized here. In order to show how these ideas are currently being applied to investigations of various aspects of hominid evolution, Shennan ends the chapter (197–205) by presenting a number of examples of recent research by archaeologists and paleoanthropologists. In the pages that follow, I briefly outline a selection of recent archaeological studies that have been informed by EP. Some of these are included in Shennan's summary, and all have particular relevance to issues of gender and human evolution.

In an article that attempts to explain the sexual division of labor in early hominid societies, Hawkes (1996) attributes differences in male and female subsistence strategies to differences in parental investment, a concept proposed by Trivers (1972) and further developed by Maynard Smith (1977) and based on the principle of "expensive egg, cheap sperm" mentioned earlier (i.e., since females are capable of reproducing at maximum about once a year, they must make a greater investment of time, energy, and resources to the production of offspring than males, for whom the costs of reproduction are relatively minimal). Hawkes argues that bipolar modes of subsistence (men/hunting, women/gathering) emerged as the result of differences between male and female reproductive biology; while hunting allowed males to maximize mating opportunities by covering a wide geographical range, gathering afforded women time and energy to required to attend to the welfare of their children. Citing a number of ethnographic examples, Hawkes (1996:297) further proposes that the particular types of foraging activities engaged in by women in a given society tend to vary in accordance with child care considerations, while hunting may not always have been undertaken by males to provide for their mates and offspring but rather to maximize mating opportunities. The methodology adopted by Hawkes in this article is identical to that of EP, involving the identification of a perceived behavioral difference between males and females (in this case, hunting vs. gathering) and "explaining" its origin by recourse to sociobiological argumentation. While the hypothetical explanations she proposes may be true, there is no way to test their validity as models for human evolution since they fail to consider the physical and cultural evidence of archaeology and paleontology. For example, they neglect to account for the more than 4 million years of prehistory during which there is little evidence of hunting as a subsistence strategy. Since human reproductive biology is unlikely to have changed during that period, the adoption of hunting-gathering lifestyle must be due, at least in part, to cultural rather than biological factors.

Articles by Power and Watts (1996), and Knight (1996) propose models of collective strategizing by ancestral hominid females for the purpose of maximizing their own reproductive success. Through tactics of "sexual manipulation" and "sham menstruation," females ensured that their mates contributed a fair share to the welfare of themselves and their offspring. According to this line of reasoning, threats or actions involving the withholding of sexual favors (through sex strikes), as well as deliberate ruses to mask fertility (sham menstruation), enabled women to enhance their ability to survive by compelling mates to engage in greater levels of parental investment, including provisioning of offspring and the establishment of home bases. Although they represent a refreshing departure from standard narratives of "active male/passive female" that portray women as weak, vulnerable, and unable to fend for themselves, the speculative nature of this type of argumentation (increasingly popular in the literature on EP), as well as the degree of conscious political machination required of actors in such scenarios, renders them as implausible as the traditional androcentric models they are meant to replace. Again, the failure to develop these models in the light of archaeological evidence seriously undermines their credibility.

In an article published in *Antiquity*, Kohn and Mithen (1999) have attempted to integrate a number of aspects of EP theory with material culture of the Pleistocene by considering the form and function of Acheulian bifacial hand axes. Acheulian bifaces have a long chronological range, first appearing about 1.4 million years ago and continuing with only slight modifications for about a million years in association with fossilized remains of *Homo erectus* and several other hominid species. Archaeologists have long been puzzled about the possible function(s) of this distinctive artifact type, particularly by some of the larger examples such as those from Olduvai, which are more than twenty-eight centimeters in length (Kohn and Mithen 1999:518). While archaeologists have traditionally interpreted Acheulian hand axes as hunting and/or butchering tools or as implements for cutting wood or processing plants, Kohn and Mithen suggest a social function, namely, that they were used as sexual symbols by males and females in processes of mate selection: in addition to functioning as signals of prodigious technical ability to prospective mates, the symmetrical form of the biface may have been a desirable feature to members of the opposite sex (518–19). Recent research in cognitive psychology suggests that individuals tend to be sexually attracted to social members whose facial and other bodily features are highly symmetrical, a physical trait regarded as indicative of "good genes" (Barrett et al. 2002:111–13). On this basis, Kohn and Mithen (1999:521) speculate that the evolution of a "perceptual bias towards symmetry" may have been transferred to elements of material culture, such as the hand axes, and that the display of these technically complex, visually stimulating artifacts may have served as an effective means of attracting potential mates. On the question of whether males or females made the bifaces, the authors cite theories of sexual selection and parental investment, discussed previously, to propose that females are likely to have been the mate selectors (they are more "fussy" because of their greater levels of parental investment); consequently, it is argued, it was probably males who made the hand axes or at least the large "impractical" examples mentioned previously (522–23). In archaeological terms, there is no way to prove whether this theory is valid, and the authors fail to propose any analytical means of testing it. Logically, however, one must question the efficacy to survival of dedicating such considerable time and effort to the manufacture of elaborate tools that afforded little practical value apart from their possible use as sex charms. In addition, one questions whether the brains of protohumans such as *H. erectus* were capable of such sophisticated stratagems. If so, it seems that a million years of toolmaking might have been more profitably devoted to the development of improved strategies for survival (such as learning how to hunt) that would have been more likely to result in reliable outcomes for the "maximizing of reproductive success."

Although archaeological applications of EP have emerged only recently and have been undertaken thus far by a relatively small group of authors, it is nonetheless important to address some of the weaknesses of this research as it has been formulated to date. With the exception of the article by Kohn and Mithen, the bulk of "evidence" used to substantiate the longevity of proposed interfaces between the biological and social aspects of human behavior in the examples cited previously takes the form of speculative reconstructions that begin in the modern industrial present and purport to take a great leap backward into the (likewise modern) hunter-gatherer "past." While ethnographic studies are occasionally included in these discussions, there is a general lack of concern with integrating archaeological data. As a consequence, we are left with "just-so" stories about the past that succeed only in creating "cardboard caricatures of female activities" (Fausto-Sterling 2001:182). The study of Acheulian hand axes by Mithen and Kohn constitutes a rare attempt to integrate cognitive theory with archaeological evidence; however, more rigorous and detailed testing of their hypothesis, including contextual analysis, is needed to strengthen their case.

A number of important questions regarding the compatibility of archaeological evidence with the speculative models outlined previously were raised nearly a decade ago by Lake (1996). As archaeological inferences concerning early hominid social and economic organization must be based on careful excavation, dating, and taphonomic reconstruction of chronologically overlapping, bona-fide sites, there are enormous obstacles to overcome in order to test the hypotheses being proposed by EP models, particularly as the paleolandscape is comprised of "a series of discontinuous sediments that are extremely difficult to correlate" (Lake 1996:185–88). Whereas some psychologists have baldly pronounced the attempt to consider archaeological data (such as fossil evidence and chronology) as unnecessary and counterproductive (e.g., Miller 2001:22) and others merely pay lip service to the need to substantiate evolutionary models of human behavior with empirical evidence (e.g., Campbell 2002:12), one would expect the archaeological proponents of Darwinian models to ground their arguments in the fossil, material, and environmental record of the prehistoric past. However, this has not often proved to be the case.

In order to overcome what he sees as "the mismatch between goals and data" in interpretations of human evolution, Lake (1996:184) advocates the use of computer simulation techniques to test the validity of hypothetical reconstructions. As an example of the potential of this technique, he uses computer simulation to test hypotheses of cultural transmission and cultural learning as proposed by Boyd and Richerson (1985). In a series of computer-generated charts diagramming temporal dimensions of individual and cultural learning, such as changes in frequency of genotypes for cultural learning over 200 generations and qualitative effects over time of relationships between individual and cultural learning (Lake 1996:figs. 6.2–6.5), Lake draws several provisional conclusions about the relative impact of cultural and individual learning at various stages of human evolution (202). While computer-based methodologies such as these may eventually serve as a viable means of assessing the effects of differently scaled processes such as individual and cultural learning in the evolution, further work is clearly needed in order to achieve that goal. Moreover, despite Lake's pessimistic assessment of the ability of more traditional methods of archaeological analysis to test the validity of evolutionary models, archaeologists intent on constructing convincing interpretations of human social behavior, including gender relations, must at the very least make more rigorous attempts to do so—or run the risk of being relegated to the theoretical dustbin of evolutionary debate.

Sexing the Prehistoric Brain: Gender and Human Cognition

In addition to EP, a number of recent approaches in cognitive psychology are beginning to have an impact on archaeological research on human evolution, and some are of potential importance for issues of gender. It is surprising, however, that the first comprehensive investigation of the evolution of the human mind was written not by an archaeologist or anthropologist (or even a psychologist) but by philosopher Merlin Donald, whose *Origins of the Modern Mind*, published in 1991, has had a tremendous impact on cognitive archaeology. Reflecting on earlier theories of human cognition, Donald notes that interpretative models of higher cognitive function, regardless of whether they follow diachronic trajectories that begin with the present and work backward to nonhuman primates or vice-versa, are either "modular" or "unitary" in their approach (6). "Modular" approaches (e.g., Fodor 1983; Sperber 1996; Tooby and Cosmides 1992) take the view that the mind is comprised of a number of specific, discrete domains that operate independently of one another (the standard example used to illustrate the modular approach is the Swiss army knife). In contrast, traditional "unitary" approaches (e.g., Anderson 1983) argue for a single, integrated structure dedicated to achieving a general-purpose cognitive capacity. As an alternative to these more traditional approaches to cognition, Donald (1991:chaps. 6–8) investigates processes of human cognition within an evolutionary framework in which the minds of apes and protohumans are seen to evolve from "modular" to "unitary" structures that mirror the increase in brain size throughout the chronological range of the genus *Homo*. The most accelerated period of cognitive development, he argues, occurred with the earliest populations of *Homo sapiens* perhaps as early as 200,000 years ago and is associated with the evolution of art, language, sophisticated and varied tool technology, and the emergence of more complex levels of social organization such as the sexual division of labor (Donald 1991:208ff.). Detailed responses to some of the key ideas in *The Origin of the Modern Mind* have appeared in Noble and Davidson (1996) and in conference volumes edited by Mellars and Gibson (1996) and Renfrew and Scarre (1998).

Many of the central concepts of Donald's work have been further developed by Steve Mithen, a cognitive archaeologist whose book *The Prehistory of the Mind* (1996a) has made a valuable contribution to research on the origins and development of human cognition. According to Mithen, the "big bang" of cognitive development did not occur until about 60,000 years ago and resulted from the coalescence of multiple specialized intelligences into a single interactive unit characterized by what he terms "cognitive fluidity" (chap. 4). As Mithen has stated, "the transition to a fluid mind was neither inevitable or pre-planned," but once the transition occurred, there was no turning back (240). More significantly, it is the human capacity for cognitive fluidity that most effectively distinguishes human from nonhuman primates since it has freed cognitive processes from the rigid straitjacket of modular thought and hence from the deterministic constraints of ultra-Darwinian models such as we have just been considering.

In a more recent work, Mithen (2001:102) has posed the somewhat rhetorical question, "Why should archaeologists be concerned with the evolution of mental modularity?" He believes there are at least three good answers: first, by examining the origins and development of human cognition, we can more fully comprehend the modern human mind; second, by engaging in this research we can test the proposal that the human mind evolved in a modular fashion against the evidence of the archaeological record; and, finally, such investigation will allow us to "reconstruct" the prehistory of the mind. For the purposes of this chapter, however, it is necessary to pose a different question: why should those interested in the archaeology of gender be concerned with issues of cognitive evolution? In order to answer this question, we must first take a brief detour into recent research in cognitive psychology, which, for the past thirty years or so, has been concerned (or increasingly obsessed, it has sometimes been suggested) with cognitive differences between males and females.

Research on cognitive sex differences can be traced back to the nineteenth century to Darwin's proposal of a hierarchy of mental functions, which placed males at the higher end of the scale (reason and imagination), while women were consigned to the lower end (intuition, emotion, and instinct) (Appleman 2001:234–35). The fact that a recent book by a prominent professor at Cambridge is based on the premise that female brains are "empathizing" while male brains are "systematizing" suggests that, in some quarters at least, little has changed over the past 150 years (Baron-Cohen 2003). In addition to the proliferation of the idea of "essential differences" in male and female cognitive abilities by the media and in books on "pop psychology," a great deal of research time and funding has been expended on the attempt to demonstrate that this is the case (for detailed critiques of this research, see Fausto-Sterling 2000:chap. 5; Tavris 1992). By the same token, research emphasizing cognitive similarities between the sexes has until recently been largely ignored, and attempts in the 1970s by Ruth Bleier, former professor in neurophysiology at the University of Wisconsin, to publish critical reviews of "brain sex" research in the prestigious journal *Science* were repeatedly rejected.

Meanwhile, over the past thirty years, a virtual raft of studies employing a wide variety of methodologies, including IQ testing, PET and MRI scans, and postmortem analysis of cerebral hemispheres and the intermediary corpus callosum, as well as an even wider range of techniques applied to the brains and genitalia of rodents and other animals, have been conducted in research laboratories across Europe and the United States (for a detailed summary, see Fausto Sterling

2000:chaps. 6–8). As Tavris (1992:5) has noted, most of this research is binary in its outlook, and there has been an increasingly widespread view that cognitive differences between the sexes begin in the womb and are strongly influenced by prenatal hormones, implying that such differences are innate (see also Fausto-Sterling 2000:chap. 6). Particular attention has been focused on studies of brain lateralization that have attempted to show that males excel in right-hemisphere functions, such as visual-spatial tasks and mathematical abilities, while females are associated either with left-hemisphere functions (verbal abilities) or with a combination of both hemispheres that results in weaker right-hemisphere performance (e.g., Benbow and Stanley 1980; Geary 1996; Macoby and Jacklin 1974; Shaywitz et al. 1995; Silverman and Eals 1992; Silverman and Phillips 1998; but for opposing views, see Alper 1985; Fausto-Sterling 2000). While a detailed critique of these studies lies beyond the aims of this chapter (and in fact has been undertaken by a number of authors in recent years, including Bleier 1984; Fausto-Sterling 1992, 2000; Halpern 1992; Rosenberg 1982; Tavris 1992), it is important to emphasize a recent trend in the literature away from a focus on difference to a more balanced view that accommodates previously neglected factors, such as sampling methods, the date when the studies were carried out, and the age(s) of individuals used as test subjects, and that acknowledges the need for more cross-cultural research, as very few studies of cognitive sex differences have been conducted outside of the industrialized West (Fairweather 1976). Halpern (1992:246) argues for a "biopsychosocial perspective" that can move beyond generic, binary categories (such as right/left hemisphere, male/female, spatial/verbal, nature/nurture, and so on) by incorporating a multiplicity of biological, psychological, and social factors. Computer-assisted techniques, such as meta-analysis (e.g., Feingold 1988; Linn and Petersen 1985; Voyer et al. 1995) have also served to reverse or substantially revise many of the conclusions of earlier research on gender and cognition by factoring in a number of these variables and thereby improving the statistical base of comparison (McGuinness 1998:70–74). Today, it is far from certain that differential results in cognitive performances of males and females have any real meaningful correlation with innate mental capacities, and it is certainly the case that greater efforts are being made to devise cognitive tests that are less prone to gender bias. As research on "sexing the brain" is gradually undermined by revealing its theoretical and methodological weaknesses and as its impact on the social sciences begins to wane, scientists might now be more likely to agree with the prophetic statement made by Bleier more than twenty years ago that cognitive psychology's attempt to sex the brain was "the modern equivalent of 19th century craniology" (Bleier 1984:11–12; see also Gould 1981:103–7).

Despite the improvements in research methods cited previously, binary approaches to the study of gender and cognition continue to appear and have been given a new lease of life by the growth of EP and Darwinian archaeology. Since the models generated by this research are based on the assumption that cognitive differences between males and females arose as adaptive responses to survival mechanisms in the remote past and hence are part of "human nature," it is important for prehistorians to engage in these debates and to evaluate their strengths and weaknesses from an archaeological perspective. Mithen (2001:113) has already acknowledged the dearth of research on gender and cognitive evolution and has emphasized the need for archaeological input into these discussions in order to introduce contextual constraints of time and space, factors that are normally ignored or underplayed by psychologists. And to Isaac's often-stated belief that only archaeology is capable of directly testing theories of early hominid behavior, we now need to add that only archaeology can transform the "cardboard caricatures" of current cognitive theory into real, palpable social actors and can articulate the dynamics of gender relations in nonessentialist terms.

Gender and Human Evolution: Directions for Future Research

As we have seen in the preceding sections, the speculative narratives of early hominid behavior generated by "Man the Hunter," as well as by current approaches in evolutionary psychology and Darwinian archaeology, are implicitly based on narratives of male and female relations that reflect stereotypical gender patterns of modern industrial societies. This presentist, ethnocentric outlook, combined with a neglect of archaeological data and its requisite temporal and spatial contingencies, has resulted in generic reconstructions of the past that sever human behavior from the particular historical contexts in which identity and behavior are embedded (Bleier 1984:71; Mishler 1979; Parlee 1979). As Barrett (2000:30–31) observes, "Gender is constituted in historically and culturally specific ways . . . hence it is important to understand the specific conditions under which gender constructs are brought into being." The failure of sociobiological research to address the specific conditions under which gender relations are constructed has also fostered what Rose et al. (1984:chap. 10) have termed a "poverty of reductionism" in which complex structures such as molecules or societies are defined in terms of the discrete units of which they are composed rather than as complex totalities and in which the wide range of human adaptive behaviors is constricted to a small range of topics centering on a narrowly defined range of reproductive behaviors (see also Gould 1977).

For some proponents of neo-Darwinism, reductionism is regarded as a "necessary evil," an analytical tool that, although not ideal, furnishes the only practical, viable means of interpreting, rather than merely describing, social phenomena (Campbell 2002:17; Miller 2001:22–24). Opponents of sociobiological argumentation think differently, however, viewing humans as "creatures who are constantly re-creating our own psychic and material environments, and whose individual lives are the outcomes of an extraordinary multiplicity of intersecting causal pathways" (Rose et al. 1984:290). Reductionism reduces the richness and variety of human life and in doing so creates narratives of social behavior that dehumanize human actions (Shanks and Tilley 1987:56). As Mithen (in Boone and Smith 1998:S163) pithily noted some time ago, cognitive approaches in archaeology need to move beyond the "food and sex stuff" to consider aspects of human evolutionary history that address issues beyond the narrow confines of reproductive success.

One way that archaeologists might begin to overcome many of the "dehumanizing" tendencies of sociobiological narratives of gender and evolution would be to introduce concepts of agency into debates about human origins (for recent examples, see Dobres 1995; Dobres and Robb 2000; Johnson 2000; McNay 2000; but for potential dangers of incorporating agency theory into gender studies, see Gero 2000). While there is clearly more work to be done to define concepts of gender and agency in archaeology, both theoretically and methodologically, and to contextualize those ideas within the framework of the archaeological record, the ability of agency theory to mediate between binary categories such as nature/culture, public/private, male/female, and individual/society provides a valuable means of modeling human behavior in evolution (both individually and in groups) from a nonreductionist perspective. For example, the concept of social agency could potentially be linked to research on cultural transmission, such as models of social learning (e.g. Boyd and Richerson 1985), or to approaches that favor concepts of egalitarianism and complementarity rather than hierarchy and dominance in the evolution of human social behavior (e.g., Erdal and Whiten 1996; Graves-Brown 1996). Agency theory can also help us appreciate more fully the temporal dimensions of social change over long periods of time as well as during the short-term changes associated with various phases of the life cycle (see the following discussion). By considering trajectories of social change at these different temporal scales, we might begin to construct narratives of gender and evolution that transcend the narrowly defined, deterministic parameters of current models by acknowledging a role for individuals and groups as agents in their own life histories.

In assessing the value of archaeological contributions to the topic of gender and human evolution, it is essential to acknowledge the important work of a number of feminist and other archaeologists who have considered these issues, either generally or in more narrowly defined contexts, in some detail. These include Conkey (1991), Gero (1991), Nelson (1997:chap. 4), articles in Hager (1997), Sørensen (2000:chap. 10), and Conkey and Spector (1984). Individually and collectively, this wide-ranging research constitutes a valuable contribution to the gendered perspective on human evolution by drawing attention to the many gender biases of traditional archaeological models of human evolution. While critical appraisals of androcentric research constitute a fundamental first step in engendering human prehistory, they need to be reinforced by the construction of new models that transcend the theoretical and methodological biases of earlier research. In the remainder of this section, therefore, I wish to consider three particular approaches to human evolution that could be integrated with current gender theory and thereby avoid the pitfalls of determinist and reductionist thinking. While these proposed areas of research are by no means new and have yielded results that could now be used in research on gender and evolution, they have yet to explicitly address issues of gender in prehistoric contexts: 1) studies of the evolution of human life history that acknowledge the importance of multiple phases of the life cycle to adaptation and survival; 2) studies of gender, technology, and material culture that focus on cooperation rather than separation of male and female subsistence activities; and 3) studies of gender and cognitive evolution that do not assume from the start the existence of significant cognitive differences between males and females.

Gender and the Evolution of Human Life Histories

Life history perspectives in human evolution embrace a wide range of interactions between physical, behavioral, and social dimensions of human life and chart their fluctuation throughout the various stages of the life cycle in accordance with environmental constraints and adaptive needs (see Bogin and Smith 2000; Fedigan 1997; Gardiner 1995; Gilchrist 2000; Key 2000; Morbeck 1997). While life history narratives are based to a considerable extent on variable aspects of male and female anatomy and could therefore be regarded as sociobiological in orientation, their focus on the dynamic and flexible nature of human behavior and decision making, as well as on the specific strategies undertaken by individuals as they negotiate their way through the life course, links them with theories of social agency and enables them to circumvent the rigid determinism and reductionism of standard sociobiological models (Morbeck 1997:6; Vitzhum 1997).

When, why, and how did modern human life cycles evolve? And in what ways did differences in the life cycles of males and females shape our evolutionary history? These are questions that form the basis of much of the current research in the field, and the results of this research are of course relevant to an understanding of gender and human evolution. Answers to these questions are complex and demand recourse to recent research on life histories of nonhuman primates, particularly those of higher primates, such as chimpanzees and bonobos, whose genetic structures closely replicate those of modern humans (Streier 2001). By the same token, the behavior of early hominids (such as *Ardipithecus* and the various species of *Australopithecus*) more closely resembles pongid behavior than that of humans, with bipedal locomotion being the only significant difference between them (Wrangham 2001). Consequently, a great deal of attention is now being paid to the role of primate behavior in the construction of life history models of human evolution (e.g., Fedigan 1997; McLeod 1997; Morbeck 1997; Streier 2001; Wrangham 2001).

As a mitigating factor to potential gender bias in this research, Fausto-Sterling (2001:49–51) has noted the increased attention given to female subjects in primatological studies during the past thirty years, a development that she feels reflects the greater numbers of female researchers who have revised or completely overturned earlier androcentric interpretations of female primate behavior. The result has been that we now know a great deal about the life histories of male and female primates, and this information can be applied to research on the reproductive and survival strategies of early hominid groups. One particularly important example is provided by longitudinal studies of Japanese macaques (Fedigan 1997; Pavelka 1997). The careful observation and study of these primates over several generations suggest that female reproductive success is most closely linked to longevity, with the key to reproductive success being not a high birthrate but the steady production of offspring with adequate interbirth intervals over a long period of time. This contradicts traditional narratives of reproductive success in which fertility rather than longevity is deemed the key adaptive element, and it consequently suggests that one of the most important elements in female reproductive fitness is the ability of females to live long and healthy lives.

Life history approaches can also contribute to an understanding of the evolution of the human mating system, a topic that has been the subject of so much recent discussion in evolutionary psychology. When did human mating behavior emerge in its present form? Wrangham (2001:40) has argued that it is likely to have occurred at a time when there was a marked decrease in sexual dimorphism of body mass since great differences (i.e., large males and smaller females) imply male competition for mates and have behavioral correlates that do not fit the human pattern. Since there is only one point in evolutionary history where a significant male reduction and female increase in body mass occur (about 1.9 million years ago with the evolution of *H. erectus*), it is highly likely that modern human mating systems also emerged at that time. More important, this example demonstrates that human evolution is a dynamic process in which physical characteristics and their behavioral correlates evolved in a mosaic rather than a unilinear fashion, and it underscores the need to analyze various types of adaptive behavior within particular temporal and spatial frameworks.

While a detailed summary of the wide array of additional research on the evolution of the human life cycle lies beyond the scope of this chapter, mention should be made of several recent life history approaches to human reproduction that have a particular bearing on gender relations. These include research on novel features of the human reproductive system, such as long periods of gestation and infancy (e.g., Ellison 2001; Key 2000), both of which are likely to have evolved as the result of encephalization (Falk 1990; Robson 2004); the considerable energy requirements of gestating females that may have played a key role in the evolution of bipedality by enhancing females' ability to nourish themselves and their offspring (Leonard and Robertson 1997); short periods of lactation in order to reduce energy demands on postpartum females that became possible as the result of the greater levels of social interaction among human primates and are likely to have had an impact on social organization (Key and Aiello 1999); and the long female postreproductive stage (menopause) that is currently being interpreted as an adaptive advantage by enabling older, experienced females to contribute to the survival of offspring and grand-offspring (for the so-called grandmothering hypothesis, see Bogin and Smith 2000:416–18; Hawkes et al. 2000). In addition, several recent studies stress the reciprocal relationships between strategies of reproduction, survival, and cognition since the ability to survive and successfully reproduce within an evolving system of complex social interactions would have placed greater demands on cognitive abilities (Erdal and Whiten 1996; Lee 1996).

The emergence of a visible archaeological record with the appearance of the earliest known stone-tool assemblages associated with the genus *Homo* provides evidence for investigating the important role of material culture in the adaptive strategies of early human populations during later phases of their evolution. Interactions between people and material culture (e.g., the manufacture and manipulation of tools in order to enhance survival) thus became an integral part of human life history from about 2.6 million years ago on. Unfortunately, life history approaches have not yet been widely adopted in archaeological research on human evolution. Mithen (2001) notes the particular lack of archaeological attention to issues of childhood and cognition in premodern societies; given the importance of childhood for the cultural transmission of gender constructs, there is also a need to develop interdisciplinary approaches between archaeology, anthropology, and developmental psychology through which we might begin to investigate how gender constructs are formed, transformed, and transmitted within particular social contexts.

Gender, Technology, and Social Organization

The potential for archaeology to contribute to our understanding of the evolution of gender relations was raised nearly a decade ago by Graves-Brown (1996). In place of the classic gendered division of labor proposed by so many earlier models, he introduced the paradigm of "complementarity" as a force in human evolution, a process by which individuals and groups fulfill different roles in the completion of a task, such as cooperative hunting and gathering by single-sex groups, cooperative child care behavior among females, and economic activities that involve both sexes. He attributes the persistence of traditional models of sexual division of labor (in particular, male provisioning models, such as Lovejoy's hypothesis) to the overstated distinction between hunting and gathering (349). In response to more recent models in evolutionary psychology, he observes, "If women could organize a sex-strike they could organize themselves to get their own food, and of course they do" and that "defense against predators is better accomplished in a group than a pair bond" (350). Female reproductive success, he believes, should be predicated on the continuous exploitation of reliable sources of nutrition rather than behaviors associated with fertility and fecundity (350; on this point as well, see Hamilton 1984).

Similar conclusions have been drawn by Key and Aiello (1999) in an article that addresses the importance of cooperative behavior in human social life. Cooperation can take many forms other than the traditional narrative of the male–female pair bond, including bonds between brothers and sisters, grandmothers and grandchildren, and parents and children as well as the bonds of friendship between individuals who are not related at all by kinship ties. While high degrees of cooperative behavior have been observed among nonhuman primates, particularly chimpanzees, nowhere has cooperation reached the level of importance achieved by humans, among whom it is highly diversified and widespread. Key and Aiello emphasize the biological bases of the evolution of cooperative behavior and demonstrate the powerful effects it is likely to have had on the evolution of human social structures. These arguments could be just as readily linked, however, to the cultural dimensions of human life, in particular to the development of tools and technology in association with the emergence of the genus *Homo*.

The socially embedded nature of technology in early human societies has been emphasized by a number of scholars in recent years (e.g., Dobres 1995; Gilchrist 1999:40–42; Ingold 1994; Lemonnier 1993; Reynolds 1993). These social approaches to material culture challenge the assumption of modern industrialists that technological achievement is largely the result of individual rather than collective endeavors since in precapitalist societies "technical relations are social" (Ingold 1994:341). Accordingly, artifacts associated with preindustrial societies should be treated as repositories of information about cultural processes involving "heterotechnic" cooperation in which technical tasks are carried out not by lone craftsmen but by a number of individuals working together (341–42). Lemonnier's (1993) concept of *chaîne opératoire* is also important in this regard for characterizing technology as a multistage process requiring the labor and skills of many individuals working interdependently. The implications of these ideas for gendered approaches to technology in human evolution are enormous since cooperative models accommodate men, women, and even children as coparticipants in technical processes.

Dobres (1995) has developed these ideas in a somewhat different direction by applying concepts of gender and social agency to the study of prehistoric technology. In a case study that considers evidence of bone and antler technologies at a number of Magdalenian sites in the eastern French Pyrénées, Dobres notes considerable intra- and intersite variation in the distribution of six artifact types as well as differences in form, function, and material. On the basis of significant local and regional variations in technical practices, she concludes that bone and antler technology was "premised on flexibility around social norms" and on this basis proposes a model of heterarchical rather than hierarchical social organization during the Upper Paleolithic (41). In addition to integrating theoretical concepts of gender and social agency with particular bodies of archaeological data, Dobres makes several important conclusions concerning gender relations in the Magdalenian without attempting to attribute specific artifacts and technical strategies to particular genders. Further application of this approach to other areas and periods of the Paleolithic would increase our understanding of the interfaces between gender and technology in other phases of human evolution and could serve as a productive methodological basis for overcoming some of the doubts expressed by Gero (2000) concerning the application of theories of social agency to archaeological studies of gender.

Gender, Evolution, and Cognition

As Mithen (2001:116) has recently asserted, archaeologists "can and must play a role in the discussions and debates about cognitive evolution" both in order to more fully understand the past mentality of humans and in order to make a significant contribution to interdisciplinary debates currently going on in the cognitive sciences. Since the latter, as we have seen earlier, have adopted a decidedly polarized model of gender relations, it is important that archaeologists become engaged in research on cognitive evolution in order to challenge the stereotypical portrayals of males and females that continue to prevail in current models of human origins.

Although the increasingly tenuous evidence for sex differences in cognitive abilities should not be entirely dismissed (Gilchrist 1999:13), the gradual erosion of earlier arguments contending that male and female brains are "hardwired differently" should now begin to encourage the development of new models of cognitive evolution based on greater degrees of sexual parity. Instead of attributing presumed cognitive differences between males and females in modern populations to differential reproductive strategies that evolved in the ancestral past, we might now begin to adopt radically different approaches that do not assume the a priori existence of cognitive sex differences and that are supported by paleobiological and archaeological data. Foley (1996:63) has traced patterns of encephalization by measuring the neocortex of extinct hominid taxa relative to modern humans. Correlation of these results with archaeological data suggests that advances in technical skills, such as improved toolmaking abilities, did not always evolve in direct proportion to enlargement of cranial capacity but that different skills and capacities evolved at different rates and times in a mosaic and nonunilinear fashion. This poses significant challenges to current theories of male and female cognition that presume that there is little or no difference in the structure of the modern human mind and that of hominids who emerged in the so-called environment of evolutionary adaptation (Tooby and Cosmides 1992). In fact, there were many adaptive environments in human prehistory, and a complex consideration of the origins and development of cognitive differences between the sexes, if those differences have indeed existed, needs to treat cognition as a dynamic process rather than a static, reified entity.

Another area of potential importance for understanding the interfaces between gender and cognition is the "creative explosion" among early modern sapient populations during the Upper Paleolithic period. While a great deal of scholarly attention has been devoted to revealing and challenging the androcentric biases of earlier interpretations of parietal and portable art (e.g., Bahn and Vertut 1997; Bailey 1994; Conkey 1991; Conkey and Williams 1991; Rice 1981; Russell 1998; Tringham and Conkey 1998), there is now a need for innovative research on the use of art and symbolism in the construction of early human social identities. Recent discoveries of a rich and complex series of cave paintings at Chauvet, skeletons painted with red ocher and sculpted images of females at Cussac (some nearly five meters in length), and large intact living floors at La Garma near Altamira replete with refuse, bone and stone tools, batons, and rudimentary stone enclosures (Bahn 2004) furnish new evidence with which to interpret the rich "iconic vocabulary" of ancestral images from a gendered perspective (Gamble 1998). In place of earlier androcentric hypotheses such as "hunting magic" to account for the apparent sudden outburst of art and creativity of early *H. sapiens*, we might begin to consider more wide-ranging explanations involved the unprecedented use of visual symbolism, by women as well as men, in the creation of social identities (for the use of red ocher as body paint in the Middle Stone Age, see, e.g., Watts 1999). These will also help reverse the marginal role traditionally granted to women in the development of art, religion, language, and other symbolic systems—cognitive achievements that have come to be regarded as hallmarks of the creativity and success of our species.

Prospects for Engendering Human Evolution: The Need for Interdisciplinary Research

While very few archaeologists are guilty of the "biophobia" attributed to "traditional social scientists" by some evolutionary psychologists (e.g., Campbell 2002:1–8; Pinker 2002; Thornhill and Palmer 2000:chap. 5; Tooby and Cosmides 1992:24), it is fair to state that archaeological contributions to human evolution have often been parochial in their overriding focus on chronology and typology as well as their lack of sufficient attention to relevant research in other fields (e.g., evolutionary biology, primatology, and cognitive psychology). Current research in the cognitive sciences is particularly important in view of some of the hypotheses that have recently been proposed in the field of evolutionary archaeology (e.g., Kohn and Mithen 1999; Shennan 2002; Steele and Shennan 1996). Here the concept of embodiment is of potential importance for integrating rather than dichotomizing the physical and cognitive aspects of human behavior (Butler 1990:chap. 1; Foucault 1978; Meskell 1998, 2000). As Gilchrist (1999:13) has recently observed, "Whether gender, social cognition or sexuality are dependent fully on biology *or* culture is no longer the issue. The interesting questions are how biological and/or cognitive difference is interpreted culturally, how this varies between societies, and how the mind and body may evolve in response to cultural definitions of gender."

In attempting to construct new models of human evolution that integrate archaeological, biological, and psychological research, there is also a need to build closer links between archaeologists, anthropologists, evolutionary biologists, and psychologists through multidisciplinary studies that can be validated through the rigorous application of empirical evidence. The potential for this type of interdisciplinary research has been demonstrated in a number of papers during the past decade (e.g., Erdal and Whiten 1996; Foley 1996; Robson-Brown 1996; Toth and Schick 1994) that integrate archaeological evidence with research in the biological and social sciences in the attempt to generate viable models for the evolution of human behavior. Unfortunately, almost all this research so far has failed to incorporate issues of gender. Since, as Thomas (1998:151) states, "the defining characteristic of humanity is not the hardware within, but the relationships between persons" and since human relationships lie at the very core of attempts to engender the prehistoric past, these are precisely the issues that research on gender and human evolution should now begin to address.

Acknowledgments

I would like to thank Sarah Nelson for inviting me to contribute to this important volume. Clive Bonsall and Eddie Peltenburg kindly read through a preliminary draft of the text and offered a number of useful and constructive comments. I naturally assume responsibility for the contents, including any errors or oversights that may occur.

References

Aiello, L. C., and J. C. K. Wells
    2002   Energetics and the Evolution of the Genus Homo. *Annual Review of Anthropology* 31:323–38.
Alper, J. S.
    1985   Sex Differences in Brain Asymmetry: A Critical Analysis. *Feminist Studies* 11(1):7–37.
Anderson, J. R.
    1983   *The Architecture of Cognition.* Cambridge, MA: Harvard University Press.
Appleman, P., ed.
    2001   *Darwin.* Norton Critical Edition. 3rd ed. New York: Norton.
Bahn, P.
    2004   New Developments in Ice-Age Art. Unpublished lecture delivered at the Department of Archaeology, University of Edinburgh, November 22.
Bahn, P., and J. Vertut
    1997   *Journey through the Ice Age.* London: Weidenfeld & Nicolson.
Bailey, D. W.
    1994   Reading Prehistoric Figurines as Individuals. *World Archaeology* 25:321–31.

Baron-Cohen, S.
    2003   *The Essential Difference.* London: Penguin.
Barrett, J. C.
    2000   Fields of Discourse: Reconstituting a Social Archaeology. In *Interpretive Archae-
            ology: A Reader.* J. Thomas, ed. Pp. 23–32. London: Leicester University Press.
Barrett, L., R. Dunbar, and J. Lycett
    2002   *Human Evolutionary Psychology.* Basingstoke: Palgrave.
Bartholomew, G., and J. Birdsell
    1953   Ecology and the Protohominids. *American Anthropologist* 55:481–98.
Benbow, C. P., and J. C. Stanley
    1980   Sex Differences in Mathematical Ability: Fact or Artifact? *Science*
            210:1262–64.
Bergounioux, F. M.
    1961   Notes on the Mentality of Primitive Man. In *Social Life of Early Man.* S. L.
            Washburn, ed. Pp. 106–18. London: Methuen.
Binford, L.
    1968   Methodological Considerations of the Archaeological Use of Ethnographic
            Data. In *Man the Hunter.* R. B. Lee and I. DeVore, eds. Pp. 268–73. Chicago:
            Aldine.
    1981   *Bones: Ancient Men and Modern Myths.* New York: Academic Press.
    1985   Human Ancestors: Changing Views of Their Behavior. *Journal of Anthropological
            Archaeology* 4:292–327.
    1986   Commentary on Bunn and Kroll's "Systematic Butchery by Plio-Pleistocene
            Hominids at Olduvai Gorge." *Current Anthropology* 27:444–46.
    1988   Fact and Fiction about the *Zinjanthropus* Floor: Data, Arguments and Interpre-
            tations. *Current Anthropology* 29:123–35.
    1989   *Debating Archaeology.* New York: Academic Press.
Bleier, R.
    1984   *Science and Gender: A Critique of Biology and Its Theories on Women.* New York: Perga-
            mon Press.
Blumenschein, R. J.
    1991   Breakfast at Olorgesailie: The Natural History Approach to Early Stone Age
            Archaeology. *Journal of Human Evolution* 21:307–27.
Bogin, B., and B. H. Smith
    2000   Evolution of the Human Life Cycle. In *Human Biology: An Evolutionary and Bio-
            cultural Perspective.* S. Stinson, B. Bogin, R. Huss-Ashmore, and D. Rourki, eds.
            Pp. 377–424. New York: Wiley-Liss.
Boone, J. L., and E. A. Smith
    1998   Is It Evolution Yet? A Critique of Evolutionary Archaeology. *Current Anthro-
            pology* 39:S141–73.
Boyd, R., and P. J. Richerson
    1985   *Culture and the Evolutionary Process.* Chicago: University of Chicago Press.

Buss, D. M.
    1999   *Evolutionary Psychology: The New Science of the Mind*. Needham Heights, MA: Allyn
            and Bacon.
Butler, J.
    1990   *Gender Trouble: Feminism and the Subversion of Identity*. New York: Routledge.
Campbell, A.
    2002   *A Mind of Her Own: The Evolutionary Psychology of Women*. New York: Oxford
            University Press.
Campbell, B. G.
    1992   *Humankind Emerging*. 6th ed. New York: HarperCollins.
Cartmill, M.
    1993   *A View to a Death in the Morning: Hunting and Nature through History*. Cambridge,
            MA: Harvard University Press.
Conkey, M.
    1991   Contexts for Action, Contexts of Power: Material Culture and Gender in the
            Magdalenian. In *Engendering Archaeology: Women and Prehistory*. J. M. Gero and
            M. W. Conkey, eds. Pp. 57–92. Oxford: Blackwell.
Conkey, M. W., and J. D. Spector
    1984   Archaeology and the Study of Gender. In *Advances in Archaeological Theory and
            Methods*. Vol. 7. M. Schiffer, ed. Pp. 1–38. New York: Academic Press.
Conkey, M., with S. H. Williams
    1991   Original Narratives: The Political Economy of Gender in Archaeology. In
            Gender at the Crossroads of Knowledge: Feminist Anthropology in the Postmodern Era. M.
            di Leonardo, ed. Pp. 102–39. Berkeley: University of California Press.
Cronin, H.
    1991   *The Ant and the Peacock: Altruism and Sexual Selection from Darwin to Today*. New
            York: Cambridge University Press.
Dahlberg, F., ed.
    1981   *Woman the Gatherer*. New Haven, CT: Yale University Press.
Dawkins, R.
    1976   *The Selfish Gene*. Oxford: Oxford University Press.
Dennett, D.
    1995   *Darwin's Dangerous Idea*. London: Allen Lane/Penguin.
Dobres, M.-A.
    1995   Gender and Prehistoric Technology: On the Social Agency of Technical Strat-
            egies. *World Archaeology* 27(1):25–49.
Dobres, M.-A., and J. Robb, eds.
    2000   *Agency in Archaeology*. London: Routledge.
Donald, M.
    1991   *Origins of the Modern Mind*. Cambridge, MA: Harvard University Press.
Dunnell, R. C.
    1980   Evolutionary Theory and Archaeology. In *Advances in Archaeological Method and
            Theory*. Vol. 3. M. Schiffer, ed. Pp. 35–99. New York: Academic Press.

Ellison, P. T.
   2001   *On Fertile Ground: A Natural History of Human Reproduction*. Cambridge, MA: Harvard University Press.
Ember, C. R., and M. Ember
   1993   *Anthropology*. 7th ed. Englewood Cliffs, NJ: Prentice Hall.
Erdal, D., and A. Whiten
   1996   Egalitarianism and Machiavellian Intelligence in Human Evolution. In *Modelling the Early Human Mind*. P. Mellars and K. Gibson, eds. Pp. 139–50. Cambridge: McDonald Institute for Archaeological Research.
Estiokio-Griffin, A., and P. Bion Griffin
   1981   Woman the Hunter: The Agta. In *Woman the Gatherer*. F. Dahlberg, ed. Pp. 121–51. New Haven, CT: Yale University Press.
Fairweather, H.
   1976   Sex Differences in Cognition. *Cognition* 4:231–80.
Falk, D.
   1990   Brain Evolution in *Homo*: The "Radiator" Theory. *Behavioral Brain Science* 13:333–81.
   1997   Brain Evolution in Females. In *Women in Human Evolution*. L. D. Hager, ed. Pp. 114–36. London: Routledge.
Fausto-Sterling, A.
   1992   *Myths of Gender: Biological Theories about Women and Men*. New York: Basic Books.
   2000   *Sexing the Body: Gender Politics and the Construction of Sexuality*. New York: Basic Books.
   2001   Beyond Difference: Feminism and Evolutionary Psychology. In *Alas Poor Darwin: Arguments against Evolutionary Psychology*. H. Rose and S. Rose, eds. Pp. 174–89. London: Vintage Books.
Fedigan, L.
   1986   The Changing Role of Women in Models of Human Evolution. *Annual Reviews of Anthropology* 15:25–66.
   1997   Changing Views of Female Life Histories. In *The Evolving Female: A Life-History Perspective*. M. E. Morbeck, A. Galloway, and A. L. Zihlman, eds. Pp. 15–26. Princeton, NJ: Princeton University Press.
Feingold, A.
   1988   Cognitive Gender Differences Are Disappearing. *American Psychologist* 43:95–103.
Fodor, J.
   1983   *The Modularity of Mind*. Cambridge, MA: MIT Press.
Foley, R. A.
   1996   Measuring Cognition in Extinct Hominids. In *Modelling the Early Human Mind*. P. Mellars and K. Gibson, eds. Pp. 57–65. Cambridge: McDonald Institute for Archaeological Research.

Foucault, M.
    1978   *The History of Sexuality.* London: Routledge.
Gamble, C.
    1998   Foreword. In *Ancestral Images: The Iconography of Human Origins.* S. Moser. Pp.
            ix–xxiv. Ithaca, NY: Cornell University Press.
Gardiner, J. K.
    1995   *Provoking Agents: Gender and Agency in Theory and Practice.* Urbana: University of
            Illinois Press.
Geary, D. C.
    1996   Sexual Selection and Sex Differences in Mathematical Abilities. *Behavioral and
            Brain Sciences* 19:229–84.
Gero, J.
    1985   Socio-Politics of Archaeology and the Woman-at-Home Ideology. *American
            Antiquity* 50(2):342–50.
    1991   Genderlithics: Women's Roles in Stone Tool Production. In *Engendering
            Archaeology: Women and Prehistory.* J. M. Gero and M. W. Conkey, eds. Pp. 163–
            93. Oxford: Blackwell.
    2000   Troubled Travels in Agency and Feminism. In *Agency in Archaeology.* M.-A.
            Dobres and J. Robb, eds. Pp. 40–50. London: Routledge.
Gilchrist, R.
    1999   *Gender and Archaeology: Contesting the Past.* London: Routledge.
    2000   Archaeological Biographies: Realizing Human Lifecycles, -Courses and -His-
            tories. *World Archaeology* 31(3):325–28.
Gould, S. J.
    1977   Biological Potentiality vs. Biological Determinism. In *Ever since Darwin.* S. J.
            Gould. Pp. 251–59. New York: Norton.
    1981   *The Mismeasure of Man.* New York: Norton.
Graves-Brown, P.
    1996   Their Commonwealths Are Not as We Supposed: Sex, Gender and Material
            Culture in Human Evolution. In *The Archaeology of Human Ancestry: Power, Sex
            and Tradition.* J. Steele and S. Shennan, eds. Pp. 347–60. London: Routledge.
Hager, L. D., ed.
    1997   *Women in Human Evolution.* London: Routledge.
Halpern, D. F.
    1992   *Sex Differences in Cognitive Abilities.* 2nd ed. Hillsdale, NJ: Lawrence Erlbaum
            Associates.
Hamilton, M. E.
    1984   Revising Evolutionary Narratives: A Consideration of Alternative Assump-
            tions about Sexual Selection and Competition for Mates. *American Anthropolo-
            gist* 86:651–62.
Hamilton, W. D.
    1964   The Genetical Evolution of Social Behaviour. *Journal of Theoretical Biology*
            7:1–52.

Haraway, D.
  1978a   Animal Sociology and a Natural Economy of the Body Politic, Part I: A Political Physiology of Dominance. *Signs* 4(1):21–36.
  1978b   Animal Sociology and a Natural Economy of the Body Politic, Part II: The Past Is the Contested Zone: Human Nature and Theories of Production and Reproduction in Primate Behavior Studies. *Signs* 4(1):37–60.
  1989   *Primate Visions: Gender, Race and Nature in the World of Modern Science.* London: Routledge.
Haviland, W. A.
  2000   *Human Evolution and Prehistory.* 5th ed. Orlando: Harcourt College.
Hawkes, K.
  1996   Foraging Differences between Men and Women: Behavioural Ecology of the Sexual Division of Labour. In *The Archaeology of Human Ancestry: Power, Sex and Tradition.* J. Steele and S. Shennan, eds. Pp. 283–305. London: Routledge.
Hawkes, K., J. F. O'Connell, N. Blurton-Jones, H. Alvarez, and E. L. Charnov
  2000   The Grandmother Hypothesis and Human Evolution. In *Adaptation and Human Behavior.* L. Cronk, N. Chagnon, and W. Irons, eds. Pp. 237–58. New York: Aldine de Gruyter.
Ingold, T.
  1994   Introduction (Part V). In *Tools, Language and Cognition in Human Evolution.* K. R. Gibson and T. Ingold, eds. Pp. 337–45. Cambridge: Cambridge University Press.
Isaac, G. Ll.
  1968   Traces of Pleistocene Hunters: An East African Example. In *Man the Hunter.* R. B. Lee and I. DeVore, eds. Pp. 253–61. Chicago: Aldine.
  1971   The Diet of Early Man: Aspects of Archaeological Evidence from Lower and Middle Pleistocene Sites in Africa. *World Archaeology* 2:278–99.
  1978   The Food Sharing Behavior of Protohuman Hominids. *Scientific American* 238:90–108.
Johnson, M.
  2000   Conceptions of Agency in Archaeological Interpretation. In *Interpretive Archaeology: A Reader.* J. Thomas, ed. Pp. 211–27. London: Leicester University Press.
Jolly, C. J., and R. White
  1995   *Physical Anthropology and Archaeology.* 5th ed. New York: McGraw-Hill.
Jurmain, R., H. Nelson, L. Kilgore, and W. Trevathan
  2000   *Introduction to Physical Anthropology.* 8th ed. Stamford, CT: Wadsworth/Thomson Learning.
Jurmain, R., H. Nelson, and W. A. Turnbaugh
  1990   *Understanding Physical Anthropology and Archaeology.* 4th ed. St. Paul, MN: West.
Key, C.
  2000   The Evolution of Human Life History. *World Archaeology* 31:329–50.

Key, C. A., and L. C. Aiello
    1999   The Evolution of Social Organization. In *The Evolution of Culture*. R. Dunbar,
            C. Knight, and C. Power, eds. Pp. 15–33. Edinburgh: Edinburgh University
            Press.
Kingdon, J.
    2003   *Lowly Origin*. Princeton, NJ: Princeton University Press.
Knight, C.
    1996   Darwinism and Collective Representations. In *The Archaeology of Human Ancestry:
            Power, Sex and Tradition*. J. Steele and S. Shennan, eds. Pp. 331–46. London:
            Routledge.
Kohn, M., and S. Mithen
    1999   Handaxes: Products of Sexual Selection? *Antiquity* 73:518–26.
Kottak, C. P.
    2000   *Anthropology: The Exploration of Human Diversity*. 8th international ed. London:
            McGraw-Hill Higher Education.
Lake, M.
    1996   Archaeological Inference and the Explanation of Hominid Evolution. In *The
            Archaeology of Human Ancestry: Power, Sex and Tradition*. J. Steele and S. Shennan,
            eds. Pp. 184–206. London: Routledge.
Leacock, E.
    1978   Women's Status in Egalitarian Society: Implications for Social Evolution.
            Current Anthropology 19(2):247–75.
    1983   Interpreting the Origins of Gender Inequality: Conceptual and Historical
            Problems. *Dialectical Anthropology* 7(4):263–84.
Lee, P. C.
    1996   Inferring Cognition from Social Behaviour in Non-Humans. In *Modelling the
            Human Mind*. P. Mellars and K. Gibson, eds. Pp. 131–38. Cambridge:
            McDonald Institute for Archaeological Research.
Lee, R. B.
    1968   What Hunters Do for a Living, or, How to Make Out on Scarce Resources.
            In *Man the Hunter*. R. B. Lee and I. DeVore, eds. Pp. 30–48. Chicago: Aldine.
    1979   *The !Kung San: Men, Women and Work in a Foraging Society*. New York: Cambridge
            University Press.
Lee, R. B., and I. DeVore, eds.
    1968   *Man the Hunter*. Chicago: Aldine.
Lee, R. B., and I. DeVore
    1976   *Kalahari Hunter-Gatherers*. Cambridge, MA: Harvard University Press.
Leibowitz, L.
    1975   Perspectives on the Evolution of Sex Differences. In *Toward an Anthropology of
            Women*. R. R. Reiter, ed. Pp. 20–35. New York: Monthly Review Press.
Lemonnier, P.
    1993   Introduction. In *Technological Choices: Transformation in Material Cultures since the
            Neolithic*. P. Lemonnier, ed. Pp. 1–34. London: Routledge.

Leonard, W. R., and M. L. Robertson
    1997   Rethinking the Energetics of Bipedality. *Current Anthropology* 38(2):304–9.
Linn, M. C., and A. C. Petersen
    1985   Emergence and Characterization of Sex Differences in Spatial Ability: A Meta-Analysis. *Child Development* 56:1479–98.
Linton, S.
    1971   Woman the Gatherer: Male Bias in Anthropology. In *Women in Perspective: A Guide for Cross-Cultural Studies.* S.-E. Jacobs, ed. Pp. 9–21. Urbana: University of Illinois Press.
Lovejoy, O.
    1981   The Origin of Man. *Science* 211(23 January):341–49.
    1988   Evolution of Human Walking. *Scientific American*, November, 82–89.
Low, B.
    2000   *Why Sex Matters.* Princeton, NJ: Princeton University Press.
Lyman, R. L., and M. J. O'Brien
    1998   The Goals of Evolutionary Archaeology: History and Explanation. *Current Anthropology* 39(5):615–52.
Maccoby, E. E., and C. N. Jacklin
    1974   *The Psychology of Sex Differences.* Stanford, CA: Stanford University Press.
Maynard Smith, J.
    1977   Parental Investment—A Prospective Analysis. *Animal Behaviour* 25:1–9.
McGuinness, C.
    1998   Cognition. In *Gender and Psychology.* K. Trew and J. Kremer, eds. Pp. 66–81. New York: Arnold.
McLeod, B.
    1997   Life History, Females and Evolution: A Commentary. In *The Evolving Female: A Life-History Perspective.* M. E. Morbeck, A. Galloway, and A. L. Zihlman, eds. Pp. 270–75. Princeton, NJ: Princeton University Press.
McNay, L.
    2000   *Gender and Agency: Reconfiguring the Subject in Feminist and Social Theory.* Cambridge: Polity Press.
Mellars, P., and K. Gibson, eds.
    1996   *Modelling the Early Human Mind.* Cambridge: McDonald Institute for Archaeological Research.
Meskell, L.
    1998   The Irresistible Body and the Seduction of Archaeology. In *Changing Bodies, Changing Meanings: Studies on the Human Body in Antiquity.* D. Montserrat, ed. Pp. 139–61. London: Routledge.
    2000   Writing the Body in Archaeology. In *Reading the Body: Representations and Remains in the Archaeological Record.* A. E. Rautman, ed. Pp. 13–21. Philadelphia: University of Pennsylvania Press.

Miller, Geoffrey
    2001   *The Mating Mind: How Sexual Choice Shaped the Evolution of Human Nature.* London: Vintage Books.

Mishler, E. G.
    1979   Meaning in Context: Is There Any Other Kind? *Harvard Educational Review* 49:1–19.

Mithen, S.
    1990   *Thoughtful Foragers: A Study of Prehistoric Decision Making.* Cambridge: Cambridge University Press.
    1996a   *The Prehistory of the Mind: A Search for the Origins of Art, Religion and Science.* London: Phoenix.
    1996b   Social Learning and Cultural Tradition: Interpreting Early Palaeolithic Technology. In *The Archaeology of Human Ancestry: Power, Sex and Tradition.* J. Steele and S. Shennan, eds. Pp. 207–29. London: Routledge.
    2001   Archaeological Theory and Theories of Cognitive Evolution. In *Archaeological Theory Today.* I. Hodder, ed. Pp. 98–121. Cambridge: Polity Press.

Morbeck, M. E.
    1997   Life History, the Individual and Human Evolution. In *The Evolving Female: A Life-History Perspective.* M. E. Morbeck, A. Galloway, and A. L. Zihlman, eds. Pp. 3–14. Princeton, NJ: Princeton University Press.

Nelson, S. M.
    1997   *Gender in Archaeology: Analyzing Power and Prestige.* Walnut Creek, CA: AltaMira Press.

Noble, W., and I. Davidson
    1996   *Human Evolution, Language and Mind: A Psychological and Archaeological Inquiry.* Cambridge: Cambridge University Press.

Parlee, M. B.
    1979   Psychology and Women. *Signs* 5:121–33.

Pavelka, M. S. M.
    1997   The Social Life of Female Japanese Monkeys. In *The Evolving Female: A Life-History Perspective.* M. E. Morbeck, A. Galloway, and A. L. Zihlman, eds. Pp. 76–85. Princeton, NJ: Princeton University Press.

Pinker, S.
    1997   *How the Mind Works.* London: Penguin.
    2002   *The Blank Slate: The Modern Denial of Human Nature.* London: Allen Lane.

Power, C., and I. Watts
    1996   Female Strategies and Collective Behaviour: The Archaeology of Earliest *Homo sapiens sapiens.* In *The Archaeology of Human Ancestry: Power, Sex and Tradition.* J. Steele and S. Shennan, eds. Pp. 306–30. London: Routledge.

Renfrew, C., and C. Scarre, eds.
    1998   *Cognition and Culture: The Archaeology of Symbolic Storage.* Cambridge: McDonald Institute for Archaeological Research.

Reynolds, P. C.
    1993   The Complementation Theory of Language and Tool Use. In *Tools, Language and Cognition in Human Evolution*. K. R. Gibson and T. Ingold, eds. Pp. 407–28. Cambridge: Cambridge University Press.

Rice, P. C.
    1981   Prehistoric Venuses: Symbols of Motherhood or Womanhood? *Journal of Anthropological Research* 37:402–14.

Ridley, M.
    1993   *The Red Queen: Sex and the Evolution of Human Nature*. London: Penguin.
    2003   *Nature via Nurture: Genes, Experience and What Makes Us Human*. London: Fourth Estate.

Robson, S. L.
    2004   Breast Milk, Diet and Large Human Brains. *Current Anthropology* 45(3): 419–25.

Robson-Brown, K. A.
    1996   Systematics and Integrated Methods for the Modeling of the Pre-Modern Human Mind. In *Modelling the Early Human Mind*. P. Mellars and K. Gibson, eds. Pp. 103–17. Cambridge: McDonald Institute for Archaeological Research.

Rose, H., and S. Rose, eds.
    2001   *Alas Poor Darwin: Arguments against Evolutionary Psychology*. London: Vintage Books.

Rose, S.
    1998   *Lifelines: Biology, Freedom, Determinism*. London: Penguin.

Rose, S., R. C. Lewontin, and L. J. Kamin
    1984   *Not in Our Genes: Biology, Ideology and Human Nature*. Harmondsworth: Penguin.

Rosenberg, R.
    1982   *Beyond Separate Spheres*. New Haven, CT: Yale University Press.

Russell, P.
    1998   The Paleolithic Mother-Goddess: Fact or Fiction? In *Reader in Gender Archaeology*. K. Hayes-Gilpin and D. S. Whitley, eds. Pp. 261–68. London: Routledge.

Shanks, M., and C. Tilley
    1987   *Re-Constructing Archaeology*. Cambridge: Cambridge University Press.

Shaywitz, B. A., S. E. Shaywitz, K. R. Pugh, R. T. Constable, P. Skudlarski, R. K. Fulbright, R. A. Bronen, J. M. Fletcher, D. P. Shankweller, L. Katz, and J. C. Gore
    1995   Sex Differences in the Functional Organization of the Brain for Language. *Nature* 373:607–9.

Shennan, S.
    2002   *Genes, Memes and Human History*. London: Thames and Hudson.
    2004   Analytical Archaeology. In *A Companion to Archaeology*. J. Bintliff, ed. Pp. 3–20. Oxford: Blackwell.

Silverman, I., and M. Eals
   1992   Sex Differences in Spatial Abilities: Evolutionary Theory and Data. In *The Adapted Mind: Evolutionary Psychology and the Generation of Culture*. J. H. Barkow, L. Cosmides, and J. Tooby, eds. Pp. 533–49. Oxford: Oxford University Press.
Silverman, I., and K. Phillips
   1998   The Evolutionary Psychology of Spatial Sex Differences. In *Handbook of Evolutionary Psychology*. C. Crawford and D. L. Krebs, eds. Pp. 595–612. Mahwah, NJ: Lawrence Erlbaum Associates.
Slocum, S.
   1975   Woman the Gatherer: Male Bias in Anthropology. In *Toward an Anthropology of Women*. R. R. Reiter, ed. Pp. 36–50. New York: Monthly Review Press.
Smith, E. A., and B. Winterhalder, eds.
   1992   *Evolutionary Ecology and Human Behaviour*. New York: Aldine de Gruyter.
Sørensen, M. L. S.
   2000   *Gender Archaeology*. Cambridge: Polity Press.
Sperber, D.
   1996   *Explaining Culture: A Naturalistic Approach*. Oxford: Blackwell.
Stanford, C. B.
   2001   The Ape's Gift: Meat-Eating, Meat-Sharing and Human Evolution. In *Tree of Origin: What Primate Behavior Can Tell Us about Human Social Evolution*. F. B. M. de Waal, ed. Pp. 97–117. Cambridge, MA: Harvard University Press.
Steele, J., and S. Shennan, eds.
   1996   *The Archaeology of Human Ancestry: Power, Sex and Tradition*. London: Routledge.
Stein, P. L., and B. M. Rowe
   1993   *Physical Anthropology*. 5th ed. New York: McGraw-Hill.
Stern, J. T., and R. Sussman
   1983   The Locomotor Anatomy of *Australopithecus afarensis*. *American Journal of Physical Anthropology* 60:279–317.
Streier, K. B.
   2001   Beyond the Apes: Reasons to Consider the Entire Primate Order. In *Tree of Origin: What Primate Behavior Can Tell Us about Human Social Evolution*. F. B. M. de Waal, ed. Pp. 71–93. Cambridge, MA: Harvard University Press.
Tague, R., and O. Lovejoy
   1986   The Obstetric Pelvis of A. L. 288-1 (Lucy). *Journal of Human Evolution* 15(4):237–55.
Tanner, N., and A. L. Zihlman
   1976   Women in Evolution. Part I: Innovation and Selection in Human Origins. *Signs* 1(3):104–19.
Tavris, C.
   1992   *The Mismeasure of Woman*. New York: Touchstone.
Teleki, G.
   1973   *The Predatory Behavior of Wild Chimpanzees*. Lewisburg, PA: Bucknell University Press.

Thomas, J.
  1998   Some Problems with the Notion of External Symbolic Storage, and the Case
          of Neolithic Material Culture in Britain. In *Cognition and Culture: The Archaeology
          of Symbolic Storage*. C. Renfrew and C. Scarre, eds. Pp. 149–56. Cambridge:
          Cambridge University Press.
Thornhill, R., and C. T. Palmer
  2000   *A Natural History of Rape: Biological Bases of Sexual Coercion*. Cambridge, MA: MIT
          Press.
Tooby, J., and L. Cosmides
  1992   The Psychological Foundations of Culture. In *The Adapted Mind*. J. Barkow, L.
          Cosmides, and J. Tooby, eds. Pp. 19–136. New York: Oxford University
          Press.
Toth, N., and K. Schick
  1994   Early Stone Industries and Inferences regarding Language and Cognition. In
          Tools, Language and Cognition in Human Evolution. K. R. Gibson and T. Ingold,
          eds. Pp. 346–61. Cambridge: Cambridge University Press.
Tringham, R., and M. Conkey
  1998   Rethinking Figurines: A Critical View from Archaeology of Gimbutas, the
          "Goddess" and Popular Culture. In *Ancient Goddesses*. L. Goodison and C.
          Morris, eds. Pp. 22–45. London: British Museum Publications.
Trivers, R. L.
  1972   Parental Investment and Sexual Selection. In *Sexual Selection and the Descent of
          Man*. B. Campbell, ed. Pp. 136–79. Chicago: Aldine.
Vitzhum, V. J.
  1997   Flexibility and Paradox: The Evolution of a Flexibly Responsive Reproduc-
          tive System. In *The Evolving Female: A Life-History Perspective*. M. E. Morbeck, A.
          Galloway, and A. L. Zihlman, eds. Pp. 242–58. Princeton, NJ: Princeton
          University Press.
Voyer, D., et al.
  1995   Magnitude of Sex Differences in Spatial Abilities: A Meta-Analysis and Con-
          sideration of Critical Variables. *Psychological Bulletin* 117(2):250–70.
Washburn, S. L.
  1951   The Analysis of Primate Evolution with Particular Reference to the Origin
          of Man. *Cold Spring Harbor Symposia on Quantitative Biology* 15:67–78.
Washburn, S. L., and V. Avis
  1958   Evolution of Human Behavior. In *Behavior and Evolution*. A. Roe and G. G.
          Simpson, eds. Pp. 421–36. New Haven, CT: Yale University Press.
Washburn, S. L., and I. DeVore
  1961   Social Behavior of Baboons and Early Man. In *Social Life of Early Man*. S. L.
          Washburn, ed. Pp. 91–105. London: Methuen.
Washburn, S. L., and C. S. Lancaster
  1968   The Evolution of Hunting. In *Man the Hunter*. R. B. Lee and I. DeVore, eds.
          Pp. 293–303. Chicago: Aldine.

Watts, I.
  1999   The Origin of Symbolic Culture. In *The Evolution of Culture*. R. Dunbar, C. Knight, and C. Power, eds. Pp. 113–36. Edinburgh: Edinburgh University Press.
Wilson, E. O.
  1975   *Sociobiology: The New Synthesis*. Cambridge, MA: Harvard University Press.
Wrangham, R. W.
  2001   Out of the Pan, into the Fire: How Our Ancestors' Evolution Depended on What They Ate. In *Tree of Origin: What Primate Behavior Can Tell Us about Human Social Evolution*. F. B. M. de Waal, ed. Pp. 121–43. Cambridge, MA: Harvard University Press.
Wright, R.
  1994   *The Moral Animal: Why We Are the Way We Are*. London: Abacus.
Yanagisako, S., and C. Delaney
  1995   *Naturalizing Power: Essays in Feminist Cultural Analysis*. London: Routledge.
Zihlman, A. L.
  1978   Women in Evolution Part 2: Subsistence and Social Organization among Early Hominids. *Signs* 4(1):4–20.
  1981   Women as Shapers of the Human Adaptation. In *Woman the Gatherer*. F. Dahlberg, ed. Pp. 75–120. New Haven, CT: Yale University Press.
  1997a   The Paleolithic Glass Ceiling: Women in Human Evolution. In *Women in Human Evolution*. L. D. Hager, ed. Pp. 91–113. London: Routledge.
  1997b   Women's Bodies, Women's Lives: An Evolutionary Perspective. In *The Evolving Female: A Life-History Perspective*. M. E. Morbeck, A. Galloway, and A. L. Zihlman, eds. Pp. 185–97. Princeton, NJ: Princeton University Press.
  1998   Woman the Gatherer: The Role of Women in Early Hominid Evolution. In *Reader in Gender Archaeology*. K. Hays-Gilpin and D. S. Whitley, eds. Pp. 91–105. London: Routledge.

Gender Dynamics in Hunter-Gatherer Society: Archaeological Methods and Perspectives

6

HETTY JO BRUMBACH AND ROBERT JARVENPA

W HAT IS THE NATURE OF gender difference and gender relations in hunter-gatherer society? More pointedly, what is our understanding of gender dynamics in hunter-gatherer societies of the past as interpreted through archaeology?

Addressing such questions is to acknowledge some formidable obstacles. Not the least of these, for most archaeologists, is the absence of living cultural systems from which to model female and male behaviors. Conventional archaeology lacks living, breathing consultants who may offer their own interpretations of female and male lives from a cultural insider's vantage point. Ethnoarchaeological studies, as well as judicious use of analogy and inference from the ethnographic and ethnohistoric record, hold promise for bridging some of these gaps. Even so, deciphering gender patterns in societies of the remote past may be akin to "working without a net."

Based in part on biological reproductive behaviors and in part on negotiated ideology and social relations, gender is deeply rooted in all societies. As Sassaman (1992:71) argues, "Gender is the primary social variable of the labor process in forager or hunter-gatherer societies." Indeed, it may be the oldest and most fundamental distinction shaping human experience. Gender dynamics among hunter-gatherers in prehistory, therefore, are central to our understanding of the human condition at large. Since 90 percent of our species' evolutionary history occurred in the context of hunting, fishing, and foraging economies, in the absence of domestication and food production, the kinds of relationships forged between women and men in those contexts are fundamental precedents in the development of human sociocultural systems generally.

To help clarify these precedents, this chapter reviews some major themes in research on gender among prehistoric hunter-gatherers.[1] What kinds of evidence or *assumptions* have archaeologists marshaled in this effort? The distinction between evidence and assumption is not trivial. As Conkey and Spector (1984:2) observe, the archaeological literature is "permeated with assumptions, assertions, and purported statements of 'fact' about gender" despite, until recently, a disinterest in formal analysis of such matters. Because hunter-gatherers occupied the earliest and longest span of prehistory, the chasm between ethnographic-ethnohistoric patterns on the one hand and the archaeological record on the other is most daunting. This gap presents formidable challenges for analysis and uses of analogy.[2] Accordingly, we seek an understanding of both overt and implicit interpretations of gender by archaeologists and the kinds and quality of information, if any, they are based on. Several broad questions emerge from and may be asked of the literature on prehistoric hunter-gatherers:

1. What is known of the sexual division of labor?
2. Are women's and men's tools and tool kits and their uses decipherable?
3. How are women's and men's activities situated in households and other spaces?
4. What do skeletal analyses reveal about the biological, demographic, and social dimensions of women's and men's lives?

While these issues are interconnected, specific studies or particular authors may focus initial attention on one question or another. Much of the literature has a frankly materialist bias, emphasizing ecological-economic infrastructure and the social relations of production that support it.[3] What are the strengths, limitations, and omissions in this literature? What more do we need to know? Are dimensions of power, prestige, and vantage point accessible to researchers?

The Great Divide? Sexual Divisions of Labor

Perhaps more than any other topic regarding prehistoric hunter-gatherers, the sexual division of labor has been a lightning rod for inappropriate analogies, muddled models, misconceptions mired in myth, and misrepresentations of data. In part, this is because what women and men did in their daily lives—or what archaeologists think they should have been doing—is an emotional projection screen inviting a plethora of hopes, fears, and biased assumptions embedded in the gender ideology of the West (Kent 1998:39).

In conventional usage, "the sexual division of labor" refers to the rules and norms that govern assignment of work to men and women in any society. Unfortunately, much discourse on this topic, particularly when related to hunting and foraging peoples, is marred by an exclusionary tone. That is, the sexual division of labor is often presented as a list of things that women cannot do, should not do, or are prohibited from doing by men (Jarvenpa and Brumbach, in press; Nelson 1997:85–111).

Gerrymandering Gender

Some landmark anthropological literature in the 1960s crystallized prevailing attitudes of the time but also influenced a subsequent generation of archaeologists. Faithful to its title, the 1968 *Man the Hunter* volume (Lee and DeVore 1968) rather dogmatically portrayed "hunting" as the exclusive role of males. In this vision of cultural evolution, men were characterized as "cooperative hunters of big game, ranging freely and widely across the landscape" (Washburn and Lancaster 1968). This exclusively male hunter model was constructed, in part, by ignoring contradictory evidence presented in the original symposium by several ethnographers and by a questionable manipulation of the content of the five original codes for subsistence economy in Murdock's (1967:154–155, cited in Lee 1968:41) *Ethnographic Atlas.*[4]

Participants in the "Man the Hunter" symposium simply reclassified the pursuit of large aquatic animals as hunting rather than fishing, and they also redefined shellfishing as gathering rather than fishing (Lee 1968:41–42). Thus, gathering now included the harvest of wild plants, small land fauna, and shellfish. Hunting was more narrowly construed to highlight the pursuit of large and mobile animals, presumably those species capable of challenging and validating a male hunter's "masculinity." In essence, by narrowing and redefining the scope of "hunting," the symposium participants eliminated women's contributions and obscured women's very real participation in a behaviorally and culturally complex enterprise.

Dahlberg's (1981) edited volume *Woman the Gatherer* served as something of a rejoinder but did this by highlighting the role of women as the gatherers of plant foods, which often contributed more than half of some foraging peoples' subsistence in tropical and temperate environments. Thus, while one of its essays demonstrated the importance of female hunters among the Agta of the Philippines (Estioko-Griffin and Griffin 1981), the volume at large has come to be best known for its discussion of women as plant gatherers "par excellence." Unfortunately, such extreme views, rendered as mutually exclusive "man the hunter" versus "woman the gatherer" models, have come to sum up the way many archaeologists interpret the economic roles of women and men.

Despite a growing literature on the topic (Endicott 1999; Estioko-Griffin and

Griffin 1981; Kelly 1995:262–70; Leacock 1981; Nelson 1980; Turnbull 1981; Watanabe 1968), the ethnographic evidence for women as hunters, and the reality of highly flexible work roles for women and men, such information has had negligible impact on archaeologists interpreting artifacts, features, and other residues at prehistoric sites. As Conkey and Spector (1984:8) have pointed out, there is a deep-seated assumption that women in prehistory were "immobilized" by pregnancy, lactation, and child care and therefore needed to be left at a home base while the males "ranged freely and widely across the landscape."

More recently, Brightman's (1996) critique of the division of labor as presented in the literature on foraging societies persuasively rejects biological or physiological determinants of gender roles. Rather, he interprets sexual divisions of labor as somewhat arbitrary ideological constructions that operate primarily to exclude women from arenas of power and prestige dominated by men (i.e., "hunting") and that women actively collude in reproducing gender asymmetries since such arrangements may be interpreted by women not as exclusion but as entitlement and complementarity.

Brightman's constructivist argument is useful in recognizing malleability in the sexual division of labor. Yet his analysis is problematic in several ways. First, women often do not accept male ideas about gender differences within their own cultures (Buckley 1982; Counts 1985), thereby calling into question the saliency of Brightman's ideas about female exclusion or marginalization, or of women's "collusion" in such matters. Second, similar to the "Man the Hunter" symposium participants, he narrowly construes "hunting" as killing, not, as we would argue, as *a comprehensive range of logistics, pursuit, dispatch, processing, and storage activities necessitating interdependent female and male labor* (Brumbach and Jarvenpa 1997b; Jarvenpa and Brumbach 1995). Even in contexts where women directly harvest or dispatch game, Brightman (1996:723) interprets these as "exceptional" or abnormal circumstances rather than flexible, adaptive behaviors. Finally, by emphasizing arenas from which women are "excluded," Brightman has perpetuated a leitmotif that has confounded research on hunter-gatherers for decades.

Why is the sexual division of labor rarely, if ever, phrased as a list of things men cannot do, should not do, or are prohibited from doing? Why are men not frequently "excluded" from vital food processing, storage, and distribution operations or from hide and clothing manufacture? In our review of the archaeological studies that follow, therefore, we invite the reader to invert familiar questions or tropes so that one may begin seeing the sexual division of labor more positively as the complex and variegated subsistence tasks *actually performed* by women and men regardless of, and sometimes in contradiction to, the normative constructions of gender fostered by their own cultures.

Behavioral Ecology Arguments

Among these tropes is the notion that specialized male hunting strategies for pro-curing meat have a long evolutionary history in the genus *Homo* (Smith 1999). One rendering of this idea by human behavioral ecologists is the "show-off" model of male hunting, viewing it essentially as a prestige activity linked to sexual selection (Winterhalder 2001). Such gene-centric paradigms raise many vexing questions that cannot be fully addressed here: Why is "showing off" (or the closely allied "costly signaling") not also provisioning? Is "prestige" simply the vehicle by which genes reproduce themselves? Is male hunting the only meaningful route to "prestige" in human society?

Other behavioral ecologists, however, note that women and men may seek different arrays of prey or resources in order to achieve different genetic fitness goals (Hill and Kaplan 1993).[5] Zeanah (2004) adopts the latter perspective for interpreting the division of labor and settlement patterns in the Late Holocene Carson Desert of western Nevada. Employing central place foraging models, he concludes that men logistically hunted out of residential bases that were situated to facilitate women's foraging activities in resource-rich wetland zones. Arguably, this arrangement was a way of reconciling conflicting subsistence interests between the sexes. This contrasts with previous views of Great Basin prehistory that have posited wholesale replacements of mobile hunters with semisedentary gathering peoples (Bettinger and Baumhoff 1982).[6]

Zeanah's argument also challenges Hildebrandt and McGuire's (2002) spe-cific hypothesis that "show-off"-style, prestige-based, large game hunting by men was increasing across California and the western Great Basin between 4000 and 1000 B.P. In prior archaeological research in California, these same authors sug-gested that a "lack of gender polarity" in the division of labor had considerable antiquity. The pervasiveness of plant and seed-grinding "milling stones" in a range of early site contexts, they argue, indicates interchangeability or a lack of task specialization by sex (McGuire and Hildebrandt 1994).

Flexibility in Women's Work

Other archaeologists, such as Wadley (1998) in South Africa and Bird (1993) in Australia, have made insightful reappraisals of the ethnographic and ethnohistoric records for their respective areas to demonstrate indigenous women's complex and widespread involvement in a range of hunting activities, including direct har-vesting of both small and large game animals, as well as toolmaking, gathering, and food processing.[7] Such fine-grained information runs counter to simple or stereotyped views of the division of labor and, thus, may be used as a source of models for more nuanced interpretations of the prehistory of South Africa and Australia. Wadley, for example, sees women's involvement as "meat providers" as highly variable and flexible. No doubt, such roles shifted along with changing gender relations linked to environmental and economic changes in Pleistocene and post-Pleistocene South Africa.

In some instances, arguments can be made for women's dominance in the direct harvest phase of activities like shellfishing, an important source of animal protein. Ethnohistoric documents attest to women's contributions in this area. Accordingly, Claassen's (1991) analysis of the Shell Mound Archaic, extending back to 8,000 B.P. in the southeastern United States, places women in a central position in the subsistence economy and society generally. Extensive shell heaps at Archaic sites, along with associated burials exhibiting preferential ritual treatment of females, suggest a prominent role for women as shellfishers. In a related study, Moss (1993) argues that while a variety of shellfish species were important food resources for prehistoric Tlingit society on the Northwest Coast, they were avoided by high-status individuals because of negative associations with laziness, poverty, and ritual impurity. There was also the danger of paralytic shellfish poisoning. Moss effectively integrates ethnographic and ethnohistoric accounts with archaeological evidence to suggest that, among Tlingit of commoner status, women depended on shellfish more than men.

While women's roles in hunting have been ignored, ironically, there is also a parallel danger in overlooking or misinterpreting the archaeological evidence for women's gathering activities. Vinsrygg (1987), for example, argues for a reinterpretation of bored or perforated stones in Stone Age sites from the Rogaland district of Norway. Rather than accepting these as "clubs" or war symbols, she interprets them as weights for digging sticks likely used by women and even children for uprooting plants in coastal areas.

Our own ethnoarchaeological work with the Chipewyan in the Canadian subarctic reveals that women's roles are far more flexible and expansive than previously believed. Women as well as men directly harvest a variety of mammals and fish. Moreover, hunting needs to be seen in context as part of a complex system of travel, preparation, and logistics preceding harvests or kills and the intricacies of butchering, processing, and distribution following kills. This full spectrum of activity is most appropriately seen as "hunting," an enterprise that produces food, clothing, tools, and other necessities of life and that requires the interdependence of female and male labor in any foraging society (Brumbach and Jarvenpa 1997b; Jarvenpa and Brumbach 1995). In a similar vein, Frink's (2002) ethnoarchaeological research among Cup'ik in western Alaska demonstrates the prominent role of women in managing multigenerational fish camps where they make complex decisions about processing and storage of fish according to species, intensity of spawning runs, and time of year. A material manifestation of this activity, albeit invisible to conventional archaeology, is women's cutting of their ownership marks on fish tails.

Ember (1975) and Hiatt (1978) assembled cross-cultural data to demonstrate an inverse correlation between men's contribution to subsistence and effective temperature. Simply put, men tend to procure more food in colder, high-latitude environments, while women's direct harvesting of food resources increases in warmer, low-latitude settings. Lee's (1968, 1979) influential work among the !Kung San, for example, demonstrates that two-thirds of the diet is plant foods gathered by women. In many other low-latitude environments, women's *and* men's plant gathering contributes significantly to the diet. Despite their prominence in gathering and also domestication of plant species from wild progenitors (Watson and Kennedy 1991), however, women receive only grudging respect for these accomplishments by archaeologists. This devaluation may derive, in part, from a Western recreational "sport hunting" model of behavior that accords prestige to those who vanquish large, dangerous animals, not to the gatherers of sessile plants.

As Halperin (1980) and Kelly (1995:262–65) argue, however, modeling subsistence as *procurement* only distorts the real labor contributions of women in processing and storing food resources, particularly in the high latitudes. Our comparative ethnoarchaeological studies in circumpolar communities reinforce this point (Jarvenpa and Brumbach 2006, in press). If archaeology is to achieve a basic understanding of women's and men's livelihoods in the past, we contend, the field must abandon Eurocentric prestige hierarchies when analyzing who did what. A preoccupation with and privileging of male hunting or even of female gathering shifts the scholarly gaze away from comprehensive social systems of provisioning toward questionable scenarios of individualistic competition and valor. We will return to these issues in the conclusion.

Tools of the Trade: Women's and Men's Gear

As discussed in the previous section, both women and men were involved in the performance of a wide range of tasks, including the harvesting of food and non-food resources, and the conversion of these items into clothing, tools, crafts items, and numerous other useful products. In order to carry out these tasks, both women and men manufactured and used a variety of tools, implements, and carriers. Part of the sexual division of labor includes the kinds and uses of such tools and facilities. Fortunately, these artifacts comprise a major part of the archaeological record left behind by hunter-gatherers.

Gender Asymmetry in Tool Visibility

Nonetheless, there appears to be significant gender asymmetry in the "visibility" of men's and women's tools and activities. Hayden (1992:42) writes, "If women have frequently been neglected in prehistory, it has largely been because of the difficulty of distinguishing their activities from males on the basis of stone tools." While this may be an accurate assessment of gender "visibility," the caution has not been applied evenly to women and men by the discipline. Most stone tools are simply assumed to have been made by men, leaving the reader to conclude that women did not make stone tools or that their tools are hard to "identify." In reviewing stone-tool manufacture, Torrence (2001:91) observes, "The gendering of hunter-gatherer stone technology has until recently been considered to be relatively unproblematic: men have been assumed to be the major, if not the only, makers and users of stone artefacts."

Some portrayals of the past have characterized the manufacture of tools and implements along stereotyped and immutable lines similar to the "man the hunter/woman the gatherer" dichotomy. For example, it has been argued that men manufactured tools of hard materials (e.g., stone, bone, antler, and ivory) while women made objects of soft items (e.g., plant fibers and animal skins) or that men made hunting and fighting weapons (e.g., knives, spear tips, and projectile points) while women produced containers and domestic items (e.g., baskets, clothing, infant carriers, and pottery). More extreme positions have emphatically argued that stone-tool manufacture was largely the occupation of men and, therefore, that most tools recovered and studied by archaeologists were made by men. Such fanciful characterizations fail to capture the behavioral realities of actual people.

While assignment of any specific tool to one gender or the other is difficult or even impossible, archaeologists rarely have problems attributing tools to men. The real crux appears to be making such attributions to women. Women are denied credit as users and producers of tools by various means. First, by (over)-emphasizing problems relating to poor preservation of organic materials, women's tools and women's production are made hard to find. Women are "hard to see" in the archaeological record, goes the argument, because women predominated in the working of soft, organic substances, which are poorly preserved. In contrast, men presumably excelled at the production of stone tools, which are more likely to be preserved. These simplistic statements about who used what materials in prehistory, however, are just as shortsighted as statements about who performed which economic activities.

Where preservation is unusually favorable, including sites characterized by extreme cold or aridity, objects of organic materials have been preserved (Ellender 1993). For example, the village site Ozette in Washington state was covered by a mud slide that preserved thousands of objects of wood and other organic material, including building materials, wooden bowls and spoons, basketry, and other craft items, thus providing a more complete picture of the material assemblage of the site's occupants. At other sites in cold and/or arid regions, preserved materials have included animal skin, wood, textiles (e.g., Ellender 1993), and even mummified remains of the people themselves. When these fuller inventories are available, it is possible to assess a broad spectrum of tools made from a variety of materials both hard and soft. Such information is a more realistic platform for interpreting the complexities of women's and men's tools and tool use.

Another way in which archaeology has colluded to exclude women from the ranks of "tool users" is by trivializing and devaluing artifacts that are attributed to women. Even when preserved, objects of organic materials are rarely accorded much respect unless they are recovered in very large numbers, such as at Ozette. For example, what is arguably the best-known bone tool from North America, the caribou leg bone hide scraper from Old Crow Flats, Yukon Territory, originally dated to 27,000 ± 3000 years B.P., was once characterized as undoubtedly "a tool created by human hands" (Jennings 1983:45). The artifact quickly faded from attention after it was more accurately dated to recent times. Yet its likely manufacture and use by a woman (the leg bone hide scraper is a quintessentially woman's tool in the ethnographic subarctic) was not considered relevant. After all, women were hard to see in the archaeological record. The object's relevance to archaeology was only its reputed antiquity.

Problems of Gender Attribution

Bird (1993:22) argues that since the economic and social roles of men and women are not biologically determined but vary both cross-culturally and through time, it "follows that in any given cultural context . . . the distribution of economic and social roles by gender should not be assumed, but rather seen as a problem worthy of exploration in its own right." Similar arguments can be made for the question of who made what tools. While gender attribution for the manufacture of specific tools may not always be possible, archaeologists should approach each situation as a fresh problem requiring a probing interpretation. This is illustrated by Wadley's (1998:80–81) residue analysis of stone tools from the South African site of Rose Cottage Cave, in which both blood and plant residues are frequently present on a single stone flake (based on Williamson's [1996] study), suggesting that a single person might be involved with both meat butchery and plant food processing. Stone flakes from another South African site, Jubilee Shelter, might have been used as arrowheads on occasion but also had plant polish on their cutting edges. Of course, the presence of plant polish does not imply that such tools were not used by men, but it does suggest that no secure gender attribution can be made (Wadley 1998:80–81).

Woman the Toolmaker

The assumption that women do not make stone tools, especially the large, formalized bifaces used for hunting and warfare, is often expressed (or implied) in the archaeological literature (see discussion in Bird 1993; Gero 1991). As Gero (1991:168) states, "The restrictive and self-fulfilling definition of stone tools as formal, standardized tools central to male activities leads to an anthropological overstatement about the importance attached to weapons, extractive tools, and hunting paraphernalia." Simply put, stone tools are *prescribed* as male by the profession. Observations of women manufacturing and using stone tools are further dismissed as "exceptions" (Bird 1993:22). In a manner parallel to gerrymandering women out of "hunting" by redefining the pursuit of small game as "collecting," the archaeological literature defines "stone tools" as elaborately produced items that are standardized, classifiable, and reproduced forms. Expedient stone tools, such as "unretouched flakes," used by women in the production of craft items are defined not as tools but as by-products from the manufacture of "real" tools (Gero 1991:165). Gero (1991), in perhaps the most influential assault on the "man the toolmaker" construct, appropriately broadens the concept of "stone tool." She insightfully notes that women can and do make stone implements but that archaeology simply does not value expedient tools as much as formalized bifaces, particularly projectile points.

Presumptions about gender hierarchy in prehistoric tool production and use parallel attitudes toward hunting and foraging work. While women may be responsible for obtaining the bulk of the food in many societies, high prestige is still accorded to the hunting of large game (particularly by archaeologists if not the hunters themselves) even when these resources provide only a small portion of a community's food supply. As a discipline, archaeology has failed to adequately address this apparent contradiction. While this issue cannot be explored in depth here, big game hunting and the apparent "prestige" that surrounds it would certainly benefit from a more probing and critical examination, one not limited by the tenets of evolutionary ecology. Gero (1991) discusses the inordinate attention paid in the literature to tools that are presumed to have been made by men for the specific purpose of killing large game animals. Such fixation on the dispatch phase of hunting is part of a Western recreational "sport hunting" model that distorts and grossly simplifies life and livelihood in hunter-forager economies (Jarvenpa and Brumbach, in press). In turn, the fascination with large, dangerous game animals has also affected, indeed compromised, archaeology's approach to the manufacture of tools.

Hunting Methods and Technologies

Archaeology's long-standing preoccupation with the dramatic confrontation of man and beast is strongly suggestive of the lurid cover art seen on some men's magazines. If hunting is to be interpreted as "male macho drama" (Gero 1993), women are excluded since a female protagonist would spoil the fun for the real men. But is this how hunting was carried out in prehistory?

More attention needs to be paid to the methods and techniques actually used by hunters of both large and small game animals. While the "man the hunter" mythos emphasizes dramatic confrontation with the large and dangerous, ethnographic and ethnohistoric accounts reveal the importance of other methods such as drives, ambushes at river crossings, poison, snares, nets, dogs, clubs, and many other techniques not characterized by direct confrontation (Casey 1998; Kehoe 1990; Kent 1998; Wadley 1998).

Kehoe (1990) notes that objects of organic materials like ropes, strings, thongs, or others she terms "lines" play pivotal roles in the harvest phase of hunting. In support of this, she cites research carried out by others, including J. E. Lips (1947), a field ethnographer among the Montagnais-Naskapi who studied critically appropriate hunting techniques. According to Kehoe (1990:27), Lips "knew that using a projectile—whether it be one pointed with stone or bone or a bullet—is the last and sometimes omitted stage of hunting, the climax after the hunters have managed to place themselves in close proximity to their prey." The devices for attaining proximity include a variety of traps, nets, and snares constructed with string, thong, and rope, that is, Kehoe's "lines." The production of ropes and lines requires the use of implements such as awls, netting shuttles, and mat and netting needles, among other tools, generally employed by women.

To illustrate the kinds of tools and implements made with the use of lines as well as tools used to manufacture the lines, Kehoe draws on Osgood's (1940) study of Ingalik material culture. More than 200 items, or almost two-thirds of the Ingalik material culture inventory, include lines in their manufacture (Osgood 1940:435; cited in Kehoe 1990:26). Kehoe believes this technology has great antiquity and demonstrates similarities between European Upper Paleolithic bone tools and the Ingalik implements described by Osgood for stripping and sewing bark and for making nets, baskets, and mats. No doubt, more awareness and study of lines would elevate women's "visibility" in the archaeological record while recognizing a larger repertoire of hunting methods and techniques employed by prehistoric peoples.

Stone-Tool Use by Women

Although fragmentary in places and often written from a male perspective, ethnohistoric and ethnographic accounts of hunter-gatherer societies document a variety of tools and materials made and used by both women and men. In societies where hunted animals make up a large part of the diet, women have been observed using large knives, hatchets, pounding stones, and other tools of hard material to butcher, pulverize, and otherwise process animal carcasses and products (Jarvenpa and Brumbach 1995, 2006). That women would attempt to butcher an animal the size of a caribou or moose, not to mention a walrus or whale, with only a utilized flake is absurd fantasy, although such tools are suitable for tailoring skin garments and other fine work. For primary butchering, large knives, hatchets, and hammerstones are far more efficient.

Bird's (1993:26) review of ethnoarchaeological studies in Australia reinforces this point. For example, Gould (1980, cited by Bird 1993:27) observes that flake knives are used by women at least as much as by men. In a related vein, Gero (1991) reviews Gould's Australian research to reveal how ethnoarchaeology can impose a male bias on stone-tool production. Thus, while Gould (1977) acknowledges use of flake knives by both genders, only males and male tasks are systematically observed.

Ethnoarchaeological research in arctic and subarctic societies demonstrates women's direct involvement in tool use and manufacture, although few stone tools are part of contemporary toolkits. Large game animals are frequently butchered by women, who use metal knives and hatchets as the tools of choice for disarticulating large sections and joints. Chipewyan women have special purpose tools for preparing animal skin hides. Today, these tools are made of wood, bone, metal, string, and leather thong (Jarvenpa and Brumbach 1995:66). Hide-making tools are wrapped in bundles of canvas, duck, or heavy cotton tightly wrapped with cord or cloth strips and stored for safekeeping.[8] The moose and caribou long bone hide scrapers in these kits are similar in form to the Old Crow Flats caribou bone flesher discussed previously. Chipewyan women also maintain log smoking and storage caches where they keep large pounding stones for pulverizing dried meat and fish and hatchets used to break up animal long bones for bone grease (Jarvenpa and Brumbach 1995:62–65).

Women in warmer, low-latitude environments also manufacture and use tools of stone and other hard materials that would be recoverable archaeologically. Gorman (1995) discusses the Andaman Islanders' interesting reversal of "traditional" sex roles in that women make stone tools, although these are used for non–food quest purposes, namely, head shaving, tattooing, and scarifying. By contrast, Andamanese men's hunting tool kits are made without lithic material but rather include implements of bamboo, wood, shell, bone, and iron.

Bird (1993:23–25) and McKell (1993) detail accounts of Australian Aboriginal women making and using tools of rough and chipped stone as well as wood. These implements were employed in a variety of tasks: cutting meat, making stone hatchets, and shaping and finishing wooden implements such as bowls, digging sticks, and fighting sticks. The hatchets were multipurpose tools used for collecting foodstuffs like honey, edible grubs, and small game. Moreover, Bird (1993:24–25) notes reports of Australian women making stone points for spears and of Tasmanian women not only making stone tools but also quarrying the stone, a toolmaking activity rarely attributed to women. Ellender (1993) describes an ossuary burial of a woman in Australia where dry conditions helped preserve organic mortuary items and other tools including a bark-fiber net bag, emu bones fashioned into split-bone knives, a quartz core, and two flakes.

A Tiwi woman on Bathurst Island used a ground edge ax while hunting that she had made herself. After describing women's use of stone tools to make digging sticks, McKell (1993:116–17) concludes, "If these stone axes were to be excavated in Australia today the archaeologist would almost always assume that they were used by men as primary tools and again by men to make secondary tools for women." As noted previously, the desire to prescribe stone tools as male is a powerful bias.

No Place Like Home: Activity Areas and Household Organization

In hunter-gatherer populations, the household is more than a reflection of society. One might argue that it *is* society. For most hunter-gatherers, the household is the center of resource production, and male–female relations form the core of economic, social, and political arrangements linking communities of households. Gender-related household or activity area analysis has been a productive research strategy for archaeologists working in arctic and subarctic contexts, for example.

Gendered Households

Reinhardt (2002) offers a statistical reanalysis and reinterpretation of a prehistoric Iñupiat subterranean dwelling destroyed by an ice override in Barrow, Alaska.

While the remarkable preservation at this well-documented site permits detailed studies of artifactual remains and architecture, Reinhardt is self-contemplative in discussing the decisions, problems, and contradictions he grappled with in converting excavated objects into quantifiable "data." He argues that the spatial distribution of artifactual material does not support earlier ideas of a clear partitioning of the dwelling into female and male "sides" or sitting areas (Newell 1984). Rather, women and children may have used most of the house floor area, with men and boys returning from a *qargi*, or men's house, to the family dwelling essentially to sleep, a pattern consistent with the ethnography of this region. Ultimately, Reinhardt urges caution in assigning gender usage or ownership to tools and residues.

In a related vein, LeMoine's (2003) analysis of Late Dorset household architecture in the eastern Canadian arctic reveals significant parallels and differences in gender roles as compared with those known from historic or ethnographic Inuit culture. In both contexts, arguably, women were the souls of the house and significant intermediaries between hunters and the animals they pursued. In the Late Dorset period, however, women may have participated more intensively in direct harvesting of small game, in sharing of labor in larger dual- or multifamily households, and in maintaining community ties during pronounced seasonal aggregations. Particularly important in this interpretation are axial features and associated hearth rows in dwellings, loci of women's activity. In LeMoine's view, women were integral to a reoccupation of the high arctic during Late Dorset times.

Whitridge (2002:172) also identifies examples of gendered space in a Classic Thule whaling village. His interpretation of the archaeological site of Qariaraqyuk, Somerset Island, identifies a detached kitchen wing he characterizes as "concealing and marginalizing a major locus of women's activities" and a *qargi* (men's communal house) that "replaced the family dwelling as the major architectural locus of men's activities." It is not entirely clear why specialized male space is interpreted as evidence for higher status while female space is interpreted as a decline in, or at least a realignment of, women's status and authority. Our own work on transformations in hunting and use of domestic space among the subarctic Chipewyan in the nineteenth and twentieth centuries indicates that increased specialization and separation of male and female economic roles does not necessarily lead to marginalization of women (Brumbach and Jarvenpa 1997a).

Asymmetries of Power?

Whitridge assumes that men derive prestige from whaling as well as from the trade goods obtained from the exchange of surplus whale products. But he makes several assumptions that need to be examined, including the notion that only men participated in the actual whale "hunt." If men indeed dominated the direct harvest phase of whale hunting, can we assume that women controlled much of the processing phases of hunting—that is, converting the carcasses into both subsistence products and valuable trade items as well as storing, managing, and distributing food? The possibility of the latter scenario gains support from ethnographic evidence from Yup'ik Eskimo communities where women not only directly harvested half the community food supply but also were regarded as the owners of the food as they dominated its storage, preparation, and distribution (Ackerman 1990). Moreover, regarding matters of domestic space, the Yup'ik men's houses actually may have contributed to men's isolation and marginalization by dispersing and separating men from their kin of both genders (Bogojavlensky and Fuller 1973).

Even so, Whitridge's work at Qariaraqyuk reminds us that the distinction between complementary gender differences and emergent asymmetries of power can be subtle. As he notes, Thule "women and men deployed their preciosities in different discursive genres, competing in effect for different kinds of cultural capital" (Whitridge 2002:190). Although this sounds like complementary gender equality, his argument about the prominent position of men in interregional systems of exchange of exotic metals points to growing differences in power and status. Whether one prefers to view this as emergent "complexity" or emergent "social asymmetry," we concur that as a fundamental structuring principle in all foraging and hunting societies, gender has been largely overlooked as a starting point for intensification and specialization in labor. We will return to the thorny issue of power and status in the concluding section of this chapter.

Somewhat different interpretations are reached in Hoffman's (2002) study of Unangan Aleut bone needles recovered from houses, among other archaeological contexts. His experiments on the production of both eyed and grooved needle forms spurred his conclusion that a change over time to grooved needles resulted from the desire of women seamstresses to produce exceptionally fine decorated clothing and gut-skin parkas. From this perspective, the garments became important status items in aboriginal trade networks and were exchanged for prestige goods like iron and amber.

Hoffman's excavations reveal concentrations of sewing needles in *large houses*, providing the connection between craft production and high-status households and, in turn, women's pivotal role in sociopolitical organization. This perspective contrasts with Whitridge in that women are seen as taking an active and conscious role in the design and production of useful tools and the crafting of high-status trade goods. In Hoffman's view, Unangan women actively participated in trade networks and gained prestige and exotic goods for themselves and their families and households.

Historical Archaeological Approaches

Other scholars have probed hunter-gatherer household organization and gender dynamics via historical archaeology and ethnoarchaeology. In such research, complementary data sets drawn from historical documents and/or native consultants' behaviors and testimony may be used to enhance interpretations of archaeological residues. Shepard's (2002) study of nineteenth-century Kuskokwim communities in Alaska analyzes changes in household social organization and division of labor triggered by European missionization. She argues that in nonstratified societies, house structures provide the clearest expression of "materialized ideology," their generalized design and layout reflecting the community's social values and ideals, a perspective shared by LeMoine (2003).

Men's and women's activities on the Kuskokwim prior to missionization were segregated into large *qasgi* (men's dormitory, communal center, and bathhouse) and small separate houses for women and children. One impact of missionization was the gradual abandonment of the *qasgi*, with the mission church becoming the focus of ceremonial life. In turn, men and women began to occupy the same domestic space, ultimately leading to a modification of dwellings and a reorientation of the spatial dimensions of activity performance.

Shepard notes that more archaeological study of mid- to late nineteenth-century houses, including the poorly documented *qasgi*, or men's house, will be needed to assess whether women's and men's living, work, and storage spaces indeed became smaller and more commingled through time. Nonetheless, Shepard's work poses a provocative question well worth pursuing in the archaeology of hunter-gatherers at large: do changes in ideas (missionization) produce changes in behavior (gender relations) that are identifiable archaeologically?

In the case of the Chipewyan of northwestern Saskatchewan, historical changes in the hunting economy, involving increased settlement centralization and logistical organization, were accompanied by a proliferation and specialization in processing and storage facilities by gender (*loretthe kwae*, or women's log smoking caches, and *t'asi thelaikoe*, or men's log storehouses)—changes that made women's special-purpose structures more visible archaeologically (Brumbach and Jarvenpa 1997a; Jarvenpa and Brumbach 1999). From this perspective, and allowing for cross-cultural differences in architecture, divergence in female and male spaces and facilities may imply increasing gender specialization but *not necessarily* marginalization of women.[9]

Household studies do not always yield clear or coherent interpretations. Shepard, for example, noted some of the unexpected patterning of faunal remains in the nineteenth-century Koyukon houses excavated by Clark (1996). In Koyukon magico-religious thought, premenopausal women are tabooed from contact with spiritually powerful bears, thus requiring an explanation for the presence of bear remains in house floors that presumably once accommodated families with women present. Aside from invoking exceptional circumstances, such as inhabiting the houses with female shamans or Iñupiat occupants, there is also the possibility—as in most societies—that some degree of behavioral flexibility operated in spite of or in contradiction to ideal norms and proscriptions.

Ambiguities and Subtleties

Indeed, the latter point is nicely reinforced by Janes's (1983) ethnoarchaeological investigations among the Willow Lake Slavey of northern Canada. While a division of labor with men as hunters and women as food processors and preparers is emphasized in Slavey ideology, *behavioral realities* are another matter. Across thirty-eight major categories of subsistence activities, nearly 35 percent of the tasks are performed by children and adults of both sexes. These include small mammal hunting, setting and checking fish nets, plucking and gutting fowl, and processing furs, among others. This flexibility and mastery of a wide range of skills by women, men, and children is highly adaptive in a demanding subarctic environment. Yet the archaeological implications may be less encouraging, at least at the intrahousehold level. As Janes (1983:79) notes, "The fact that activity areas are all nearly multifunctional at Willow Lake precludes the existence of sex-specific spaces."

In a rather novel approach to domestic space, Cooke (1998) uses hypothesized travel routes and contour lines for inferring women's and children's presence at large open prehistoric campsites in a seasonally occupied mountainous region of the Cooleman Plain of Australia. She argues that women with small children and elderly people negotiated the gentler gradients linking camps characterized by their large size and artifact diversity. While younger men may have been present at these camps, Cooke suggests they were also traversing the country via steeper routes and using camps characterized by smaller size and lesser artifact diversity.

Kent (1998) grapples insightfully with "invisibility" or lack of clear gender patterning in the spatial arrangement of residues at Late Stone Age and Early Iron Age sites in southern Africa. In the former case, she argues that early foragers simply may not have organized their culture by gender. While gendered spaces may have been of greater significance for Early Iron Age people, however, they remain elusive to the archaeologist because artifacts and features have not been provenienced with sufficient detail to allow such analysis. Kent notes that the reality of changing gender relations over time requires flexible cross-cultural ethnographic or ethnoarchaeological models for interpreting the past. Her proposition "that a consistent relationship exists between the rigidity of a division of labor that influences the use of space and objects by gender and a society's sociopolitical complexity" is an exemplar of such modeling (Kent 1998:40–41).

In a similar vein, Wadley (2000) cautions against the temptation to impose San ethnographic models on spatial patterning at Stone Age sites in South Africa. In examining the distributions of ostrich shell beads, bone points, hearths, grindstones, scrapers, flakes, and animal bone fragments, she argues that there is no compelling reason to view such spatial patterning as the product of a gendered division of labor. Rather, Wadley recommends recognition of the possibility that activities in the past may have been organized along lines of age, ability, or status, with gender distinctions playing a comparatively minor role.

Afterlife: Skeletal and Bioarchaeological Analysis

Differences in the lives of women and men often can be assessed from analyses of human skeletal remains. Cohen and Bennett (1993) summarize a range of such studies that shed light on gendered patterns of labor, physical injuries and trauma, infection and disease, nutrition, childhood stress, reproduction, and mortality, among other processes. Nonetheless, gender differences can be difficult to interpret by such means. Not enough is known about "natural" patterns to confidently differentiate between the effects of gender constructs and biological patterns. For example, there is uncertainty about how the sexes absorb nutrition, how they respond to stress, the manner in which stress is recorded, differential nutritional needs between males and females, and the confounding influence of greater stresses on women due to pregnancy and lactation (Cohen and Bennett 1993:283–84). However, despite these challenges, skeletal analysis may be a productive and insightful way of comparing the lives of women and men.

Gendered Patterns of Arthritis

Gender-specific patterns of degenerative arthritis and/or robusticity of the skeleton is one method of determining the presence and rigidity of a division of labor (Cohen and Bennett 1993). The pattern or location of degenerative joint disease may also allow inferences concerning the nature of the activities that a person engaged in while living.

Because of the difficulties of distinguishing "natural" patterns from gendered and/or cultural patterns, many studies compare skeletal health of hunter-gatherer populations with that of later agricultural peoples in the same area. According to Cohen and Bennett (1993), degenerative joint disease (DJD) and osteophytosis (arthritic changes in the spine) have been shown to increase through time as agriculture is adopted and intensified, suggesting that agriculture led to an increase in workload and physical stress when compared to the work regime of hunter-gatherers. At Dickson Mounds, Illinois, rates of both DJD and osteophytosis increased over time with the adoption of agriculture and was found to be more severe for males than for females (Goodman et al. 1984, cited in Cohen and Bennett 1993:277–78). However, a different pattern was observed at sites in Kentucky. While males from the Archaic period Indian Knoll population exhibited more pronounced vertebral arthritis than males from the later Mississippian period Hardin site, rates for females remained similar over time or increased (Cassidy 1984, cited in Cohen and Bennett 1993:278). These data suggest that not all hunter-gatherer populations were subjected to similar work stresses and that the sexual division of labor was not structured similarly across all hunter-gatherer populations.

A series of sites in Illinois dating from 6000 B.C. to A.D. 1200 indicate increased severity of arthritis for women in later populations than for the earlier Archaic populations, although the *pattern* of arthritis on the skeleton did not change. Males from these sites did not display an increase in severity, but the pattern of arthritis changed. These data suggest that women performed the same kinds of activities but in intensified form with the transition to agriculture, whereas men's work tasks changed without necessarily intensifying (Cook 1984, cited in Cohen and Bennett 1993:278). The transition to agriculture appears to have contributed to increased rates and severity of degenerative arthritis for some but not all populations as well as to changes in the patterns of arthritis (Cohen and Bennett 1993:278).

Hollimon (1992) compared skeletal populations of the fishing-collecting Chumash and the agricultural Arikara and found different patterns of DJD in both populations. Hollimon attributes these differences to divisions of labor according to gender in both populations. The percentage of Chumash men and women displaying degenerative changes was roughly equal, while Arikara males displayed almost twice the rate of DJD as Arikara females. The latter statistic may be due to a roughly seven-year difference of average age at death between Arikara males and females, with the males living longer. Among the Chumash,

Early Period women had more severe arthritis in their knees and spines than did Early Period men, while the men had more severe arthritis in their shoulders, elbows, and hands. These differences are attributed to a sexual division of labor among the Early Period Chumash where women used digging sticks and grinding implements to procure and process plant foods, while men used other tools to hunt and fish. Late Period (after A.D. 1150) women and men had similar patterns of DJD, suggesting more flexibility in gender roles. Ethnographic information from the historic period indicates that women and men were members of guilds of specialists, the membership of which cross-cut age and sex categories (Hollimon 1991).

Access to Food Resources

A common assumption regarding the consequences of a sexual division of labor among hunter-gatherers is that men and women have differential access to food resources (see note 6). It has been assumed that males, being hunters, have greater access to meat or better parts of meat because they might eat portions of the kill immediately or that women are excluded from consuming the best parts of carcasses or that women have greater access to plant foods. However, access to meat or plant foods by women and men varies considerably among different hunter-gatherer populations. Ethnographic and ethnohistoric accounts indicate that men frequently gather plant foods and that women may participate in hunts or have direct access to small game, fish, shellfish, birds, turtles, and other species that they snare or collect. Chipewyan women, who predominate in rabbit snaring, for example, often take a rest at the end of their snare line and cook one of the rabbits for a meal (Jarvenpa and Brumbach 1995:69–70). In many societies where women handle most of the processing, preservation, and management of stored foods, women may have greater access to a variety of food supplies than do men. While there does not appear to be any broad pattern of differential access to foods by gender, specific populations may demonstrate gendered differences. Some of the implications of such behaviors for nutrition in prehistory can be addressed by paleopathologists and bone chemists (Cohen and Bennett 1983).

Wadley (1998) discusses stable carbon isotope composition of human bone collagen as a marker of differences in diet, attributed to gendered work patterns and gendered access to foods. A study of skeletons from Western Cape, southern Africa, revealed few gender differences in the pre-3000 B.P. material. Stable carbon isotope compositions remained similar for both pre-3000 B.P. and post-3000 B.P. samples of female skeletons. However, the bone chemistry shifted for males of the later period. These data were interpreted to suggest that after 3000 B.P., labor became more gendered and that men ate more seal meat, fish, and other marine foods away from a home base (Sealy et al. 1992, cited in Wadley 1998:77).

Despite the previously cited changes in access to resources, studies of nutritional health among hunter-gatherer and agricultural women and men demonstrate better nutrition for the former. Cohen and Bennett (1993:281) summarize several studies of women's skeletal health that demonstrate that women in prehistoric hunter-gatherer societies suffered less from a variety of problems than did their counterparts in agricultural societies. Symptoms of anemia and other nutritional disorders, pathological bone loss, and premature osteoporosis were more pronounced in women in agricultural societies. A comparison between hunter-gatherer and agricultural skeletal samples in the Levant revealed premature osteoporosis among women in the agricultural populations (Smith et al. 1984, cited in Cohen and Bennett 1993:281). In contrast, women in the earlier Paleolithic and Mesolithic populations exhibited significantly less, if any, bone loss. Even so, such trends need to be carefully evaluated to assess the impact of increased fertility and its stresses on women in agricultural populations.

The transition to agriculture also witnessed an increase in the rates of dental caries, which were rare in earlier human populations (Cohen and Bennett 1993:281). Since diets high in carbohydrates yield higher rates of caries than diets high in fats and protein, frequencies of caries can provide dietary assessments. Walker and Erlandson's (1986) study of skeletal populations from the Northern Channel, California, uses frequencies of dental caries as an index of the ratio of proteins to carbohydrates in the diet. In earlier populations (3000–4000 B.P.), females exhibit higher rates of dental caries than do males. The authors attribute this difference to a sexual division of labor in which men had greater access to high-protein animal food through hunting while women gathered plant foods. The exploitation of plant foods is evidenced by the recovery of stone digging-stick weights used for harvesting roots and tubers. In the later part of the sequence (1820–450 B.P.), the rates of caries in men and women become more similar, a change the authors attribute to a decline in the dietary significance of plant foods and an increase among both sexes of protein, especially from small fish.

Discussion and Conclusion

Several significant generalizations about gender dynamics and the nature of work among prehistoric hunter-gatherers have emerged from the research and literature to date. The division of labor was highly variable and more flexible than commonly assumed, both within and across populations. There was no rigid or universally applicable "man the hunter/woman the gatherer" protocol, even with respect to the narrower scope of food procurement (i.e., ignoring food processing, storage, and distribution). Indeed, divisions of labor occasionally followed lines of age, ability, and experience, among other factors, rather than gender per se.

The variability and flexibility in work roles noted previously is generally supported by skeletal evidence. While arthritis and other paleopathologies afflicted women and men differently within some populations, there is no consistent gender patterning in pathologies across populations that might suggest a universal or rigid separation of female and male workloads and behaviors. Moreover, the intensification and gendered patterning of some diseases accompanying the transition to agriculture only serve to underscore the more variable and fluid situation for hunter-gatherers.

Variability and flexibility in work roles is also supported by information drawn from activity area and household analyses. While female and male sitting areas, men's houses, women's kitchen wings, and other gendered spaces are occasionally decipherable in some archaeological contexts, there is also ample evidence for widespread commingling of men's and women's activities and work areas or, alternatively, organization of work and space along lines other than gender.

Assignment of static gender categories (e.g., "female" or "male") to archaeological artifacts may bear a misleading relationship to the way such materials were employed in the real world. At best, the assignments reflect normative patterns culled from ethnohistory and ethnography. At worst, they are a kind of "best-guess" gender stereotyping based on internalized assumptions from our own cultural background. Fine-grained ethnoarchaeological accounts of actual implements and facilities in living context, including scrupulous tracking of women's and men's behaviors vis-à-vis these use histories and processing cycles, are needed to interpret how gender dynamics generate the static residues in the archaeological record. As Whitridge (2002) notes, to say that a lamp is "female" and a harpoon "male" may reflect meaningful symbolic or iconic associations. Yet these associations may obscure rather than illuminate the myriad ways such materials were actually manufactured, utilized, curated, recycled, and discarded by both women and men.

Arguably, archaeological approaches to the tools and technologies of prehistoric hunter-gatherers deserve major rethinking. The pervasive view of large stone projectile points and blades as quintessential male tools for slaying big dangerous animals is tied too closely to the Western iconic "man conquers snarling beast" cover art gracing men's magazines. At the same time, the tendency to interpret "hunting" as the fleeting moment of dispatch, or the kill, seriously distorts the complex behaviors and technologies in hunter-gatherer economies. Following Kehoe (1990), we recommend a renewed attention to "lines" and other nonlithic technologies involving preparations, travel, logistics, and management of animal movements that, ultimately, made the moment of dispatch possible. The full repertoire of procurement technologies and strategies, no doubt, required the complementary labor of women, men, and children.

If the preharvest procurement side of hunting has been seriously distorted, the postkill processing dimension of hunting has virtually been ignored by archaeologists. Ethnoarchaeological research is useful for demonstrating how postkill butchering, food processing, and storage arrangements for converting carcasses into useful food products, clothing, and implements made survival in adverse conditions possible for communities of hunter-gatherers (Jarvenpa and Brumbach 2006, in press). Much of the processing phases of hunting were managed by women. Indeed, the time investment of women's labor in such activity increases dramatically with the package size of hunted prey and is a compelling reason for decreased participation of women in the direct harvest phase of hunting in some high-latitude societies. Women were simply too busy converting carcasses into vital subsistence products. Facile arguments about women's "marginalization" and/or men's "high prestige" tend to wither in the face of such behavioral realities. Accordingly, we believe the archaeology of hunter-gatherers can come of age only with serious study of the material correlates of postkill processing, storage and distribution of food, and the implications of these dynamics for gender relations.

The last point cannot be overemphasized. Without compelling analysis of what women and men actually accomplished in their daily lives, questions about power, status, and prestige differences between the sexes cannot be addressed. Ideas about prestige hierarchies are particularly prone to contamination by gender stereotypes and biases from our own culture. Lest there be doubts on this score, one may recall how the "Man the Hunter" symposium "gerrymandered" women out of hunting by semantic manipulation of definitions. Similarly, archaeology has "downsized" or "redlined" women out of stone-tool manufacture by disassociating them from big formal lithic tools, purportedly the domain of male hunters only. Finally, the contributions of women's work in producing strings and cordage (or "lines," as noted previously) and the role these items play in hunting strategies are too often overlooked. As we have seen, the profession has a history of interpreting hunter-gatherer society in terms of women's marginalization and exclusion.

We submit that these interpretations have little resemblance to hunter-gatherer gender relations in the past or in recent history. If we inverted the logic, one might well argue that men's "show-off" or "costly-signaling" kills of large game are neither inherently prestigeful nor displays of genetic fitness but rather attempts to avoid exclusion or marginalization by women and children who represent the nurturing epicenter and future of society. Conceivably, we could build models of women's "show-off" food processing or "show-off" storage. However, there is little to be gained by replacing one set of questionable assumptions with another. Surely, *both women and men* actively negotiated their existence in hunter-gatherer societies, strategizing, coping, and making numerous decisions that facilitated their lives and livelihoods. Until the discipline removes Western gender ideology from its analysis, there can be no compelling archaeology of hunter-gatherers.

Acknowledgments

We are grateful to Sarah M. Nelson for her intellectual support and for inviting us to write this chapter. Our thinking on many of the issues discussed in this chapter has benefited from recent comparative ethnoarchaeological research generously supported by the National Science Foundation (NSF), Arctic Social Sciences Program (grant OOP-9805153). We also thank the Canadian Studies Faculty Research Grant Program, Academic Relations Office, Canadian Embassy, and the Faculty Research Awards Program, University at Albany, State University of New York, for funding an early component of our work. Special thanks are due to Fae Korsmo at NSF for her kind assistance. Our international colleagues Elena Glavatskaya, Carol Zane Jolles, and Jukka Pennanen have our gratitude for their creative collaborations. Our most profound debt is to the local people and consultants who have shared their lives and wisdom, especially to the Chipewyan of the English River First Nation, Saskatchewan, but also to the Métis of Ile à la Crosse, Saskatchewan; the Cree of Pinehouse Lake, Saskatchewan; the Khanty of the Trom'Agan area of the Surgut region of Siberia, Russia; the Sámi of Kultima, Finland; and the Iñupiaq of Little Diomede Island, Alaska. Thank you all.

Notes

1. Our survey is selective rather than exhaustive, using key monographs, journal articles, and chapters from edited symposia that best illustrate several broad themes emerging in the published literature.

2. While archaeological research is the focus of this discussion, what is known of women's and men's lives and relationships from ethnography and ethnohistory will be used to highlight, reinforce, or question arguments, themes, and analogies in the archaeological literature. By the same token, fine-grained models of gender relations derived from

ethnoarchaeological studies of living hunter-gatherers offer useful contexts for evaluating arguments about gender in the prehistoric past.

3. Arguably, a fifth question with more symbolic resonance could be added to this discussion: how are women and men identified, defined, or represented in prehistoric rock art, Upper Paleolithic cave paintings, "Venus" figurines, and other aesthetic forms? The gendered dimensions of hunter-gatherer society as expressed in art is a large and specialized area of scholarship beyond the scope of this chapter. However, see chapter 3 in this volume.

4. See Nelson (1997:86) for a discussion of the gender polarizing assumptions in Murdock's work.

5. Jochim (1988) also discusses the possibility of developing separate optimal foraging models for men and women based on their purportedly different genetic fitness goals, distinct foraging strategies, and divergent adaptive constraints. Such modeling views the individual rather than the male–female pair or some larger social form as the adaptive unit. From the vantage point of real-life hunter-gatherer families and communities, such exercises might appear oddly reductionistic. More troubling, perhaps, is that optimal foraging models fixate on energy capture, plain and simple, while ignoring the dynamics of energy flow in subsistence economies in toto, including the vast corpus of food processing, storage, and distribution activities generally handled by women.

6. See Walshe's (1998) critique of Bettinger and Baumhoff's (1982) model of Numic expansion into the Great Basin of California. She argues that their notion of a "male-rich" hunting society, marked by elaborate art and complex stone technology, being replaced by "female-rich" seed processors, with less impressive material culture, has less to do with archaeological data than with unanalyzed gender bias.

7. Similarly, Gleeson (1995) surveys ethnographers about Aboriginal Australian uses of fire with an eye toward archaeological implications. While women and men use fires somewhat differently in hunting, cooking, and toolmaking activities, the greatest gender specificity may occur in contexts involving initiation and the maintenance of large tracts of landscape defined as "female" or "male" via ritualized burning (or cleansing). In another insightful use of ethnographic evidence, Gorman's (1995) discussion of Andaman Island female stone knappers provokes a rethinking of rigid models of prehistory associating men with stone tools and meat.

8. Women in another Athapaskan-speaking group, the Tahltan of northern British Columbia, also make and use a variety of implements, including bone tools for hide preparation, which are curated as part of special-purpose "tool kits" (Albright 1999).

9. The Chipewyan historical trend toward specialized gender-segregated spaces reverses the pattern Shepard (2002) suggested for mainland western Alaskan Eskimo. The fact that the *qasgi* was not part of indigenous social structure in the central subarctic no doubt has some bearing on these divergent patterns. Even so, Whitridge's Thule kitchen and *qargi* complex could be interpreted as signs of increased specialization and separation of female and male economic roles but *not necessarily* marginalization of women.

References

Ackerman, Lillian A.
   1990   Gender Status in Yup'ik Society. *Etudes/Inuit/Studies* 14(1–2):209–21.
Albright, Sylvia
   1999   A Working Woman Needs a Good Tool Kit. In *Feminist Approaches to Pacific Northwest Archaeology*. Katherine Bernick, ed. Northwest Anthropological Research Notes, vol. 33(2):183–90. Moscow, ID.
Bettinger, R. L., and M. A. Baumhoff
   1982   The Numic Spread: Great Basin Cultures in Competition. *American Antiquity* 47(3):485–503.
Bird, C. F. M.
   1993   Woman the Toolmaker: Evidence for Women's Use and Manufacture of Flaked Stone Tools in Australia and New Guinea. In *Women in Archaeology: A Feminist Critique*. Hilary du Cros and Laurajane Smith, eds. Pp. 22–30. Canberra: Australian National University.
Bogojavlensky, Sergei, and Robert W. Fuller
   1973   Polar Bears, Walrus Hides, and Social Solidarity. *Alaska Journal* 3(2):66–76.
Brightman, Robert
   1996   The Sexual Division of Foraging Labor: Biology, Taboo, and Gender Politics. *Comparative Studies in Society and History* 38(4):687–729.
Brumbach, Hetty Jo, and Robert Jarvenpa
   1997a   Ethnoarchaeology of Subsistence Space and Gender: A Subarctic Dene Case. *American Antiquity* 62(3):414–36.
   1997b   Woman the Hunter: Ethnoarchaeological Lessons from Chipewyan Life-Cycle Dynamics. In *Women in Prehistory: North America and Mesoamerica*. Cheryl Claassen and Rosemary A. Joyce, eds. Pp. 17–32. Philadelphia: University of Pennsylvania Press.
Buckley, Thomas
   1982   Menstruation and the Power of Yurok Women. *American Ethnologist* 9:47–90.
Casey, Joanna
   1998   Just a Formality: The Presence of Fancy Projectile Points in a Basic Tool Assemblage. In *Gender in African Prehistory*. Susan Kent, ed. Pp. 83–103. Walnut Creek, CA: AltaMira Press.
Cassidy, Claire M.
   1984   Skeletal Evidence for Prehistoric Subsistence Change in the Central Ohio River Valley. In *Paleopathology at the Origins of Agriculture*. Mark N. Cohen and George J. Armeelagos, eds. Pp. 307–46. New York: Academic Press.
Claassen, Cheryl
   1991   Gender, Shellfishing and the Shell Mound Archaic. In *Engendering Archaeology: Women and Prehistory*. Joan M. Gero and Margaret W. Conkey, eds. Pp. 276–300. Oxford: Basil Blackwell.

Clark, A. McFadyen

    1996   Who Lived in This House? Mercury Series, Archaeological Survey of Canada Paper 153. Hull, Quebec: Canadian Museum of Civilization.

Cohen, Mark Nathan, and Sharon Bennett

    1993   Skeletal Evidence for Sex Roles and Gender Hierarchies in Prehistory. In *Sex and Gender Hierarchies*. Barbara Diane Miller, ed. Pp. 273–96. Cambridge: Cambridge University Press.

Conkey, Margaret W., and Janet D. Spector

    1984   Archaeology and the Study of Gender. In *Advances in Archaeological Method and Theory*. Vol. 7. Michael B. Schiffer, ed. Pp. 1–38. New York: Academic Press.

Cook, Delia

    1984   Subsistence and Health in the Lower Illinois Valley: Osteological Evidence. In *Paleopathology at the Origins of Agriculture*. Mark N. Cohen and George J. Armelagos, eds. Pp. 237–70. New York: Academic Press.

Cooke, Helen

    1998   Fieldwork, Mothering and the Prehistoric People of Blue Water Holes, Kosciuszko National Park. In *Redefining Archaeology: Feminist Perspectives*. Research Papers in Archaeology and Natural History, no. 29. Mary Casey, Denise Donlon, Jeannette Hope, and Sharon Wellfare, eds. Pp. 55–62. Canberra: ANH Publications, Research School of Pacific and Asian Studies, Australian National Museum.

Counts, Dorothy

    1985   Tamparonga: The Big Women of Kaliai (Papua New Guinea). In *In Her Prime: A New View of Middle-Aged Women*. J. Brown and V. Kerns, eds. Pp. 49–64. South Hadley, MA: Bergin & Garvey.

Dahlberg, Frances, ed.

    1981   *Woman the Gatherer*. New Haven, CT: Yale University Press.

Ellender, Isabel

    1993   Gender in Aboriginal Burial Practices: Evidence from Springfield Gorge Cave, Victoria. In *Women in Archaeology: A Feminist Critique*. Hilary du Cros and Laurajane Smith, eds. Pp. 104–13. Canberra: Australian National University.

Ember, Carol R.

    1975   Residential Variation among Hunter-Gatherers. *Behavior Science Research* 10:199–227.

Endicott, Karen I.

    1999   Gender Relations in Hunter-Gatherer Society. In *The Cambridge Encyclopedia of Hunters and Gatherers*. Richard B. Lee and Richard Daly, eds. Pp. 411–18. Cambridge: Cambridge University Press.

Estioko-Griffin, Agnes, and P. Bion Griffin

    1981   Woman the Hunter: The Agta. In *Woman the Gatherer*. Frances Dahlberg, ed. Pp. 121–51. New Haven, CT: Yale University Press.

Frink, Lisa
    2002   Fish Tales: Women and Decision Making in Western Alaska. In *Many Faces of Gender: Roles and Relationships through Time in Indigenous Northern Communities*. Lisa Frink, Rita S. Shepard, and Gregory A. Reinhardt, eds. Pp. 93–108. Boulder: University Press of Colorado.
Gero, Joan
    1991   Genderlithics: Women's Roles in Stone Tool Production. In *Engendering Archaeology: Women and Prehistory*. Joan M. Gero and Margaret W. Conkey, eds. Pp. 163–93. Oxford: Basil Blackwell.
    1993   The Social World of Prehistoric Facts: Gender and Power in Paleoindian Research. In *Women in Archaeology: A Feminist Critique*. Hilary du Cros and Laurajane Smith, eds. Pp. 31–40. Canberra: Australian National University.
Gleeson, C. T.
    1995   Gender and Aboriginal Fire-Use in Australia: A Preliminary Analysis of the Results of a Questionnaire. In *Gendered Archaeology: The Second Australian Women in Archaeology Conference*. Research Papers in Archaeology and Natural History, no. 26. Jane Balme and Wendy Beck, eds. Pp. 97–104. Canberra: ANH Publications, Research School of Pacific and Asian Studies, Australian National University.
Goodman, Alan, Debra Martin, George J. Armelagos, and George Clark
    1984   Health Changes at Dickson Mounds, Illinois (A.D. 950–1300). In *Paleopathology at the Origins of Agriculture*. Mark N. Cohen and George J. Armelagos, eds. Pp. 271–306. New York: Academic Press.
Gorman, Alice
    1995   Gender, Labour and Resources: The Female Knappers of the Andaman Islands. In *Gendered Archaeology: The Second Australian Women in Archaeology Conference*. Research Papers in Archaeology and Natural History, no. 26. Jane Balme and Wendy Beck, eds. Pp. 87–91. Canberra: ANH Publications, Research School of Pacific and Asian Studies, Australian National University.
Gould, Richard A.
    1977   Ethno-Archaeology: Or, Where Do Models Come From? In *Stone Tools as Cultural Markers*. R. V. S. Wright, ed. Pp. 162–77. Canberra: Australian Institute of Aboriginal Studies.
    1980   *Living Archaeology*. Cambridge: Cambridge University Press.
Halperin, Rhoda
    1980   Ecology and Mode of Production: Seasonal Variation and the Division of Labor by Sex among Hunter-Gatherers. *Journal of Anthropological Research* 36(3):379–99.
Hayden, Brian
    1992   Observing Prehistoric Women. In *Exploring Gender through Archaeology: Selected Papers from the 1991 Boone Conference*. Cheryl Claassen, ed. Pp. 33–47. Madison, WI: Prehistory Press.

Hiatt (Meehan), Betty
    1978   Woman the Gatherer. In *Woman's Role in Aboriginal Society*. F. Gale, ed. Pp.
            4–15. Canberra: Australian Institute of Aboriginal Studies.
Hildebrandt, William R., and Kelly R. McGuire
    2002   The Ascendance of Hunting during the California Middle Archaic: An Evo-
            lutionary Perspective. *American Antiquity* 67(2):231–56.
Hill, Kim, and H. Kaplan
    1993   On Why Male Foragers Hunt and Share Food. *Current Anthropology* 34:701–6.
Hoffman, Brian W.
    2002   Broken Eyes and Simple Grooves: Understanding Eastern Aleut Needle Tech-
            nology through Experimental Manufacture and Use of Bone Needles. In *Many
            Faces of Gender: Roles and Relationships through Time in Indigenous Northern Communities*.
            Lisa Frink, Rita S. Shepard, and Gregory A. Reinhardt, eds. Pp. 151–64.
            Boulder: University Press of Colorado.
Hollimon, Sandra
    1991   Health Consequences of Divisions of Labor among the Chumash Indians of
            Southern California. In *The Archaeology of Gender*. Proceedings of the 22nd
            Annual Chacmool Conference. Dale Walde and Noreen D. Willows, eds. Pp.
            462–69. Calgary: Department of Archaeology, University of Calgary.
    1992   Health Consequences of Sexual Division of Labor among Prehistoric Native
            Americans: The Chumash of California and the Arikara of the North Plains.
            In *Exploring Gender through Archaeology: Selected Papers from the 1991 Boone Conference*.
            Cheryl Claassen, ed. Pp. 81–88. Madison, WI: Prehistory Press.
Janes, Robert R.
    1983   Archaeological Ethnography among Mackenzie Basin Dene, Canada. Techni-
            cal Paper, no. 28. Calgary: Arctic Institute of North America.
Jarvenpa, Robert, and Hetty Jo Brumbach
    1995   Ethnoarchaeology and Gender: Chipewyan Women as Hunters. *Research in
            Economic Anthropology* 16:39–82.
    1999   The Gendered Nature of Living and Storage Space in the Canadian Subarctic.
            In *From the Ground Up: Beyond Gender Theory in Archaeology*. Nancy L. Wicker and
            Bettina Arnold, eds. Pp. 107–23. BAR International Series 812. Oxford:
            British Archaeological Reports.
    2006   *Circumpolar Lives and Livelihood: A Comparative Ethnoarchaeology of Gender and Subsis-
            tence*. Lincoln: University of Nebraska Press.
    In press   The Sexual Division of Labor Revisited: Thoughts on Ethnoarchaeology
            and Gender. In *Integrating the Diversity of 21st Century Anthropology: The Life and
            Intellectual Legacies of Susan Kent*. Wendy Ashmore, Marcia-Anne Dobres, Sarah
            Nelson, and Arlene Rosen, eds. Archaeological Papers of the American
            Anthropological Association 17. Washington, DC: American Anthropologi-
            cal Association.

Jennings, Jesse D., ed.
   1983   *Ancient North Americans*. San Francisco: W. H. Freeman.
Jochim, Michael A.
   1988   Optimal Foraging and the Division of Labor. *American Anthropologist* 90:130–36.
Kehoe, Alice B.
   1990   Points and Lines. In *Powers of Observation: Alternative Views in Archeology*. Sarah M. Nelson and Alice B. Kehoe, eds. Pp. 23–37. Archaeological Papers of the American Anthropological Association 2. Washington, DC: American Anthropological Association.
Kelly, Robert L.
   1995   *The Foraging Spectrum: Diversity in Hunter-Gatherer Lifeways*. Washington, DC: Smithsonian Institution Press.
Kent, Susan
   1998   Invisible Gender—Invisible Foragers: Southern African Hunter-Gatherer Spatial Patterning and the Archaeological Record. In *Gender in African Prehistory*. Susan Kent, ed. Pp. 39–67. Walnut Creek, CA: AltaMira Press.
Leacock, Eleanor B.
   1981   *Myths of Male Dominance*. New York: Monthly Review Press.
Lee, Richard B.
   1968   What Hunters Do for a Living, or How to Make Out on Scarce Resources. In *Man the Hunter*. Richard B. Lee and Irven DeVore, eds. Pp. 30–48. Chicago: Aldine.
Lee, Richard B.
   1979   *The !Kung San: Men, Women and Work in a Foraging Society*. Cambridge: Cambridge University Press.
Lee, Richard B., and Irven DeVore, eds.
   1968   *Man the Hunter*. Chicago: Aldine.
LeMoine, Genevieve
   2003   Woman of the House: Gender, Architecture, and Ideology in Dorset Prehistory.
          Arctic Anthropology 40(1):121–38.
Lips, J. E.
   1947   *The Origin of Things*. New York: A. A. Wyn.
McGuire, Kelly R., and W. R. Hildebrandt
   1994   The Possibilities of Women and Men: Gender and the California Milling Stone Horizon. *Journal of California and Great Basin Archaeology* 16(1):41–59.
McKell, Sheila
   1993   An Axe to Grind: More Ripping Yarns from Australian Prehistory. In *Women in Archaeology: A Feminist Critique*. Hilary du Cros and Laurajane Smith, eds. Pp. 115–20. Canberra: Australian National University.

Moss, Madonna L.
  1993   Shellfish, Gender, and Status on the Northwest Coast: Reconciling Archaeo-
          logical, Ethnographic, and Ethnohistoric Records on the Tlingit. *American
          Anthropologist* 95(3):631–52.
Murdock, George P.
  1967   The Ethnographic Atlas: A Summary. *Ethnology* 6(2):109–236.
Nelson, Richard K.
  1980   Athapaskan Subsistence Adaptations in Alaska. In *Alaskan Native Culture and
          History*. Senri Ethnological Studies, no. 4. Y. Kotani and W. Workman, eds.
          Pp. 205–32. Osaka: National Museum of Ethnology.
Nelson, Sarah Milledge
  1997   *Gender in Archaeology: Analyzing Power and Prestige*. Walnut Creek, CA: AltaMira
          Press.
Newell, Raymond R.
  1984   The Archaeological, Human Biological, and Comparative Contexts of a Cata-
          strophically Terminated Kataligaaq House at Utqiagvik, Alaska (BAR-2).
          Arctic Anthropology 21(1):5–51.
Osgood, Cornelius
  1940   Ingalik Material Culture. Yale University Publications in Anthropology, no.
          22. New Haven, CT: Yale University Press.
Reinhardt, Gregory A.
  2002   Puzzling Out Gender-Specific "Sides" to a Prehistoric House in Barrow,
          Alaska. In *Many Faces of Gender: Roles and Relationships through Time in Indigenous
          Northern Communities*. Lisa Frink, Rita S. Shepard, and Gregory A. Reinhardt,
          eds. Pp. 121–50. Boulder: University Press of Colorado.
Sassaman, Kenneth
  1992   Gender and Technology at the Archaic-Woodland Transition. In *Exploring
          Gender through Archaeology: Selected Papers from the 1991 Boone Conference*. Cheryl
          Claassen, ed. Pp. 71–79. Madison, WI: Prehistory Press.
Sealy, J. C., M. K. Patrick, A. G. Morris, and D. Alder
  1992   Diet and Dental Caries among Later Stone Age Inhabitants of the Cape Prov-
          ince, South Africa. *American Journal of Physical Anthropology* 88:123–34.
Shepard, Rita S.
  2002   Changing Residence Patterns and Intradomestic Role Changes: Causes and
          Effects in Nineteenth Century Western Alaska. In *Many Faces of Gender: Roles
          and Relationships through Time in Indigenous Northern Communities*. Lisa Frink, Rita
          S. Shepard, and Gregory A. Reinhardt, eds. Pp. 61–79. Boulder: University
          Press of Colorado.
Smith, Andrew B.
  1999   Archaeology and the Evolution of Hunters and Gatherers. In *The Cambridge
          Encyclopedia of Hunters and Gatherers*. Richard B. Lee and Richard Daly, eds. Pp.
          384–90. Cambridge: Cambridge University Press.

Smith, Patricia, Ofer Bar-Yosef, and Andrew Sillen
    1984   Archaeological and Skeletal Evidence for Dietary Change during the Late
            Pleistocene/Early Holocene in the Levant. In *Paleopathology at the Origins of Agri-
            culture*. Mark N. Cohen and George J. Armelagos, eds. Pp. 101–36. New
            York: Academic Press.
Torrence, Robin
    2001   Hunter-Gatherer Technology: Macro- and Microscale Approaches. In *Hunter-
            Gatherers: An Interdisciplinary Perspective*. Catherine Panter-Brick, Robert H. Lay-
            ton, and Peter Rowley-Conwy, eds. Pp. 73–98. Cambridge: Cambridge Uni-
            versity Press.
Turnbull, Colin M.
    1981   Mbuti Womanhood. In *Woman the Gatherer*. Frances Dahlberg, ed. Pp. 205–
            19. New Haven, CT: Yale University Press.
Vinsrygg, Synnove
    1987   Sex-Roles and the Division of Labour in Hunting-Gathering Societies. In
            Were They All Men? An Examination of Sex Roles in Prehistoric Society. Reidar Ber-
            telsen, Arnvid Lillehammer, and Jenny-Rita Naess, eds. Pp. 23–32. Sta-
            vanger: Arkeologisk Museum i Stavanger.
Wadley, Lynn
    1998   The Invisible Meat Providers: Women in the Stone Age of South Africa. In
            Gender in African Prehistory. Susan Kent, ed. Pp. 69–81. Walnut Creek, CA:
            AltaMira Press.
    2000   The Use of Space in a Gender Study of Two South African Stone Age Sites.
            In *Gender and Material Culture in Archaeological Perspective*. Moira Donald and Linda
            Hurcombe, eds. Pp. 153–68. Hampshire: Macmillan.
Walker, Philip L., and Jon M. Erlandson
    1986   Dental Evidence for Prehistoric Dietary Change on the Northern Channel
            Islands, California. *American Antiquity* 51(2):375–83.
Walshe, Keryn
    1998   Breeding Processors and Moribund Travellers. In *Redefining Archaeology: Feminist
            Perspectives*. Research Papers in Archaeology and Natural History, no. 29.
            Mary Casey, Denise Donlon, Jeannette Hope, and Sharon Wellfare, eds. Pp.
            37–40. Canberra: ANH Publications, Research School of Pacific and Asian
            Studies, Australian National University.
Washburn, Sherwood, and C. S. Lancaster
    1968   The Evolution of Hunting. In *Man the Hunter*. Richard B. Lee and Irven
            DeVore, eds. Pp. 293–303. Chicago: Aldine.
Watanabe, Hitoshi
    1968   Subsistence and Ecology of Northern Food Gatherers with Special Reference
            to the Ainu. In *Man the Hunter*. Richard B. Lee and Irven DeVore, eds. Pp.
            68–77. Chicago: Aldine.

Watson, Patty Jo, and Mary C. Kennedy
   1991   The Development of Horticulture in the Eastern Woodlands of North America: Women's Role. In *Engendering Archaeology: Women and Prehistory.* Joan M. Gero and Margaret W. Conkey, eds. Pp. 255–75. Oxford: Basil Blackwell.

Whitridge, Peter
   2002   Gender, Households, and the Material Construction of Social Difference: Metal Consumption at a Classic Thule Whaling Village. In *Many Faces of Gender: Roles and Relationships through Time in Indigenous Northern Communities.* Lisa Frink, Rita S. Shepard, and Gregory A. Reinhardt, eds. Pp. 165–92. Boulder: University Press of Colorado.

Williamson, B. S.
   1996   Preliminary Stone Tool Residue Analysis from Rose Cottage Cave. *Southern African Field Archaeology* 53:36–44.

Winterhalder, Bruce
   2001   The Behavioural Ecology of Hunter-Gatherers. In *Hunter-Gatherers: An Interdisciplinary Perspective.* Catherine Panter-Brick, Robert H. Layton, and Peter Rowley-Conwy, eds. Pp. 12–38. Cambridge: Cambridge University Press.

Zeanah, David W.
   2004   Sexual Division of Labor and Central Place Foraging: A Model for the Carson Desert of Western Nevada. *Journal of Anthropological Archaeology* 23:1–32.

Gender and Early Farming Societies   7

JANE D. PETERSON

G ENDER STUDIES OF prehistoric farming societies are perched precariously between the detailed, often text-aided studies of complex societies and the more speculative, techno-environmental reconstructions associated with Paleolithic archaeology. Neolithic and Formative villagers often left behind an assortment of tantalizing clues—from burials, human remains, architecture, artifacts, and images—so that archaeologists feel they ought to be able to address some fairly substantial questions about the gender systems of early farmers. And these are important issues, seeing that making the transition to an agricultural economy is commonly perceived as one of the major, transformational events in the human career. How the first farmers organized their work, how they structured their relationships with family and community, and how their ideational systems shaped and reinforced gender concepts were undoubtedly critical features in the success or failure of their ventures. Yet the promise of reconstructing the gender systems from the fragmentary and static prehistoric remains has remained often illusive.

My intent is to chart the sometimes uneven progress of gender research concerning early agricultural societies. The discussion is limited to those societies that *did* depend on domesticated plants or a mix of domestic plants and animals for their livelihood but *did not* exist as part of larger state-level entities that involved institutionalized hierarchical structures. I will forefront those studies that, by virtue of theoretical insight and methodological innovation, have advanced and challenged how we think about gender in early farming societies. By doing so, I hope to provide some suggestions about conceptualizing sex roles and gender and how to overcome problems that continue to plague gender studies.

Two important trends unfold in the course of these discussions. First, while the "Neolithic Revolution" was clearly a transformative process wherever it took hold, results of gender studies suggest that the inception of settled, village farming life led to few outcomes that can be viewed as broadly generalizable across regions. Despite the strongly seductive metaphor of evolutionary change, universal (or even regional) descriptions of the effects and outcomes of the agricultural developments inevitably falter in the light of local data sets and detailed analyses. So it may seem to some that there is little we can say with certainty about gender during the rise of agriculture. I would offer, alternatively, that the variation is less a symptom of theoretical inadequacy or lack of methodological rigor but more a reflection of the stunning variety present in the data themselves—in terms of both the diversity of gender systems in place and the material ways these systems are imbued with meaning (Crown 2000a). Frequent reinterpretations and active debates indicate the incremental, sometimes awkward development of archaeological knowledge in an arena that is still experiencing substantial growing pains. Second, the past twenty years have also reminded us of the truism in anthropology that culture is holistic. It is difficult to talk about sexual roles or the sexual division of labor, for example, without considering social, economic, political, and ideological categories of gender (Dobres 2004). So it becomes increasingly clear that the most compelling studies consider multiple cultural spheres and integrate diverse data sets in their discussions of sex and gender.

I suggest that there is no one, simple solution to moving gender studies forward because there is not, one uniform limitation. Some shortcomings continue to have their roots in stereotypical projections of Western gender patterns into the past. Gender clichés are perpetuated by archaeologists who continue to claim that the search for gender is a futile pursuit and then inject assumptions about sex and gender freely into their interpretations. Yet authors who express sympathy to feminist goals and familiarity with feminist theory have sometimes presented naive, formulaic accounts as well. The archaeological record and variable preservation can also have an impact. Yet if we search out the most robust, well-preserved data sets, we do not necessarily find the most advanced gender studies. Confronting these challenges constitutes the next stage for gender studies among farming societies. And there is still an enormous potential for insightful, engendered archaeological analyses. The incentives to build a more coherent and less stereotypical gendered past are strong. As prone as we are to situate the present in the past, a more complete and unbiased view of that past clearly paves the way for thoughtful reflection and action concerning our gendered future.

Domesticating Gender

As the arbiters of culture change over the vast expanse of prehistory, we have never been hesitant about modeling gender roles, relationships, and ideologies in sweeping terms. First came the universally-applied essentialist assumptions about the roles of women and men rooted firmly in their biology and the limitations those were thought to imply. Women in farming societies were increasingly stressed by the demands imposed by larger families. Increasing sedentism fully tethered them to the "domestic" sphere. And women were less likely than ever to contribute to the technological or political developments of a group. These assumptions—and the reconstructions of Neolithic society that emerged from them—provided fodder for a first wave of critical analysis.

In 1970, Boserup published the tremendously influential study *Women's Role in Economic Development*. This pathbreaking work documented African women's massive contribution to agricultural economies and also formulated an engendered model for changing agricultural production. She claimed that women did the bulk of agricultural work in tribal societies where population levels were low, land was both abundant and collectively owned, and technology was handheld (hoe). Her typology from extensive to increasingly intensive farming was evolutionary, with demographic change and land pressure precipitating intensification and technological advance. Increased male participation coincides with the introduction of the plow.

Boserup's "female farmer" model seemed to demonstrate that women made significant productive contributions in the subsistence economy of extensive farmers. The "female farmer" model provided a basis for responding to those who supposed that modern divisions of labor were rooted in the biological limitations imposed on women by the rigors of bearing and nurturing children. And it was a powerful inferential tool for feminist researchers who were predisposed to structural-Marxist analyses (Leacock 1978, 1981; Martin and Voorhies 1975; Sacks 1974; Schlegel 1977). For many archaeologists, the model relied on technological and economic behaviors that were likely to leave material clues. Boserup's categories seemed to correspond not only with technological trajectories identifiable in the past (hoe to plow) but also with widespread social conditions in the present. This combination proved irresistible for many, and the outlines of Boserup's model are still resonant in gender accounts of prehistoric farming societies to this day.

The decline in women's agricultural contribution was viewed as a starting point for social declines. Some interpreted Boserup's model as supporting the notion that women's relegation to the domestic realm and their declining status was a historically late phenomenon associated more with the rise of private property and the state (Silverblatt 1988). Other historians and archaeologists projected the African trajectory wholesale much deeper into the prehistoric past. The onset of domestication economies served as a trigger for institutionalized sexual labor roles and further sowed the seeds of widespread social inequality between the sexes (Aaby 1977; Chevillard and LeConte 1986; Divale and Harris 1976; Ehrenberg 1989; Lerner 1986; Mears 2001; Meillassoux 1981). Accounts, often not overly burdened by data, posit a unlineal devolution of women from autonomous, valued agents to subordinate, disenfranchised objects corresponding with the rise and development of agricultural societies.

Despite its influence, Boserup's model has not survived the past thirty-five years unscathed. And the range of critiques is highly relevant to archaeological research. Foremost, the evolutionary link between an ethnographically based era of "female farming" in Africa and primitive agricultural systems writ large has crumbled under the weight of ethnographic evidence. As one example, Guyer's (1991) work among the Beti of Cameroon skillfully demonstrates how the "female farmer" model is more an artifact of the volatile social and economic conditions in the past two centuries than a result of long-term, evolutionary processes. The Beti's ancient stable crops of millet, yams, and sorghum were never produced by female labor alone. In the case of millet, men cut back tree branches, and women stacked the branches. Men placed the seeds in the ground, and women covered them with soil. Men fenced the fields, and women tended the growing crop. Only reaping was the sole domain of women. Each of these tasks took place in a ritualized context, sometimes set to music and literally choreographed. It was only with the introduction of maize and cassava and the colonial policies that encouraged their production that cultivation took on "female farming" mantle (Guyer 1991).

Results from the first wave of ethnographic research, spawned by a growing feminist interest in women's roles, reinforced Guyer's critique. Numerous geographically far-flung examples can be cited in which the productive tasks in agricultural societies do not conform to the universal, sex-segregated patterns Boserup envisioned (Bacdayan 1977; Cloud 1985; Peters 1978; Trenchard 1987). Furthermore, conceptualizing complex sets of related tasks as monolithic entities such as "farming," "hunting," or "exchange" rather that suites of smaller, related tasks often masks dual participation, complementarity, and interdigitation of men's and women's lives (i.e., Brumbach and Jarvenpa 1997 regarding hunting). These observations have not been lost on all archaeologists (see Fish 2000; Szuter 2000). But it remains all too common for archaeologists to constitute activity as monolithic chunks to be assigned to either "male" or "female" columns. Inevitably, these same accounts "snowball" into formulaic reconstructions of labor, social relationships, and power structures. From a theoretical position informed by feminism, this style of evolutionary argument is no less problematic than biological imperative models. It still maintains that gender roles are somehow rooted in fixed, essentialist capacities in men and women that map out their progress in a predetermined way over vast expanses of time and space. In sum, there are a plethora of reasons to approach evolutionary models with skepticism. My point is not that there can be no variables that are widely influential in forecasting gender but only that evolutionary models do an inadequate job of explaining known gender variability and patterning, let alone the variety likely to have been present in precolonial and preindustrial agricultural settings (sensu Leacock 1978).

In keeping with broader trends in the social sciences, archaeological gender studies increasingly embrace perspectives that stress human agency, practice, and historical contingency more than evolution (Hegmon 2003; Meade and Wiesner-Hanks 2004; Sørensen 2000). We have been reminded of Schlegel's (1977) important message that separate domains of activity and influence between the sexes do not necessarily imply a hierarchy of values associated with those domains (Claassen 1997). And the dangers of projecting etic, Western concepts of worth onto productive tasks are more often avoided (Crown 2000a). While recent studies tend to be more theoretically sophisticated and nuanced, the road is still bumpy. The process of switching paradigms has not always been graceful, nor has it ensured coherent accounts of gender. Many of the studies are aptly characterized as involving rapid intellectual reappraisal rather than deep logical consideration (Guyer 1995:26).

Lamphere (2000) has provided one particularly effective modeling effort in her synthesis of evidence from the pre-Hispanic Southwest. This model focuses on a concept of hegemony defined as both *ideas* about prestige and value and also the *practice* of exercising power (sensu Ortner 1996), combining elements of productive labor, status, and ideology. She situates the source of hegemonic influence in the realm of ritual power; which, when defined emically, should be broadly applicable to prehistoric agricultural societies outside the Southwest.

Gender relationships can be played out on a field characterized by either balanced or hierarchical hegemony. Balanced hegemony prevails when the "power associated with ritual is widely dispersed among kin groups and among men and women, and where there is little control over productive resources by kin groups whose leaders are 'important' people" (Lamphere 2000:389). Gender balance can be maintained in situations where the sexual labor is either shared or segregated (overlapping or complementary in Lamphere's words). Hierarchical hegemony, her Ritual Power Model, exists in situations where a more limited number of ritual practitioners have access to the higher prestige roles. Productive labor is likely to be more sex segregated and reinforces growing social and ideological divides. She makes a compelling case that elements of hegemony can be wrested from a range of archaeological data, albeit indirectly. I find Lamphere's model valuable as a framework to discuss a number of gender studies among prehistoric farming groups. In doing so, we are able to highlight variation in prehistoric gender systems and suggest the applicability of this model to studies outside the pre-Hispanic Southwest.

Regional Gender Case Studies

My approach in organizing a more detailed investigation into recent research trends is to highlight several broad, geographic regions. The logic of this choice rests in the publication of several influential gender volumes that review and synthesize bodies of regional data for China, Africa, North and South America, and Mesoamerica and North America (Bruhns and Stothert 1999; Claassen and Joyce 1997; Kent 1998; Linduff and Sun 2004). This format also facilitates a discussion of the influence regional research traditions has played in developing gender studies. Admittedly, the choice of the regional case studies also reflects my own familiarity with the archaeological record. My hope is that the range of Old and New World regional case studies is representative of research developments in the study of gender and farming. For readers with interests in farming societies not covered here, I direct them to the chapters in part 4 of this volume. These chapters will provide important supplemental information.

Europe (with an Emphasis on the Mediterranean Region)
The architecture of longhouses, a large corpus of figurines, mortuary data, and diverse ethnographic gleanings feature prominently in the Neolithic gender research of Europe. Economic and ideological realms have often been considered by separate authors in separate articles. There is evidence of both more sophisticated and nuanced treatments of gender and also the retention of some unproductive lines of inquiry.

One well-known vision of a pan-European gendered past was offered by Gimbutas (1974, 1989) in her examination of female figurines. Gimbutas interprets the numerous figurines as representing a religious system centered on a Great Mother Goddess, who represents concepts of fertility and life force in societies that, while egalitarian, were matrilineal and "matrifocal." There are echoes of a biological imperative model as women's position in society is centered primarily on their reproductive role. Women's downfall comes in the Bronze Age with the onslaught of male herders from the East. Archaeologists have criticized Gimbutas's data, methods, and theory related to the Goddess Culture of Old Europe (Meskell 1995). But we will limit our discussions to reworkings of the gendered implications of the figurine data.

Gimbutas's model, stretching as it does over thousands of miles and thousands of years, overlooks substantial variation in the figurines of Neolithic Europe. So it is predictable that scholars have mounted critiques of her model by analyzing the uses and meanings of specific assemblages. Concerns with fertility, particularly as it is connected with agriculture, have persisted, but alternative interpretations include considerations of figurines as territorial markers, toys, teaching aids, self-representations, good-luck charms, votives, and effigies. Talalay (1987) offers one such alternative hypothesis to explain a distinctive assemblage drawn from five sites in the northern Peloponnese. The group consists of eighteen individual female legs that appear to be as parts of broken leg pairs. A review of ethnographic and historic sources suggests that broken, paired tokens often served to identify partners in social or economic exchanges in preliterate and classical societies. Given that the legs are all sexed female, one possibility is that the legs represent the relocation of women through an exogamous marriage system (Talalay 1987:168).

Binary conceptions of sex and gender that many have imposed on figurine data have also come under fire. Talalay (2000) documents the variation in the Greek corpus. Although female figurines are the most numerous and varied—in terms of decoration, material, and position—male, dual-sexed, and sexless figurines also occur. The same is true of eastern European Neolithic figurines (Hamilton 2000). A number of possibilities in conjunction with the sexless figurines are reviewed. The figures may represent 1) individuals who subsumed or transcended sexual/gender classification (e.g., child, shaman, and so on), 2) the irrelevance of sexual classification to the image portrayed, 3) items that took on sex by the addition of perishable clothing or ornaments, or 4) individuals with sexed information that we cannot "read." Whatever the case, their interpretation is not straightforward. And these discussions encourage us to envision gender systems in which sex and gender are conceived of and represented as more multifaceted, potentially fluid categories than previously envisioned.

A second pan-European model of gender systems was put forward in Ehrenberg's *Women in Prehistory* (1989). Her reconstruction of the European Neolithic owes much to Boserup in that it identifies diminished economic production at the crux of women's disenfranchisement over time. During the Early Neolithic, women across Europe are lauded not only as the innovators of agriculture and the technologies that farming required (lithic and ceramic) but also as the main source of labor in a mixed agropastoral economy. They were socially supported by an extended matrilocal kin network and economically empowered by their control of domestic products. But by the end of the Neolithic, with the advent of the plow and increases in the importance of milk and wool, their lives had been transformed by men usurping their economic roles and relegating them to the constant drudgery of making and raising babies and the repetitive, mindless tasks of cooking and textile production. By this process, the groundwork was laid for the modern gender asymmetries seen in Western society today (Ehrenberg 1989:77). The most detailed analysis discusses the connections between family size, family structure, postmarital residence patterns, and the architectural variability of European longhouses.

There are serious problems implicit in the detailed, dichotomous sexed labor scenario on which the model is founded. Most significant, it is unsupported by any archaeological data. And since the causal mechanism for change rests in the reallocation of productive resources and labor input, these are telling. Ehrenberg is not alone in facing this dilemma. Archaeologists have been exhorted to establish an empirical basis for assigning tasks to one sex, the other, or both (Conkey and Spector 1984; Spector 1983). It is through this basic step that patterns of artifacts and features take on gendered meaning. However, this has proven a more difficult task than many first imagined. There is substantial ambiguity in our understanding of sex roles with respect to farming and herding task sets. The utility of the ethnographic record is hampered by the very diversity of sexed labor scenarios that it describes.

Whitehouse's (2002) gendered look at the data from southern Italy faces some of the same problems in discussing gendered tasks and spatial domains. Yet her model, which seeks to describe role, status, and ideology by synthesizing a wider range of archaeological materials and entertaining multiple interpretations of those data, is a good deal more satisfying. Based on grave treatments, figurines from settlement and cave deposits, and paintings on cave walls, she describes a spatially segregated but complementary gender system in which the roles, relations, and ideology of men and women were balanced (Whitehouse 2002:40–41). Men are associated with hunting by virtue of painted depictions at cave and rock-shelter locations. Only female figurines are found at settlements. Images and figurines from caves depict both males and females. And there is no evidence of status differences between the sexes from grave goods. Men and women are interpreted as having separate (off-site vs. village-based) activity spheres that also serve as the loci of ritual activity. The lack of differentiation in graves suggests that both domains are socially valued.

This preliminary engendered model is highly reminiscent of the balanced hegemony scenario previously outlined and speaks well for the value of applying Lamphere's scheme outside the pre-Hispanic Southwest. Second, the value of considering less binary classificatory systems for studying gender in Neolithic societies is reinforced. Southern Italy has its own dual-sex and sexless figurines.

Furthermore, the one significant correlation of sex in burials is that men tend to be buried on right sides and women their left. However, the rule is far from universal, as 26 percent of males and 31 percent of females are buried on the wrong side. And the lack of strict differentiation along sex lines has led authors to speculate about possible disconnects between sex and gender (Robb 1994a, 1994b). Finally, Whitehouse admits her difficulty in assigning economically important subsistence tasks by gender. Nonetheless, her discussion belies a tendency to segregate tasks by sex and lump complex task sets together. Thus, women become the cultivators, potters, and weavers and men the hunters, herders, traders, and stone-tool makers (Whitehouse 2000:39). The clear association of women's tasks with the areas close to the house and village and men's tasks to areas at greater distances affirms rather than supports her conclusion.

In looking for potential activity sphere's or specific tasks that can more safely be associated with women's work in Europe, spinning and weaving are good candidates for some regions. A Hallstatt vase from Hungary depicts groups of women spinning and weaving to musical and dance accompaniment (Barber 1994:88). Textiles themselves bear the traces of communal weaving. Crisscrossing weft threads from a man's burial cloak from Trinhoj in Jutland (ca. 1300 b.c.) demonstrates that three weavers, passing the bobbins back and forth between them, produced the garment (Barber 1994:86–87). Well-preserved textile fragments, spindle whorls, weights, and loom emplacements have begun to yield gendered insights about the social and economic contexts of weaving at the Neolithic Swiss Lake Dwelling of Robenhausen (Lillis 2004).

Africa

Archaeological gender studies are in their infancy throughout most of Africa, although the application of ethnoarchaeology, ethnohistory, and linguistics hold great promise. I know of no studies focusing on gender from early farming sites in the Sahara-savanna zone of Africa that produced the first indigenous domesticates—millet, sorghum, and African rice. A gender study of the Early Iron Age Urewe communities along Lake Victoria's lakeshore and vicinity (ca. 500 b.c.) has been conducted (Maclean 1998). Indirect evidence for farming includes the location of Urewe sites on the most fertile lands in the region and palynological sequences suggestive of human-induced deforestation. Domestic cattle and caprovine remains suggest a mixed agropastoral economy that approximates Neolithic conditions elsewhere. However, a well-developed iron-smelting technology was in place here as well and makes this case unique.

Maclean identifies four new activity sets in Urewe Early Iron Age communities: ceramic production, iron production, agricultural production, and pot cooking. Who produced the ceramics is ambiguous, although regional ethnographic accounts suggests household production is overwhelming assigned to one sex or the other. A system of joint control of agricultural production is achieved by men clearing the land and women providing all other labor. Local linguistic and ethnographic evidence support this division (Maclean 1998). The author describes pot cooking and iron smelting as a pair of emergent technologies—equally complex and equally powerful—that are linked conceptually in a developing belief system with females responsible for cooking and males for smelting. Cooking and smelting are both perceived as acts of procreation in which the application of heat changes natural objects into cultural objects (plants/animals into food and stone/ore into iron) in the same way blood and semen, when heated, produce a child (Maclean 1998:173).

The study is of note for several reasons. Maclean's emic appreciation for the social value and power associated with pot-cooking technology is important. Producing a range of cooked, nutritious foods required skills and knowledge. As the providers of cooked meals, women would have had the power to withhold food, manipulate food to cause poor health, and pollute food. Communal occasions involving cooked food would have provided arenas for displaying these skills publicly (Brumfiel 1992; Maclean 1998). The joint discussion of productive labor, technology, and symbolism produces a foundation for describing Urewe gender relations in terms of its hegemonic tendency. Lacking a discussion of ritual power per se, Maclean seems to be well on her way to describing a balanced system in which the value of men's and women's productive and symbolic realms were both intimately connected and valued.

Northern China

China presents an interesting anomaly to the historical and theoretical trends already outlined. Shelach (2004) argues that the Chinese archaeologists of the Marxist era (1960–1980) were actively discussing gender and that this concern has become less mainstream in post-Marxist times. Researchers agree that the predominant Marxist paradigm problematized the study of gender by glossing over variation in the name of universal patterns and assuming set temporal trajectories for men's and women's status. Yet Shelach describes the gender discussions of the Marxist era as producing robust, empirically based debates as well (Shelach 2004). Political agendas in the post-1980, nationalistic era have tended to marginalize gender interpretations, focusing instead on situating "Chinese-ness" in the Neolithic past (Barnes and Guo 1996; Shelach 2004). The recent publication of Linduff and Sun's *Gender and Chinese Archaeology* (2004) represents a significant event in the reintegration of gender studies into Chinese archaeology. Reexamination of robust mortuary data sets, ceramic images, figurines, and statuary feature most prominently is recent discussions.

Marxist-era models for the plethora of regional cultures identified across China typically equated Early Neolithic periods with matrilineal, egalitarian society, while Late Neolithic periods were associated with the emergence of patrilineal and patriarchal societies in which gender and social stratification emerged (Pearson and Underhill 1987). Sexual labor scenarios were constructed to accommodate the assumption that men usurped women's role in the productive economy during the Late Neolithic. As such, the expectation was that stone tools associated with cultivation (adzes and stone plowshares) would be found in males' graves and tools associated with domestic chores found in females'. Spindle whorls were typically singled out as female grave goods. Extensive samples from the Late Neolithic cemeteries of the Yangshao culture (north-central China) area and the Qijia culture (northwestern China) demonstrate that this correlation is not supported (Jiao 2001; Sun and Yang 2004). Either utilitarian grave goods are not good indicators of sexed labor patterns, or there were significant overlaps in sexed labor. In contrast, grave goods from the Late Neolithic cemetery of Dadianzi (Xiajiadian culture of eastern Inner Mongolia) lend support to traditional sexual labor divisions, as axes and arrowheads pattern consistently with males and the majority of spindle whorls occur in female graves (Wu 2004). The presence of spindle whorls in a relatively small number of male graves is never discussed, nor is the regionally variability in artifact:sex correlations.

Mortuary analyses of body position, number and type of grave goods, and labor investment in burial pits suggest that the Late Neolithic involved significant social restructuring in several parts of northern China. The distribution of grave goods and increasing numbers of exotic finds in a limited number of burials during the Late Neolithic certainly seems to suggest the emergence of distinctions between important and common people in some regions (Sun and Yang 2004; Wu 2004). How gender features in the emergent stratification is often unclear. The consideration of male/female patterning is often limited to a small subset of the burials. Double burials of adult males and females have received considerable attention in discussions of gender relations (Jiao 2001; Sun and Yang 2004; Wu 2004). During the Marxist era, this emphasis stemmed from their assumed association with the arrival of patriarchy, establishment of monogamous marriage patterns, and the resulting loss of social and economic independence for women (Sun and Yang 2004:31–32). Subsequently, they have also been used to trace changes in the status balance between the sexes. In some of the Qijia double burials, for example, female burials with skeletal elements either missing or out of anatomical position are interpreted as wives, slaves, or concubines sacrificed as part of the burial ritual (Jiao 2001; Sun and Yang 2004).

Yet mixed-sex double burials are a short-lived phenomenon limited to certain regions. In the Late Neolithic alone, single burials predominate—even at the sites with double burials. There are documented examples of double burials involving adults and children as well. And finally, mixed- and single-sex multiple burials are also part of the tradition (Jiao 2001). Thus, while site-specific cases for emerging social (and possibly gender) stratification can be built (Wu 2004), any attempt to generalize broadly about gendered mortuary patterns is quite premature.

The only discussion of human imagery on ceramics I know of briefly introduces Early Neolithic examples from the Majiayao culture. Male, female, and sexless figures occur on ceramics in burials. Images of figures that hold hands encircling bowl interiors are described as indicating men's and women's ritual dances associated with harvest, fertility, and sexual potency. One anthropomorphic jar has a female image on one side and a male on the other. This dual-sexed image and the association of both male and female painted representations on ceramics in graves suggests to some a complementary and unified conception of gender in the Majiayou Early Neolithic and is contrasted with the succeeding Late Neolithic Qijia, with its evidence for asymmetrical treatment of males and females in burials and lack of human iconography on pottery (Sun and Yang 2004:444–45).

Two ritual sites uncovered in the 1980s in northeastern China contain fascinating female-sexed figurative imagery. Both belong to the Hongshan culture of northeastern China, which flourished from 6,000 to 4,500 years ago. While most Hongshan sites consist of unpretentious Neolithic-style village sites, Dongshanzui and Niuheliang contain unique evidence of ritual elaboration and hierarchical social development in early farming contexts (Nelson 1995, 2002). Dongshanzui is a ritual site consisting of a cluster of house floors, stone platforms, and enclosures. Among these features are spread twenty clay figurine fragments, several of which are described as nude, probably pregnant females and a third that may be nursing (Jiao 2001; Nelson 2002; Pearson and Underhill 1987). Fragments of larger statues, at least one life sized, are in some cases sexed female (Jiao 2001).

Niuheliang is more accurately described as a ritual complex rather than a single site. It consists of tombs, structures, and compound enclosures stretching over eighty square kilometers. The complex does not contain a settlement component. It lies across from a low mountain shaped like the head of an animal (Barnes and Guo 1996). The tombs are considered to be elite resting places because of the effort required for their construction as well as the wealth of exotic and finely made grave goods—particularly intricate jade pieces (Barnes and Guo 1996; Nelson 1991, 2004). A large cruciform pit structure with elaborate construction and painted designs is described as the "Goddess Temple." Among the stunning finds within the temple were a painted clay mask with inlaid jade eyes and fragments of at least seven large clay statues, one estimated to be three times life size. At least one statue can be sexed female, given the presence of a breast fragment. A radiocarbon date of about 3500 B.C. situates the site in the Late Neolithic of the Hongshan culture and suggests that it may pre-date the first life-size human sculptures previously known from 3200 B.C. in Egypt (Barnes and Guo 1996).

One interpretation of Niuheliang simply assumes that the mask and statues within the complex represent the worship of female deities on which the Hongshan culture's religion centered (Jiao 2001:60). In a series of publications, Nelson has explored the political and religious significance of these images in more detail (Nelson 1991, 1995, 1996, 2002, 2004). She notes as relevant the absence of male figures at these ceremonial sites. Based on Sanday's (1981) cross-cultural research concerning gender formulations in origin myths and other religious contexts, it is difficult to deny females social power in the Hongshan cultural system where female symbolism predominates (Nelson 1991, 1996). Both ancient texts and ethnohistoric data suggest clues as to the possible sources of this power. Women may have exercised considerable leadership in spiritual life as shamans (Nelson 1996, 2002). Furthermore, women may have played important roles in the management and husbandry of pigs. While the economic importance of pig declines over the course of the Hongshan, its cultural significance is magnified as manifest through increased pig imagery and evidence for pig feasts (Nelson 1995, 2004). Working from the figurative evidence, Nelson builds compelling arguments that women were influential agents in elite Hongshan cultural circles.

Sexing the individuals in the elite tombs will certainly provide relevant data; however, results of these analyses are currently unavailable (Nelson, personal communication). If women are among the important people buried at Niuheliang, then credence is lent to a discussion of their role as central figures in elite spheres. If the burials contain only males, then the appropriation and manipulation of female imagery by males may become appropriate paths of future inquiry.

Southern Levant

As recently as 1998, well-respected figures in Levantine prehistory were cautioning that gender was all but impossible to recognize in the early prehistory of the Middle East (Bar-Yosef and Belfer-Cohen 1998:279–80). I disagree with this pessimistic forecast in light of a growing corpus of bioarchaeological work that has provided considerable insight into the activities of early farming populations. In addition to well-preserved skeletal material, the Levant boasts spectacular architectural preservation of both domestic and ritual structures. Figurative representations painted on ceramics, molded from clay, and formed with plaster on skulls are all open to gendered analyses.

In a research tradition dominated by technological and environmental analyses, statements about internal social dynamics are scarce and about sex and gender even more scarce. When pushed to consider women's activities in Neolithic societies, authors sometimes provide a litany of women's economic tasks including house construction, food preparation, water and wood gathering, planting fields, tending crops, harvesting, caring for domestic animals, cleaning, and refuse disposal (Bar-Yosef and Belfer-Cohen 1998:283). In this same account, no similar list is provided for the men. We are also told to expect that productive labor will become increasingly sex segregated with the establishment of farming communities as women are described as having new agricultural tasks and additional child care duties added to their workload. Men, meanwhile, would be increasingly involved in long-distance trade (Bar-Yosef 1995). Not only are tasks not shared, but they are spatially separate. A related point suggests that the appearance of female figurines during the Neolithic is a cultural expression for a growing dichotomy between males and females (Bar-Yosef and Belfer-Cohen 1992). The authors' recent statements regarding the inaccessibility of gender have not kept them from making some fairly specific statements on the subject in the past.

Despite these gloomy projections, a number of researchers have found productive venues to explore gender. The skeletal material from Abu Hureyra, a site in the Euphrates River valley of present-day northern Syria, was analyzed with specific attention paid to markers of occupational stress (Molleson 1994, 2000). A suite of morphological changes to the skeleton (joint faceting, degeneration of joints, and pronounced muscle attachment sites) suggested to Molleson that women spent a considerable amount of time kneeling on the floor with their toes tucked up under their feet, probably processing grain at querns. She also identified groups of females who, by virtue of distinctive dental use-wear patterns and enlarged mandibular joint surfaces, were probably involved in processing quantities of tough plant material to obtain fibers (Molleson 1994, 2000). Based on Molleson's research and the evidence showing that more women than men were buried beneath house floors, the excavators hypothesize that women's labor was closely associated with the household. They extrapolate that men would have been involved in agriculture and herding and further that men and women would have likely cooperated in labor-intensive, tightly scheduled activities like communal game drives and harvesting (Moore et al. 2000).

Two multisite analyses of Neolithic skeletal remains have suggested that Levantine sexual labor patterns might be highly localized (Eshed et al. 2003; Peterson 2002). The authors agree that Neolithic farmers had more physically demanding lifestyles than their Natufian predecessors and that new kinds of activities influenced musculature. However, they disagree on sexual divisions of labor. Osteological material from nine sites indicates to Peterson (2002) that there is little clear evidence to support a pronounced sexual division of labor during the Neolithic, as both males and females appear to have used similar muscle groups at similar levels and in similar ways. Perhaps a large number of labor-intensive tasks were shared by both sexes, or male and female tasks differed to some degree but produced similar musculature signatures. Eshed et al. (2003), in contrast, find that males in their Neolithic sample retain a high degree of muscle asymmetry in contrast to the more bilaterally symmetrical musculature of females. Since the majority of their sample comes from the coastal site of Atlit Yam (now underwater), the author proposes that paddling boats might have been a significant contributor to male musculature. The collective results suggest that sexual labor patterns varied with respect to local environments within the southern Levantine setting. Both studies provide results that occasionally suggest specific activities but more often reconstruct general activity patterns and levels. Nevertheless, even coarse-grained patterns add substantially to the discussion of sexual labor patterns.

Wright's analysis of the social contexts of food preparation and dining in Neolithic societies discusses changing men's and women's roles over time. She describes grinding and cooking as women's tasks, citing osteological and ethnographic evidence. During the earliest phase of food production (Pre-Pottery Neolithic A), grinding tools and hearths are found both indoors and outdoors representing fluid and unstructured boundaries between house and common spaces. By the Late Pre-Pottery Neolithic B, these same tools and features are found increasingly inside larger, more complicated houses in spaces that Wright describes as less accessible and out of the public eye. Following Hastorf (1991), she associates a spatial restriction of food-processing artifacts as a circumscription and control of female activities (Wright 2000:114).

This is a fascinating line of inquiry but one that needs to consider several points before its potential is fully actualized. For one, most of the structures that Wright examines have good evidence of being multistoried. The analysis of interior spaces and artifact distributions succumbs to a "tyranny of the floor plan." By this I mean that archaeologists have difficulty, in all but the most rare cases, reconstructing the arrangements of space and artifacts that occurred anywhere except on the ground floor (Peterson 2004). Furthermore, the conclusion that female activities are being controlled and circumscribed, to me, seems predicated on the notion that men are operating in different social and spatial contexts. Aside from hunting, which is becoming much less economically significant as sheep and goat domestication provide most of the needed protein, we do not have any archaeological or bioarchaeological evidence for what the men were doing. Recent osteological evidence from Çatalhöyük suggests that men were spending as much time in the smoky interior spaces as women were (Hodder 2005). Finally, our etic notions of interior spaces as "inferior," "dark," and "cramped" need to be critically examined. Considering the placement of burials under house floors, might not ground-floor rooms have been "sacred" and "powerful"?

Figurative imagery increases during the Neolithic of the southern Levant. The sculpted assemblage divides logically into larger, plaster and clay statues (thirty or more centimeters) typically found in ritual caches and smaller figurines made from clay and stone and found in domestic areas and refuse deposits. The larger statues have been interpreted as having roles in public rituals, as their size, stylized features (big eyes), and probable added garments would have made them highly visible (Garfinkel et al. 2002; Schmandt-Besserat 2004b). Examples of the large plaster statues have been described from Jericho, Nahal Hemar Cave, and 'Ain Ghazal. The most extensive collection (parts of approximately thirty-four statues) comes from two caches at 'Ain Ghazal. Morphologically, most are sexless, although three have sexual characteristics that indicate that they are female (Tubb and Grissom 1995). Examples of female images predominate among the figurines, although examples of both male and sexless figurines occur there as well (Bar-Yosef and Belfer-Cohen 1992; Miller 2002).

A recent interpretation of the proliferation of anthropomorphic images during the Neolithic revolution suggests that their meaning can be broadly interpreted. Cauvin (1997) maintains that the Neolithic revolution, rather than having its genesis in climate change or economic need, derived from a symbolic revolution grounded in a religious beliefs that placed women and bulls jointly at the apex of the prehistoric pantheon. Cauvin's position is evocative of Gimbutas at some levels, and the response to the sweeping explanatory framework in the Levant has been similar to that in Europe.

More nuanced treatments of the representations have been offered by individuals looking at the context, technology, clay composition, range of sexed types/combinations, and standardization in specific assemblages. Schmandt-Besserat describes one alternative suggested from early Babylonian texts—that the plaster statuary from 'Ain Ghazal might have functioned in ghost rituals. Ghosts featured in rituals as 1) beneficent spirits called on to remove pain by taking it with them to the underworld, 2) diviners, and 3) malevolent spirits to be exorcised

(Schmandt-Besserat 2004a). Both morphological features and contextual associations of the archaeological assemblage resonate with early historical accounts and make this hypothesis worthy of further consideration.

The largest assemblage of figurines to date comes from Sha'ar Hagolan, a village near the Sea of Gallilee (Garfinkel et al. 2002). Among the 200 figurines, a subset of seventy-four seated clay figurines has received special attention. They are designated "cowrie eyed" by virtue of their most prominent feature: long elongated oval eyes with diagonal slits. The cowrie-eyed seated figurines stand out because they appear substantially more standardized in facial and body features, apparel, and body position than the other figurines at Sha'ar Hagolan and those at other Levantine Neolithic sites as well (Miller 2002). Miller interprets the figurines as representing the Matron of Sha'ar Hagolan. As for the matron's authority, she assumes that the seated posture is linked with a position of power—as it is often assumed for male figures. Given the domestic context of finds, the matron's authority and power may hold sway primarily within the household. As to her maturity, Miller interprets the generous proportions of the lower torso and legs as being linked not with youth but with the joint effects of gravity, childbearing, and sedentism on a middle-aged body.

This interpretation is interesting and plausible but forgoes any discussion of the male cowrie-eyed figure mentioned but not illustrated (Garfinkel et al. 2002:195). In addition, there has been considerable discussion of the dual-sexed nature of these and similar figurines in the Levant and Cyprus. While the figurines have female anatomical details on the front, their overall outline and profile, when viewed from the rear, resemble phalli and glandes (Gopher and Orelle 1996; Miller 2002). Casual observations of the photographs and drawings of examples from the Sha'ar Hagolan assemblage substantiate possible dual-sex imagery in the cowrie-eyed assemblage as well. Consideration of the dual-sex interpretations does not enter into Miller's final assessment.

Less numerous than the figurines and statues from Neolithic sites are a set of figurative representations engraved on stone vessels or slabs; incised, painted, and molded in relief on ceramics; and painted on plaster floors. Garfinkel (2003) argues that these are best understood as "dancers" in religious rituals and surveys the distribution and frequency of similar imagery across the Near East and Europe from the eighth to the fourth millennium B.C. The emergence and increase in dancing motifs, beginning in the Neolithic, marks the intensification of ritual practice that would have provided the needed cohesion among members of growing agricultural villages. The decline in dancing motifs during the fourth millennium is viewed as signifying the reduction in prominence of dance in public, ritual life concomitant with the emergence of religious specialists and centralized authority. The Neolithic examples are widely distributed over space and relatively scarce. The celebrants are female, male, and sexless. While I do not always agree with the author's sex assignments (Peterson 2005), I think it is safe to say that females constitute the majority. From Neolithic objects, all-female and mixed-sex groups occur, but there are no clear examples of all-male groups. Accepting Garfinkel's premise that these are dancers, it seems reasonable to suggest that women played a significant role in Neolithic ritual sphere. But Garfinkel astutely reminds us that these images are not the equivalent of photographs of ancient rituals. The depictions on ritual and commemorative objects are realistically interpreted as reflecting the concepts *behind* the dance. The consistent uniformity in appearance, size, and posture of grouped figures is suggestive of an egalitarian ethic in which male, female, and sexless bodies had similar representational meaning at some level(s) (Garfinkel 2002).

In contrast with the communal ethic represented among the dancers, the production of plastered skulls seems to have been a Neolithic ritual that focused on the maintenance of individual identity. The postmortem removal of the skull was a common part of the Pre-Pottery Neolithic mortuary ritual. Certain of these removed skulls were slated for special treatment and subsequent reinterment. Plaster was applied to create distinctive facial features. Along with the application of pigment and inlaid items, it seems that there was an attempt to re-create individual likenesses. While this may be true, the widely held belief that these skulls represented an ancestor cult focusing on revered, male ancestors can no longer be sustained. Both CT scans and DNA analysis now indicate that skulls from women, men, and children all received this special treatment (Bonogofsky 2004). This ritual sphere is also inclusive in terms of both age and sex categories.

There is, I would argue, little evidence for a hegemonic gender hierarchy in the southern Levant. Detailed mortuary studies provide no evidence for status differentiation along sex lines during the Neolithic (Grindell 1998). Men and women are jointly participating in range of physically strenuous, habitual activities. Some sexual divisions of labor seem to be present with grinding and fiber processing being done by females and ungulate hunting probably being done by men. But there is no evidence of the bulk of agricultural work being borne by one sex or the other. Females were actively involved in domestic and community rituals that featured plaster statuary, skull plastering, and household figurines. There is some evidence for increasingly cloistered context for women's food preparation activities, but analyses need to consider both men's spaces, roof spaces, and possible emic meanings of ground-floor spaces before conclusions about the emergence of differential access to and use of public and private spaces can be sustained.

Coastal Ecuador

The Early Formative Valdivia culture of coastal Ecuador maintained sedentary village life based on multicrop agriculture. Domesticates included maize, beans, squash, and manioc. Fishing and shellfishing were important dietary components as well. During the 2,800 years that mark its development (ca. 4400–1600 B.C.), there is some evidence for emergent hereditary inequality as sites become more internally complex, evidence for ceremonialism increases, and mortuary data provides some evidence of social ranking (Zeidler 2000). Recent studies have suggested that symbolic separation between the sexes characterized household spaces and, less convincingly, daily tasks. But it is equally clear that neither separate household spheres nor the onset of incipient complexity removed females from a wide range of political and religious roles.

Efforts to differentiate the primary economic tasks of Valdivian culture are the least satisfying of recent gender efforts. Ethnographic and Spanish ethnohistoric sources have been used to establish a sexed labor pattern for the primary economic tasks. The sources are accepted grudgingly but without much critical analysis and no independent archaeological support (Bruhns and Stothert 1999). Not surprisingly, a highly segregated labor scenario emerges with men and women taking on different tasks and carrying these tasks out in different spaces. Women worked in the fields doing most of the agricultural work. They also maintained kitchen gardens and collected fish and shellfish in the mangrove swamps. Textile and, possibly, pottery production were female domains as well. Men cleared virgin agricultural land, fished in the bays and estuaries, constructed houses, hunted, and trapped (Bruhns and Stothert 1999:108). It has been suggested that a broadly diversified economy, like that of the Valdivians, would have labor and scheduling requirements likely to involve a pronounced sexual division of labor (Pearsall, in Bruhns and Stothert 1999:114).

An interest in household social organization has long been a staple of Latin American archaeology thanks to the pioneering work of Flannery, Winter, Wilk, and others. In keeping with this tradition, several attempts have been made to map gendered activities into domestic spaces and village structure. Village layout at the site of Loma Alta is described as U-shaped, with houses forming three sides around an open plaza area (Damp 1984). Using presumed associations between objects, tasks, and sexual labor divisions, Damp identifies a woman's spinning area from spindle whorls just outside the front door of one structure. Interior hearths are also assumed to be women's food production areas. Lithic debris and a broken tool on an exterior side of the house delimits a men's zone according to the author. A structural separation of male and female spheres is expanded in the interpretation of village layout using ethnographic data from the Ge Bororo of central Brazil. Damp maintains that the open plaza area, associated with the public and ceremonial aspects of village life, is associated with the "male," while the female sphere centers on the house and is considered peripheral (Damp 1984:582). While the separation of household space into male and female realms garners support from a second study, the interpretations associating male:public and female:household have been more recently challenged.

Ethnoarchaeological work among the Achuar of southeastern Ecuador has provided a basis for interpreting household spaces as well. A conceptual and functional division of house space into male and female areas is identified. Feature placement, artifact distribution, and microassemblages trampled into earthen floors from the archaeological site of Real Alto have produced parallel patterns to those observed and excavated from ethnographic settings (Stahl and Zeidler 1990; Zeidler, in Bruhns and Stothert 1999). These patterns suggest that both men and women use houses, with women's activities centering on the hearth and men's activities along the periphery. While these provide some insights into gender organization and symbolism, one might ask whether a complete picture of men's and women's lives can be constructed emphasizing households and domestic structures. In the case of Valdivia, the answer would be an emphatic no.

Real Alto (Phase 3, ca. 2800–2400 B.C.) contains several ceremonial structures on earthen platforms located in the central ceremonial district. The Charnel House stands on one of these mounds and contained a female skeleton in the central crypt, which was lined with fragmented manos and metates. The tomb complex also contained partially disarticulated and secondary interments of seven males. The group has been interpreted, most recently, as a high-status family. A hereditary component to status is suggested by the inclusion of subadults in the burials. The female burial stands out primarily because of its placement in the central ceremonial precinct of the large village (Zeidler 2000:167–68). Bruhns and Stothert (1999:100) ponder whether this woman might not have been sacrificed when the building was dedicated. While this alternative is plausible, I would note the infrequency with which male burials in similar contexts would be considered sacrificial victims.

A second inhumation from San Isidro (Phase 8, ca. 1800–1600 B.C.) is distinctive by virtue of its grave goods. A young female (age fifteen to twenty) was buried with a suite of tools highly suggestive of a shaman's ritual paraphernalia, including bat bones, a miniature incised vessel, ceremonial pieces of ground stone, and a cape or poncho made from a medium-sized feline with portions of the maxilla and mandible intact. Inside the mouth of the feline was a small figurine. It has been suggested that Valdivia figurines functioned as the repositories for spirits visited by shaman during trance (Stahl, in Zeidler 2000). Together, the burials from Real Alto's Charnel House and San Isidro suggest that women were highly visible in politico-religious aspects of Valdivian society and definitely not concerned only with preparing family meals and spinning. The archaeological evidence also mounts a substantial challenge to Damp's interpretation of women's spheres and the use of the Ge Bororo as an appropriate analogue.

The final data set to be considered are the Valdivia figurines, which have typically been interpreted as female fertility symbols. While female-sexed images predominate, once again there are examples of male and sexless images as well (Zeidler 2000:172). Figurines are found in a variety of contexts: domestic, mortuary, and ceremonial. One alternative to the fertility hypothesis describes some of the seated female figures as representations of powerful ritual practitioners (Bruhns and Stothert 1999:116). Zeidler proposes a third interpretation, suggesting that they were ritual paraphernalia used in shamanic rites, curing, and rites of passage. The predominance of female figurines suggests that a number of shamanic rituals were female focused related to life cycle changes, illness, and dangerous events like childbearing (Zeidler 2000:174). Alternatives to the fertility hypothesis reinforce the notion that women were highly visible actors in Valdivian society and support Zeidler's interpretations of the mortuary data from Real Alto's Charnel House and the San Isidro "shaman" burials.

Pre-Hispanic Southwest

Claassen (1997:77) noted that little gendered work had been conducted in southwestern archaeology. But Crown's edited volume *Women and Men in the Prehispanic Southwest* (2000b) provides readers a compilation of thoughtful studies written by researchers with long-standing interests in using gender to explore prehistoric farming societies. The Southwest is fortunate to have tremendously diverse and generally well-preserved archaeological data sets, robust regional databases, and contemporary Puebloan groups as possible analogues. Researchers have avoided some of the shortcomings discussed earlier in this chapter by a conservative approach emphasizing the "particular" over the "general."

In the context of sexual labor divisions, rather than assuming a task division for agricultural work, researchers admit that the production and distribution of corn has yet to be engendered (Spielmann 1995). Fish (2000:176–77) suggests that men and women likely shared responsibility and control for different stages of production and use of intensively managed plants. She views it likely that men's labor was pulled into agricultural pursuits as crops became a major share of diet, a view with some osteological support. Measures of cortical thickness and area indicate that Black Mesa males and females were not significantly dimorphic with respect to skeletal robusticity or muscularity. Both males and females had physically demanding lifestyles that could have resulted from participating either in the same tasks or in different tasks that required similar amounts and types of physical exertion (Martin 2000:282). Mixed-sex participation in hunting also seems likely if we view "hunting" more broadly to include small game drives, trapping, and the like (Szuter 2000:199–200).

There is wide acceptance and substantial archaeological support for assigning several tasks to one sex or the other. Bioarchaeological evidence, sex-patterned mortuary offerings, sculpted images, and regional ethnographies support sex role divisions in which women ground corn using manos and metates and men hunted using bows and arrow (Crown 2000a:224; Szuter 2000:207). The attribution of pottery production to women and loom weaving to men is more dependent on southwestern ethnography (Hegmon et al. 2000; Mills 2000; Mobley-Tanaka 1997). The argument has been made that women produced pottery vessels in response to changing sources of food and food preparation requirements (Crown and Wills 1995). These associations between sex and task provide the material bases (artifacts and features) for exploring the gendered use of space and changing gender relationships.

Issues of productive labor and status have been approached by locating the spatial domains of work within villages. Crown (2000c) argues that although women across the Southwest spent an increasing amount of time and energy preparing food, this work was valued as being critical to society's well-being and resulted in complementary status hierarchies for men and women. When status is viewed multidimensionally (as prestige, autonomy, and power), variable trajectories are uncovered for the Mogollon-Mimbres, Hohokam, and Puebloan sequences (Hegman et al. 2000). Mills (2000) makes a similar observation, finding that the increased demand for craft items in Puebloan and Hohokam settings led to different organizational strategies with different impacts on men and women. It is noteworthy that these efforts are unfettered by the devolutionary models so influential in Europe and the Near East. The lack of plow agriculture and secondary products from domestic livestock make the application of Boserupian models far less likely.

Gender ideology and its relationship with productive labor and status has been explored through a variety of media in the Southwest: rock art; pottery, textile, and basket designs; ceramic and stone figurines; and menstrual aprons/imagery (Hays-Gilpin 2000). Mortuary remains indicate fluctuating gender hierarchies within regions and over time, with inconsistent links between the presence of gender hierarchy (male vs. female dominated) and the development of social differentiation (important people vs. commoners) (Neitzel 2000).

In a synthetic chapter concluding Crown's (2000b) volume, Lamphere (2000) suggests that four periods in the prehistory of the Southwest may have supported a more hierarchical hegemony, all of which had men at their apices. A case where hierarchical gender structures reverted to more balanced model is also included. While Lamphere's model is powerful and the database broadly integrative, there is still room for active debate about these interpretations. Discussion of a single case study illustrates this point. Relying heavily on the work by Hegmon and her coauthors, Lamphere suggests that women's prestige declined during the Pueblo IV period (post–A.D. 1300). The symbolic power of the household declined as kivas moved out of household units and into larger, aggregated community contexts. Ceremonial grinding activities, presumed to be a locus of women's power, that were once carried out in specialized mealing rooms or within kivas are increasingly secularized and carried out in open, highly visible plaza settings. This limits women's access to ritual spaces. New tools indicate that labor-intensive tortillas and piki bread making were introduced at this time, increasing women's workloads (Crown 2000c:247, 250; Hegmon et al. 2000:78–89; Mobley-Tanaka 1997:446). A hierarchical hegemony accommodates these data quite well, but the evidence from the realm of ceramic exchange networks and certain mortuary assemblages is less easy to explain.

During the Pueblo IV period, large bowls using a new glaze technology spread quickly across the Albuquerque area. Spielmann (2000:366–76) suggests that women throughout the region were integrated in a network that shared knowledge about how to make and fire these wares. At the site of Hawikku (ca. fourteenth to seventeenth centuries), dental morphology and demographic data indicate that discrete cemetery areas are associated with kin groups. Mortuary treatment and grave offerings suggest that important people (leaders) came from a small subset of the kin groups, suggesting an ascriptive element to status formation. From the 572 inhumations analyzed, eight male and three female "leaders" are identified. The male leaders consistently had grave goods that associated them with warrior roles, and two of the female leaders are described as heads of matrilines (Howell 1995). The third female "leader" had the most diverse array of grave goods, including prayer sticks, human hair (scalps), painted stones, and feathers. Zuni workmen at the site identified her as a "Medicine Priestess" based on a shrine made of shaped and painted wood, string, and feathers contained in the burial (Howell and Kintigh 1996:551). The analyses of mortuary patterns from Hawikku and glazeware ceramics from the Albuquerque area suggest that several avenues to power and prestige were still active for some women during the Pueblo IV period and may have provided considerable counterhegemonic forces.

Progress to Date

The select case studies and historical analysis of gender studies of prehistoric farming groups demonstrates remarkable (albeit uneven) progress toward more sophisticated treatments of this topic in archaeology. While a few scholars may still holdout that gender is archaeologically invisible, this position has become increasingly tenuous. As gender permeates the discussions of Neolithic and Formative societies around the globe, I sense a growing acceptance of its significance.

Task differentiation continues to pose challenges for many scholars, and it is particularly frustrating that the specifics of agricultural labor have proved so illusive. Very often we do not have a good understanding of who reaped, sowed, or milked—and arguably this may be an overly ambitious goal. The promise of fully engendering the Neolithic activity spectrum is likely to go unfulfilled. One productive trend has been to focus on more modest sets of tasks for which there are integrated data from archaeological sources, physical anthropology, and relevant ethnographies from which to infer female and male roles. Limiting the number and types of tasks discussed has left archaeologists with much to discuss. Studies that speculate on sex roles with reference to a broad range of tasks, based entirely on cross-cultural surveys or random ethnographic analogues, have failed to provide the bases for productive analyses and have tended to perpetuate unrealistic and stereotyped sexed labor scenarios.

Osteological studies of occupational stress markers have also added much to our understanding of labor patterns. The data sometimes reflect specific activities like fiber processing but often warrant more generic statements about the levels of activity, comparisons of synergistic muscle groups, or overall similarity in stress loads between males and females. Efforts to provide fine-grained interpretations from coarse-grained data leave room for injecting preconceived assumptions about labor patterns (Peterson 2002; Robb 1994c).

We can also trace a growing appreciation for the rich symbolic and ritual lives of early farmers. Researchers are actively grappling with the uses and meanings of human representations in a variety of media. Where once we had widespread acceptance that all the representations (or at least those worth depicting and discussing) were female and that all female images were fertility goddesses, we now find these same assemblages being discussed in the context of fluid gender roles, business transactions, shamanistic cures, celebrations of dance, and ghost rituals.

Evolutionary frameworks that viewed gender roles as proceeding through a series of predictable stages defined by technological, economic, and demographic variables served a generation of scholars well in their attempts to understand the processes of culture change. Unpacking the assumptions inherent in long-held theories and choosing alternatives can be an awkward process. But we have, for the most part, emerged from that process. The result is not a set of studies with a single, shared theoretical approach. They are, instead, typically informed by a variety of interests and perspectives: agency, practice theory, and the feminist critique, to name but a few. Their coherence comes not from a shared paradigm but through what Hegmon (2003:219) describes as an openness and dynamism that result from dialogue across theoretical lines. When combined with methodological rigor and an appreciation for the limitations of archaeological data, these hybrid theoretical perspectives have begun to pave the way for the next generation of gender studies.

Future Directions and Conclusions

There are several domains of inquiry that I can foresee providing fodder for future studies of gender in farming societies. The dynamic nature of gender in the human life cycle has gone largely untapped. The socialization and acculturation of children is one venue that seems promising (Morelli 1997). The role of apprenticeship in the transmission of cultural knowledge and craft is another (McClure 2004). Recently, Cannon (2004) has drawn attention to mortuary patterns suggestive of mother–daughter inheritance practices as well.

The new social roles and relationships that emerged between men and women during the Neolithic have typically been approached by trying to "gender" objects. A shift in perspective that examines how gender is made material could be a productive alternative. I am particularly drawn to studies that examine the ways in which identity is communicated through dress and adornment (Arnold 2004; Harlow 2004; Sørensen 2000). While the perishable aspects of clothing (textile, fur, and skin/hide) are often lost to time, nonperishable items can be preserved. Stone and shell items that are sewed onto clothing and headpieces or worn as jewelry can sometimes be identified. This line of inquiry might be of interest in any number of Neolithic and Formative contexts with fine-grained mortuary data sets.

Finally, in recent years, radiogenic isotopes of strontium have been used to identify immigrants among ancient populations. Strontium levels from a burial population in West Heslerton that included Neolithic/Early Bronze Age individuals suggested that some of the adult men and women were nonlocal (Montgomery et al. 2005). This method could be applicable elsewhere where the underlying geology has been mapped and is sufficiently variable to differentiate strontium signatures. The value of the application at a microregional level, the one of most significance to prehistorians interested in documenting exogamous marriage patterns for example, has yet to be documented.

The primary focus of this chapter has been to highlight the stunning variation in gender arrangements suggested by a set of geographically dispersed case studies. Historical developments provide the context for tracking the increasing theoretical eclecticism and methodological sophistication being brought to bear on archaeological gender studies. My very sincere wish is that we avoid, in the rush and pressure to generalize, the very real risk of ignoring the conspicuous variability of gender systems among early farming groups that sets our work apart as truly interesting and important.

References

Aaby, Peter
 1977   Engels and Women. *Critical Anthropology* 3(9–10):25–53.
Arnold, Bettina
 2004   Embodied Gender Performances in Early Iron Age Mortuary Ritual. Paper presented at the Chacmool Conference: Que(e)rying Archaeology—The 15th Anniversary Gender Conference, University of Calgary, Alberta, November.
Bacdayan, A. S.
 1977   Mechanistic Cooperation and Sexual Equality among the Western Bontoc. In *Social Stratification*. A. Schlegel, ed. Pp. 270–91. New York: Columbia University Press.
Barber, Elizabeth Wayland
 1994   *Women's Work: The First 20,000 Years*. New York: Norton.
Barnes, Gina, and Dashun Guo
 1996   The Ritual Landscape of "Boar Mountain" Basin: The Niuheliang Site Complex of North-Eastern China. *World Archaeology* 28:209–19.
Bar-Yosef, Ofer
 1995   Earliest Food Producers—Pre-Pottery Neolithic (8,000–5,500). In *The Archaeology of Society in the Holy Land*. T. E. Levy, ed. Pp. 190–201. New York: Facts on File.
Bar-Yosef, Ofer, and Anna Belfer-Cohen
 1992   From Foraging to Farming in the Mediterranean Levant. In *Transitions to Agriculture in Prehistory*. A. B. Gebauer and T. D. Price, eds. Pp. 21–48. Madison, WI: Prehistory Press.
 1998   Views of Gender in African Prehistory from a Middle Eastern Perspective.

In *Gender in African Prehistory*. S. Kent, ed. Pp. 279–84. Walnut Creek, CA: AltaMira Press.

Bonogofsky, Michelle
2004   Including Women and Children: Neolithic Modeled Skulls from Jordan, Israel, Syria and Turkey. *Near Eastern Archaeology* 67:118–19.

Boserup, Ester
1970   *Woman's Role in Economic Development*. New York: St. Martin's Press.

Bruhns, Karen Olsen, and Karen E. Stothert
1999   *Women in Ancient America*. Norman: University of Oklahoma Press.

Brumfiel, Elizabeth M.
1992   Distinguished Lecture in Archaeology: Breaking and Entering the Ecosystem—Gender, Class and Faction Steal the Show. *American Anthropologist* 94:551–67.

Brumbach, Hetty Jo, and Robert Jarvenpa
1997   Ethnoarchaeology of Subsistence Space and Gender: A Subarctic Dene Case. *American Antiquity* 62:414–36.

Cannon, Aubrey
2004   Mortuary Expressions of Mother-Daughter Inheritance and Identity. Paper presented at the Chacmool Conference: Que(e)rying Archaeology—The 15th Anniversary Gender Conference, University of Calgary, Alberta, November.

Cauvin, Jacques
1997   *Naissance des Divinités Naissance de l'Agriculture*. Paris: CNRS.

Chevillard, N., and S. LeConte
1986   The Dawn of Lineage Societies. In *Women's Work, Men's Property*. S. Coontz and P. Henderson, eds. Pp. 76–107. London: Verso.

Claassen, Cheryl
1997   Changing Venue: Women's Lives in Prehistoric North America. In *Women in Prehistory*. C. Claassen and R. A. Joyce, eds. Pp. 65–87. Philadelphia: University of Pennsylvania Press.

Claassen, Cheryl, and Rosemary A. Joyce, eds.
1997   *Women in Prehistory*. Philadelphia: University of Pennsylvania Press.

Cloud, K.
1985   Women's Productivity in Agricultural Systems: Considerations for Project Design. In *Gender Roles in Development Projects*. C. Overholt, M. B. Anderson, K. Cloud, and J. R. Austin, eds. Pp. 17–56. West Hartford, CT: Kumarian Press.

Conkey, Margaret W., and Janet Spector
1984   Archaeology and the Study of Gender. *Advances in Archaeological Method and Theory* 7:1–38.

Crown, Patricia L.
2000a   Gendered Tasks, Power, and Prestige in the Prehispanic American Southwest.

In *Women and Men in the Prehispanic Southwest*. P. L. Crown, ed. Pp. 3–41. Santa
Fe, NM: School of American Research Press.

Crown, Patricia L., ed.

2000b   *Women and Men in the Prehispanic Southwest*. Santa Fe, NM: School of American
Research Press.

Crown, Patricia L.

2000c   Women's Role in Changing Cuisine. In *Women and Men in the Prehispanic Southwest*. P. L. Crown, ed. Pp. 221–66. Santa Fe, NM: School of American
Research Press.

Crown, Patricia L., and Wirt H. Wills

1995   The Origins of Southwestern Containers: Women's Time Allocation and
Economic Intensification. *Journal of Anthropological Research* 51:173–86.

Damp, Jonathan E.

1984   Architecture of the Early Valdivia Village. *American Antiquity* 49:573–85.

Divale, William, and Marvin Harris

1976   Population, Warfare, and the Male Supremacist Complex. *American Anthropologist* 78:521–38.

Dobres, Marcia-Anne

2004   Digging Up Gender in the Earliest Human Societies. In *A Companion to Gender
History*. T. A. Meade and M. W. Wiesner-Hanks, eds. Pp. 211–26. Oxford:
Blackwell.

Ehrenberg, Margaret R.

1989   *Women in Prehistory*. Norman: University of Oklahoma Press.

Eshed, Vered, Avi Gopher, Ehud Galili, and Israel Hershkovitz

2003   Musculoskeletal Stress Markers in Natufian Hunter-Gatherers and Neolithic
Farmers in the Levant: The Upper Limb. *American Journal of Physical Anthropology*
122:303–15.

Fish, Suzanne K.

2000   Farming, Foraging, and Gender. In *Women and Men in the Prehispanic Southwest*.
P. L. Crown, ed. Pp. 169–96. Santa Fe, NM: School of American Research
Press.

Garfinkel, Yosef

2003   *Dancing at the Dawn of Agriculture*. Austin: University of Texas Press.

Garfinkel, Yosef, Naomi Korn, and Michele A. Miller

2002   Art from Sha'ar Hagolan: Visions of a Neolithic Village in the Levant. In
Sha'ar Hagolan 1. Y. Garfinkel and M. A. Miller, eds. Pp. 188–208. Oxford:
Oxbow Books.

Gimbutas, Marija

1974   *The Gods and Goddesses of Old Europe*. Berkeley: University of California Press.

1989   Figurines and Cult Equipment: Their Role in the Reconstruction of Neolithic Religion. In *Archilleion: A Neolithic Settlement in Thessaly, Greece, 6400–5600*

BC. M. Gimbutas, S. Winn, and D. Shimabuku, eds. Monumenta Archaeologica 14. Los Angeles: Institute of Archaeology, University of California.

Gopher, A., and E. Orelle
1996   An Alternative Interpretation for the Material Imagery of the Yarmukian, a Neolithic Culture of the Sixth Millenium BC in the Southern Levant. *Cambridge Archaeological Journal* 9:133–37.

Grindell, Beth
1998   Unmasked Equalities: An Examination of Mortuary Practices and Social Complexity in the Levantine Natufian and Pre-Pottery Neolithic. Ph.D. dissertation, University of Arizona; Ann Arbor: University Microfilms International.

Guyer, Jane I.
1991   Female Farming in Anthropology and African History. In *Gender at the Crossroads of Knowledge*. M. di Leonardo, ed. Pp. 257–77. Berkeley: University of California Press.
1995   Women's Farming and Present Ethnography: Perspectives on a Nigerian Restudy. In *Women Wielding the Hoe*. D. F. Bryceson, ed. Pp. 25–46. Washington, DC: Berg.

Hamilton, Naomi
2000   Ungendering Archaeology: Concepts of Sex and Gender in Figurine Studies in Prehistory. In *Representations of Gender from Prehistory to the Present*. M. Donald and L. Hurcombe, eds. Pp. 17–30. New York: St. Martin's Press.

Harlow, Mary
2004   Dress and Identity at the End of the Roman Empire. Paper presented at the Chacmool Conference: Que(e)rying Archaeology—The 15th Anniversary Gender Conference, University of Calgary, Alberta, November.

Hastorf, Christine
1991   Gender, Space and Food in Prehistory. In *Engendering Archaeology*. J. Gero and M. Conkey, eds. Pp. 131–62. Oxford: Blackwell.

Hays-Gilpin, Kelley
2000   Gender Ideology and Ritual Activities. In *Women and Men in the Prehispanic Southwest*. P. L. Crown, ed. Pp. 91–135. Santa Fe, NM: School of American Research Press.

Hegmon, Michelle
2003   Setting Theoretical Egos Aside: Issues and Theory in North American Archaeology. *American Antiquity* 68:213–43.

Hegmon, Michelle, Scott G. Ortman, and Jeanette L. Mobley-Tanaka
2000   Women, Men, and the Organization of Space. In *Women and Men in the Prehispanic Southwest*. P. L. Crown, ed. Pp. 43–90. Santa Fe, NM: School of American Research Press.

Hodder, Ian
2005   Women and Men at Çatalhöyük. *Scientific American* 15(1):34–41.

Howell, Todd L.
  1995   Tracking Zuni Gender and Leadership Roles across the Contact Period in the Zuni Region. *Journal of Anthropological Research* 51:125–47.
Howell, Todd L., and Keith W. Kintigh
  1996   Archaeological Identification of Kin Groups Using Mortuary and Biological Data: An Example from the American Southwest. *American Antiquity* 61:537–54.
Jiao, Tianlong
  2001   Gender Studies in Chinese Neolithic Archaeology. In *Gender and the Archaeology of Death*. B. Arnold and N. L. Wicker, eds. Pp. 51–62. Walnut Creek, CA: AltaMira Press.
Kent, Susan, ed.
  1998   *Gender in African Prehistory*. Walnut Creek, CA: AltaMira Press.
Lamphere, Louise
  2000   Gender Models in the Southwest: A Sociocultural Perspective. In *Women and Men in the Prehispanic Southwest*. P. L. Crown, ed. Pp. 379–401. Santa Fe, NM: School of American Research Press.
Leacock, Eleanor
  1978   Women's Status in Egalitarian Society: Implications for Social Evolution. *Current Anthropology* 19:247–75.
  1981   History, Development, and the Division of Labor by Sex. *Signs* 7:474–91.
Lerner, Gerda
  1986   *The Creation of Patriarchy*. New York: Oxford University Press.
Lillis, Jackie E.
  2004   Women and the Production of Textiles at the Neolithic Swiss Lake Dwelling Site of Robenhausen. Paper presented at the Chacmool Conference: Que(e)rying Archaeology—The 15th Anniversary Gender Conference, University of Calgary, Alberta, November.
Linduff, Katheryn M., and Yan Sun, eds.
  2004   *Gender and Chinese Archaeology*. Walnut Creek, CA: AltaMira Press.
Maclean, Rachel
  1998   Gendered Technologies and Gendered Activities in the Interlacustrine Early Iron Age. In *Gender in African Prehistory*. S. Kent, ed. Pp. 163–77. Walnut Creek, CA: AltaMira Press.
Martin, M. Kay, and Barbara Voorhies
  1975   *Female of the Species*. New York: Columbia University Press.
Martin, Debra L.
  2000   Bodies and Lives: Biological Indicators of Health Differentials and Division of Labor by Sex. In *Women and Men in the Prehispanic Southwest*. P. L. Crown, ed. Pp. 267–300. Santa Fe, NM: School of American Research Press.
McClure, Sarah B.
  2004   "Variability around the Template": Cultural Inheritance Theory and an

"Engendered" Neolithic Ceramic Technology. Paper presented at the Chacmool Conference: Que(e)rying Archaeology—The 15th Anniversary Gender Conference, University of Calgary, Alberta, November.

Meade, Teresa A., and Merry E. Wiesner-Hanks

2004   Introduction. In *A Companion to Gender History*. T. A. Meade and M. W. Wiesner-Hanks, eds. Pp. 1–7. Oxford: Blackwell.

Mears, John A.

2001   Agricultural Origins in Global Perspective. In *Agricultural and Pastoral Societies in Ancient and Classical History*. M. Adas, ed. Pp. 36–70. Philadelphia: Temple University Press.

Meillassoux, Claude

1981   *Maidens, Meals, and Money*. New York: Cambridge University Press.

Meskell, Lynn

1995   Goddesses, Gimbutas and "New Age" Archaeology. *Antiquity* 69:74–86.

Miller, Michele A.

2002   The Function of the Anthropomorphic Figurines: A Preliminary Analysis. In *Sha'ar Hagolan I*. Y. Garfinkel and M. A. Miller, eds. Pp. 221–33. Oxford: Oxbow Books.

Mills, Barbara J.

2000   Gender, Craft Production, and Inequality. In *Women and Men in the Prehispanic Southwest*. P. L. Crown, ed. Pp. 301–43. Santa Fe, NM: School of American Research Press.

Mobley-Tanaka, Jeanette L.

1997   Gender and Ritual Space during the Pithouse to Pueblo Transition: Subterranean Mealing Rooms in the North American Southwest. *American Antiquity* 62:437–48.

Molleson, Theya I.

1994   The Eloquent Bones of Abu Hureyra. *Scientific American*, August, 70–75.

2000   People of Abu Hureyra. In *Village on the Euphrates*. A. M. T. Moore, G. C. Hillman, and A. J. Legge, eds. Pp. 301–24. Oxford: Oxford University Press.

Montgomery, Janet, Jane A. Evans, Dominic Powlesland, and Charlotte A. Roberts

2005   Continuity or Colonization in Anglo-Saxon England? Isotope Evidence for Mobility, Subsistence Practice, and Status at West Heslerton. *American Journal of Physical Anthropology* 126:123–38.

Moore, A. M. T., G. C. Hillman, and A. J. Legge, eds.

2000   *Village on the Euphrates*. Oxford: Oxford University Press.

Morelli, Gilda A.

1997   Growing Up Female in a Farmer Community and a Forager Community. In *The Evolving Female*. M. E. Morbeck, A. Galloway, and A. L. Zihlman, eds. Pp. 209–19. Princeton, NJ: Princeton University Press.

Neitzel, Jill E.

2000   Gender Hierarchies: A Comparative Analysis of Mortuary Data. In *Women and*

Men in the Prehispanic Southwest. P. L. Crown, ed. Pp. 137–68. Santa Fe, NM: School of American Research Press.

Nelson, Sarah M.

1991   The "Goddess Temple" and the Status of Women at Niuheliang, China. In *The Archaeology of Gender.* Proceedings of the 22nd Annual Chacmool Conference. D. Walde and N. D. Willows, eds. Pp. 302–8. Calgary: Department of Archaeology, University of Calgary.

1995   Ritualized Pigs and the Origins of Complex Society: Hypotheses regarding the Hongshan Culture. *Early China* 20:1–16.

1996   Ideology and the Formation of an Early State in Northeast China. In *Ideology and the Formation of Early States.* H. J. M. Claessen and J. G. Oosten, eds. Pp. 153–69. New York: E. J. Brill.

2002   Performing Power in Early China: Examples from the Shang Dynasty and the Hongshan Culture. In *The Dynamics of Power.* M. O'Donovan, ed. Pp. 151–67. Occasional Paper 30. Carbondale: Center for Archaeological Investigations, Southern Illinois University.

2004   *Gender in Archaeology: Analyzing Power and Prestige.* Walnut Creek, CA: AltaMira Press.

Ortner, S. B.

1996   *Making Gender: The Politics and Erotics of Culture.* Boston: Beacon Press.

Pearson, Richard, and Anne Underhill

1987   The Chinese Neolithic: Recent Trends in Research. *American Anthropologist* 89:807–22.

Peters, E. L.

1978   The Status of Women in Four Middle East Communities. In *Women in the Muslim World.* L. Beck and N. Keddie, ed. Pp. 311–50. Cambridge, MA: Harvard University Press.

Peterson, Jane

2002   *Sexual Revolutions: Gender and Labor at the Dawn of Agriculture.* Walnut Creek, CA: AltaMira Press.

2004   Around the House: The Use of Space in Late Pre-Pottery Neolithic B Villages in the Southern Levant. Paper presented at the 69th Annual Meeting of the Society for American Archaeology, Montreal, April.

2004   Review of *Dancing at the Dawn of Agriculture.* *Near Eastern Archaeology* 67:117–18.

Robb, John

1994a   Burial and Social Reproduction in the Peninsular Italian Neolithic. *Journal of Mediterranean Archaeology* 7:27–71.

1994b   Gender Contradictions, Moral Coalitions, and Inequality in Prehistoric Italy. *Journal of European Archaeology* 2:20–49.

1994c   Issues in the Interpretation of Muscle Attachments. Paper presented at the Annual Meeting of the Paleoanthropology Society, Anaheim, CA, April.

Sacks, Karen
    1974   Engels Revisited: Women, the Organization of Production, and Private Prop-
            erty. In *Women, Culture and Society*. M. Rosaldo and L. Lamphere, eds. Pp. 207–
            22. Stanford, CA: Stanford University Press.
Sanday, Peggy Reeves
    1981   *Female Power and Male Dominance: On the Origins of Sexual Inequality*. Cambridge:
            Cambridge University Press.
Schlegel, Alice
    1977   Toward a Theory of Sexual Stratification. In *Sexual Stratification: A Cross-
            Cultural Review*. A. Schlegel, ed. Pp. 1–40. New York: Columbia University
            Press.
Schmandt-Besserat, Denise
    2004a   'Ain Ghazal Monumental Figures: A Stylistic Analysis. Electronic document,
            http://link.lanic.utexas.edu/menic/ghazal/ChapVI/dsp.html, accessed
            November 15, 2004.
    2004b   A Stone Metaphor of Creation. Electronic document, http://link.lanic.utexas
            .edu/menic/ghazal/ChapIV/chapter4.html, accessed November 15, 2004.
Shelach, Gideon
    2004   Marxist and Post-Marxist Paradigms for the Neolithic. In *Gender and Chinese
            Archaeology*. K. M. Linduff and Y. Sun, eds. Pp. 11–27. Walnut Creek, CA:
            AltaMira Press.
Silverblatt, Irene
    1988   Women in States. *Annual Review of Anthropology* 17:427–60.
Sørensen, Marie Louise Stig
    2000   *Gender Archaeology*. Cambridge: Polity Press.
Spector, Janet D.
    1983   Male and Female Task Differentiation among the Hidatsa: Toward the
            Development of an Archaeological Approach to Gender. In *The Hidden Half:
            Studies of Plains Indian Women*. P. Albers and B. Medicine, eds. Pp. 77–100.
            Washington, DC: University Press of America.
Spielmann, Katherine A.
    1995   Glimpses of Gender in the Prehistoric Southwest. *Journal of Anthropological
            Research* 51:91–102.
    2000   Gender and Exchange. In *Women and Men in the Prehispanic Southwest*. P. L. Crown,
            ed. Pp. 345–77. Santa Fe, NM: School of American Research Press.
Stahl, Peter W., and James A. Zeidler
    1990   Differential Bone-Refuse Accumulation in Food-Preparation and Traffic
            Areas on an Early Ecuadorian House Floor. *Latin American Antiquity* 1:150–69.
Sun, Yan, and Hongyu Yang
    2004   Gender Ideology and Mortuary Practice in Northwestern China. In *Gender
            and Chinese Archaeology*. K. M. Linduff and Y. Sun, eds. Pp. 29–46. Walnut
            Creek, CA: AltaMira Press.

Szuter, Christine R.
    2000   Gender and Animals: Hunting Technology, Ritual, and Subsistence in the Greater Southwest. In *Women and Men in the Prehispanic Southwest*. P. L. Crown, ed. Pp. 197–220. Santa Fe, NM: School for American Research Press.

Talalay, Lauren E.
    1987   Rethinking the Function of Clay Figurine Legs from Neolithic Greece: An Argument by Analogy. *American Journal of Archaeology* 91:161–69.
    2000   Archaeological Ms.conceptions: Contemplating Gender and the Greek Neolithic. In *Representations of Gender from Prehistory to the Present*. M. Donald and L. Hurcombe, eds. Pp. 3–16. New York: St. Martin's Press.

Trenchard, E.
    1987   Rural Women's Work in Sub-Saharan Africa and the Implications for Nutrition. In *The Geography of Gender in the Third World*. J. H. Momsen and J. Townsend, eds. Pp. 153–72. Albany: State University of New York Press.

Tubb, Kathryn Walker, and Carol A. Grissom
    1995   Ayn Ghazal: A Comparative Study of the 1983 and 1985 Statuary Caches. In *Studies in the History and Archaeology of Jordan V*. Pp. 435–47. Amman: Department of Antiquities.

Whitehouse, Ruth D.
    2002   Gender in the South Italian Neolithic: A Combinatory Approach. In *In Pursuit of Gender: Worldwide Archaeological Approaches*. S. M. Nelson and M. Rosen-Ayalon, eds. Pp. 15–42. Walnut Creek, CA: AltaMira Press.

Wright, Katherine I.
    2000   The Social Origins of Cooking and Dining in Early Villages of Western Asia. *Proceedings of the Prehistoric Society* 66:89–121.

Wu, Jui-man
    2004   The Late Neolithic Cemetery at Dadianzi, Inner Mongolia Autonomous Region. In *Gender and Chinese Archaeology*. K. M. Linduff and Y. Sun, eds. Pp. 47–91. Walnut Creek, CA: AltaMira Press.

Zeidler, James A.
    2000   Gender, Status, and Community in Early Formative Valdivia Society. In *The Archaeology of Communities*. M. A. Canuto and J. Yaeger, eds. Pp. 161–81. New York: Routledge.

Women, Gender, and Pastoralism   8

PAM CRABTREE

T HE TRANSITION FROM FORAGING to farming represents one of the most significance changes in all of human prehistory. The nineteenth-century evolutionary anthropologists used food production, including both agriculture and animal husbandry, to distinguish savagery from barbarism in their schemes of universal social evolution. For V. Gordon Childe (1936) writing in the middle of the twentieth century, plant and animal domestication marked the beginning of the agricultural revolution. Drawing an analogy with the industrial revolution, Childe argued that the agricultural (or first) revolution represented a change in subsistence technology that affected all other aspects of human life, including settlement patterns, social relations, and ideology. Moreover, the agricultural revolution provided the economic basis for the urban (or second) revolution that produced complex, urban societies in Mesopotamia, the Indus Valley, Egypt, and the Mediterranean region (Childe 1950).

In the Eastern Hemisphere, domesticated herd animals, including sheep, goats, and cattle, played a crucial role in both Neolithic and later complex societies. Since the end of World War II, Old World archaeologists have worked diligently to identify the beginnings of animal domestication and to trace the spread of these animal domesticates throughout Eurasia. Less attention has been paid to social context in which early animal domestication took place. This chapter will attempt to examine the roles played by both women and men in early agropastoral societies. It will begin with a definition of pastoralism and a review of the archaeological evidence for the origins and spread of pastoralism in the Middle East and Europe. This chapter will then examine the roles that women and men may have played in early agropastoral societies in Eurasia and the ways that these roles may have changed through time as a result of the use of animals for secondary products, such as milk, wool, and traction (Sherratt 1981, 1983).

Pastoralism

While there is debate in the anthropological literature over the definition of pastoralism, I will follow Chang and Koster (1994:8) and define pastoralists as people "who keep herd animals and who define themselves and are defined by others as pastoralists." This is a very broad definition of pastoralism that includes nomadic pastoralism, transhumant pastoralism, and agropastoralism.

Pastoral nomads are people who practice little or no agriculture and who move their herds from place to place on a seasonal schedule. A classic ethnography of pastoral nomads is Barth's (1961) study of the Basseri in Iran. The Basseri move to high mountain pastures in the Zagros Mountains during the summer and return to the lowlands of southern Persia during the winter. Since pastoral nomads practice little or no agriculture, they are dependent on village farmers for cereals and other necessities. The rise of urbanism in the fourth millennium B.C.E. may have provided new opportunities for specialized pastoralists who could sell their excess meat and other animal products to nonfarming city dwellers (Zeder 1991).

Transhumant pastoralists combine fixed-field agriculture with mobile herding strategies. While part of the community remains in the farming village on a year-round basis, some members of the community move to seasonal pastures with their flocks and herds. Historical and ethnographic records indicate that seasonal transhumance has been practiced in the Swiss Alps since the Middle Ages (Netting 1996). In the Swiss Alps, permanent farming villages are located on the slopes. During the summer, when the high Alpine pastures are free of snow, the flocks from an entire farming village are relocated to these high pastures. The flocks are tended by a small number of men from the village who milk them and make cheeses in bulk (Netting 1996:226). Most of the population remains in the village to carry out hay making and other vital tasks. Historical and archaeological sources suggest that transhumant pastoralism may have a long history in the mountainous parts of southeastern Europe and the Alpine regions of central Europe. Transhumance, known locally as booleying, was also practiced in northwestern Ireland before the potato famine (Shanklin 1994).

Agropastoralists combine both agriculture and animal husbandry in permanent village locations. While those who favor a more restrictive definition of pastoralism may not view agropastoralists as "true" pastoralists,[1] historical evidence suggests that animal husbandry played a critical role in many ancient agropastoral societies in Eurasia. For example, in *De Bello Gallico*, Caesar remarks on the importance of cattle in both Gaul and Germany. In early Christian Ireland (from the fifth to the eighth century C.E.), historic sources indicate that "land was measured in terms of the cows it could maintain, legal compensation was reckoned in terms of cattle, a man's standing in society was determined by his wealth in cattle, and cattle raiding was a recognized form of warfare and adventure for young nobles" (Ó Curráin 1972:53). Agropastoralism has a long history in Eurasia. Archaeological evidence indicates that agropastoral villages were established about 10,000 years ago in the Middle East and that agropastoralism had spread to southeastern Europe by about 7000 B.C.E.

While pastoral societies are characterized by a wide range of mobility strategies, what all these societies have in common is that their livelihood depends on herd animals and their products. Chang and Koster (1994:9) note that "keeping herd animals requires human beings to shape their lives—socially, culturally, economically, and ideologically—in ways that are structured by an interdependence with their animals." This interdependence distinguishes pastoral societies not only from hunter-gatherer societies but also from communities that combine agriculture with hunting, such as the Mississippians of eastern North America. In order to explore the ways in which animal keeping transforms human lives, we will begin by examining the archaeological evidence for the beginnings of animal domestication in the Near East.

Identifying Animal Domestication in the Archaeological Record

Hunters and herders view animals in very different ways. Hunters are interested in acquiring dead animals and their primary products—meat, hides, sinew, and bone. Herders, on the other hand, are interested in live animals and their offspring. The shift from acquiring dead animals to maintaining flocks of live animals marks the beginning of animal domestication (Meadow 1989:81). While this represents a useful behavioral definition of animal domestication, the problem that has vexed archaeologists for over half a century is how to recognize evidence for early animal domestication in the archaeological record.

Most of our evidence for early animal domestication comes from butchered animal bones that were discarded at archaeological sites. These fragmentary remains represent refuse from meat consumption. They are therefore an indirect reflection of animal production strategies. Zooarchaeologists have used a number of criteria to identify early animal domestication in the archaeological record (for a review, see Crabtree 1993). These criteria include the appearance of an animal outside its natural range, morphological changes in the animal bones themselves, and changes in the demographic profiles or age and sex distribution of the animals that were selected for slaughter. While all these criteria have been used success-fully to identify early animal domestication, each criterion has its limitations.

The appearance of animals outside their natural ranges is an obvious indica-tion that animals are under some form of human control. Since wild goats and wild sheep are not native to Europe, the appearance of sheep and goats in south-eastern Europe beginning about 9,000 years ago indicates the beginnings of pas-toralism in that region. However, experiments with animal domestication are most likely to have occurred in regions where the wild ancestors of early domestic animals are found, so this criterion cannot be used to identify the earliest attempts to domesticate animals.

Morphological changes that have been used to identify animal domestication include overall body size reduction, changes in the form of the horn cores (the bones that underlie the horns), reduction in the size of the teeth and jaws, and evidence for pathological changes that may be the result of penning or tethering. The most commonly used of these criteria is overall size reduction since measure-ments can be taken on a wide variety of anatomical elements (Driesch 1976). Tchernov and Horowitz (1991) have suggested that size reduction may have been the result of selection for animals that would mature more quickly and reproduce more rapidly, especially in the anthropogenic environments that surrounded early farming villages. However, recent research by Zeder (2001) has indicated that, at least for goats, the supposed size reduction that accompanied early domestication may be a result changing demographic profiles of the slaughtered herds.

Demographic profiles have been used to identify early animal domestication since the 1960s. Zooarchaeologists suggested that hunting populations, interested in the dead animal and its primary products, would focus their attention on prime adult animals. Those animals would provide the highest-quality meat as well as fat and pelts (Perkins and Daly 1974:80). Herders, on the other hand, would need to maintain a small breeding population of primarily female animals. Most males would be slaughtered in late adolescence, when most of their growth had been completed. A high proportion of immature animals was therefore seen as a signature of early animal domestication.

This criterion was used rather indiscriminately in the 1960s to identify early domestic animals. Perkins (1964), for example, identified possible domestic sheep at Zawi Chemi Shanidar in northern Iraq, dating to the ninth millennium B.C.E., based on a small sample of morphologically wild sheep bones that includes a high percentage of immature specimens. Legge (1972) even suggested that gazelles might have been domesticated in Israel during the Late Pleistocene, based on a high proportion of immature animals at the Natufian site of Nahal Oren. Today, both these claims for early animal domestication are viewed with suspicion. The small sample size and the absence of morphological changes make sheep domestication at Zawi Chemi unlikely (for a critique of the evidence for sheep domestication at Zawi Chemi, see Uerpmann 1987:62–63). Although gazelles can be tamed, they cannot be herded in groups or with dogs, and they are therefore unsuitable for pastoral adaptations (Clutton-Brock 1980:171). The high proportions of young gazelles found at many Late Pleistocene sites in the Near East may be the result of hunting techniques that focused on entire herds of animals (see, e.g., Campana and Crabtree 1990; Henry 1975; Legge and Rowley-Conwy 1987).

Modern studies use demographic profiles to identify animal domestication in far more sophisticated ways. In sexually dimorphic species such as goats, measurement data can be combined with data on aging to construct demographic profiles for each species. Since a focus on live animals and their progeny leads herders to treat male and female animals differently (Meadow 1989), differences in age profiles for male and female animals may reflect the transition from hunting to herding (Hesse 1984; Zeder 2001).

The Archaeological Evidence for Early Animal Domestication in the Near East and Europe

Zooarchaeological data indicate that goats and sheep were first domesticated about 8000 B.C.E. in the Near East. Detailed analyses of the demographic data for early goats from the early eighth-millennium site of Ganj Dareh in western Iran indicates that goats were first domesticated there at about 7900 B.C. (Hesse 1984; Zeder and Hesse 2000). Early domesticated goats appear in the southern Levant at about the same time. Goats from Jericho show changes in the shape of their horn cores that may indicate incipient domestication (Clutton-Brock 1979), while a majority of the goats from the Neolithic site of 'Ain Ghazal in Jordan were killed before they reached adulthood. In addition, some of the goats from 'Ain Ghazal show evidence for arthritis, which may have resulted from poor husbandry conditions (Köhler-Rollefson et al. 1988). It is not entirely clear whether goats were independently domesticated in the southern Levant or whether they were introduced to the region from the Zagros.

Sheep appear to have been domesticated at approximately the same time as goats in the Near East. Early evidence for domestic sheep comes from a number of eighth-millennium B.C.E. sites in Syria and Anatolia. For example, the sheep from the Early Neolithic site of Bouqras in Syria show significant size decrease at a time when their numbers are increasing, leading Clason in Akkermans et al. (1983) to suggest that they were early domesticates. Recent DNA studies

(Hiendleder et al. 2002) suggest that modern domesticated sheep are derived from two different subspecies of wild mouflon (*Ovis orientalis*), indicating that the pattern of sheep domestication may be a complex one involving multiple centers of domestication.

DNA studies have shown that the pattern of cattle domestication in the Old World is quite complex. Both faunal evidence and DNA studies suggest that cattle were independently domesticated in the eastern Sahara between 8,000 and 10,000 years ago (Bradley 2003; Bradley et al. 1998; Gautier 1987). The molecular data also point to an independent domestication of zebu (humped cattle) in South Asia. The DNA evidence points to a third center for the domestication of Near Eastern and European cattle, although the location of this center has not been determined archaeologically. Domesticated cattle appear at a number of sites in the eastern Mediterranean at about 7000 B.C.E.

The cultural context in which early animal domestication took place is equally important. While early scholars such as Childe saw plant and animal domestication as a single process of transformation from foraging to farming, archaeological research conducted over the past twenty-five years has shown clearly that in the Middle East plant cultivation clearly preceded animal domestication (see, e.g., Bar-Yosef and Belfer-Cohen 1991; Moore 1982). In Syria, cereal cultivation may have begun as early as the Late Pleistocene. Hillman et al. (2001) have argued that the residents of Abu Hureyra may have begun to cultivate rye in response to a decline in the availability of wild plants during the Younger Dryas climatic event (around 11,000 B.C.E.). Evidence for early sheep and goat domestication does not appear until Period 2A (about 8000 B.C.E.), millennia after the appearance of cultivated cereal crops. In the southern Levant, plant cultivation was established during the Pre-Pottery Neolithic A (9750–8550 B.C.E.), while early animal domestication does not appear until the Middle Pre-Pottery Neolithic B (8150–7300 B.C.E.).[2] A cluster of Pre-Pottery Neolithic A sites in the lower Jordan Valley, including Gilgal (Noy 1989) and Netiv Hagdud (Bar-Yosef and Kislev 1989; Zohary 1989), has provided evidence for early barley cultivation, but these sites provide no evidence for animal domestication (Tchernov 1994). In short, in the Middle East, animal domestication was adopted by sedentary communities that had already begun to cultivate cereal crops.

The issue of why early cereal cultivators in the Middle East adopted sheep and goat pastoralism remains an important but largely unanswered question. Moore et al. (2000:497) suggest that early agricultural communities in the Middle East experienced significant population increases. As these early farming populations increased, they increased their predation of gazelle herds. As gazelles became less available to these early farming communities, Neolithic farmers turned to domestic sheep and goats as sources of meat. Using an approach based on evolutionary ecology, Alvard and Kuznar (2001:298) have suggested that animal husbandry is a form of prey conservation and that conservation is most likely to occur when long-term returns from husbandry are "higher than short term returns from hunting." In addition, a number of scholars have suggested that early domestic animals served as "walking larders" (Clutton-Brock 1989) that were used to store agricultural surpluses. Livestock manure may have also served to maintain the fertility of small agricultural plots (Halstead 1996:302).

The Near Eastern sequence of plant and animal domestication is in marked contrast to the pattern that has been established for Africa. Both archaeological evidence and DNA studies suggest that cattle pastoralism was established in eastern Africa just south of the Sahara about 8,000 to 10,000 years ago. However, agriculture was not established in the region until about 4000 B.P. Marshall and Hildebrand (2002:111) have suggested that hunter-gatherers in the eastern Sahara may have begun to domesticate cattle "to ensure their predictable availability as a food source." The highly mobile lifestyles of these early pastoralists, especially in marginal areas, worked against the adoption of cereal cultivation. Since the African pattern of animal domestication is so different from the pattern seen in the Middle East and Europe, the remainder of this chapter will focus on early pastoralists in Eurasia.

Women in Early Agropastoral Societies in the Middle East

What roles did women and men play in early agropastoral societies in the ancient Near East? While many studies of early animal domestication have focused on interpretation of the faunal data and have treated humans who domesticated these animals as "a lot of faceless blobs" (Tringham 1991:94), two early studies, one by Robert Braidwood and a second by Charles Reed, envisioned very different roles for women in early animal domestication.

Robert Braidwood was a pioneer in the study of animal and plant domestication in the Near East. In his studies of early animal and plant domestication in northern Iraq and Anatolia, he was one of the first archaeologists to make use of a multidisciplinary research team including zooarchaeologists, paleoethnobotanists, and geoarchaeologists. While Braidwood is best known for scholarly works (e.g., Braidwood and Howe 1960), he is also the author of the aptly named *Prehistoric Men* (Braidwood 1967), which served as an introductory text for archaeologists in the late 1960s and the early 1970s. The text provides the following description of life in an Early Neolithic village:

Children and old men could shepherd the animals by day or help with the lighter work in the fields. After the crops had been harvested the younger man might go hunting and some of them would fish, but the food they brought in was only an addition to the food in the village; the villagers wouldn't starve, even if the hunters and fishermen came home empty-handed. (Braidwood 1967:113)

One wonders what Early Neolithic women and girls were doing while the men and boys planted crops, herded livestock, fished, and hunted the occasional wild animal. Presumably, the women were engaged in child care and food preparation. This vision of early agropastoral societies owes more to the world of Ozzie and Harriet in the 1950s than to the archaeological evidence for life in the Early Neolithic period.

While Braidwood's view of early agropastoral societies is an essentially andro-centric one, Charles Reed, a founding father of zooarchaeology, suggests that women and girls may have played a more active role in early animal domestica-tion. Reed (1977, 1986) notes that taming is a necessary prerequisite for animal domestication and that it is relatively easy to tame wild animals. In order for pastoralism to develop, however, a critical change in human behavior was neces-sary. Reed (1986:12) argues that "as long as the successful male hunter was the hero, the human social ideal, there could be no real relationships between humans and animals other than that of hunter and hunted." Reed (1977) suggests that since men were hunters, women—and especially little girls—took the first steps toward animal domestication by taming wild animals. He argues that

little girls, increasingly as they grow, have estrogens coursing in their bloodstream; little girls play with dolls, have maternal instincts. They are not yet, as their mothers would be, inured to killing and the necessities of killing; a little girl might well adopt, protect, and tend a weaned lamb, kid, or baby pig, thus establishing that one-to-one social relationship nec-essary for the abolition of the flight reaction. (Reed 1977:563)

While this model allows women to play a more active role in early Near Eastern pastoralism, the model rests on untested assumptions about men's roles as hunters and the nurturing nature of women and little girls.

Reed is not alone in assuming that men were hunters and women were plant collectors in preagricultural societies in the ancient Near East. As noted pre-viously, Henry (1975) and others have argued that preagricultural populations in the Near East hunted entire herds of gazelles. Henry (1989:215) further suggests that while these hunting strategies "would have required a substantial party of hunters, there would have been little difficulty in mustering the necessary number of adult males in a Natufian village." Henry (1989:217) further suggests that gathered cereals and nuts would have provided the bulk of the Natufian diet. Plant collecting is often assumed to have been women's work in the preagricultural Near East. For example, an illustration of plant gathering that accompanies an article on skeletal remains from the site of Abu Hureyra in Syria depicts a woman collecting plants during the Epipaleolithic, even though the skeletal remains themselves provide no evidence that women collected plants in Late Pleistocene Syria. In the Early Neolithic, men are shown as both plant cultivators and as herders of goats and sheep (Molleson 1994:75).

There is little direct archaeological evidence to suggest that men hunted animals and women gathered plants in the Near East during the Late Pleistocene. The assumption that men hunted and women gathered must be based on ethnographic parallels, especially analogies with the !Kung San as described by Lee (1968). While Lee's carefully documented study of !Kung San foraging practices has colored archaeological interpretation of ancient hunter-gatherers for over a generation, the !Kung are a particularly inappropriate analogue for ancient Near Eastern foragers. Plant remains, especially the staple mongongo nuts, are available on a year-round basis in the Kalahari, while wild wheats and barleys have a short season of availability in the Middle East. !Kung hunters generally form small hunting parties, while Near Eastern hunters stalked entire herds of gazelles. Since !Kung subsistence practices differ significantly from Epipaleolithic practices, it is unlikely that these two populations practiced similar divisions of labor.

In fact, the nature of Epipaleolithic subsistence, which is well documented archaeologically, might indicate that men and women cooperated in both hunting and gathering activities (Crabtree 1991). Hunting entire herds of animals requires substantially more labor than hunting individual animals. The animals must be driven into some kind of net, trap, or surround, and then the entire herd must be killed. Ethnographic data indicate that men and women often cooperate in communal hunting activities (see, e.g., Downs 1966). Similarly, Epipaleolithic plant-collecting activities focused on wild cereals such as wild wheats and barleys. These cereals ripen during a short three- to four-week period in the spring (Harlan 1971) and must be stored for use throughout the year. It is likely that all members of the community—men, women, and children—cooperated to maximize the harvest of these important plant resources. The nature of Late Paleolithic subsistence in the Near East does not support a strict division of labor by sex. If there is no real evidence for a sexual division of labor for preagricultural populations in the ancient Near East, then we should be highly skeptical of models for the origins of pastoralism that are based on the assumption of male hunting and female gathering.

More recent attempts to identify the sexual division of labor in early agropast-oral societies have focused in human skeletal remains since repetitive activities may leave traces on bones (Molleson 1994, 2000). Molleson examined the human bones recovered from the Epipaleolithic and Early Neolithic site of Abu Hureyra in Syria. She identified changes on the articular surface of the first meta-tarsal that she argued were associated with prolonged use of a saddle quern to grind grain. Since a majority of these pathological changes were seen on smaller (presumably female) metatarsals, she concluded that "most of the food prepara-tion was carried out by women" (Molleson 2000:314). She further concluded that there must have been a sexual division of labor within Early Neolithic house-holds and that "males may have been more involved in hunting and procuring meat" (322), even though there was no specific osteological evidence to support male hunting. Molleson's conclusions have been appropriately criticized by Gilch-rist (1999:44), who notes that "other explanations for the bone pathologies are not explored, and the possibility of more flexible, seasonal, or perhaps age-based divisions of labor are not considered." For our purposes, none of the osteological data shed any light on the roles that women and men (and/or boys and girls) may have played in early animal husbandry. The assumption that men played a major role in early animal husbandry (see, e.g., the image in Molleson 1994:74) is simply an assumption.

Molleson's model of the sexual division of labor in the Early Neolithic sug-gests that women were engaged in tasks inside the household, including not only grinding grain but also basketry and the preparation of hides. Men were engaged in a range of outside activities, including pastoralism, agriculture, and hunting. This scenario bears a striking similarity to Hodder's (1990) model for the Early European Neolithic where he contrasts the *domus*, or interior of the household, with the *agrios*, or exterior world. The model also shows similarities to the early work on the anthropology of gender that suggested that male/female dichotomies and gender hierarchies were grounded in the contrast between the world inside the household (the domestic sphere) and the outside world (the public sphere) (see Moore 1988:21–24 and references therein). Moreover, Molleson (2000:322) argues that women's "role specialization in food preparation at Abu Hureyra can be seen as a natural and inevitable development of nurturing that provided for older children and fathers." Reed used almost the same argument nearly twenty-five years earlier to explain the role of women in early animal domestication.

As an archaeological model of early agropastoral communities, Molleson's model presents several interpretive problems. First, Molleson's assumption that women were engaged primarily in food preparation rests almost entirely on a single line of evidence—that pathologies that appear to be associated with the use of a saddle quern appear more commonly on the foot bones of individuals who appear to be female. Gilchrist (1999:53) has shown that "the most convincing and nuanced readings of gender have been developed from multiple lines of evidence." Second, Molleson fails to address the roles that children might have played in early agropastoral societies. This is a striking omission since the skeletons from Abu Hureyra show that adolescents carried heavy loads, probably on their heads (Molleson 1994:71). Moreover, ethnographic and historical data suggest that children and adolescents often play important economic roles in pastoral and agricultural societies. Third, and most important from our perspective, Molleson fails to address the important question that was first raised by Reed (1977) nearly thirty years ago: how were the male gazelle hunters of the Epipaleolithic transformed into the male shepherds and goatherders of the Early Neolithic? As Reed noted many years ago, this change involves both the development of the technological knowledge involved in animal husbandry and a transformation of the ideology that surrounds animals and human–animal relationships.

The Secondary Products Revolution

The difficulty that archaeologists have had in creating models for women's and men's roles in early agropastoral societies in the Near East and Europe are highlighted when archaeologists attempt to examine the secondary products revolution (SPR) (Sherratt 1996a, 1996b) and its effects on women in early pastoral societies in Eurasia. Sherratt argued that during the mid- to late fourth millennium B.C.E., a series of fundamental changes took place in the ways that Eurasian pastoralists made use of their animals. Domestic animals, including cattle, sheep, and goats, were no longer seen primarily as sources of meat. Instead, they were used for a variety of secondary products, including milk, wool, and traction. Sherratt (1996:160–61) suggests that the SPR "separates two stages in the development of Old World agriculture: an initial stage of hoe cultivation, whose technology and transportation systems were based upon human muscle power, and in which animals were kept purely for meat; and a second stage in which plough agriculture and pastoralism can be recognized, with a technology using animal sources of energy." The use of domesticated animals for a variety of different purposes would also have increased the importance of the pastoral component in ancient economies. Since Sherratt's original model was developed more than twenty years ago, we will begin with a brief review of the archaeological evidence for the SPR (for a concise review of this evidence, see Russell 2004).

The use of animals for traction represents one of the most important technological developments of the later Neolithic (fifth and fourth millennia B.C.E.) in
Eurasia. The use of animals, primarily oxen or castrated bulls, to pull light plows
or ards[3] allowed farmers to expand the amount of land under cultivation. Evidence for early plowing includes plow marks preserved in buried soil surfaces and
images of plowing that appear in Bronze Age rock art. In addition, zooarchaeologists have identified a series of morphological changes on cattle bones that result
from traction activities (Bartosiewicz et al. 1997). In Europe, zooarchaeological
evidence for traction pathologies suggests that plowing may have been established
in eastern Europe as early as 4500 B.C.E. Plowing was established in northwestern
Europe by 4000 B.C.E., and pictographic evidence indicates that plowing was
widespread by 2500 B.C.E. (Russell 2004). Images of light plows are also well
known from mid-third-millennium contexts in the eastern Mediterranean (Sherratt 1996a:165–67). The other main use for draft animals was for transportation.
A wide range of archaeological data, including images and models of carts and
wheel ruts, indicate that wheeled vehicles first appeared in Europe and the Near
East at about 3500 B.C.E.

While the early history of animal-drawn wheeled vehicles in Eurasia is well
documented and well dated, the history of early dairying is less well known. Most
archaeological evidence for dairying is indirect, including ceramic vessels that may
have been used for dairy products and faunal assemblages that include a high
percentage of very young animals under six months of age. The faunal argument
is based on the assumption that dairy herds will include a high percentage of
adult female animals and that excess male calves will be slaughtered at very young
ages. Sherratt (1981) initially argued that dairying was part of the SPR on the
basis of changes in pottery vessel forms. He suggested that the appearance of
vessels such as jugs and cups in the Late Neolithic was associated with the manipulation of liquids, including milk. Bogucki (1984, 1986), however, suggested that
dairying might have a much greater antiquity, at least among temperate European
pastoralists. Bogucki suggested that ceramic sieves, which are commonly recovered
from Early Neolithic (ca. 5500–5000 B.C.E.) Linearbandkeramik sites in central
Europe, may have been used for cheese making. While Sherratt (1996b:206) subsequently acknowledged the possibility that some dairying may have occurred in
Early Neolithic societies, he argued that the quantities of milk produced must
have been quite small. Following McCormick (1992), Sherratt argued that until
recent times, calves must have been present in order for a cow to let down her
milk. Therefore, McCormick (1992) suggested that prehistoric archaeological
sites that have produced evidence for the slaughter of large numbers of very young
cattle do not indicate dairying since the absence of the young calves would pre-

vent females from lactating. This argument is problematic for several reasons. First, a cow can be induced to let down her milk by other means, such as stimulating her vagina or presenting her with a surrogate calf (Russell 2004:327). Second, ethnohistoric and archaeological sources do not confirm McCormick's assertion that faunal assemblages that include a high proportion of very young cattle indicate a meat rather than a dairy economy. For example, the archaeological and historical data for medieval Iceland and Greenland, where cattle were kept almost exclusively for dairying from the initial Viking-period settlement, consistently produce large numbers of very young cattle under six months of age (see, e.g., McGovern et al. 1996, 2001). Third, recent studies of organic residues recovered from pottery vessels from the British Isles provide direct evidence for widespread Early Neolithic dairying in northwestern Europe (Copley et al. 2003). The residue evidence indicates that dairying was established, at least in parts of Europe, well before the SPR.

The antiquity of dairying may also have important implications for our understanding of women's roles in early pastoral societies in Europe. Ethnohistoric data indicate that women played a major role in dairy production in many parts of Europe from the early Middle Ages on (see the following discussion). If women also engaged in dairying in prehistoric European societies, then women may have played an active and integral role in pastoral economies beginning in the Early Neolithic.

The final aspect of the SPR is wool production. Wild sheep and early domesticated sheep were hairy rather than woolly; their short undercoats were shed each spring. In order for sheep to be reared for wool production, genetic changes were necessary so that the wooly undercoat grew longer and was maintained throughout the year. Occasional finds of preserved textiles indicate that sheep's wool first appeared in the Middle East about 3000 B.C.E. and in Europe about 2500 B.C.E. (Russell 2004:327).

The Gender Implications of the SPR

The SPR model, as envisioned by Sherratt (1981, 1996a), has important implications for gender roles in later Neolithic agropastoral societies in Europe and the Near East. Sherratt, unlike Molleson, assumes that women would have played a primary role in Early Neolithic horticulture. He argues that "in simple hoe agriculture, the major subsistence contribution comes from female labor in sowing, weeding, and harvesting" (Sherratt 1996a:194). The SPR led to a fundamental change in the sexual division of labor. It "produced an economy dominated by men, who played a dominant role in handling large livestock either as herds or in plowing. Women became increasingly relegated to the domestic sphere" (Sherratt 1996a:196). Since women were freed from their role as food producers, they could spend more time on activities such as textile production.

The effect of this model is the same as Molleson's and even Braidwood's model for the Early Neolithic—it removes women from primary roles as pastoral producers. This model is problematic for several reasons. First, it assumes that women would have been the primary agricultural producers in Early Neolithic societies in the Middle East and Europe, and there is no clear archaeological evidence to support this assertion. Second, it assumes that men would have taken a major role in both plowing and pastoral production beginning in the Late Neolithic. While medieval historical sources from many parts of Europe indicate that plowing was a male activity, these same sources indicate that women often played a primary role in dairying. Third, it assumes that the introduction of wool sheep would have led to a new role for women as textile producers. It is important to note that while wool sheep may not have been developed until the Late Neolithic or Early Bronze Age, textiles have a much greater antiquity in Eurasia. Neolithic textiles in both the Middle East and Europe were made of flax or linen. At the site of Tybrind Vig in Denmark, Mesolithic textiles made of strings of lime and willow have recently been discovered (Anderson 2004:143), and engravings on Upper Paleolithic figurines suggest that textiles made of plant fibers may have been manufactured in the European Upper Paleolithic (Soffer et al. 2000). Textile production is not a new industry in the Late Neolithic, and the introduction of wool sheep is not likely to have radically changed women's roles. Moreover, early medieval historical sources indicate that women were often engaged in both dairying and textile production (see the following discussion).

Historical Models for Women's Roles in European Pastoral Economies

While no one wants to envision early Eurasian pastoralists as a group of faceless blobs, some alternatives are even worse. The effect of almost all the models reviewed in this chapter is to remove women from a primary role in agropastoral production. In Molleson's model for the Neolithic of the Near East, men are pastoralists and cultivators, while women are engaged in household tasks such as food preparation, basket making, and hide working. Sherratt's model for the SPR envisions men as herders and plowmen, while women are engaged in "spinning, weaving, and textile production" (Sherratt 1996a:195). Unfortunately, there is very little archaeological data to support these gender attributions. These models reify the domestic sphere/public sphere dichotomy and relegate women to a secondary role in pastoral (and agricultural) production. This need not be the case.

The historical record for medieval Europe provides evidence that women played an active role in pastoral production in many regions of the continent. As noted previously, booleying is a form of transhumance that was practiced in parts of Ireland until the early twentieth century. In the spring or early summer, cattle were moved from their winter pastures in the lowlands to summer pastures or booleys, which were often located in wooded, highland areas. Historical accounts of prefamine Ireland describe young women and men accompanying cattle and sheep to the summer pastures along with dairying vessels, spinning and carding equipment, and cooking pots (Shanklin 1994:109–10). Historical records trace the practice of booleying back to the early medieval period (ca. 400–850 c.e.).[4] The early Irish sources associate the practice of booleying with women and children and often with women of low economic and social status (Boyle 2004:95; see also Brady 1994:131; Patterson 1994:90–91). In Ireland, women and children remained in the booleys with the livestock throughout the summer, while men returned to the lowlands to protect the crops and prepare for warfare (Patterson 1994:136). The Irish sources also identify dairying, spinning, baking, and shepherding as appropriate activities for servile women (Brady 1994:131). The Irish data thus suggest that women and children played an active role in pastoral production in early medieval Ireland.

The historical records from late medieval France identify other possible roles for women in medieval agropastoral societies. In late medieval France, plowing was carried out exclusively by men. However, women were not excluded from a direct role in animal production. While men cared for the plow teams, women were responsible for the smaller livestock, such as sheep and goats as well as poultry.

Conclusion

While it would be a mistake to project models of medieval labor organization onto prehistoric Eurasian pastoral communities, the medieval data do suggest ways in which women may have played more active roles in animal husbandry and pastoral production. At present, we do not have adequate archaeological data to identify the roles played by men and women in early agropastoral communities in Eurasia. Nuanced studies of gender must be based on multiple lines of archaeological evidence, not on assumptions about the nature of women as nurturers. Zooarchaeologists have worked for forty years to develop a suite of criteria that can be used to identify early animal domestication in the archaeological record.

We need to address questions about the social organization of pastoral production with equal vigilance.

Notes

1. Dyson-Hudson and Dyson-Hudson (1980), for example, define pastoralists as individuals who rely heavily on domestic herd animals and who move their animals to pasture.

2. These dates are based on Kuijt and Goring-Morris (2002:366).

3. Light plows or ards simply scratch the surface of the soil. Heavy plows, which include a coulter, plowshare, and moldboard, do not appear in Europe and the Mediterranean until about 2,000 years ago.

4. Historical records first appear in Ireland in the early fifth century, but it is likely that the practice of booleying is even older. Only a few possible booleying sites have been identified archaeologically (Boyle 2004:95).

References

Akkermans, P. A., J. A. K. Boerma, A. T. Clason, S. G. Hill, E. Lohot, C. Meiklejohn, M. Le Mière, G. M. F. Molgot, J. J. Roodenberg, W. Waterbolk-vanRooyen, and W. Van Zeist
   1983   Bouqras Revisited: Preliminary Report on a Project in Eastern Syria. *Proceedings of the Prehistoric Society* 49:335–71.
Alvard, Michael S., and Lawrence Kuznar
   2001   Deferred Harvests: The Transition from Hunting to Animal Husbandry. *American Anthropologist* 103(2):295–311.
Anderson, S. H.
   2004   Tybrind Vig. In *Ancient Europe: 8000 B.C.–A.D. 1000: Encyclopedia of the Barbarian World*. Vol. I. Peter Bogucki and Pam J. Crabtree, eds. Pp. 141–43. New York: Charles Scribner's Sons.
Barth, Frederik
   1961   *Nomads of South Persia: The Basseri Tribe of the Khamseh Confederacy*. Boston: Little, Brown.
Bartosiewicz, L., Wim Van Neer, and A. Lentacker
   1997   *Draught Cattle: Their Osteological Identification and History*. Annales du Musée Royale de l'Afrique Centrale, Sciences Zoologiques. Tervuren: 281.
Bar-Yosef, O., and A. Belfer-Cohen
   1991   From Sedentary Hunter-Gatherers to Territorial Farmers in the Levant. In *Between Bands and States*. S. A. Gregg, ed. Pp. 181–202. Carbondale, IL: Center for Archaeological Investigations.

Bar-Yosef, O., and M. E. Kislev
    1989   Early Farming Communities in the Jordan Valley. In *Foraging and Farming: The Evolution of Plant Exploitation.* D. R. Harris and G. C. Hillman, eds. Pp. 632–42. London: Unwin and Hyman.

Bogucki, Peter
    1984   Ceramic Sieves of the Linear Pottery Culture and Their Economic Implications. *Oxford Journal of Archaeology* 3:15–30.
    1986   The Antiquity of Dairying in Temperate Europe. *Expedition* 28(2):51–58.

Boyle, James W.
    2004   Lest the Lowliest Be Forgotten: Locating the Impoverished in Early Medieval Ireland. *International Journal of Historical Archaeology* 8(2):85–99.

Bradley, Daniel G.
    2003   Genetic Hoofprints: The DNA Trail Leading Back to the Origin of Today's Cattle. *Natural History* 112(1):36–41.

Bradley, D. G., R. T. Loftus, P. Cunningham, and D. E. MacHugh
    1998   Genetics and Domestic Cattle Origins. *Evolutionary Anthropology* 6(3):79–86.

Brady, N.
    1994   Labor and Agriculture in Early Medieval Ireland: Evidence from the Sources. In *The Work of Work: Servitude, Slavery, and Labor in Medieval England.* A. J. Frantzen and D. Moffatt, eds. Pp. 125–45. Glasgow: Cruithne Press.

Braidwood, R. J.
    1967   *Prehistoric Men.* 7th ed. Glenview, IL: Scott, Foresman.

Braidwood, R. J., et al.
    1960   *Prehistoric Investigations in Iraqi Kurdistan.* Chicago: University of Chicago Press.

Campana, D. V., and P. J. Crabtree
    1990   Communal Hunting in the Natufian of the Southern Levant: The Social and Economic Implications. *Journal of Mediterranean Archaeology* 3(2):223–43.

Chang, Claudia, and Harold A. Koster
    1994   Introduction. In *Pastoralists on the Periphery: Herders in a Capitalist World.* Claudia Chang and Harold T. Koster, eds. Pp. 1–15. Tucson: University of Arizona Press.

Childe, V. G.
    1936   *Man Makes Himself.* London: Tavistock.
    1950   The Urban Revolution. *Town Planning Review* 21(1):3–17.

Clutton-Brock, Juliet
    1979   The Mammalian Remains from Jericho Tell. *Proceedings of the Prehistoric Society* 45:135–57.
    1980   *Domesticated Animals from Early Times.* London: British Museum (Natural History) Press.

Clutton-Brock, Juliet, ed.
    1989   *The Walking Larder: Patterns of Domestication, Pastoralism, and Predation.* London: Unwin Hyman.

Copley, M. S., R. Berstan, S. Docherty, A. Mukherjee, V. Straker, S. Payne, and R. P. Evershed
    2003   The Earliest Direct Evidence for Widespread Dairying in Prehistoric Britain. *Proceedings of the National Academy of Sciences* 100(4):1524–29.

Crabtree, Pam J.
    1991   Gender Hierarchies and the Sexual Division of Labor in the Natufian Culture of the Southern Levant. In *The Archaeology of Gender*. Proceedings of the 22nd Annual Chacmool Conference. D. Walde and N. D. Willows, eds. Pp. 384–99. Calgary: Department of Archaeology, University of Calgary.
    1993   Early Animal Domestication in the Middle East and Europe. In *Archaeological Method and Theory*. Vol. 5. M. B. Schiffer, ed. Pp. 201–45. Tucson: University of Arizona Press.

Downs, J. F.
    1966   *The Two Worlds of the Washo*. New York: Holt, Rinehart and Winston.

Driesch, Angela von den
    1976   *A Guide to the Measurement of Animal Bones from Archaeological Sites*. Peabody Museum Bulletin 1. Cambridge, MA: Peabody Museum of Archaeology and Ethnology, Harvard University.

Dyson-Hudson, R., and N. Dyson-Hudson
    1980   Nomadic Pastoralism. *Annual Review of Anthropology* 9:15–61.

Gautier, A.
    1987   Prehistoric Men and Cattle in North Africa: A Dearth of Data and a Surfeit of Models. In *Prehistory of Arid North Africa*. A. E. Close, ed. Pp. 163–87. Dallas: Southern Methodist University Press.

Gilchrist, Roberta
    1999   *Gender and Archaeology: Contesting the Past*. London: Routledge.

Halstead, Paul
    1996   The Development of Agriculture and Pastoralism in Greece: When, How, Who and What? In *The Origins and Spread of Agriculture and Pastoralism in Eurasia*. D. Harris, ed. Pp. 296–309. Washington, DC: Smithsonian Institution Press.

Harlan, J.
    1971   A Wild Wheat Harvest in Turkey. *Archaeology* 20(3):197–201.

Henry, Donald O.
    1975   The Fauna in Near Eastern Archaeological Deposits. In *Problems in Prehistory: North Africa and the Levant*. F. Wendorf and A. E. Marks, eds. Pp. 379–85. Dallas: Southern Methodist University Press.
    1989   *From Foraging to Agriculture: The Levant at the End of the Ice Age*. Philadelphia: University of Pennsylvania Press.

Hesse, Brian
    1984   These Are Our Goats: The Origins of Herding in West Central Iran. In *Animals and Archaeology: 3. Early Herders and Their Flocks*. J. Clutton-Brock and C.

Grigson, eds. Pp. 243–64. BAR International Series 202. Oxford: British Archaeological Reports.

Hiendleder, S., B. Kaupe, R. Wassmuth, and A. Janke
  2002   Molecular Analysis of Wild and Domestic Sheep Questions Current Nomenclature and Provides Evidence for Domestication from Two Different Subspecies. *Proceedings of the Royal Society of London B: Biological Sciences* 269(1492): 893–904.

Hillman, G., R. Hedges, A. Moore, S. Colledge, and P. Pettit
  2001   New Evidence of Lateglacial Cereal Cultivation on the Euphrates. *The Holocene* 11(4):383–93.

Hodder, Ian
  1990   *The Domestication of Europe*. Oxford: Blackwell.

Köhler-Rollefson, I., W. Gillespie, and M. Metzger
  1988   The Fauna from Neolithic 'Ain Ghazal. In *Prehistory of Jordan: The State of Research in 1986*. A. N. Garrard and N. H. Gebel, eds. Pp. 423–30. Oxford: British Archaeological Reports, International Series 398(i).

Kuijt, Ian, and Nigel Goring-Morris
  2002   Foraging, Farming, and Social Complexity in the Pre-Pottery Neolithic of the Southern Levant: A Review and Synthesis. *Journal of World Prehistory* 16(4):363–440.

Lee, R. B.
  1968   What Hunters Do for a Living, or How to Make Out on Scarce Resources. In *Man the Hunter*. R. B. Lee and I. Devore, eds. Pp. 30–48. Chicago: Aldine.

Legge, A. J.
  1972   Prehistoric Exploitation of the Gazelle in Palestine. In *Papers in Economic Prehistory*. E. S. Higgs, ed. Pp. 119–24. Cambridge: Cambridge University Press.

Legge, A. J., and P. Rowley-Conwy
  1987   Gazelle Killing in Stone Age Syria. *Scientific American* 238(8):88–95.

Marshall, F., and E. Hildebrand
  2002   Cattle Before Crops: The Beginnings of Food Production in Africa. *Journal of World Prehistory* 16(2):99–143.

McCormick, Finbar
  1992   Early Faunal Evidence for Dairying. *Oxford Journal of Archaeology* 11(2):201–9.

McGovern, T. H., T. Amorosi, S. Perdikaris, and J. W. Woolett
  1996   Zooarchaeology of Sandnes V51: Economic Change at a Chieftain's Farm in West Greenland. *Arctic Anthropology* 33(2):94–122.

McGovern, T. H., Sophia Perdikaris, and Clayton Tinsley
  2001   Economy of Landman: The Evidence of Zooarchaeology. In *Westward to Vinland*. U. Bragason et al., eds. Pp. 154–65. Reykjavik: Nordahl Institute.

Meadow, R. H.
  1989   Osteological Evidence for the Process of Animal Domestication. In *The Walking Larder: Patterns of Domestication, Pastoralism, and Predation*. Juliet Clutton-Brock, ed. Pp. 80–89. London: Unwin Hyman.

Molleson, Theya
  1994   The Eloquent Bones of Abu Hureyra. *Scientific American* 271(2):70–75.
  2000   The People of Abu Hureyra. In *Village on the Euphrates: From Foraging to Farming at Abu Hureyra.* A. M. T. Moore, G. C. Hillman, and A. J. Legge. Pp. 301–24. Oxford: Oxford University Press.
Moore, A. M. T.
  1982   A Four-Stage Sequence for the Levantine Neolithic, ca 8500 B.C.–3750 B.C. *Bulletin of the American Schools of Oriental Research* 246:1–34.
Moore, A. M. T., G. C. Hillman, and A. J. Legge
  2000   *Village on the Euphrates: From Foraging to Farming at Abu Hureyra.* Oxford: Oxford University Press.
Moore, Henrietta L.
  1988   *Feminism and Anthropology.* Minneapolis: University of Minnesota Press.
Netting, Robert McC.
  1996   What Alpine Peasants Have in Common: Observations on Communal Tenure in a Swiss Village. In *Case Studies in Human Ecology.* Daniel G. Bates and Susan H. Lees, eds. Pp. 219–31. New York: Plenum.
Noy, T.
  1989   Gilgal I. A Pre-Pottery Neolithic Site, Israel. The 1985–1987 Seasons. *Paléorient* 15(1):15–22.
Ó Curráin, D.
  1972   *Ireland Before the Normans.* Dublin: Gill and McMillan.
Patterson, N. T.
  1994   *Cattle-Lords and Clansmen: The Social Structure of Early Ireland.* 2nd ed. Notre Dame, IN: University of Notre Dame Press.
Perkins, Dexter, Jr.
  1964   Prehistoric Fauna from Shanidar, Iraq. *Science* 144:1565–66.
Perkins, Dexter, Jr., and Patricia Daly
  1974   The Beginnings of Food Production in the Near East. In *The Old World: Early Man to the Development of Agriculture.* R. Stigler, ed. Pp. 71–97. New York: St. Martin's Press.
Reed, Charles A.
  1977   A Model for the Origin of Agriculture in the Near East. In *The Origins of Agriculture.* C. A. Reed, ed. Pp. 543–67. The Hague: Mouton.
  1986   Wild Animals Ain't So Wild, Domesticating Them Not So Difficult. *Expedition* 28(2):8–15.
Russell, Nerissa
  2004   Milk, Wool, and Traction: Secondary Animal Products. In *Ancient Europe: 8000 B.C.–A.D. 1000: Encyclopedia of the Barbarian World.* Vol. 1. Peter Bogucki and Pam J. Crabtree, eds. Pp. 325–33. New York: Charles Scribner's Sons.

Shanklin, Eugenia
1994   "Life Underneath the Market": Herders and Gombeenmen in Nineteenth-Century Donegal. In *Pastoralists on the Periphery: Herders in a Capitalist World.* Claudia Chang and Harold T. Koster, eds. Pp. 103–21. Tucson: University of Arizona Press.
Sherratt, A. G.
1981   Plough and Pastoralism: Aspects of the Secondary Products Revolution. In *Pattern of the Past: Studies in Honour of David Clark.* I. Hodder, G. Isaac, and N. Hammond, eds. Pp. 261–305. Cambridge: Cambridge University Press.
1983   The Secondary Exploitation of Animals in the Old World. *World Archaeology* 15:90–104.
1996a   Plough and Pastoralism: Aspects of the Secondary Products Revolution. In *Economy and Society in Prehistoric Europe: Changing Perspectives.* Andrew Sherratt, ed. Pp. 158–98. Princeton, NJ: Princeton University Press.
1996b   The Secondary Exploitation of Animals in the Old World. In *Economy and Society in Prehistoric Europe: Changing Perspectives.* Andrew Sherratt, ed. Pp. 199–228. Princeton, NJ: Princeton University Press.
Soffer, O., J. M. Adovasio, and D. C. Hyland
2000   The "Venus" Figurines. *Current Anthropology* 41:511–37.
Tchernov, Eitan
1994   *An Early Neolithic Village in the Jordan Valley, Part II: The Fauna from Netiv Hagdud.* Cambridge, MA: Peabody Museum of Archaeology and Ethnology, Harvard University.
Tchernov, Eitan, and L. K. Horowitz
1991   Body Size Diminution under Domestication: Unconscious Selection in Primeval Domesticates. *Journal of Anthropological Archaeology* 10:54–75.
Tringham, Ruth E.
1991   Households with Faces: The Challenge of Gender in Prehistoric Architectural Remains. In *Engendering Archaeology: Women and Prehistory.* Joan M. Gero and Margaret W. Conkey, eds. Pp. 93–131. London: Basil Blackwell.
Uerpmann, Hans-Peter
1987   *Probleme der Neolithisierung des Mittelmeerraums.* Wiesbaden: Dr. Ludwig Reichert.
Zeder, Melinda A.
1991   *Feeding Cities: Specialized Animal Economy in the Ancient Near East.* Washington, DC: Smithsonian Institution Press.
2001   A Metrical Analysis of a Collection of Modern Goats (*Capra hircus aegargus* and *C. h. hircus*) from Iran and Iraq: Implications for the Study of Caprine Domestication. *Journal of Archaeological Science* 28(1):61–79.
Zeder, Melinda A., and Brian Hesse
2000   The Initial Domestication of Goats (*Capra hircus*) in the Zagros Mountains 10,000 Years Ago. *Science* 287:2254–57.

Zohary, D.
  1989   Domestication of Southwest Asian Neolithic Crop Assemblage of Cereals, Pulses, and Flax: The Evidence from Living Plants. In *Foraging and Farming, the Evolution of Plant Exploitation*. D. R. Harris and G. C. Hillman, eds. Pp. 358–73. London: Unwin Hyman.

Index

Aboriginal peoples, and tool use, 76, 181
Abu Hureyra, 216, 242
Acheulian bifacial hand axes, 140
Achuar society, farming and gender in, 222
adolescents, in agropastoralist societies, 247
Africa: animal domestication in, 243; farming and gender in, 211–12
African Americans: at Clifton Plantation, 12–20; and midwifery, 4, 41–42; and mothering, 13
age, gender identity and, 104–5
agency theory: and evolution, 147; and farming, 207
agricultural revolution, 237
agropastoralists, 238–39; women and, 243–47
Agta society, hunting in, 128, 171
'Ain Ghazal, 218, 241
Alberti, Benjamin, 69–102
Andaman Islands, tool use in, 181
androcentrism: and evolutionary theory, 119, 122–25, 130, 133–34; and hunter-gatherer studies, 169–201; and primatology, 126–27
animal domestication, 237; in archaeological record, 239–41; in Near East and Europe, 241–43
'aqi, 106
archaeobiography, 5–6; case study in, 6–11
archaeology: and masculinity, 69–102; of personhood, 1, 5–6; of sexuality, theorizing, 38–39; sexuality in, 33–68
architecture: Cheyenne/Anglo, 10; and sexu-

ality, 49–51; and third/other genders, 111–12; Zuni, 45
Ardipithecus, 149
Arikara society, joint diseases in, 187–88
arthritis, gendered patterns of, 186–88
Ashanti society, personhood in, 3–4
Athapaskan society, third/other genders in, 105
Atum, 56
Australia, tool use in, 181; men and, 76
Australopithecus spp., 121, 149

balanced hegemony, 207–8, 212, 224–25
beads: Cheyenne and, 8; at Clifton Plantation, 19–20
bears, 185
behavioral ecology, on hunter-gatherers, 173
behavioral realities, versus gender roles, 185–86
berdache, 34, 43, 105. See also third/other genders
Bergounioux, F. M., 123
Beti society, farming in, 206
Binford, Lewis, 124–25, 129, 133
bioarchaeology: on hunter-gatherers, 186–89; on third/other genders, 109–11
biopsychosocial perspective, 145
bipedality, and evolution, 129–31
birth intervals, and reproductive success, 131, 149
Blackdog burial site, 107
Bleier, Ruth, 144–45

259

About the Contributors

Benjamin Alberti received his Ph.D. in archaeology form Southampton University in 1998. He has written on the representation of sexual difference at Late Bronze Age Knossos, Crete, and has begun to research gender, art, and materiality in late pre-Inca Northwest Argentina. He was a lecturer in archaeology at the Universidad Nacional de la Provincia de Buenos Aires, Argentina, 1999–2001, and is currently an assistant professor of anthropology at Framingham State College.

Diane Bolger is a research fellow in archaeology at the University of Edinburgh in Scotland and ceramic specialist for the university's projects in Cyprus and Syria. Her research interests include ceramic production and craft specialization in the prehistoric Near East and the archaeology of gender. Her main published works on gender are *Gender in Ancient Cyprus* (2003) and *Engendering Aphrodite: Women and Society in Ancient Cyprus* (2002), the latter coedited with N. Serwint. She received her Ph.D. from the University of Cincinnati in 1985.

Hetty Jo Brumbach is an associate curator at the University of Albany, State University of New York, and Museum Associate at the New York State Museum. She is a graduate of the Buxton School, Hunter College, and the University of Albany, where she received a PhD in anthropology. Her research has focused on the Northeast United States and Canada, with interests in social archaeology, material culture and ethnicity, ceramic analysis, ethnoarchaeology, and gender. She has conducted ethnoarchaeological and ethnographic fieldwork in circumpolar communities and archaeological work in the Eastern Woodlands. Her publications include *Gaskin's Reef and River Edge South: A Multicomponent Woodland Site on the Seneca River, New York* (2003) and *Circumpolar Lives and Livelihood: A Comparative Ethnoarchaeology of Gender and Subsistence* (with Robert Jarvenpa, 2006).

Bonnie J. Clark is an assistant professor of anthropology at the University of Denver. She serves on the board of the National Collaborative for Women's History Sites. For over a decade, she has investigated a range of historical archaeology in western North America. She is interested in what the material record of daily life can tell us about the way people live their ethnic, gender, and class identities. She was one of the authors of *Denver: An Archaeological History* (2001).

Pam Crabtree is an associate professor at the Center for the Study of Human Origins of the Department of Anthropology, New York University. She is a zoo-archaeologist who has worked on faunal materials from late prehistoric and medieval Europe, the Near East and South Asia, and historic North America. She coauthored *Exploring Prehistory: How Archaeology Reveals Our Past* (with Douglas Campana, 2005) and coedited *Ancient Europe: Encyclopedia of the Barbarian World 8000 BC–1000 AD* (with Peter Bogucki, 2004).

Sandra E. Hollimon is a lecturer at Sonoma State University. Her Ph.D. is from the University of California, Santa Barbara. Her research interests include gender, shamanism, and emerging complexity in prehistoric California societies, especially the Chumash. Her most recent publication is "Hide Working and Changes in Women's Status among the Arikara, 1700–1862" (in *Gender and Hide Production*, 2005).

Robert Jarvenpa is a professor and former chair of anthropology at the University of Albany, State University of New York. His research and publications focus on ecology and culture, political ecology, social and economic change, interethnic relations, sociospatial organization, decision making, and gender. He has conducted research in circumpolar communities as well as Costa Rica and the United States. He is author of *Northern Passage: Ethnography and Apprenticeship among the Subarctic Dene* (1998) and coauthor and coeditor with Hetty Jo Brumbach of the forthcoming *Circumpolar Lives and Livelihood: A Comparative Ethnoarchaeology of Gender and Subsistence*.

Sarah Milledge Nelson is a John Evans Professor at the University of Denver. She works mostly in Asian archaeology. Her current project is in Liaoning Province, China, where she is surveying sites of the Hongshan period. Books include *Korean Social Archaeology* (2004) and *Gender in Archaeology, Analyzing Power and Prestige* (2nd ed., 2004). Edited books include *Ancient Queens* (2003) and *The Archaeology of the Russian Far East* (with Y. V. Kuzmin, R. Bland, and A. Dervianko, 2006).

Jane D. Peterson is an associate professor of anthropology at Marquette University. Her research interests focus on questions of social organization among early farming groups, particularly those in arid zones. Her analysis of household labor patterns in the Pre-Pottery Neolithic of the southern Levant led her to explore both bioarchaeological patterns in markers of occupational stress and architectural changes. Her current field site is Khirbet Hammam in southern Jordan.

Barbara L. Voss is an assistant professor of cultural and social anthropology at Stanford University. She received her doctorate from the Department of Anthropology at the University of California, Berkeley, with a designated emphasis on women, gender, and sexuality. Her previous work includes *Archaeologies of Sexuality* (coedited with Robert A. Schmidt, 2000) and "Feminisms, Queer Theories, and the Archaeological Study of Past Sexualities" and "Sexual Subjects: Identity and Taxonomy in Archaeological Research" (in *The Archaeology of Plural and Changing Identities*, ed. Eleanor Conlin Casella and Chris Fowler, 2005). She currently directs the Tennessee Hollow Watershed Archaeological Project at the Presidio of San Francisco and the Market Street Chinatown project in San Jose, California.

Laurie A. Wilkie is an associate professor of anthropology at the University of California, Berkeley. Her research interests include archaeological considerations of the construction of engendered, racialized, and ethnic identities in the recent past. Her published works include *Creating Freedom: Material Culture and African American Identity at Oakley Plantation, Louisiana, 1840–1950* (2000; winner of the 2001 James Mooney Book Award), *The Archaeology of Mothering: An African American Midwife's Tale* (2000; winner of the 2005 James Deetz Book Award), and, with Paul Farnsworth, *Sampling Many Pots: An Archaeology of Memory and Tradition at a Bahamian Plantation* (2005).